The Subject's Tragedy

The Subject's Tragedy

Political Poetics, Feminist Theory, and Drama

Linda Kintz

Ann Arbor

THE UNIVERSITY OF MICHIGAN PRESS

Copyright © by the University of Michigan 1992
All rights reserved
Published in the United States of America by
The University of Michigan Press
Manufactured in the United States of America

1995   1994   1993   1992   4   3   2   1

A CIP catalogue record for this book is available from the British Library.

Library of Congress Cataloging-in-Publication Data

Kintz, Linda, 1945–
    The subject's tragedy : political poetics, feminist theory, and
drama / Linda Kintz.
        p.   cm.
    Includes bibliographical references (p.   ) and index.
    ISBN 0-472-10385-7 (alk. paper)
    1. Drama—20th century—History and criticism. 2. Greek drama
(Tragedy)—History and criticism. 3. Women in literature.
4. Feminism and literature. 5. Kennedy, Adrienne—Criticism and
interpretation. 6. Norman, Marsha—Criticism and interpretation.
7. Castellanos, Rosario—Criticism and interpretation.   I. Title.
PN1861.K48   1992
809.2'512—dc20   92-36504
                                                              CIP

For Chase and Brook

Acknowledgments

Parts of this study were supported by grants from the University of Oregon Center for the Study of Women in Society and the Oregon Humanities Center. Versions of parts of the manuscript appeared in "The Sanitized Spectacle: What's Birth Got to Do With It?: Adrienne Kennedy's *A Movie Star Has to Star in Black and White*," *Theatre Journal* (Spring 1992); and "Gendering the Critique of Representation: Fascism, the Purified Body, and Theater in Adorno, Artaud, and Maria Irene Fornes," *Rethinking Marxism* 4, no. 3 (Fall 1991).

My work has been encouraged by Marilyn Farwell and Irving Wohlfarth, and at a critical moment by Thelma Greenfield, who understood what it meant to be both a mother and a graduate student. Stephen Rendall and Wolf Sohlich supported and encouraged my work and made scholarship collegial and impassioned. Page duBois, Nancy Armstrong, and Cheris Kramarae generously gave me support and encouragement. Namascar Shaktini, Iris Young, and Sue-Ellen Case have given me help at important moments.

I would also like to thank Karla and Kurt Schultz for their steady, elegant support and Maria dePriest and Nikki for their cheer and care. And I have been very lucky to have the warmth, friendship, and intellectual encouragement of Ann Laskaya, Judith Raiskin, Aletta Biersak, Barbara Pope, Gloria Johnson, Julia Lesage, Ellen Seiter, Kathleen Rowe, and Lee Taylor. William Rossi, Tres Pyle, and Randall McGowan provided cheerfulness and support, and George Rowe spent time commenting on my writing. Mary Wood's compassion and honesty have given me a model of feminist scholarship; Suzanne Clark has kept me thinking for many years, and her friendship inspires me. Claudia Yukman's insights and affection have modeled another kind of feminism for me.

I also thank Frankie Westbrook for her grace at a difficult time when this book was a victim of the canon wars at the University of Texas, proving that the Right has its own version of political correctness. Though the editorial board of the University of Texas Press approved the publication of this book, which deals with multiculturalism and feminism, in 1990, the board's decision was overruled and reversed the next day by a note from an administrator. In the early stages of that process, Jan Swearingen's and Sandra Messinger Cypess's readings were of great help to me, and I have since been fortunate to have Leann Fields's generous editorial advice at the University of Michigan Press and especially Christina Milton's careful readings. I also want to thank Diane Hunsaker, Mike Stamm, Marilyn Reid, Phyllis Warner, and Evelyn Marczuk in the English Department of the University of Oregon for their help and good spirit.

I owe the most to my mother, Mozelle Pruitt Urbanczyk, and my father, Bennie Urbanczyk—she for making sure I knew how to use the library, he for teaching me to drive a tractor. And my thanks to my sisters, Karen, Marsha, Roseann, and Lisa, whose talk I depend on, and my brothers, Joel, Kevin, and Jan. Chase and Brook have seen this book through many difficult moments, when it interrupted their lives in too many ways. And finally, I thank Joe for his quiet support and for patiently picking up the pieces when I dropped things.

Contents

Introduction: Real Fictions and True Delusions

There is a fictive moment at the genesis of every science, a generative fiction (a hypothesis) at the foundation of every theory.
                                                              —Shoshana Felman

Culture can emanate only from the centralizing significance of an art or work of art.
                                                              —Friedrich Nietzsche

To articulate the past historically does not mean to recognize it "the way it really was." . . . It means to seize hold of a memory as it flashes up at a moment of danger.
                                                              —Walter Benjamin

In the history of Western representation theater, theory, and concepts of the body have been linked in the most intricate and intimate ways, and poststructuralist theories of subjectivity and performance now circulate among them. An important though invisible feature of this linkage is the way the specific *generic* requirements of Greek tragedy continue to function as the hidden structural model for theories of subjectivity as well as for theories of drama in general, in spite of both feminist and Brechtian anti-Aristotelian theory. The generic features of tragedy produce a dramatic and theoretical discourse that in many ways requires that there be no female agency as it guarantees the masculinity of both the protagonist and the theorist.

In order to investigate the continuing, invisible, and, at least for feminist criticism, troubling influence of tragedy a certain risk has to be taken in this study, one that involves jumping the centuries to link Greek tragedy to a study of performance, subjectivity, and three twentieth-century women dramatists—Adrienne Kennedy, Marsha Norman, and Rosario Castellanos. Perhaps such a jump is legitimate if it is based on Froma Zeitlin's claim that tragedy provides Western culture with its "epistemological form par excellence" (Zeitlin 1985, 72).

Developing the implications of Zeitlin's claim and taking the historical leap it requires finds further justification in a particular problem feminist theory encounters every time the question of history arises. On the one hand, a study of historical context and specificity is, of course, indispensable to feminist study. Yet something unsettlingly predictable happens when historical specificity alone drives the study. As historical differences show up, broad, long-term similarities among periods seem to fade from view. Clyde Taylor, an African-American film critic, in a discussion of the history of the aesthetic, has made a similar argument about the erasure of analyses of race. While the privilege of the aesthetic has been demystified by poststructuralist and Marxist critics, all too often such studies have found themselves reengaged in what appears to be either a formalist or a historicist description of the differences among the ruses of representation at various historical moments. But these descriptions of differences, while necessary, almost inevitably overlook important *similarities,* which construct an invisible, larger frame for the work being analyzed, a frame that seems to disappear. In particular, as Taylor argues in the case of cinema, "many distinctions and interpretations of narrative representation in western cinema shrink in significance beside their coherence in functioning to uphold racial hierarchies" (Taylor 1988, 97).

Another film critic, Patrice Petro, makes a similar argument about gender in response to new historicist criticism of speculative feminist theory for its lack of historical rigor, yet she argues that such criticism begs the question, for

> the methods and approach of traditional histories have proven problematic for feminists, not least of all because so many documents preserved from the past offer only limited traces of women's presence, while presenting massive evidence of their marginality and repression. But what is fundamentally at issue here is not a lack of adequate documentation. . . . It also involves submitting regimes of visibility to a general critique of objectivity and subjectivity in the

writing of film history, and rethinking critical methods and theoretical procedures. (1990, 9)

I want to argue that a similar case can be made in relation to gender
hierarchies in the history of drama and, in particular, in relation to the
genre of tragedy which links Western metaphysics to Western aesthetics.
A study of the differences between the classical Greek stage and the stage
of the late twentieth century can be juxtaposed to an analysis that shows
how historical differences "shrink in significance" beside the symbolic
power of their continuation of gender hierarchies. Underlying this symbolic power are long-lived and striking similarities that have to do with
organizing and ordering the body in preparation for a particular form
of heterosexual marriage that founds the political space of the Greek
city-state and constructs the legitimate speaking subject as masculine.
Homosexual relations among men in the polis, though highly complex,
nevertheless accompany the simultaneous heterosexual organization of
family and property through marriage, which brought together the ordering of the state and the form of sexuality that would ensure both its
cultural and physical reproduction. The goal of this study will be to
provide a double-handed analysis of the history and theory of tragedy,
one that tries to "submit regimes of visibility to a general critique of
objectivity and subjectivity," while also juggling and keeping in sight
structural similarities that persist over a long period of time. It will also
attempt to reconceptualize certain notions of the performative in both
drama and dramatic theory.

This study will return initially to what would seem to be overly
familiar names—Oedipus and Aristotle—in order to show how their
sociosymbolic effects continue to handicap both the production and the
reception of feminist theory and theories of drama and performance.
Though the symbolic weight of both Oedipus and Aristotle has been
under discussion for some time, the parameters they set for concepts of
subjectivity are still not recognized by many theorists, even and especially poststructuralist and Marxist ones. In particular, what is overlooked are the oedipal and Aristotelian influences on the theorist's own
position as a producer of knowledge. While many poststructuralist and
Marxist readings of texts have been of great importance to feminism,
they have too often stopped with the rigorous isolation of the constructions of gender hierarchy *within* the texts. But the same rigor has not

been applied to the legitimacy of the theorist's own enunciative site of knowledge production. In fact, a rigorous analysis of gender construction on the page and in the media or performance text, on the one hand, is very often accompanied, on the other, by the assumption of a kind of Habermasian public space of critical discourse, where differences are acknowledged then bracketed, so that "we" all may speak together equally. There is here a curious erasure or denial of the effects of the performance of theory, a split between content (or the statement) and the praxis that determines form (the conditions within which the discussion may take place at all). Oedipus theoretically disclaims his privilege while hanging onto an institutional "objectivity." As a result, a study of theories of subjectivity as performance will of necessity have to do with the performance of theory as well as the theory of performance.[1]

A rereading of Oedipus, Aristotle, and tragedy as they influence theoretical, or rational, sites of knowledge production might help develop a way to read these enunciative positions through a concept of subjectivity as performance—or better, performances—that is, subjectivity as a series of subject positionings in which the discourse that produces those sites is activated by specific kinds of bodies which perform themselves as real fictions. At this stage of poststructuralism, now that all meaning can be seen to be constructed, there is a pressing need to argue that different kinds of constructed bodies enter discursive spaces differently. "What is called a man" and men coexist in the space of performance theory and theories of performance in a way that "what is called woman" and women do not. There is a difference here that is not at all enigmatic but has to do with symbolic violence, as I will argue.

The sociosymbolic parameters of this "stage" of reason that still haunts discourse originates in the Greek polis, and it is structurally linked to the more abstract and metaphysical discursive stage upon which contemporary embodied subjects can speak and mean. My focus here will be on the epistemological constraints of both philosophical discourse and dramatic theory, in spite of the fact that John J. Winkler, in *The Constraints of Desire: The Anthropology of Sex and Gender in Ancient Greece,* has importantly called into question studies of ideas without a simultaneous study of social practices, in particular in relation to classical Greece. The history of ideas, he argues, should not give ideas a weight, power, and dominance they did not possess within the culture under study. And yet this very warning by Winkler enforces the need to trace ideas. As he argues, the debates of intellectuals and philosophers cannot tell us much about "the beliefs and practices of the population at large"; such a study would require anthropology and ethnography as well as the study of philosophical and literary texts. This kind of study of ideas instead has much to tell us "about the formation of a class of intellectuals and about competition for ideological hegemony" (Winkler 1990, 44). Thus, my own attempt to talk about Greek tragedy and twentieth-century theater has had to confront at every turn the constraints caused by precisely the kind of history Winkler finds to be a partial one—the history of the formation of a class of intellectuals who have provided the historical and theoretical texts available to us, with all the omissions and oversights of women that mark such texts.

And though this study will put in the foreground the development and construction of certain ideas by that class of intellectuals, part of its project will be to open up the possibilities and definition of what counts as intellectual work. In the phobically anti-intellectual climate of North American culture, it seems unhelpful and even dangerous to suggest that we simply set up another binary in opposition to intellectuals, rather than attempt to retheorize and reclaim the very field of intellectual activity. One model for this reformulation of the role of the intellectual is the work of bell hooks, whose work refuses the tragic binary that separates theory and practice.

Because both drama and psychoanalysis rest precisely on the aesthetic relation between bodies and symbols, where figurations or tropes cover over the basic unit of signification—*relations* within systems of differences—a critique of Oedipus and Aristotle's relation to the ordering of the Greek polis inevitably implicates Freud's reading of a drama, *Oedipus the King*. That reading still powerfully describes the effects of institutions of normalization and technologies of power that are involved in the construction of "decent" and proper subjects embodied in very specific ways, as they provide an underlying logic for the modern nation-state. My argument assumes that a critical analysis of Freud's privileging of the subject position of the son and the oppressive history of the institution of psychoanalysis need not give up the indispensable resources of psychoanalytic theory for analyzing the way desiring bodies come to perform themselves within textual and symbolic systems, which are always political.

What will be at issue throughout this study is an attempt to make visible the effects on dramatic theory of a seemingly neutral, ungendered rational space of knowledge production, or enunciation, that constantly forgets its own embodiment. It remains so visible it is *in*visible, a visible invisibility that is nowhere more pronounced than in the situatedness of analyses of drama and subjectivity upon a foundation based on the generic requirements of tragedy, with its dramatic agon. Tragedy enforces its own privilege in a way made most obvious by the gendered hierarchy that can always be found in a list of those genres supposedly inferior to tragedy: comedy, melodrama, sentimental fiction, soap operas, sitcoms, and so forth.

Tragedy in the Twentieth Century

But before turning to several early versions of the tragic oedipal story, which associates man with subjectivity, activity, and force and woman with objectivity and passivity and constructs her as matter or medium, it helps to see why retelling these stories might be important at this historical moment in the late twentieth century. A sense of impending tragedy currently structures debates about fragmentation in North American culture and politics, with suggestions that a community, a "we," is no longer possible because "special interests" have fragmented any hope of collective identity. This concern crosses boundaries from Right to Left, from Dinesh D'Souza to Alexander Cockburn and Fredric Jameson, its rhetoric still relying on a somber, tragic model of community. Even the tone of the debate suggests a sigh and a sad, tragic submission to fate, for it seems to be fate that will consign us all to inevitable tragic misunderstanding if we don't come together and agree on One interpretation of meaning.

But for whom will this fragmentation be tragic? And what if the binary opposition unity/fragmentation that underlies the discussion is itself the problem? Marginalized groups have always recognized, in a way dominant groups have not, the dangers of models of unity which, invisibly and subtly, take the dominant group as the model and require that everyone else remold themselves to fit in. A reexamination of the requirements of oedipal subjectivity might be motivated by a refusal of this tragic sigh that is still based on binary logic—and *any* binary rests on the structural presuppositions of tragedy. Such a refusal makes possible a focus on other models of unity that cannot be couched in terms of tragedy's requirements; the models, in fact, depend on dismantling those very requirements. If, at the moment, we are still locked in a tragic model of cultural politics, it is important to see what kind of assumptions continue to handicap even the most radical theorists of political and cultural change.

For there are very different models of unity available.[2] An investigation of them can be aided by a review of the tragic view of the world, which will constitute the first two chapters of this book—chapter 1 devoted to a rereading of *Oedipus the King,* chapter 2 to *The Women of Trachis.* After a transitional chapter 3 which sets out a way of bringing those readings of tragedy together with various feminist and poststructuralist theories of subjectivity, the second half of the book looks at three twentieth-century dramatists who are dissecting that tragic view in the interests of something else, some other way of conceptualizing solidarity and community that does not simply leave us stranded in fragmentation or schizophrenia as a revolutionary possibility or as bit players in the male-bonding dramas of oedipal revolutionaries.

The plays of Adrienne Kennedy, an African-American playwright, are radical experiments with subjectivity and theatrical form; they show how the very notion of the unity of character or of autonomous subjectivity is simply artificial, even phobic, in a culture in which subject positions are always multiple. This is particularly true in North America where African Americans come to be subjects through a long process of identification with white cultural models of literacy and popular culture and through identifications within a strong and complex African-American culture, where the artificiality of the normative middle-class nuclear family is constantly evident. In Kennedy's plays it is the very insistence on a unified model of character, or subjectivity, that proves to be abnormal, rather than the resistance to that artificial unity. Kennedy's kaleidoscopic characters deconstruct the stage, the character, the author, and a social contract based on the privilege of purity that sacrifices feminized others, both male and female. She brings into the discussion a much more specific way of investigating gender and the problems of psychological colonization in a culture organized around white supremacy.

Marsha Norman, a white North American playwright, shows how drama based on the oedipal protagonist has serious trouble staging the conflicts and relations of a mother and daughter and the everyday "trivia" of the lives of homemakers. One of her plays has become a kind of feminist litmus test that elicits very different feminist readings. The tense contradictions among these readings are important to North American feminism, as her nondescript housewives undo the claim that class definitions are the same for women as they are for men. They also reveal the costs exacted by the private, domestic space on the women exiled within it and show how the invisibility of women's domestic work in political theory is related to the invisibility of female agency in the Aristotelian dramatic tradition as well as, often, in feminist theory. Her play provides a way to talk about what Michel de Certeau calls "the practices of everyday life," the kinds of resistances that cannot be accounted for in heroic, revolutionary, or tragic terms. My reading attempts to show how Oedipus still limits both the dramatist's options and the ability of academic feminist criticism to deal with housewives and mothers.

Rosario Castellanos, a Mexican playwright, sets out a broader historical panorama in which a twentieth-century Mexican woman watches as various recreations of women in Mexican history are staged by other women, most of them based on actual historical personages. Castellanos's use of farce and Brechtian foregrounding of the apparatus of representation shows the artificiality of the forms used to reconstruct these women and simultaneously the artificiality of received versions of history. She also undercuts the stereotypes of women and men in Mexico by showing the complexity those stereotypes hide. Women's relationship to Catholicism or women and men's relationship to a supposed "macho" culture are not seen as one-dimensional but, rather, as relational, or dialectical, historical constructs. These complex cultural forms make possible various kinds of agency as well as, at other moments, supporting domination, her play both acknowledging and dissecting the effects of patriarchy, colonialism, imperialism, and representation on Mexican women.

This study of the dramaturgy of the subject will conclude by turning to Virginia Woolf's meditation on the relation between the privatized subject of the novel and the collective or anonymous subject of communal drama in *Between the Acts,* a novel written on the eve of the Second World War that experiments with the genre of the novel as well as of drama. In an experimental form that might be called a "performative novel" what proves to be most significant is what goes on "between the acts" and in the specific sites of enunciation which make an interpretation of the play available to the reader and/or spectator. In reacting against the privatized, copyrighted Author of the English novel, Woolf deconstructs that Author, who is here a lesbian playwright determined to hide in the bushes so that the spectators, the actors, and even nature must also be "authors" of meaning. What goes on between the acts, what in some way completely disrupts the notion of acts and of a stage separated off from the world, has to do with those things that are usually marginalized and purified out—the feminine, the body, materiality, nature, death, even a cesspool, as well as critiques of patriarchy, militarism, fascism, and imperialism on the eve of war. This war is also intimately connected to the love and war that goes on throughout the novel between a husband and wife "performing" the gendered roles required of them by a patriarchal First World social contract determined to enforce the heterosexual nuclear family as norm. The political structure proves to be inseparable from bodies and the cultural production of desire.

Woolf's novel links considerations of authorship and the specific sites of performance to the contemporary search for an ethical model for feminist theory after authorship and subjectivity have been deconstructed in both poststructuralist theory and the postmodern economic structures described by that theory. Her little group of spectators, actors, and nature offer a possible model for a heterogeneous notion of subjects coming together in a different kind of "we," an ethical model of solidarity that does not fall back into a reliance on the now deconstructed autonomous subject that has for so long underwritten the Eurocentric "we" of the social contract. The very different and very difficult model of unity she proposes will be discussed in more detail in the afterword, but it is dependent on a different kind of identity suggested in this phrase: "Dispersed are we; who have come together" (Woolf 1941, 196).

That it also has to do with dramatized identity, or identity as performance, is noticed by audience members whose reactions are found in a long paragraph composed of fragments of statements and ellipses, suggesting an identity (a unity, an audience) that is, nevertheless, not identifiable in atomistic, static terms. Neither, however, does the static identity of the group override distinct, separate individualities, which are nonetheless nameless. This is a community trying to figure out the meaning of a highly unusual, decentered play about community, a play whose author, Miss Latrobe, referred to by everyone as Miss Whatshername, refuses to claim ownership of its meaning. As the Audience, in its separate but not atomistic individualities, says: "He said she meant we all act. Yes, but whose play? Ah, that's the question! And if we're left asking questions, isn't it a failure, as a play? I must say I like to feel sure if I go to the theatre, that I've grasped the meaning. . . . Or was that, perhaps, what she meant? . . . Ding dong. Ding . . . that if we don't jump to conclusions, if you think, and I think, perhaps one day, thinking differently, we shall think the same?" (200). But, of course, if we all thought differently in order to think the same, the *same would have been completely redefined,* and subjectivity would no longer be equated with identity. A radical possibility of difference in unity underlies this ostensibly naive statement by Woolf's audience.

In relation to this question of community and of thinking the same differently in a postmodern context is another binary that often leaves those involved in cultural politics at an impasse, the opposition between deconstructed subjects and autonomous ones, an opposition that suggests that, once the notion of subjectivity has been shown to be historical and constructed, we all risk floating away because we have no subjectivity anymore. Because historically powerless groups have been denied legitimate forms of subjectivity, many people have understandably not embraced the notion of deconstructed subjectivity as liberating. Though these resistances to deconstruction have sometimes been too abrupt, they have nevertheless pointed to a serious conceptual failure within poststructuralist theory itself, a failure to theorize subjectivity in a way that can simultaneously describe constructedness as socially and textually determined *and* as filled with possibilities for agency, where each subject, though still a construction, is unique, active, and historically specific. Investigations of what Woolf calls dispersion in unity, or individuality in decenteredness, are important if we are ever to reconceptualize community in a way that can dispense with the inevitably tragic agon of a certain kind of subjectivity tragically performed on both the Left and the Right.

In this determination to look around and beyond the constraints of tragic subjectivity Julia Kristeva's concept of *thetic* subjectivity is helpful, depending as it does on an extended theorizing of language that insists that language can only be analyzed in terms of performances involving materiality, that is, performances that are enunciations by embodied subjects who are, of course, also subjec*ted* by that performance. Thinking of the performance of subjectivity as a discursive, poetic matrix might help link the materiality of bodies, social and political structures, and aesthetic form. Perhaps in such a project, what might be called a postaesthetic aesthetics, we could also include the way bodies are trained to be certain kinds of subjects through rhythm, sound, touch, and visual forms as well as through spoken language.

Kristeva's work also shows what kind of First World social structure is engaged in retroactively producing particular kinds of families in order to provide itself with the kinds of subjects—and bodies—it needs for its own reproduction. Her extended analysis of the construction of the legitimate speaking subject and its "clean and proper body" provides a way to look at a symbolic, cultural logic of purity that structures gender and race in Christian capitalist society, organizing the bodies of its proper, purified subjects, and she rereads Freud against the Hegelian Christianity of Lacanian readings, revising the notion of the mirror stage and radically recovering the "texture" of the maternal body, what Cynthia Chase calls "coagulation," even though Kristeva has yet to take advantage of her own insights that might lead to a theory of the female speaking subject. But just as socialist feminists use Marx, even though he had little to say about female subjectivity or reproduction, feminists writing about subjectivity might also push Kristeva's insights beyond themselves.

This attempt to join the work of Kennedy, Norman, Castellanos, Woolf, and Kristeva is motivated by a deep concern to bring into the foreground the very tense and problematic differences in feminist theory that circle around discussions of female agency or specificity because these discussions have relied on retheorizing the relation to the maternal body. My study, because of its reliance on Kristeva's theory of a cultural logic, will also depend very heavily on retheorizing the maternal, as it will depend on a very particular, personal relationship to theories of gender similar to one described by Susan Rubin Suleiman: if a woman is the mother of sons, as I am, "she may also, very likely, be unwilling to consider the other sex as always and only 'other'" (1990, xvii). And she also may be unwilling to leave the maternal body, perhaps her own, out of theory either because it is too threatening or too boring; mothers must engage in this theorizing as well as daughters.[3]

Part of my interest in this study results from my own experience growing up on a farm in West Texas, where my models were strong aunts, grandmothers, and mother, none of whom were college educated and all of whose identities in many important ways rested on their own situatedness as housewives, not housewives of the suburban stereotype but, rather, women whose married lives were lived as mothers, housekeepers, and, to some degree, farm laborers. Some of them were second-generation Polish Catholic women in the heart of the Bible Belt who had seen the Klan burn crosses in their pastures; others came out of backgrounds made difficult by economic hardship. Leaving attempts to theorize the maternal out of feminist theory because of the dangers of essentialism or biologism simply erases the significance of a good part of the lives of these very diverse, very active, and strong women.

But to the very serious risk of *not* theorizing the maternal must be added the risks of reinscribing all women's bodies as, in some sense, potentially pregnant, a return of the biological model in which feminine specificity is equated with the possibilities of reproduction. Many discussions of female agency do find themselves uneasily requiring some notion of the specificity of reproductive functions, as those functions mark a difference between female and male bodies in terms of working conditions (i.e., as Emily Martin describes, in *The Woman in the Body: A Cultural Analysis of Reproduction* (1987), the way the organization of working space is based on the physical needs of men's bodies, leaving women to have to figure out ways to deal with menstrual cycles, time off for childbirth, flexibility during menopause, etc., quite on their own).[4] Another aspect of feminist theory in which this biology/construction tension is very immediate is the attempt to provide specific categories for women in legal discourse, analyzed in such studies as that of Zillah Eisenstein, *The Female Body and the Law* (1988). In particular, Eisenstein attempts to conceptualize the specific kinds of interruptions menstruating or menopausal or pregnant bodies introduce into legal categories that are based on autonomous male subjects. Similarly, I want to ask about the kinds of interruptions such bodies, culturally constructed as they are, introduce into performative notions of gender.

My concern in this study will thus be to attempt to extend a study of the construction of gender while trying to retheorize some notion of specificity in describing and conceptualizing the continuing effects of the relation to the maternal body, which seems far too often to lead to either a denial or a repudiation of mothers. This repudiation uneasily coexists with the cultural requirements that turn a *description* of the maternal into a *prescription* that requires every woman to be, or to desire to be, a mother, even though—and this is the point that too often gets lost in feminist concerns about the heterosexual privilege enjoyed by mothers— the idealization of motherhood in this society coexists with *contempt* for actual mothers. Acknowledging the dangers of conflation between prescription and description does not justify giving up the attempt.

This study will, as a result, attempt to analyze those places in discussions of the maternal that constitute a danger site that threatens a "return of the real," where physiology threatens to intrude as "real" and the split subject of textuality itself becomes equated with the pregnant body, though the notion of "essentialism" itself needs to be historicized, for a warning against it most often shows up as a distrust of femininity. Another side of the dangers of the return of the real is developed by Judith Butler in *Gender Trouble: Feminism and the Subversion of Identity*. Her study of gender as performance develops the radical possibilities of lesbian and gay theory yet also argues against a different return of the real, suggesting that neither heterosexuality nor homosexuality can claim a privileged relation to figurative language as the site of contesting "the compulsory syntax and semantics that construct 'the real'" (1990, 128).

There are here two intense sites of resistance which are also, of necessity, located precisely where bodies and symbols come together, which also means that they are sites where the return of the real threatens: the maternal and the lesbian—though, of course, those categories are themselves in no way mutually exclusive nor are they, in any sense, unambiguous concepts. Because my interest is in reclaiming the possible radical dimensions of retheorizing the maternal, this study will focus primarily on that issue, though I wish Minnie Bruce Pratt had written a play that discusses the intersection between motherhood and lesbian sexuality and identity in the way her book of poetry, *Crime against Nature,* does. Virginia Woolf's novel about a play includes both the question of the wife/mother and the resistant lesbian author as well as a meditation about a sister. Perhaps the intersection between theorizing the maternal and theorizing lesbian sexuality, theoretical projects that cannot be collapsed into one another but must be worked out separately and specifically, might provide a powerful and productive site within feminism because they are both—differently—affected by the most intense pressures arising out of the repudiation of the feminine.

The Subject's Tragedy

A study of tragedy must look at the site of what Régis Durand calls the subject's dramaturgy, its theatrical art, finding in the political and aesthetic structure of *Oedipus the King* a matrix that has organized the possibilities for subjectivity in Western culture.[5] These possibilities might be referred to figuratively as character roles, or dramatis personae. This particular Greek tragedy thus functions as the matrix for sign systems that possess, as Daniel Peri Lucid argues, "the capacity literally to mold or 'model' the world in its own image, shaping the minds of society's members to fit its structure" (1977, 87). Performance in this semiotic theater has little to do with mimesis as a copy of something already existing but is, instead, as Aristotle describes it, an imitation of the material activity of making.

But the activity of making produces "true delusions." For, as Nietzsche says,

> [when] the same image has been generated millions of times and has been handed down for many generations and finally appears on the same occasion every time for all mankind, then it acquires at last the same meaning for men it would have if it were the sole necessary image and if the relationship of the original nerve stimulus to the generated image were a strictly causal one. (1979, 87)

There is a familiar assumption here—that this is a problem having to do with "man." If Aristotle finds the story of Oedipus to be the most nearly perfect aesthetic production and if Western culture finds that the fate of Oedipus is the fate of every subject, a universal human experience, then Luce Irigaray's question is still urgent: Is every theory of the subject masculine?[6] Or in terms of the questions raised in this study which might at least glimpse a way out of this impasse, is every theory of the subject that is *tragic* masculine?

The sanctioned ignorance of the knower as masculine is related to an obvious historical characteristic of theories of meaning; they are descriptions of masculine experience by males as knowers, based on an Aristotelian circle, or tautology. The way to decide what is appropriate, proper, or true in history, according to this circularity, is to ask the question of someone who is appropriate and proper. Within this tautology we conclude that what we know is what there was to be known by appropriate knowers, i.e., what we know coincides with what there was to be known.[7] Or as Roland Barthes said, what was noted was notable.

This universalized masculine, tautological perspective works through the simultaneous *elimination* and *maintenance* of difference:

> One can in effect read the terms of reason's desire which animates *homo rationalis* in the maxims he inscribes on the fronts of his courts. One can read the terms of that desire equally well in the signs he traces on the bodies of the people upon whom he inflicts corporal punishment [*supplice*] or in the disgrace and shame with which he

charges those he wants to exclude. In one of these cases one reads what he poses for himself as the infinity of his own desire. In the other, what must be produced so that that desire can be maintained. (Gravel 1980, 70; my translation)

In rethinking the effects of Oedipus and Aristotle, this subject, or *homo rationalis*, will have to be considered in two different ways. First, it cannot fully know itself; it loses itself because it has an unconscious, and, second, it identifies itself in language, a pre-existent system into which a subject is "subjected," or interpellated, to use Althusser's term.[8]

But the subject can also transform its position; it occupies a series of thetic positions. That is, it presumes a temporary form of subjectivity, or agency, in a thesis that enables it to speak the grammatical "I" and posit a momentary identity, then to dissolve that thesis and respeak another contextually specific "I." (In psychoanalytic theory this mobile contextualization can be compared to the structure of transference.)

The supposedly static subject is thus both definition and process. It might better be described according to an expanded notion of dramatic character as a collection of events in time, each of which marks the intersection of various identifications and representations. It is a process "according to which all the play of identification becomes possible . . . a register of passage, a movement of inscription" (Gravel 1980, 59) that both (a) *happens to* a subject in a historical situation, and (b) *is changed by* the subject's activity. This is a process of subjectivity that is both determinate and changeable.

Allegory of the Stages

Any subject requires limits within which it can make sense. In this study the metaphor of the stage refers to the economy which constitutes those limits, *Oedipus the King* providing a heuristic model for an allegory of the stage(s). The male actor in this allegory represents Man as subject. In Greek tragedy all the actors were men who wore masks; thus, all the female characters were masculine. In this case every theory of the character was, to paraphrase Irigaray, masculine.

The male actor's position was thus overdetermined in terms of its "acts": (1) his was a masculine body onstage; (2) as a man, he was, anyway, only "acting" like a man because of his situatedness in language and in relation to the unconscious; (3) he may have been a male actor acting a male character role; (4) he may have been a male actor acting a female character role; and (5) as we will see, he was a particular kind of Greek citizen being initiated into the responsibilities of the polis, an aesthetic/political actor. Rather than a play within a play, his subject position was a play within a subject, his multiple subject positions a series of theatrical performances.

There is only a trace of women left here, an "échonomie."[9] What this trace is (and what it is not) can be made clearer by the myth of Echo and Narcissus.[10] The nymph Echo was persuaded by Zeus to chatter and sing to distract Hera and keep her from noticing Zeus's seduction of other nymphs. Hera's discovery of Echo's ruse led her to deprive Echo of speech, condemning Echo to repeat only the last syllable of words spoken in her presence. Her "own" earlier speech had, of course, been possible only at the bidding of Zeus. After her punishment her speech was copy of man's, enforced by the phallic mother figure of a patriarchal pantheon.

Echo then fell in love with Narcissus, a Thespian, who refused her advances.[11] Her attentions made possible for Narcissus a specular mirroring of himself by a woman, but he preferred instead auto-affection without female participation. In one version of the myth she "hid her grief in solitary caverns" and died of a broken heart, leaving behind only the trace of her voice in echoes, which still linger about enclosed spaces.

The gods punished Narcissus for refusing Echo, disciplining him by privileging a form of heterosexual narcissism as opposed to a homosexual one, causing him to fall in love with his own image, directly reflected back to him without Echo's intervention. This homo-sexual form of narcissism kills him. In a movement that reappears in Lacan's version of the subject's tragedy Narcissus died when he finally saw himself in the water, a death the soothsayer Teresias, who will also be involved in the fate of Oedipus, had predicted. The sight of Narcissus's own face caused him to fade away: "He died there of languor."[12]

The trace of Echo's speech lingers over the allegory of the Greek stage and links that stage to twentieth-century theories of the subject. The concept of the echo will be linked eventually to the excess constituted by attempts to represent female agency, an excess that will continue to trouble theories of history and subjectivity.[13]

The Play of Exclusion

What looks like an old, tired oedipal story and a too familiar myth of an echoing woman are repeated in the poststructuralist work of Michel Foucault and Roland Barthes. Yet Barthes, in what will prove to be a blinded lament over the inevitable force and power of the tragic oedipal position, nevertheless points to a way out, a way to theorize female agency, when he inadvertently describes what he calls "naive history." In an essay entitled "Taking Sides" Barthes seems sorrowfully to accept the futility of trying to change the particular system of representation Foucault traces. That futility, however, results from the fact that he does not question the gendered site of knowledge production, instead viewing the system of representation from an ungendered, tragic model of knower.

"Taking Sides" traces Foucault's *Histoire de la folie* as it reexamines "Otherness" to show that exclusion is a technique of reason (Barthes 1972). Foucault goes beyond a traditional structural examination of the exclusion that works by means of binary oppositions to show how the knowledge produced in such an opposition also produces what come to be called excluded knowledges as discourse. That is, the discourse that talks about the excluded "Other" or its resistances to that exclusion is also a product of the power responsible for the exclusion in the first place. But Foucault, too, overlooks the gendered production of knowledge by claiming that the discourse of excluded knowledges exhausts its object—that what knowledge knows of the Other constitutes all the symbolic possibilities available to that Other.[14] That would suggest that all Echo can ever do is echo. She is caught within the ruses of reason which constrain and even produce her resistances to that entrapment.

Women have been associated with madness in the West because of the isomorphic relation between terms in binary oppositions: reason / madness, men/women, culture/nature, speech/silence.[15] Because of the substitutions within these series of oppositions, it is possible to read Barthes's text about madness and temporarily insert the words *women* or *the female* as echoes wherever he writes *madness* in order to show how he presumes a generic subject position. The passage could just as easily be rewritten with the binary pair First World/Third World to foreground the Manichaean impasse of First World critics who also "lament" the silence of the colonized or subaltern subject. In a later chapter the symbolic effects of colonization will be discussed in relation to an expanded notion of the gendered pair—active/passive, the One/Other. Barthes's text and the addition of an echo foreground the similarity between the ways the history of women and the history of Others have been written by authorized knowers, men of reason.

Madness (the female), says Barthes, is only "what it is *said* to be (and what else could we decide, since there is no discourse of madness [women] about reason, corresponding to the discourse of reason about madness [women]" (1972, 165). This *saying* must be "treated literally, and not as the outmoded phenomenon about which we now know the truth at last." This act of saying constitutes a true delusion, in Nietzsche's terms. Barthes continues:

> And on the other hand . . . [Foucault] here studies an object whose objective character he deliberately puts in parenthesis; not only does he describe collective representations (still rarely done in history), but he even claims that without being mendacious these representations somehow exhaust their object; we cannot reach madness [women] outside the notions of men of reason (which does not mean, moreover, that these notions are illusory; it is therefore neither on the side of (scientific) reality nor on the side of the (mythic) image that we shall find the historical reality of madness [women]: it is on the level of the interconstituent dialogue of reason and unreason, though we must keep in mind that this dialogue is faked; it involves a great silence, that of the mad [women]; for the mad [women] possess no metalanguage in which to speak of reason. (165)

This is a dialogue that is only *acting* like a dialogue because it is basically still what we might call a monologue with symptoms; it is not reciprocal. Its alternations, its meanings and losses, do not occur freely in both directions:

> For the constitutive observation of madness [women] by men of reason is very quickly seen to be a simple element of their *praxis*: the fate of the mad [women] is closely linked to the society's needs with regard to labor [in the case of women, reproduction and eroticism, as well as labor], to the economy as a whole . . . *simultaneous* with these needs appear representations which establish them in nature. (Barthes 1972, 166)

These representations of the mad and of women acquire an effective force; they become discursive facts which define a field in which identifications and exclusions become possible and are enforced. Barthes arrives at what is for him the most disturbing paradox of this structured situation, this trap of reason: the accounts of exclusion can only be written by one of the "two humanities participating" because nomination by the knower produces both the known and the knower (Barthes 1972, 166). Man, like Adam, "communicates his own mental being (insofar as it is communicable) by naming all other things," says Walter Benjamin. "*It is therefore the linguistic being of man to name things,*" and by so doing, "*he* communicates himself by naming *them*" (Benjamin 1982, 317). Though there are other kinds of language than the language of naming, language as a concept in the Western tradition has most often referred to the notion of linguistic Being, which is itself equated with mental being: "The quintessence of this intensive totality of language as the mental being of man is naming. Man is the namer . . ." (Benjamin 1982, 317).

This metaphysical tradition that equates linguistic Being with mental being rests on a fundamental exclusion, and Man's attempts to describe this exclusion in a critical way falls into a kind of "bewilderment," a "vertigo," because, as he studies and names the excluded Outside, his stance and position are reinscribed on the side of the Inside:

> In the couple constituted by reason and madness [women], by included and excluded, knowledge is a taking of sides; the very act which apprehends madness [femininity, woman] no longer as an object but as the other face which reason rejects, thereby proceeding to the extreme verge of intelligence, this act, too, is an act of darkness: casting a brilliant light on the couple constituted by madness [women] and reason, *knowledge* thereby illuminates its own solitude and its own particularity: manifesting the very history of the division, it cannot escape it. (Barthes 1972, 168)

There is, says Barthes, a structural paradox: men have accepted the historicity of the forms of reason, "but there has never been a corresponding history of *unreason* in this couple, outside of which neither term can be constituted, one of the partners is historical, participates in the values of civilization, escapes the fatality of being, conquers the freedom of doing; the other partner is excluded from history, fastened to an essence, either supernatural, or moral, or medical . . . " (Barthes 1972, 168, 169).

Even when madness [woman] is constituted as an inspired or respectable object, such as in the works of Hölderlin or Nietzsche (or when the feminine becomes a metaphor for textual ambiguity),[16] it is limited and subject to exchange among men of reason. Barthes continues:

> To discourse about madness [women] starting from knowledge, whatever extreme one reaches, is therefore never to emerge from a functional antinomy whose truth is thus inevitably situated in a space as inaccessible to the mad [women] as to men of reason; for to conceive this antinomy is always to conceive it starting from one of its terms: distance here is merely the ultimate ruse of reason.

Knowledge cannot escape this exclusion, reinforcing the exclusion "often just when it thinks it is being most generous." Foucault is critical of progressivist attempts that convert madness into an object, thus "masking the functional antinomy of two humanities." He continues: "the history of madness [women] could be 'true' only if it were naïve, i.e., written by a madman [a woman]; but then it could not be written in terms of history, so that we are left with the incoercible bad faith of knowledge" (1972, 170).

By remembering Echo's plight and her relation to the exclusiveness of reason in the Western tradition to which Barthes refers, his text can be brought to comment on itself because it makes audible an ironic silence that is, paradoxically but importantly, *not* muteness. There is, on the one hand, Echo as Woman repeating masculine words. But, on the other hand, there are women who have spoken from the cultural and historical particularity of female knowledge all through history, yet they were not "heard" by reason. There is an excess here, a difference. Woman as spoken does not exhaust women speaking.

Looking more closely at what Barthes says about history helps unsettle what he calls the bad faith of knowledge, whose particularity is that it is a version of knowledge having to do with masculine experience. But "the history of [women] could be 'true' only if it were naive, i.e., written by [a woman], but then it could not be written in terms of history." Barthes's despair over the impossible dizziness of knowledge makes sense if we presume that men (or the supposedly neuter, or generic, "man") are the only agents of history and knowledge, that the mad, nature, and women merely wait to be named and that men are always trapped in their identity as namers; they just can't help themselves. This is the despair repeated in discussions of colonial discourse in which First World theorists wring their hands at the futility of writing about the Third World because they find they must simply recolonize it, their symbolic representations exhausting all there is to be said about colonized subjects. It might be more productive, however, to recognize that, because "naive history" *cannot* be written in terms of history, it has some chance of being written differently. Colonized subjects and women can and do write and speak and know. They are neither mute nor mysterious, nor do they patiently wait for man as Namer to tell their story. Barthes's despair, paradoxically, has functioned to reassure Man the namer of his centrality in the face of naive threats.

The stories women and colonized subjects might tell of naive history and the stories white men have told may have very little similarity because of the different positions of subjectivity, the different sites of enunciation, out of which they arise. Men and women, First World and Third, may, in fact, occupy (at least) two very different spheres, which need an aesthetic story to connect them. As Nietzsche says:

> Between two absolutely different spheres, as between subject and object, there is no causality, no correctness, and no expression: there is at most an aesthetic relation: I mean a suggestive transference, a stammering translation into a completely foreign tongue—for which there is required, in any case, a freely inventive intermediary sphere and mediating force. (Nietzsche 1979, 86)

The history of Oedipus and Western metaphysics lies in this passage locating meaning in an aesthetic relationship between words and things. Its interpretation is accomplished by a mediating *force,* which requires an intermediary sphere, a *medium.* In the *Timaeus* Plato sets out just such a model of the cosmos: Being, which results from the originary force of the Demiurge, or Divine Craftsman, must be interpreted by the privileged interpreter, the philosopher, as it makes its forms or paradigms intelligible within the *chora,* the intermediary, feminized sphere or space.

Backgrounds for a Family Story

All twentieth-century dramatists must wrestle with the heritage that underlies discussions of bodies in performance, a heritage that has to do with the cultural construction of the family, which grounds the most resolutely abstract and metaphysical discussions. For Plato Being comes to be interpreted by the philosopher according to a model of biological reproduction. Being is analagous to the father, Becoming is the son, and the medium within which Being becomes intelligible is the receptacle, the womb, the mother. This story of reproduction continues in a surprisingly similar way in the twentieth century in the work of Lévi-Strauss, whose work was fundamental to poststructuralism. Lévi-Strauss told a story about how it was that "a stammering translation" of the real world by means of symbolic thought, or a language that was the sedimented history of a social grouping, came about: "The emergence of symbolic thought must have required that women, like words, should be things that were exchanged." This exchange was the only way to deal with an original symbolic incompatibility, the fact that "the same woman was seen under two incompatible aspects: on the one hand, as the *object* of personal desire, thus exciting sexual and propietal instincts; and, on the other, as the *subject* of the desire of others, and seen as such, i.e., as the means of binding others through alliance with them" (1969, 496). Women here are still the medium of the men's production of knowledge by way of symbolic thought. In every society, according to Lévi-Strauss, certain individuals figure incompatible syntheses or compromises; their marginal position does not, however, keep them from being integral to the system.

The woman is, thus, both object and means of binding society together. For Lévi-Strauss, it is because of the double nature of woman that the relations between the sexes "have preserved that affective richness, ardour and mystery which doubtless originally permeated the entire universe of human communications" (497). He describes those relations as a "duet." But the duet, like Barthes's dialogue between reason and unreason, is faked. Marriage as duet is perhaps the most prestigious fiction of all; our defenses should go up everytime we hear marriage used as a metaphor, for there are usually very unequal things being joined when that metaphor is used. Lévi-Strauss's duet story is about marriage as an activity that takes place among men. Following Emile Benveniste's tracing of the Indo-European terminology for *marriage* helps see what is going on in this marriage story.

First of all, Benveniste points out that, in the vocabulary of kinship, particularly concerning conjugality, "the situation of the man and that of the woman have nothing in common" (Benveniste 1973, 193). There is, in fact, no connection between the derivation of the verb *to marry* and the noun for the condition of being married, or *matrimony*. This independence of derivation is marked by the different connotations of the two strains of development: one refers to men, the other to women. "For the man the terms are verbal, and for the woman nominal." For the man the verb has to do with an act; for the woman the noun has to do with a site where she is to be found, with a function she is given—reproduction, receptivity to the male who gives her and her offspring an identity.

Benveniste goes on to say: "If we now search for terms employed to designate the 'marriage' from the woman's point of view, we find that there exists no verb denoting in her case the fact of marrying which is the counterpart of the expressions mentioned ['to take, to lead, to give' as male actions]. The only verb which can be cited is the Latin *nubere*. But apart from being confined to Latin, *nubere* properly applies only to the taking of the veil" (193). For the woman, then, there is no active verb having to do with her entry into this marriage situation. Following etymologies, as Derrida and Nietzsche have shown, does not give us origins or truths. Rather, it provides a social history of *usage* and helps set out a description of grammar as sedimented social history.

There are only verbal forms marking the woman as the object and not the subject, what Benveniste calls a "negative lexical situation" for the woman. Legally, she is led into wifehood, "the condition to which the young woman accedes." That condition, named *matrimonium*, signifies "legal status of the *mater*"; it gets its full sense from "the point of view of the father, from the husband's point of view, and lastly from the woman's point of view," but only as a condition, not as an act. Her only act is, paradoxically, passive, the "taking of the veil." She does not appropriate it or grasp it but accedes to it because she herself has already been taken. This veil she accedes to sets up her unveiling at marriage. That unveiling can, of course, only occur because she has previously been veiled, the terminology here echoing Western philosophy's discussions of blindnesses and insights.

The Spatial Ordering of the Family of Man: Building the Stage

Lévi-Strauss's comparison of marriage to the original fullness of human communication is ironic because it denies dual participation by two members in the marriage unit, then it erases that denial by calling the unit a duet. This rich, passionate duet becomes even more disturbing, however, as he continues. His countermodel to the repressions the nature/culture split requires is a longing for a time when "women will no longer be exchanged" (1969, 497), a time of full presence. But this is hardly a feminist utopia, for he goes on to describe it as a time when one can "enjoy without sharing," when "one might keep to oneself," what formerly had had to be exchanged. Because "one" here can only be masculine in this kinship model, we find here mystified a startling romanticization of incest. It is daughters and sisters whom one can "enjoy without sharing."

The ironic metaphor of the domestic duet thus idealizes and covers over what has been left out of history, but, long before the domestic duet assumed its metaphoric power in Lévi-Strauss, the marriage metaphor was important to Western reason. The fact that we can skip back and forth between historical periods here is important. There are obviously important differences between twentieth-century France and classical Greece, but Barthes's and Lévi-Strauss's texts (and later Lacan's) share certain assumptions with Aristotle about the naturalness of the family founded on a particular form of marriage.[17]

Aristotle's interest in reproduction, morphology, and embryology led to *Generation of Animals,* in which he developed his idea that animal reproduction, the continuity of the species, and the continuity of the cosmos are united in an organic relation. The specific female contribution to this continuum is allotted to the biological sphere of particularity, while that of the male is located in the rational sphere, where it is capable of being generalized. A passage from this work sounds remarkably contemporary. As a description of natural reproduction, which is the basis for the relation between male and female, it connects male and female to the opposition between active and passive. In contemporary culture this opposition continues to organize symbolic relationships which have nothing to do with biological reproduction:

The male and female are distinguished by a certain capacity and incapacity. (For the male is that which can concoct and form and discharge a semen carrying with it the principle of form—by "principle" I do not mean a material principle out of which comes into being an offspring resembling the parent, but I mean the first moving cause, whether it have power to act as such in the thing itself or in something else—but the female is that which receives semen; but cannot form it or discharge it.) . . . Now since the one sex is able and the other is unable to reduce the residual secretion to a pure form, and every capacity has a certain corresponding organ, whether the faculty produces the desired results in a lower degree or in a higher degree, and since the two sexes correspond in this manner (the terms "able" and "unable" being used in more sense than one)—therefore it is necessary that both female and male should have organs. Accordingly the one has the uterus, the other the male organs. (Aristotle 1984, 1184)

The semen "acts and makes," while the female secretion "is made and receives the form" (1185). The male, associated with the semen, acts; the female is acted upon. In Benveniste's tracing of the etymology of *marriage* the male acts; the female is acted upon. A "natural" link seems to have been established between each of the genders and the categories of subject, or actor, and object, or the one acted upon.

There was a concomitant spatial separation in the Greek city between those who were "able," who had the capacity, to act and those who were "unable," who were acted upon. Active civic participation took place in the agora and those who were unable to participate in civic affairs engaged in other duties elsewhere. The agora was an open space in the middle of the city, and its form represented a significant change in the architecture of Athens as compared to the older architectural style of Mycenae, which had been constructed as a fortified palace. The Greek organization of urban space continues to influence our notion of the subject as active, public man and the object as domestic, passive woman. Language as a carrier and organizer of symbolic meaning intersects with the organization of *space* by means of the articulations, the dividing up into units of meaning, achieved by each.

The agora represented an urban framework that differed from the fortified palace because the activities that occurred in it relied to a great extent on the art of argumentation through speech. The art of politics, says Jean-Pierre Vernant, "became essentially the management of language" (1982, 48). Greek reason, he argues:

> was not so much the product of human commerce with things as of the relations of human beings with one another. It developed less through the techniques that apply to the world than through those that give one person power over others, and whose common instrument is language: the art of the politician, the rhetorician, the pedagogue. Greek reason is that reason which makes it possible to act practically, deliberately, and systematically on human beings, not to transform nature. (132)

In the agora citizens argued the merits of their positions according to certain codified rules of reason and persuasion; the rules of justice and wisdom were no longer handed down from on high but were the result of mediation and dialogue. As John Winkler argues, the polis was itself a kind of performance space for "the collective maneuvering of public opinion," for "social movements in a competitive game" (1990, 75).

The public space of the agora presupposed only certain participants in any debate; the simple fact of entry into this public space defined one as a rational human being. Citizens were those who had the right to speak there, though not all citizens routinely spoke; rather, speakers (rhêtores) proposed legislation and made speeches.[18] No matter how different they were in rank or function or origin, however, citizens were somehow comparable and "like" in a particular way, a "likeness" or sameness that made them eligible to be members of the *philia,* or community, as Insiders. This likeness, however, was complex.

The concept of likeness draws on the historical development of the subject in its relation to the history of the rise of the Greek city-state as a military organization. An equivalence was originally set up among fighters according to their martial qualifications, which established their right to participate in public affairs, an equivalence or correspondence "that was never again questioned" (Vernant 1982, 62). This equivalence was gradually refined, and the organization of horse soldiers was replaced by the organization of a different kind of soldier, the hoplite, a heavily armed line soldier who fought in phalanxes, or close formations. Heroic individual bravery based on *thymos,* or passion, was replaced by bravery based on *sophrosyne,* the power of self-control and discipline, which led to cooperation. Worth gradually came to be demonstrated within the formation, on the terrain of coordinated maneuvers, rather than according to the singular merits of an individual heroic act.

Later, in democratic Athens, there were two kinds of equivalences possible for individuals who were able to participate in civic activity in the polis. One was an aristocratic similarity between individuals of greater merit than the ordinary citizen. Their aristocratic status was reinforced by a level of organization in which the strong were kept in place by moderation, and the weak trusted in that moderation, a remnant of a kind of situation based on might: "The equality thus achieved remained proportional to merit" (Vernant 1982, 97). The other kind of equivalence, possible only after the first had been accounted for, was democratic, a one-to-one relationship that defined all citizens as exactly equal in relation to the law and to the punishment of crimes.[19]

Vernant suggests that the polis could thus be seen in terms of a complex rationalization of space: "The first urban planners ... were in fact political theorists: the organization of urban space was but one aspect of a general effort to order and rationalize the human world ... at bottom the sage and the politician had the same aim: to set social life in order, to bring together and unify the city" (1982, 76). The origins of Western rational thought were "bound up with the social and mental structures peculiar to the Greek city" (130), where a certain rationalized urban space coincided with the presuppositions of reason and thereafter constrained Western symbolic possibilities for those who would be "subjects."[20] The development of the agora implies that reason, language, and the state simultaneously found each other as the state escaped the hold of the aristocratic *genes* to become everybody's business.

But not quite. Vernant's tracing of the political background of *homo rationalis* is very important for feminist theorists, but in this particular argument and in his discussions of Greek tragedy, though he acknowledges women, he curiously leaves them out of attempts to conceptualize Greek society; he does this, paradoxically, by acknowledging their absence. That is, their circumstances are acknowledged—"Women, whether slaves or free, were never citizens in the Greek cities. They were beneath the city, relegated to a status of less than citizenship" (1982, 312)—but that acknowledgment is then erased. As I will argue in the next chapter, after noting women's absence, Vernant finds himself mak-

ing claims about the development of "human" knowledge in the very
site from which they were excluded, the city.

A feminist researcher thus finds herself having to function like Echo
as she works with these texts. At such moments Patrice Petro's advice
to submit "regimes of visibility to a general critique" proves its relevance. There are certain things Vernant cannot *see*. Though I am not a
classicist, perhaps, if I am careful, my rereading of this regime of visibility, a rereading that all the while tries to acknowledge the risks inherent
in such a project, can also problematize the way our very definitions of
scholarship have to be carefully and rigorously investigated,[21] for overlooking evidence about women means that the first step, what precedes
the polis, is still presumed to be natural, and mystery, ardor, enigmas,
and riddles circle around it. As Marx said, the family is "that spontaneously developed form which we find on the threshold of the history of
all civilized races," with a "natural division of labor existing in the family" (1987, 82; 1978, 151).

But marriage and the family are, of course, not natural—unless we
define *natural* as Winkler does, as "conventional"; he argues that the very
contrast between nature and culture "seems to be a product of the sophis-
tic enterprises of the fifth century B.C.E." (1990, 17). Analyzing the
ordering of the family upon which the polis rests and naturalizes itself
means looking even more closely at the effects of Sophocles, Aristotle,
and tragedy on the sociosymbolic system that brings us "nature." Aristotle considered *Oedipus the King* to be "the most nearly perfect tragedy,"
and, as Gerald Else argues, Aristotle's logic is "permeated by the convic-
tion that the best or perfect specimen *is* the species in the proper sense"
(1957, 445). Oedipus' drama *is* the species called tragedy, just as Oedipus
is the species called human being. This ironic story of a universal human
experience which very few people are entitled to have organizes an aesthetic and epistemological concept of subjectivity in which the tragic
subject sets the stage for Western reason and aesthetics. And a very
specific form of marriage founds his plot.

Chapter I

Tragedy as Marriage Strategy: The Story of Oedipus

Son, it's very plain you don't know what you're doing.
— Messenger, *Oedipus the King*

A drama is an action performed by persons, and persons necessarily enter, in some fashion and to some degree, into the visible realm.
— Gerald Else, *Aristotle's Poetics: The Argument*

Sophocles' *Oedipus the King* is about historical transitions and the attempt, during such periods of transition, to articulate and stabilize categories that reinforce social organization. It is also about the purification of defilement that interferes with fertility during a spring ritual, the Thargelia. At the time the tragedy was written Athens was in the process of changing from an oligarchical political system to a democratic one and from laws based on sacred revelations to laws that grew out of the discursive activity of the polis; a mythological pantheon that retained traces of matriliny was being replaced by a patriarchal system of gods. Central to all these shifts was the inscription and ordering of sexual difference. One of the most powerful conceptual and political structures involved in this ordering was the institution of marriage, and one of the most important sites of organizing the cultural representations of marriage and gender was tragedy.

The representations of women on the Greek stage that have come down to us were constructed by male dramatists and actors, this masculine site of knowledge production the result of the historical development of religious and political forms that relegated matriarchal influences to prehistory. Male priests also took over from female ones; the temple at Delphi was originally the temple of a matriarchal cult of priestesses, who participated in hymns and chants, but, by the time of the Bronze Age, Delphi was Apollo's, the Olympian deities having replaced the matriarchal ones. Only a single female soothsayer, the Pythia, was left in what had become a masculine cult of the oracle. She functioned as a medium, the words of her oracle interpreted and formulated by men— the male priests and seers like Tiresias who turned what the Pythia said into sensible language;[1] an incoherent utterance was translated into the intelligible language of the polis.

This particular notion of translation, as it relates to priests translating the Pythia, helps develop the linkage I have been trying to establish between classical Greece, or at least received notions of classical Greece, and the continuing influence of tragedy on poststructuralism. Nietzsche's concept of translation is historically important to this linkage because his reading of classical Greece, in *The Birth of Tragedy*, helped provide twentieth-century poststructuralism and dramatic theories of performance with insights into the constructedness of the real. His discussion of translation, from "On Truth and Lying," bears repeating. The interpretation of meaning, he argues, works according to a model of translation that depends on a relation between subject and object and seems to be about *making*:

> Between two absolutely different spheres, as between subject and object, there is no causality, no correctness, and no expression: there is at most an aesthetic relation: I mean a suggestive transference, a stammering translation into a completely foreign tongue—for which there is required, in any case, a freely inventive intermediary sphere and mediating force. (1979, 87)

Though I will eventually argue that femininity in general serves as the intermediary sphere or medium, at this point, in relation to interpretation, it is more specifically the Pythia who is the medium and the masculine priest the knower, whose interpretation provides the mediating force and whose interpretation becomes the received version, or the truth.

Sophocles and Aristotle, too, translated women,[2] and the site of intelligibility, the place where their translations could be understood by the polis at large, was the genre of tragedy that helped set the terms of the language that made such translations comprehensible; its requirements began to function as a kind of grammar. Aristotle's critical assessment of tragedy passed over a number of other tragedies with different kinds of protagonists to settle on *Oedipus the King* as the finest, his choice perhaps attributable to his focus on plot, which he considered to be the most important element in tragedy. But why plot? What does plot have to do with translated women and with what Vernant referred to as the rationalization of space? How was it bound up "with the social and mental structure peculiar to the Greek city," Vernant's notion of rationalized space? And what does it have to do with marriage?

Aristotle selected *Oedipus the King* as the most nearly perfect tragedy according to his own formal requirements set out in the *Poetics*. Only one-tenth of all Greek tragedies fit those requirements, and of the extant thirty-two, only two fit, according to Gerald Else: *Oedipus the King* and *Iphigenia in Tauris*. One of these, *Iphigenia*, in Else's opinion, is a melodrama, its selection revealing the way Aristotle allowed his preference for symmetry as the most important feature of the perfect plot to interfere with his critical appreciation of tragedy.[3] But the other, *Oedipus the King*, is different: "It so happened that the knife-edge of [Aristotle's] judgment hit square on one masterpiece, the *Oedipus*" (Else 1957, 446).

A series of judgments are thus involved in selecting the *Oedipus*. Sophocles himself had had to select the particular Oedipus story he needed from a number of variants of the legends about Oedipus and the family of Cadmus.[4] This same Greek tragedy, out of all the others, also provided Freud with an aesthetic figure to represent the universal structure of subjectivity; to paraphrase Else, the knife-edge of Freud's judgment again coincidentally hit on one masterpiece, the *Oedipus*. Freud described the particular Oedipus legend that Sophocles selected as one "whose profound and universal power to move can only be understood if the hypothesis I have put forward in regard to the psychology of children has a universal validity" (1965, 294).

Yet these selections of *Oedipus the King* have more to say about the societies which find their truths in its plot, as well as about what Winkler called "the formation of a class of intellectuals and about competition for ideological hegemony," than they do about that plot itself. The questions to be asked are why this particular plot has proved so attractive, why it and not another has been preserved. Looking at tragedy as an epistemological structure requires that questions about universality be asked somewhat differently. Rather than asking what is universal about the Oedipus legend, we might much more productively displace such a question and ask a different, more interesting one: what does it mean that a particular society asks if this plot is universal? More particularly, what does the site of knowledge production have to do with the kinds of questions asked of the *Oedipus?*[5]

The word *mythos* in the *Poetics* means tragic plot, but it had not always had that meaning. In Homer *mythos* meant a word or an utterance, and it later came to mean talk or a story about the heroic or distant past, eventually referring specifically to a mythical or fabulous tale. By Aristotle's time the use of *mythos* to refer to legends and tales was common. His application of the word to dramatic plot was innovative and new, and it may have reflected the fact that tragic poets were reconstructing legends and tales for the theater, as Gerald Else argues. The native context of this new usage of *mythos* as plot, or principle of motion, was thus theater. And theater was much more directly and openly related to the military and political organization of the state than it is today.

According to John Winkler, the audience's observance of the play ritualized an initiation of the *ephebate,* the group of young citizens in military training. The origins of Greek tragedy, he argues, were not Dionysian revelry and the overturning of hierarchies, as Nietzsche romantically suggests. They were, instead, intimately connected to military training: "It is important to underscore the fact that the *toto caelo* difference we experience between the military realm and the theatrical, between marching to war and going to a play, did not apply to the City Dionysia" (Winkler 1985, 31–32).

The performers onstage were differentiated according to age status: the chorus was performed by *ephebes,* while the main three actors were always mature men. The *ephebate* becomes what Winkler calls the "still center," the perspective symbolized by the chorus, those who will learn the lesson of the tragedy: "the events and characters portrayed in tragedy are meant to be contemplated as lessons by young citizens (or rather by the entire *polis* from the vantage point of the young citizen) and therefore makes the watchful scrutiny of the chorus structurally important as a still center from which the strange turbulence is surveyed and evaluated." The very organization of meaning depended on that still center, for "in the complex and ever-changing organization of the city Dionysia, the ephebes were both physically and analytically at the center of attention" (Winkler 1985, 38, 29).

The precision of the dance movements of the Greek chorus were most likely extensions of military gymnastics and training in disciplined movement—in particular, the movements required for hoplite formations: "the tragic chorus' formation and movements were homologous to (or aesthetic refinements of) the hoplite drill" (Winkler 1985, 43). The hoplite was a military phalanx, which had replaced the individual method of fighting celebrated in Homer; the Greek military had come to rely on disciplined, highly organized maneuvers in which no single hero stood out.

Tragedy as an initiation of young men into adulthood and, in particular, into military and civic responsibility was a social ritual, with actors representing the social differentiation between the *ephebate* and mature adult males and with the audience symbolizing the polis itself:

> The entire audience is organized in a way that demonstrates its corporate manliness as a *polis* to be reckoned with, comprising individuals who are both vigilant to assert excellence against other members of the city (tribe versus tribe) and ready to follow legitimate authority against external threats (cadet soldiers and Council). . . . The plays they watched spoke to this organization. (Winkler 1985, 32)

Mythos as plot of the dramatic work referred to the composition of the action of the play; it was the aesthetic expression of the principle of motion, the way that principle could be made perceptible to human understanding, what Nietzsche might call the translation of the principle of motion into perceptibility. This version of plot also has to do with mimesis, which was to be an imitation not of something already existing but of action itself, of the activity of making.

The construction of plot "is not an incidental duty, it is the critical, the essential part of the poet's 'making' . . . it keeps the full active sense: ποίη-σις, mak-ing, composi-tion. . . . It represents the shaping process as it guides the poet's mind, the ἀρχή which will eventuate later in the finished poem" (Else 1957, 8–9).

The poet's artistic construction would be a highly complex means of expressing the universal principle of construction, of imitating the principle of construction, activity, the process of making. The plot's organic unfolding in language involves a process of discovery: the poet recognizes and uncovers "a true relation which already exists somehow in the scheme of things" (Else 1957, 320) through a kind of dialectic involving two poles: artistic expression and universal truth. This schema does not involve the claim that a form or paradigm already exists in the scheme of things, as does Plato's metaphysics. Here, rather, the poet, in his mind's eye, discovers not a form but a relation that already exists, an aesthetic linkage between the cosmos and the possibilities of symbolic expression.

The poet was to construct something that had never existed before, thus simultaneously making something new and discovering true relations already there. These true relations could, in fact, only be said to "exist" if they were expressed, the universal truth inherent in them requiring the specific phenomenon of its expression—the work of art. This dialectical relation between the universal principle of motion and the particular phenomenon was kept from getting out of control by the claim that plot could overrule any disturbances that might inadvertently be introduced into the tragic plot by the randomness of the particular bodies or words involved in its expression. The demands of the universal principle of motion were thus presumed to overrule accidents and randomness along the way, as the sequential, linear motion of the plot (closely linked to temporality or time) achieved precedence over incidents that occurred along the way and were surpassed (the spatial dimension).

Tragic poetry, in Aristotle's mind, was actually truer than history because of this concern with universals. While historians might write about accidental particularities, the task for tragic poets was to represent kinds of occurrences that were not accidental but were necessary and probable and, thus, closer to universal truth.

Continuing this attempt to mark history off from tragedy, he distinguished between dramatic plot and narrative. Narrative corresponds to history that is reported or told as the historian gathers his material into a form in some measure forcibly structured by his narration. Dramatic plot, however, requires that the poet allow characters to speak for themselves, to enact themselves as types of human beings whose identification partially depends on visibility: "the characters will necessarily look one way rather than another" (Else 1957, 245).

Aristotle's advice to the poet to visualize his plot first means that the poet is to forget himself and "[bring] his characters on" in his mind so that he can tell whether or not they are expressing themselves appropriately: "In constructing his plots and using diction to bring them to completion, [the poet] should put [the events] before his eyes as much as he can. In this way, seeing them very vividly as if he were actually present at the actions [he represents], he can discover what is suitable, and is least likely to miss contradictions" (1987, 22). Because of this, the plots do not have to be enacted to achieve their effects; they can do so even if they are only imagined. The individual characters are, in fact, secondary to the plot, which is to be constructed first in outline form, then the names of characters supplied and episodes introduced. The poet's visualization of plot first and then his search for character names will supposedly counteract the interference of the particularity of individual human bodies into the universality of plot and character type. Character is not primary: "Character can be conveyed through speech or action—though, considering the severe limitations of the Greek stage, tragedy does it primarily through speech. Thought on the other hand, *cannot be conveyed by anything but language*" (244).

The male poet's eye and poetic language are thus fundamental elements of the sphere of intelligibility called tragic plot. Aristotle also relies on the male eye for the concept of a symmetrical whole in which action can be comprehended by the spectator. This symmetry requires that the protagonist pass from happiness to unhappiness, or, vice versa, move "from one extreme state of human fortune to the other, passing through a necessary or probable sequence of intermediary steps" (Else 1957, 487). The perfect imitation of action will be one that represents the balanced treatment of these polarities, the concept of the "whole" depending on the length of the representation that can fit the eye, a representation that the poet and later the spectator can visualize and comprehend as a kind of organic whole without losing interest: "Consequently, just as in the case of bodies and of animals these should have magnitude, but [only] a magnitude that is easily seen as a whole, so too in the case of plots these should have length, but [only] a length that is easily memorable" (Aristotle 1987, 11).

Else suggests that soul and body, spirit and biology, are linked by Aristotle in his discussion of *mythos:*

> The μῦθος is the imitation of the action, says Aristotle; he means it in the same sense that a man's soul is the man. For the plot is the *structure* of the play, around which the material "parts" are laid, just as the soul is the structure of a man. It is well known that in Aristotle's biology the soul—i.e., the form—is "prior" to the body; and we shall see that he thinks of the plot as prior to the poem in exactly the same way. By this I do not mean when we say that the "story"

or "myth" of Oedipus was there before Sophocles wrote his drama. For Aristotle the plot precedes the poem, but it too is essentially "made" by the poet, even if he is using traditional material. (242–43)

Aristotle's concept of dramatic plot proves to rest on the privilege of two concepts: masculine vision and masculine activity. Both of these privileged concepts recur in the organization of the institution called marriage. Developing the implications of this linkage will depend on Teresa de Lauretis's work showing the relationship between this kind of plot and the social construction of gender.[6] She extends Vladimir Propp's study of plot in folktales and Jurij Lotman's structuralist description of certain "universals" of plot structure, her plotting of plots describing a structure that forms part of the prehistory of the twentieth-century Western concept of the subject and its deconstruction, both inherently linked to the masculine protagonist of Greek tragedy.

The Stories of Oedipus

Propp's *Morphology of the Folktale* is his best-known work, but a more historical study is *The Historical Roots of the Fairy Tale,* published in 1946 but not yet published in English.[7] In this study Propp established the need to connect the historical origins of plots to overlapping structures of authority: "From the point of view of their content, the phenomena in themselves [the plots of tales] are not historical, but they can only be explained historically as resulting from the substitution of one social order by another and by the incongruences and contradictions which derive from that substitution" (1974, 506; my translation).

In periods of transition between matrilineal and patrilineal succession, when cultural work involved organizing the representations of the passage of authority, women's authority was in some measure connected to animals. As such, women had some influence over the success of hunting. They were also involved in divination and interpretation, associated with skills in reading the behavior of animals and the symptoms of the body.[8]

The connection between women, nature, animals, and interpretation linked women directly as contributors to the survival of the group. The Sphinx retains this female-animal connnection in her image, which represents a border that, perhaps, marks this transitional period: between nature and culture, or one kind of society and another—between animal and woman. The transition to patrilineal succession had to do with lessening the threat of that border and with organizing the role of the wife of a citizen of the polis into that of mother, rather than that of a contributor to the sustenance of the group. The society's need for organized reproduction came under the control of the city-state in more complex ways; paradoxically, as woman became mother, control of fertility became man's job. In Sophocles' drama Oedipus was responsible for restoring the fertility of three things: the land, the animals, and women.

Propp's tracing of this transition from matriliny to patriliny foregrounds the cultural organization of subject positions and of signifying possibilities directly related to political possibilities for subjectivity. Not only is the role of woman symbolically arranged by plot, but it also helps construct authority in the polis. A family triangle set out for heuristic purposes makes that organization clearer. In matrilineal societies, Propp says, the triangle's characters are father–daughter–son-in-law. In tales from the matrilineal period the daughter often had the responsibility to give the suitor tasks to perform, as the Sphinx does in Oedipus. But in patrilineal societies, passage of the throne goes from father to son. Oedipus' plot, in Propp's schema, illustrates this change; the throne is not passed to the daughter's husband (by way of the daughter) but, rather, to the son.

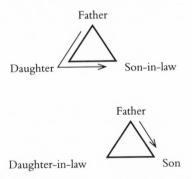

In the earlier system, when the throne was passed from the father by way of his daughter to his son-in-law, stories of regicide were possible, and, says Propp, they were likely; the son-in-law in those tales frequently killed the king and replaced him. But in the stories arising out of the new family triangle regicide is committed by the son, combining regicide and parricide. The Oedipus stories are related to Athens, on a cultural terrain in which the worst of all crimes is murder within the family, such a murder within the *philia* resulting in the pollution of society and requiring cleansing by catharsis: the body of the murderer was to be thrown outside the city gates or left naked at a crossroads, unburied.

In *Oedipus the King,* whose plot illustrates this transition in the passage of authority, leadership must be passed from father to son, from Laius to Oedipus, by way of a woman unrelated to the father by blood, the widow Jocasta, rather than by way of the father's daughter. By laying the second triangle on the first, the position of the daughter can be seen to be replaced by that of the daughter-in-law.

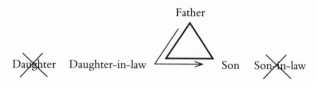

In the tales Propp analyzes the transition between kinds of authority rests on the regicide/parricide, a murder that carries such moral opprobrium yet becomes so inevitable that it acquires the characteristics of an involuntary act, its horrible necessity turned into an accident that befalls the character who commits the murder. In *Oedipus the King,* which might be seen as a tragedy of this very inevitability that simultaneously cleanses the murderer of his crime, Oedipus is described by Aristotle as innocently guilty. Because he does not intend to kill his father, he is innocent, but, because he does in fact kill him, he is guilty. The oracle has made his guilt necessary, but, through his own remorse, self-mutilation, and the unavoidability of his actions, he reveals that he is tragically innocent.

Gerald Else argues that this concept of innocent guilt illustrates a stage in the historical change from an archaic concept of blood law and its inevitable judgment of death for murderers of family members, whether or not the murderer intended the act, to the law of the polis. In democratic Greece law became the site of judgment and punishment, taking the responsibility for punishment out of the family's hands and giving it to the state, which could pardon an act of guilty innocence, of murder without the intent to murder. That is, the state through its law could *interpret,* even translate, that act. The law of the polis also became the site where the son could replace the father, freeing the social group from the instability produced by violence among its male members.

In the earlier matrilineal tales the murder of the king was always committed by a stranger, the son-in-law coming from a different extended family group. In the version of the story having to do with a transition from matrilineal to patrilineal passage of authority, however, a story like that of Oedipus, the murder of the king is still committed by a stranger. But he was a stranger only because he was unwittingly in disguise to himself as well as to the king.

The plot required that the son must have been separated from his father at an early age so that he would be thought of as a stranger, this separation brought about through the device of the oracle. In myths and stories containing remnants of the matrilineal period, Propp argues, there was no need for oracles because it was presumed that the father would die upon the accession of the son-in-law to the throne; however, "the oracle appears when the necessity of this form of substitution [father to son rather than son-in-law] begins to be unclear in the minds of men" (1974, 491; my translation). The oracle and the prophecy appeared along with patrilineal succession to deal with violent substitutions that were necessary but abhorrent. In a similar historical process the interpretation of the oracles also passed from women priestesses to male representatives of Apollo.

Just as the themes of the tales changed with the system of succession, so did the position and significance of the daughter who was equated with the princess. In a social system marked by succession by way of the daughter the tasks were often posed for the son-in-law by the daughter or her father. There were, in these tales, two types of princesses: one faithfully *waited* for the hero to save her from a serpent or monster and the other was *scheming* and vengeful, always ready to kill or rob the son-in-law claimant. In stories of the second type the hero's task generally involved overpowering and dominating the princess. Her hostility took the form of competition with him, but he generally took her violently against her will. These early matrilineal tales give her no brothers, but over time brothers began to appear in tales of transition, as the daughter's legitimate position was gradually eliminated. The allegory of the elimination of such a position is perhaps most strikingly staged in Antigone's death, her plot literally ended, as she is walled up in a cave.

The Sphinx, in *Oedipus the King,* narratively serves as the site of this ambiguous transitional female position, figuring one-half of the unstable split site of the princess. She is the remaining trace of the second possibility for princesses, the threatening, vengeful one who must be dominated, her plot ended. The other half of the princess role of the earlier triangle, that of the faithful woman who waits, is filled by Jocasta, the wife/mother.[9] She is also, however, like the daughter of matrilineal tales, the reward given to the suitor who performs the task given to him. This one remaining symbolic place within the family for all kinds of women begins to reveal its density and the intimate, overdetermined tensions that will haunt the construction of sexuality and especially women's relationships with each other.

The Sphinx retains other connotations from earlier tales, in particular the characteristics of the serpent, which is linked to the princess-sorceress of the fundamental plot structure that Propp isolates, the initiation (1974, 491). In the initiation plot, which he calls the "simple plot," the hero goes into the forest, the domain of the princess-sorceress, to endure a trial that prepares him for a higher level of existence, initiation functioning as a rite of transcendence, a passage from an immature state to a mature one. The hero in these tales frequently deprived the princess-sorceress of her power by sexual union, an act that also occurs in several of the other variations of the Oedipus myth. The female-animal in these tales is a hybrid, a kind of animal mother who nourishes the hero in her domain, the forest. As the strength of patrilineal authority became more strongly established, what Propp calls the complex Oedipus plot developed. Here the encounter with the hybrid female-animal became not the *goal* of movement as in the initiation plot but, rather, an encounter *incidental* though necessary to the son's search for the father, which becomes the goal. This encounter will be integral to the hero's larger goal, but the importance of that goal will surpass the importance of the encounter.

The two triangles thus mark two different strategies for the passage of authority and the arrangement of alliances. In spite of various changing configurations—in tales of matrilineal succession the daughter and son-in-law sometimes conspire against the father; at other times the conquered or violated daughter sides with the father; in the patrilineal Oedipus triangle father, son, and mother/wife in various ways establish and rearrange alliances—the broad structure of each kind of plot, the matrilineal and the patrilineal, remains identifiable.

Naming the Father

The tragedy of *Oedipus the King* assumes such importance in Western epistemology not because of any inherent universal truths it may contain but because those societies that found such truths in it were themselves involved in organizing the passage of authority and arranging alliances. That process is as strong in the late twentieth century as it ever was— perhaps stronger, in a period of political reaction against the gains made by feminism, lesbian and gay politics, and minority struggles.

Oedipus' search for the father, from whom the hero has been separated, revolves around the necessity of finding a proper name, which is Oedipus' goal, even though he is not aware of it; he knows his name, but he does not understand it. This particular feature of the oedipal plot, the search for the proper name, can also be historicized, using Jurij Lotman's structural approach to plot that isolates the proper name as a sign of the historical transition between mythological and nonmythological (or scientific, logical) ways of organizing meaning.[10] Though the word *logical* has come to suggest a universal and more highly developed mode of reasoning, it is highly specific, partial, and has to be historicized. It develops out of the same historical circumstances as does Aristotelian plot. These two systems of categorization, the mythological and the scientific, or logical, are chronologically different, the earlier one (the mythological) now accessible only obliquely and indirectly, perhaps only aesthetically, through structures influenced by the latter (the scientific, or logical). The symbolic place where the alternation and ambiguity of the two different systems of organization and articulation may be most clearly isolated is the proper name.

Categorization according to mythological naming, argues Lotman, works by arranging things which have in common only the fact that they share the same *name*. An arrangement of the group of things named Fido, for example, shares only the common trait of being named Fido. They share "Fido-ness." A different, nonmythological—logical—way of categorizing would be associated with the common noun *dog*. The group of things named "dog" shares traits organized by a master concept of "dogness," which would include species, visible characteristics, etc.[11]

Things that share the same name in a mythological system may be said to be isomorphic to each other, argues Lotman. They are "identical," though they are not the "Same." In the conceptual system of mythological cultures, for example, the word *Father* introduces an isomorphic set that includes God, the king or leader of the state, the phallus, and the actual father within the family. Similarly, *Mother* generates an isomorphic set that includes nature, the womb, and the actual mother. Isomorphisms "dealt not with phenomena which happened once and without reference to natural laws, but with events which were timeless, endlessly reproduced and in that sense motionless."[12]

The mythological system that remains active within proper names destabilizes nonmythological ways of organizing meaning by bothering, to some degree, the *meta*logic of logic, whose purpose is to divide things into discrete, decipherable categories of shared attributes and to arrange them in linear fashion. In phallocentric, logical cultures the meta-category of the Name of the Father distributes and delineates distinctions and attributes within an established symbolic system, this metalogic intimately related to the requirements of kinship and marriage.

Julia Kristeva's tracing of cursive and monumental time attempts to rethink these two kinds of logics in a way that extracts them from a system of binary opposition and theorizes their heterogeneity to and constant disruption of each other, a point to be developed in a later chapter (1982c, 13–35). The important concept of heterogeneity implies that each system is still at work disrupting the other as the two actually exist in a state of mixture, from which neither can be cleanly distinguished in its own right. Oedipus' search for his name and for the answer to the riddle of the Sphinx finds that the search rests precisely on the edge of the alternation between the mythological and the logical. It also rests on the edge of the sacred and the legal, the political and the aesthetic. But, though we might also expect it to be rather exquisitely balanced between the privilege of the masculine and the feminine, that struggle was already a thing of the past. *Oedipus the King* is about organizing the victory of the masculine and handing it down to posterity, to all the sons to come.

In Lotman's analysis both the mythological and the nonmythological stories involved masculine protagonists. In the mythological plot the action had to do with one character and his basic project: "entry into a closed space—emergence from it" (Lotman 1974, 171). Eventually, as this kind of mythological plot became more complex, this initial single situation concerning one hero and one object or obstacle was dispersed, first into doubles then into more and more characters or even various complex identities within the same character. All of these built on the textual material of the initial, simple situation, but they varied it in infinite ways; this simple, basic model of hero and object serves now as a "universal" structure. It is separated from specific contents, but it serves as structural material for textual construction: "Looked at typologically, the initial situation is that a certain plot space is divided by a *single* boundary into an internal and an external sphere, and a *single* character has the opportunity to cross that boundary" (167).

Any doubles of the male hero will remain in the active masculine plot space, even if they happen to be women; in the twentieth century this is the site of the generic "he." This model of the basic structure of the mythological text continues to structure all plots, argues Lotman, playing the "role of a normalizing mechanism, situated on a meta-level in relation to all the other texts of a given culture" (173). The normalizing mechanism is, to repeat, the entry into a closed space and emergence from it, and it presupposes an active hero or subject or function defined by what it is *not*. And what it is not are those things that are characteristics of the object, things that in the myth text are isomorphic to one another as the not-man: a cave, the grave, a house, a woman, death, the forest, conception, a return home.

This text-generating mechanism of the mythological text which helped produce the nonmythological, or logical, text is similar to the description Aristotle gave of the difference between the sexes, a difference that has to do with reproduction; one gender does, or acts; the other is done to, or receives. One is activity; the other is passivity. One is verbal; the other nominal. As de Lauretis says in her influential description of this textual mechanism:

> [Oppositions are] predicated on the *single* figure of the hero who crosses the boundary and penetrates the other space. In so doing the hero, the mythical subject, is constructed as human being and as male; he is the active creator of differences. Female is what is not susceptible to transformation, to life or death; she (it) is an element of plot-space, a *topos,* a resistance, matrix and matter. (1984, 119)

Mobility and the lack of it prove to be constituent features of this structure, as she points out:

> It is not difficult to notice that characters can be divided into those who are mobile, who enjoy freedom with regard to plot-space, who can change their place in the structure of the artistic world and cross

the frontier, the basic typological feature of this space, and those who are immobile. . . . (121)

Her description of this mechanism universalizes it to *all* plot, but Propp's model and Lotman's description make it possible to historicize this mechanism, locating its development in Greek and Judeo-Christian culture and in particular forms of social transformations from matrilineal to patrilineal succession. The plot mediates between the heterogeneous spheres of mythological and nonmythological and between the masculine and the feminine, "a mapping of differences, and specifically, first and foremost, of sexual difference into each text; and hence, by a sort of accumulation, into the universe of meaning, fiction, and history." Its guarantee of sexual difference (the masculinity and activity of the hero, the femininity and passivity of the object) mediates "and ultimately reconciles the mythical and historical, norm and excess, the spatial and temporal orders, the individual and the collectivity" (de Lauretis 1984, 120).

These active-passive differences, and their secure location in relation to gender, is this particular historically specific plot's *ground*.[13] As the privileged sphere of intelligibility where masculine knowers function as the mediating force doing the translating, or mapping differences into the universe of meaning, plot can be connected back to the description Nietzsche gave of interpretation as it depends on an aesthetic relation between subject and object, whose relationship arises out of "no causality, no correctness, and no expression" but, rather, out of an aesthetic relation "for which there is required . . . a freely inventive intermediary sphere and mediating force" (Nietzsche 1977, 86). There are broad similarities between Nietzsche and Aristotle which overwrite their very considerable differences.

Plot, for Lotman and Aristotle, organizes order out of the arbitrary and the accidental, and Oedipus' story proves to be one that takes him through encounters that lie in the plot space of randomness and arbitrary, unexpected interruptions. These interruptions, however, are always contained, kept in check by their association with characters who are themselves isomorphic with femaleness, with the passive female function. Their essential characteristic is that they *wait*, that they will be in a place where they will be *found* then surpassed by the hero, their possible danger to him already circumscribed by the privilege of his inevitable temporal movement through and beyond their space. While the oedipal linear movement may be disturbed, it is never seriously threatened as movement. As Else argues about Aristotle's plot, which links up with his logical system as a whole, "the unspoken premise is that the best things come last in the order of development" (1957, 301).

Contemporary Oedipus

A feminist researching this cultural organization produced by Oedipus encounters, time and again, oedipal workings in the scholarship she uses. There is a constant need to mark the "echo" effect, the doubling of subjectivity required on the part of a female critic. In an analysis of *Oedipus the King* by a twentieth-century critic Jean-Pierre Vernant mirrors Aristotle's and Sophocles' cultural logic in a particular way that helps show the difficulties for analysts who do not acknowledge the effects of the knower's subject position.

In this particular text Vernant, like Aristotle, does not acknowledge that Oedipus might not be a universal subject; as a result, he overlooks the issue that is at stake in tragedy—man feminized, made passive, by fate or the gods or logic or language. The tragedy of the masculine subject, as I will argue more fully later, lies in his recognition of his own passivity in a specific and important moment. The structure of tragedy as a genre then ultimately functions to organize meaning so that, in every *other* aspect of his life besides this primary, momentous encounter, he has associated activity with his own position of masculinity.

Vernant writes that Greek tragedy was "a spectacle open to all citizens, directed, acted, and judged by the qualified representatives of the various tribes. In this way [the city] turned itself into a theatre. Its subject, in a sense, was itself and it acted itself out before its public" (Vernant 1988, 33). This sentence, like Vernant's very important book-length study of Greek tragedy, cannot find a way to put women into its categories without disrupting the symmetry of his analysis of Oedipus. This symmetrical analysis, in particular "Ambiguity and Reversal: On the Enigmatic Structure of *Oedipus Rex*," is drawn on by Derrida in "Plato's Pharmacy" (1981, 63–171). For Vernant finds Oedipus to be the perfect representative of deconstructive man, who can know only that he cannot, finally, know. Vernant, at another point, in discussing the eighteenth century and Voltaire's discussions of the chorus, again presumes an absence he has formerly admitted then erased. Citing Voltaire, he says this: "'A chorus is only suitable in plays in which an entire people is involved,' which it most certainly is in the case of *Oedipus Rex,* as Voltaire fully realized" (377). Vernant's beautiful and perfectly balanced ironic deconstructive knowledge requires the symmetry that is only possible if there is *one* kind of subject position, that of the knower as masculine.

Women are referred to in this footnote after the phrase "the city makes itself into theatre":

> Only men could be qualified representatives of the city; women are alien to political life. That is why the chorus (not to mention the actors) are always and exclusively males. Even when the chorus is supposed to represent a group of young girls or women, as is the case in a whole series of plays, those who represent it are men, suitably disguised and masked. (418n)

What is at issue here is what Derrida calls "the city's body *proper*" (Derrida 1981, 133).

Having acknowledged the exclusion of women, Vernant nevertheless goes on to talk of the ironic nature of *all* human knowledge. First, women's absence is cited; then that absence is overlooked in a discussion of the universal nature of Oedipus' knowledge of the irony of knowing. What one knows is the impossibility of knowledge. The logical conclusion for any reader paying attention can only be that, if Oedipus is the exemplary model of humanity, then all *human* knowledge is masculine, the female still assigned to the nonhuman sphere outside human knowledge, even in Vernant's contemporary argument. Or as Derrida says about the similar theatrical scene of Plato's Pharmacy:

> This scene has never been read for what it is, for what is at once sheltered and exposed in its metaphors: its *family* metaphors. It is all about fathers and sons, about bastards unaided by any public assistance, about glorious, legitimate sons, about inheritance, sperm, sterility. Nothing is said of the mother, but this will not be held against us. (143)

Maybe not, maybe so. Both Vernant's and Derrida's scholarly communications resemble the duet of marriage described by Lévi-Strauss, and dramatic criticism needs to take this point seriously. These communications take place among men; they are about men; they do not allow for reciprocity; and, as the chorus says, "There is besides only an old faint story."[14]

In a later chapter I will argue that this privileged rhetorical trope, the oxymoron, inhibits theories of performance by not admitting what it really is—a metathesis, or transposition of letters, sounds, or syllables *within* a word, as in the shift from the Old English *brid* to modern English *bird*. The oedipal oxymoron guards its limits in an increasingly subtle but nonetheless virile symbolic violence that refuses form to oppositional subjects, all the while blind to the guaranteed masculinity of the subject position of the theorist, the guarantee of one particular invisible *form* of formlessness, the phallus. While the phallus has been shown to be hollow, empty, impotent, its figuration and its power have nevertheless been subtly *reinforced* by that very claim of impotence.[15]

Oedipus the King

The ambiguities and reversals that structure *Oedipus the King* are even more ironic than they might at first seem. Oedipus comes before Thebes as a savior of the city, though both we and a Greek audience know that he is actually the cause of its troubles. The irony of our knowing what he does not is overdetermined, for a female reader or spectator, by her realization that she knows something else his male critics do not. No matter what other disruptions and reversals he may face, Oedipus is always guaranteed the posssibility of being the active character on the stage. Even if, in twentieth-century readings of Oedipus like that of Vernant or Derrida, the nature of subjectivity itself is in question, Oedipus is nevertheless guaranteed the space of activity in making that discovery. The reversals and ambiguities he experiences occur within certain limits precisely because they lie within the structure of a masculine plot, which Oedipus never leaves.

His plot involves securing the linkage between masculinity and activity, drawing on the biological model in which a particular model of procreative sexual intercourse comes to mark one of the participants as active, the other as passive. In *Oedipus the King* the Sphinx can momentarily be his double because she retains some connection with the activity of the hostile, competitive daughter from the matrilineal tales. But her activity has been reduced to arriving at the place where she will wait motionless for Oedipus in order to provide him with an initiation task to accomplish. He will then leave behind his immaturity and move beyond his encounter with her, as the male initiation plot and the search for the father come together in the same oedipal plot. The ostensibly active movement by the Sphinx has actually taken place only in order for her to arrive at the place in the plot where the hero will find her. Her activity is of a different quality from that of Oedipus.

The site of the Sphinx in the plot functions to organize a number of meanings. For Vernant her status as half-human monster at the beginning foreshadows Oedipus' eventual discovery that he, too, is a kind of monster; that is, he will find out that he is not one of the equals before the law, one of the *isoi,* who are entitled to participate in the polis. He will instead discover himself to be what Vernant calls "un être *apolis."* Having broken the most important laws of the polis, he ultimately will not be defined as human because the definition of *human being* refers to one who is a member of the polis. That definition as inhuman, however, will ultimately and paradoxically be reinscribed and transcended as a part of his tragedy.

Oedipus proves to be inhuman for two reasons. First, not only does he occupy the site of activity, but also he claims too much of it, and, because of this, he threatens to become a tyrant, a man who takes himself to be superior to the other citizens and who, like the Homeric hero, is a threat to the democratic polis because he figures a semidivine inhumanity. And, second, he falls *below* the level of equal citizens to a bestial level because he has killed his father and slept with his mother. (For Lévi-Strauss the incest taboo was the dividing line between nature and civilization, or mating and reproduction. Oedipus has blurred those divisions, falling into a bestial inhumanity.)

The Sphinx, too, is part beast, embodying the carnal animal-woman who balances Jocasta, the faithful mother/wife "incarcerated," to use Alice Jardine's term, in the oedipal family. The Sphinx awaits Oedipus at the intersection of three roads, a semiotically loaded site. As the priestesses' roles in Greek religion were taken over by men, one of their only remaining duties was as *kaledones,* shouting women who stood at the crossroads once a month to invoke the powers of the moon through their shouting or singing. The etymology of the word *prostitute* also refers to crossroads, to women who waited at intersections of well-traveled roads to ply their trade, and crossroads were also the place where the bodies of people who had committed a murder of a blood relative were thrown, headless, naked, unburied, in order to purify the city of murder within a family. In the mythologies of many cultures the metaphor of the crossroads also refers to the navel of the world, and in this tragedy the sacred site at Delphi is called the crossroads, or navel, of the earth. And the crossroads were known as the "haunt of Hecate." Hecate, so the story goes, was banished to the underworld because she had hidden in the house of a woman who was giving birth. Because of her contamination by this contact, she was plunged into the underworld, where she became queen of the dead, of magic, and of the night, frequently haunting crossroads, tombs, and scenes of crimes, accompanied by her "infernal dogs." Her image was frequently found at crossroads on columns of stone with three faces called "triple Hecates," where offerings were left on the eve of the full moon.[16]

The importance of the crossroads, however, was different for the Sphinx than for Oedipus. The Sphinx, with her characteristics of the hostile, unmarried daughter of the folktale, finds that the crossroads and the encounter there constitute a deadend, a termination of her dominance as questioner posing questions, even though she does succeed momentarily in tricking him. For Oedipus, on the other hand, the crossroads lead to a temporary horrible realization of his monstrosity, but that realization is eventually followed by another crossroads in *Oedipus at Colonus,* where he miraculously joins the gods in a kind of Assumption at a crossroads in the hills just across the border of Thebes. The site of his death then becomes a secret that can only be passed from Theseus to his most cherished son and then down through history from father to son, setting up a transcendent masculine knowledge.

In some stories the Sphinx throws herself from a cliff when she discovers that Oedipus has solved her riddle; her half-human story is ended with a death that is final. But Oedipus transcends his bestiality with a death in *Oedipus at Colonus* that is *fatal* but not *final.* His family, or tribal line, is ended: both his sons are killed, and Antigone's death, like the Sphinx's, marks the end of the power of the unmarried daughter. But Oedipus as Man, in general, will continue in all men. His genealogy will transcend familial particularity to the universality of the public sphere, beyond biological limitation to the spiritual link of immortality, the interiority of the family superseded by the exteriority of the interests of civilization.

At the beginning of *Oedipus the King* Oedipus had already encountered the Sphinx, but problems of classification are haunting the city of Thebes, leaving it plagued by mixtures. (Chapter 3 will more extensively develop the meaning of mixtures and their threat.) As the chorus says, "the augur has spread confusion, terrible confusion" (Sophocles 1960, 131). The city is sunk in a miasma of pestilence, contagion, and sterility, which, according to an oracle, has been caused by a crime; even its suffering is represented by troubling mixtures: "The town is heavy with a mingled burden / of sounds and smells, of groans and hymns and incense" (111). As a result, "all the ship's timbers are rotten" (118).

Boundaries like the one the Sphinx represented between outside and inside the city can no longer be depended upon to divide things that should remain distinct; hymns of praise are indistinguishably mixed with lament in the people's voices, and the pleas to the gods are confused: "the hymn to the healing God rings out but with it the wailing / voices are blended" (118). Deaths of the city's inhabitants are "unnumbered" and cannot be properly mourned because of their lack of distinctness. And the season of Thargelion, which should be the time for the fertility rite of spring, is instead a time of pollution and sterility:

A blight is on the fruitful plans of the earth,
A blight is on the cattle in the field,
A blight is on our women that no children
are born to them; a God that carries fire,
a deadly pestilence . . .

(112)

A fertility rite follows the rite of purification, but the distinctions between these two rites and between fertility and pollution themselves are unclear in Thebes. In his detective work Oedipus must try to reestablish distinctions and to articulate the elements whose blending has constituted the crime responsible for the pestilence.

The audience knows the story of Oedipus and is aware of relations that have been collapsed into one in a horrible mixture, that of two isomorphic "sames," father and son. Both father and son, within the requirements of the plot, are characters with the possibility of activity, and each one of their heroic trajectories coincides in a plot space that is both *logically* identical (it is one space: activity; and not another: passivity) and *mythologically* same (in the same paradigm: God, Man, son). Their trajectories coincide in Jocasta's womb, the womb of the wife/ mother. She is, in reality, the "haven" that is common to both Laius and Oedipus, the plowed field sowed by them both, the "matter" of her position graphically represented in the play's imagery. Oedipus says: she is "this field of double sowing whence I sprang and whence I sowed my children" (166). As Oedipus becomes both brother and father, husband and son, he erases distinctions and plunges the world into chaos.

He is able to solve the Sphinx's riddle because he does not understand her question. The question she asks him has to do with separate categories—infancy, adulthood, old age. But Oedipus does not recognize that she has mixed together mythological categories that, in a logical system, should remain distinct. Thus, he gives the answer "Man" to the riddle, combining not only infancy, adulthood, and old age into one word but also the categories of son, husband, and father into the one term that he assumes will translate all those things—the name *Man*. But, in doing so, he overlooks important differences.

Attempting to fuse various levels of meaning into one (husband/son, divine subject/political subject, conscious/unconscious), Oedipus thinks of himself as unitary, singular Man. But he exists within a number of overdetermined, heterogeneous spheres. He is not singular; he is plural in his role of murderer(s): "The robbers they encountered were many and the hands that did the murder /were many; it was no man's single power" (116). Oedipus is also plural as a subject divided within itself because of an unconscious and because of the linguistic nature of subjectivity. He is in many ways multiple, though the possibility that he might also be both masculine and feminine is sharply controlled; it is a possibility that will only arise later in a way in which he nevertheless can retain control of that particular mixture. The Sphinx, as half-human monster, has set him a trap, which he falls into because he does not recognize his own multiple identities. By the end of the tragedy he does recognize difference, but it is a difference that is carefully circumscribed.

Oedipus makes a mistake in his answer because he has not been adequately "written" in relation to the transcendental metaphor that guarantees a social system in which the discourse of the family, "the rules of kinship and marriage [,] dictate the positions and possibilities open to all members of the group," as Kaja Silverman argues: "The discourse of the family produces the subjects it needs by aligning them with the symbolic positions of 'father' and 'mother'" (1983, 182). That metaphor is what Lacan calls the "Name of the Father," which articulates the identities of members of the patrilineal contract, an articulation dependent on two taboos: one, the taboo on the murder of a family member; the other, the taboo of incest. Both taboos, at least in the theoretical worlds of Lévi-Strauss and Freud, inaugurate culture and its symbolic systems and forestall violent substitution of fathers by sons. Individuals are thus gendered, marked as male or female, like or unlike the father when they are named, their name assigning them a particular place within the family. And the places available within the family are organized retroactively by a phallocentric social order *that needs subjects*. The discourse of the family, as Silverman says, "produces the subjects it needs" (182).

By marking the son as son, the father's name also arranges possible sexual partners for that son, prohibiting to the son sexual relations with his mother or sister or brother. It also requires that he go outside the immediate family for a mate; by doing so, he will participate in the community of alliances with other men. Language symbolically puts the incest taboo into circulation.

But Oedipus has not been identified with the name of the father. As an infant, he was carefully placed on a "pathless hillside" after his mother, Jocasta, heard the oracle foretelling the murder of Laius.[17] Without a path, or writing, as a system of organizing articulations, Oedipus has difficulty finding his way back to the father he has to kill. But Oedipus was only physically separated from his mother and father; he was not marked by society's separation: the entry into language as a symbolic system articulating him according to the centrality of masculinity.

In a mythological system, unlike a logical one, Oedipus' answer could be correct. Man *would be* the same as son, father, husband. But *Oedipus the King* is about, among other things, cleaning up categories in the transition to logical organization from mythological, and, because of this transition, distinctions or differences among the various possibilities for Man must be made. Because he has not been properly written himself, Oedipus does not know how to "write" or "read" those differences and is, thus, unable to recognize his mother and his father. His inscription into the logical system of differences based on the father's name will not occur until he is able to see blindly, accepting his vulnerability to the father's name.

Oedipus' answer to the Sphinx presumes a "literal," or mythological, metaphor, one he enacts by becoming Man/husband/son in a mixture of nonmythological categories. This fusion is the cause of both his tragedy and Thebes' distress. But, while he must disarticulate these categories, Jocasta, in the female plot space, is *required* to function as mythological fusion. In fact, the plot movement could not occur unless she had already become the fused Woman/wife/mother. This symmetrical story of the universal ambiguity of knowledge is only possible *on condition* that she function as such a fusion; its symmetry requires one kind of knower. The complex but symmetrical oedipal plot that moves in perfect balance from one state to its opposite, from ignorance to knowledge, could not find its symmetry and ironic perfection that could fit "the mind's eye" if it did not have a medium within which to work. And the medium is Jocasta. Her womb, not her knowledge, provides the closure of his story and allows the beginning of his plot, his ignorance, to circle around to meet its end. His story will "come together," find its closure here in the literal intersection of Oedipus and Laius, the substitution of father by son taking place at the crossroads at the navel of the world.

In Oedipus' case the fusion of characters into one (Man, husband, son) produces tragedy for the city. But the fusion of different characters into one in Jocasta's case (Woman, wife, mother) is required, fundamental to *his* story as a man and to the story of the city, or civilization. It is a story that is immediately linked to the family story of the oedipal triangle—father, daughter-in-law (wife/mother), son—and reinforced by Aristotle's list of the characters who are proper to tragedy. For the greatest of the arts of the polis finds its material in intimate family violence: "When the painful deed is done in the context of close family relationships, for example, when a *brother* kills or intends to kill a *brother*, or a *son* a *father*, or a *mother* a *son*, or a *son* a *mother*, or does something else of that kind—those are the acts one should look for" (Else 1957, 413).

The characters who can participate in these intimate family relationships are remarkably familiar; they are the ones who figured in Propp's transitional triangles.

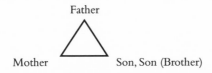

The daughter is nowhere to be found, the woman's position neatly circumscribed into that of reproducer, the wife/mother, the body, or womb, as opposed to Man as Knower. Oedipus as Man progresses into a logical system; Jocasta as Woman remains locked in a mythological one. What remains of the Sphinx will become clearer in the next chapter in a discussion of the concept of the enigma.

While the fusion of separate characters into Jocasta as wife/mother proves to be the norm in the oedipal triangle, the fusion that Oedipus enacts between the son/husband leads to a reversal, or peripeteia, from happiness to unhappiness due to a mistake in the recognition of the identity of a family member (*anagnoresis*). But the reversals Oedipus experiences can only be called "limited reversals" because this is the concept of reversal that underwrote the structure that showed up in Barthes's lament about the bad faith of knowledge, in Lévi-Strauss's duet, and in Vernant's description of human knowledge. Each occurs on a plane *beyond,* or *after,* the establishment of the privilege of masculinity, that establishment itself shrouded in an unanalyzed, untheorized mystery. As an example, the paradigm for describing Oedipus' role in the crime of incest in this perfectly ironic tragedy is "begetter and begot." The fusion of son/husband means that Oedipus will both beget and be begotten in the same place, Jocasta's womb. But if we try to decide how a daughter might fill this universal role, we see right away that she cannot, that it is always already too late for her. She can be begotten, i.e., she can receive action, but only the son can initiate it and preserve the symmetrical opposition of the masculine paradox, or oxymoron, with which Oedipus is associated.

The oxymoron, a rhetorical figure characterized by the conjunction of two contradictory terms, thus comes to mark the figure of Oedipus, who appropriates difference into the masculine plot space; this particular rhetorical feature has become the deconstructive trope par excellence. This particular alternation of begetter and begot structures a series of other alternations in the tragedy: savior/villain, tyrant/*pharmakos,*[18] stranger/native, law-abiding citizen/murderer, knower/known. Each term in these oppositions logically excludes the other. But the terms require each other to make sense, as they establish difference at the same time that they limit how wide that difference might range; they are "played on the boundary line between inside and outside" (Derrida 1981, 133), as they ceaselessly retrace and constitute that boundary.

Vernant's discussion of the oxymoronic nature of Oedipus, which Derrida cites, suggests that the ostracism of Oedipus works in symmetry with the fertility ritual of Thargelia, which opened the play: "When [the city] establishes ostracism, it creates an institution whose role is symmetrical to and the inverse of the ritual of the Thargelia. . . . It takes the proper measure of the human in opposition on one side to the divine and heroic, on the other to the bestial and monstrous" (Derrida 1981, 131n). Their symmetry reinforces rather than threatens limits, the possible differences between the terms of these oppositions merely different versions of masculinity, or activity.[19] Their alternations occur *after* masculinity has appropriated activity to itself, this struggle for identity limited to masculine participants (or, in the twentieth century, those who can disguise themselves as masculine. Such disguises will be discussed in later chapters.) This struggle for identity, like marriage in Benveniste's description, reveals that "the situation of the man and that of the woman have nothing in common" (1973, 193).

If oxymorons such as "begetter and begot" really are the exemplary tragic figures, structuring the perfectly balanced irony of the exemplary tragedy, then the greatest of all tragedies would be unbalanced if Oedipus were feminine, and it would, in fact, not even be a tragedy. The ultimate root of tragedy, says Else, "is ignorance and its conversion into knowledge" (1957, 420), this perfectly symmetrical knowledge and ignorance possible only in the oedipal active plot space. Those who can engage in this tragic activity are those who possess the *symbolic capacity* for it, those characters who can occupy the symbolic space of the active subject. (The feminist echo can be heard again here, but only momentarily. If oedipal knowledge can only take place from the site of masculine knowledge production, then, as in Barthes's claim that a different history might only be written from a place where that history cannot be written, perhaps Aristotle and Sophocles here reveal the theoretical gap within which something besides an oedipal subject is being written from a different site of knowledge production.)

Oedipus' transcendence—while certainly not pleasant in *Oedipus the King,* though glorious in *Oedipus at Colonus*—has had disastrous effects on the *matter* of his knowledge. The Sphinx, as the story goes, kills herself after he answers the riddle. And Jocasta, whose plot space allows her to wait,[20] finds her sphere limited to the circumscribed place around another traditional motif associated with the female plot space in all kinds of plots from the folktale to the Hollywood movie, and that is the *bed,* the place where she can frequently be found waiting: "And then she groaned and cursed the bed in which she brought forth husband by her husband, children by her own child, an infamous double bond" (1960, 166). She too commits suicide.

Their knowledge does not produce a transcendence for them, only death; they remain immobile in their already immobile segments, or spaces, of the plot. Oedipus' trajectory is associated with temporal movement forward, Jocasta's immobility with spatiality. His movement must go through her and the Sphinx as feminized spaces.

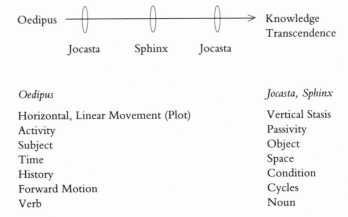

Oedipus	*Jocasta, Sphinx*
Horizontal, Linear Movement (Plot)	Vertical Stasis
Activity	Passivity
Subject	Object
Time	Space
History	Condition
Forward Motion	Cycles
Verb	Noun

Jocasta dies cursing the bed, where everything significant has happened to her—conceptions, births, and now death, in the space of the woman that Propp described. She now must also curse her own body, the Greek word for bed and for woman interchangeable. Her sphere is circumscribed, private, enclosed, interior, important primarily as isomorphic to the site of the initiation which the active hero must enter and emerge from into a wider, more open exterior place, the polis.

Her death comes in a painful and bitter scene presented to us in one of the most telling passages in the drama. She has just killed herself, but the chorus, in its attempt to report her death, is diverted by their concern for the protagonist of the plot:

Whose troubles so reverse his life as his!
O Oedipus, the famous prince
for whom a great haven
the same both as father and son
by your generation
how, o how have the furrows ploughed

by your father endured to bear you, poor wretch
and hold their peace so long.

(164)

Jocasta's life has been absolutely reversed into death, yet in this logic
it is Oedipus' reversal of *knowledge* that merits the term *reversal*. After
this long silence on Jocasta's part even the story of her suicide as an action
requiring agency (and agency always equals activity) is obscured by
Oedipus: "How after that she died I do not know— / for Oedipus distracted us from seeing" (164). He distracts the chorus by calling for a
sword to kill her, to punish her for her crime. She ends in death, silence,
finality, obscurity.[21] He, on the other hand, is blinded, but that blinding
allows him to progress to a higher level of insight, knowledge, and
speech.

Silence, like immobility, characterizes the possibilities for the occupants of the female plot space. If they do speak, they are not understood.
The Sphinx is referred to as "the cruel singer," "the hooked taloned maid
of riddling speech" (Sophocles 1960, 166). Jocasta's warnings had cau-
tioned Oedipus about his rashness, her warnings similar to those of
Teiresias, the male interpreter of the gods, connecting her knowledge
to an intuitive divination that Oedipus has mistakenly rejected: "I solved
the riddle by my wit alone / Mine was no knowledge got from the birds"
(164). The plot lets us know, however, that his progressive movement
toward greater understanding (which is, in fact, an understanding of the
depth of his *mis*understanding) forbids his ever following her advice. For
she advised him to stop searching for the origin of the plague:

Why should man fear since chance is all in all
for him and he can clearly foreknow nothing?
Best to live lightly, as one can, unthinkingly.

(127)

He could not, as a political, rational man whose decisions were
made on the basis of universals,[22] listen to her as her words originate
from the realm of excess, chance, and particularity. But he also suggested that she spoke duplicitously for a reason that did not arise out of
a desire for truth. As she began to suspect where his detective work
would lead, her very concrete fears for his life determined what she said:

> I beg you—do not hunt this out—I beg you
> if you have any care for your own life.
> What I am suffering is enough.
>
>   (157)

Though he has been tempted by her arguments, he continues with his search—"although you talk so well, Jocasta." She can either agree with him, keep silent, or speak warnings he does not understand.

When she warned him about the dangers of knowledge ("God keep you from the knowledge of who you are!"), he concluded that she wanted to keep from discovering who she was—perhaps the wife of a peasant or slave, if it should prove that he were either of these: "Perhaps she is ashamed of my low birth / for she has all a woman's high-flown pride" (Sophocles 1960, 158); everything circles back to him. But Jocasta had discerned the truth, and in the moment of peripeteia, or reversal, she, like the Sphinx, went off to a death caused by interpretation. Oedipus, however, experienced the pleasure of interpretation, even though that interpretation was full of horror, but it was a horror that itself became more matter for interpretation in *Oedipus at Colonus* and led to his guaranteed transcendence; his twentieth-century sons will "make capital" of his horror. Had Oedipus stopped his investigation while only Jocasta knew the answer, she might have lived on, enclosing and keeping to herself, as did Teiresias, the horrible secret.

But that would have meant the continuation of the pestilence that affected Thebes. Jocasta, like all women as Freud described them, was unable, perhaps too weak, to repress domestic concerns that conflicted with the public concerns of the city as a whole; she was limited by this inability to repress a concern for the physical and the concrete, remaining locked within the immediate sphere of the body, of life and death and the immediacy of her concern for Oedipus, "naturally" closer to the body and farther from reason. His will to know has coincided with the needs of the city; it is necessary and inevitable that the investigation be pursued to its ends in order for the public good to be served.[23] A similar will to know does not seem to drive Jocasta, whose affections threaten to sacrifice the public to the private and introduce rupture and instability into the public contract.[24] It might, of course, also have led to a very different notion of the public contract.

There is a third encounter in Oedipus' trajectory besides the one with the Sphinx and the one with Jocasta, all of these reported rather than directly observed onstage. The third encounter is with Laius, Oedipus' father. This encounter is not on the same categorical level as the other two. The meeting with the Sphinx was a meeting with a partially active character whose trajectory could only lead her to a position in which she could be found waiting, in a category of *active passivity,* to which I will return in the next chapter. But the encounter with Laius involves two men of appropriate magnitude in equally active plot trajectories. Thus, where there is the possibility of one kind of violence in the first two encounters—that is, a violence of rape or domination—in the encounter with Laius, a different category of violence is possible and, in fact, required, as Propp reminded us. The son must violently replace the father, but he will be ignorant of the fact that he is doing so.

Encounters between superior and inferior characters are the rule in the first two examples; in the encounter with Laius two superior characters come into conflict. The natural rhythm of generations would normally find a son replacing his father after a certain period of time. But in the type of succession to power that Propp describes as characteristic of this period in the organization of patrilineal succession as lawful substitution, the son's replacement of the father will, of necessity, be violent in such a plot. In the encounter between Laius and Oedipus the plot line of the father is overtaken by that of the son, as one of the two plots must be eliminated in this plot based on a logic of the One.[25]

The father-son plot intersection occurs twice, once within Jocasta and once at another intersection of roads, this time as Oedipus and Lauis attempt to cross one path simultaneously. There is only one place to cross, not two—one main plot, and one of its claimants must be killed. Part of the difference between this encounter and the others is that, with two heroes, the hero-object relationship cannot be clearly established. Laius and his coachmen are not passive objects whose space is "entered" in an assymetrical encounter that would provide matter for transcendence. Rather than an initiation, as represented by the other two interior spaces of Jocasta and the Sphinx, the encounter with Laius constitutes a public act of rivalry. But it occurs *outside* the city's gates and represents the violence of substitution which precedes lawful substitution, or symbolic substitution,[26] suggesting the very real dangers to the polis of such active masculine rivalries and the necessity to defuse them in order to solidify the social contract among men.

Whatever horror Oedipus experiences at the discovery of the murder of Laius helps unite the polis against him, as that body sends him into exile both as *pharmakos* and tyrant, both source of pollution and savior. The public good is served and strengthened by his suffering, as he becomes the instrument of the unification, and even the salvation, of Thebes. This is a familiar story: Oedipus enacts the *Aufhebung* of the private by the public, the female by the male, the noncitizen by the citizen, the corporeal by the spiritual. And he serves as the privileged figure of that redemptive action.

At the end of the play his words to his daughters, with whom he has a "grim equality," are: "I weep when I think of the bitterness there will be in your lives, how you must live before the world" (Sophocles 1960, 174), for the oedipal plot provides very bitter options for women. They can be the Sphinx, the enigma that suggests animality and nature and which conceals a higher truth that must, however, be interpreted and deciphered by men who destroy her. Or they can be Jocasta, the wife/mother available to serve as the matter of social and biological reproduction and the means of transmission of name and property. What dooms Antigone and Ismene is the impossibility of this option for them: "Clearly you are doomed / to waste away in barrenness unmarried" (174). Their continuation in the plot clearly depends on marriage. Or women can be Antigone who, like the Sphinx, finds activity only in a doomed matrilineal plot having to do with Creon, who, as the mother's brother, is the most important male relative in societies where succession is matrilineal; that plot is literally a dead end. The enclosure of possibilities for women within this plot is symmetrical, efficient, and aesthetically unified.

But there is one last point to be made about the organization of dramatic plot. Gerald Else points out that Aristotle's description of the symmetry of the plot of *Oedipus the King* leaves out one element, which, nevertheless, intrudes into it, and, because of this, the whole is greater than the sum of its parts. Oedipus does not question *why* the gods have placed him in such a paradoxical and tragic position, which the twentieth-century critics call the tragic nature of subjectivity itself. In Aristotle's theory there is no room for any cause other than man's own faulty decisions underneath an unchangeable cosmic umbrella. Men's decisions are made according to logic, but a misrecognition of some particular (not a universal) can make the judgment turn out tragically. It is paradoxically logical that such misrecognition could occur, as tragedy is in some sense inherent in logic. It is framed and necessitated by the contradictions that arise between the concepts of the "necessary" and the "probable."

As a result, though tragedy is about the importance of activity, it is also about man's *reaction* to a universe within which tragedy is logically inevitable. His activity at the most important point of the tragedy, its climax, is shown to be contradicted by his passivity, by his vulnerability to something that is outside his control. He cannot account for what befalls him because its cause lies outside the scope of tragedy, which, says Aristotle, does not concern metaphysical questions but, rather, deals with actions men take in the world. It can, as such, only deal with *what* happens rather than *why* it happens, leaving Fate, the Cause of things, the Prime Mover—all are unfathomable—beyond human reason and beyond the scope of tragedy. Something *befalls* him—that is, he is the object of another subject, be it fate, the gods, logic, language—and the pathos of the tragedy lies in that crucial moment of the hero's passivity.

What are the implications of this model of Fate? Because *mimesis* is defined as the imitation of an *action,* it points to an inherent contradiction within the nature of tragedy. The protagonist, like the poet at a crucial moment, finds himself *passive* in relation to the Cause of things, a Cause which lies outside the practical sphere of human activity and knowledge, and it is the recognition of this moment of passivity, of this logically *feminine* moment, which seems to constitute tragic recognition. For Aristotle that recognition lies in the moment the protagonist understands the identity of a blood relative and follows from hamartia, or the ignorance of the identity of a blood relative (Else 1975, 379).

But hamartia may be more than ignorance of the identity of a blood relative. It may be the protagonist's ignorance of the nature of gender and of its construction in discourse; he misrecognizes his identity as pure masculinity and proceeds to insist on making clear distinctions that enforce that misrecognition. The stability of the polis that he creates is then built on his articulation of those distinctions, chief among them sexual difference as it assigns activity and passivity to each of the genders. Tragedy reveals Oedipus' femininity to him, while at the same time it protects him from it in every part of the social structure except the one he cannot control, his relationship to the gods and, later, in twentieth-century theory, his relationship to language. The clarity of distinctions in the face of this ultimate powerlessness makes for stability in the organization of the polis. But that stability comes at the price of the disappearance of the female subject.

The plot of *Oedipus the King* arranges the possibilities for subjects in such a way that activity is claimed for the masculine protagonist at every point as a kind of compensation for that ultimate moment of passivity, when the protagonist must be "done to" by the gods or by Fate. But there is something different about Oedipus' passivity. Not only does the plot allow him to be active in every situation except one, but the most nearly perfect tragedy *ritualizes* his passivity. We have seen that the passivity associated with women has to do with static, formless matter, their passivity a mark of inferiority in opposition to masculine activity. But when pathos results from the situation of Oedipus as Man, when something happens to him beyond his control, his experience of it inspires and structures one of the finest art forms of Greek culture. The oedipal plot thus symbolically encircles, ritualizes, and controls his experience of passivity. The impossibility of complete control, of complete activity, is recognized in the tragic climax, but there is consolation for this lack of control, the aesthetic transcendence as well as the guarantee, in the plot, of his right to the active plot space everywhere else.

Tragic plot and marriage may actually be the same organizing structure, one that valorizes and claims activity for masculine characters of the dominant race in every situation besides the one man cannot control, be it his encounter with the gods, with the unconscious, with the economy, or with language. For even if Oedipus takes Jocasta's warning seriously—"God keep you from finding out who you are"—his agony over his impossible identity is a tease. Dramatic plot, marriage, the polis, the concept of the human subject protect him from his femininity, while they simultaneously punish Jocasta for hers.

Chapter 2

The Family of Man: *The Women of Trachis*

No other man but you must ever have her
Who has lain with me at my side.
                                    —Herakles to Hyllos

In *Oedipus the King* a messenger brings evidence to help Oedipus in his interpretive task. The word *actor,* or *hypokrites* ("answerer"), was originally used to refer to the second actor, not the first; the first was called the *exarchon* ("leader-off"), or *tragôidos.* The second actor's importance lay in what he made possible for the first: "The second actor is not introduced in order to conflict or contrast with the hero; he is not a hero or even a person at all, but an instrument for extending the play in time and space."[1] He provides the poet with the time and space necessary to change or sharpen the hero's situation. In another of Sophocles' dramas, *The Women of Trachis,* messengers move back and forth between the hero, Herakles, and his wife, Deianeira, who never speak directly to each other. One messenger tries to bring about some communication between the husband and wife—which means he tries to make clear to the wife what the husband has to say. The other tries to prevent that communication, knowing that the truth will destroy her.

Herakles and Deianeira mark two very different character sites joined by the institution of marriage, which was not situated on the needs of communication between males and females but, instead, on requirements for the organization of the city. The dramatic poet's task was to portray these two different character sites appropriately, with appropriateness determined by the principle of goodness. That is, a certain concept of goodness connects the protagonist, who is a "good man," to the citizens in the audience who are "like" him, this likeness ensuring that he merits their identification and sympathy. The spectators will then make judgments about two things—whether or not the protagonist is "like" them and whether or not he deserves what happens to him: "the mechanisms of our emotion grant sympathies to some and refuse it to others even though the change of fortune they undergo is the same."[2] These judgments are of central importance, bringing into view the etymology of the word *ethics,* from *ethos,* or "custom, disposition, trait," its etymology closely related to *ethnos,* a band of people living together, or "people of one's own kind."[3] Ethical concerns must struggle with this very early and long-lived structuration of sameness as a foundation for empathy, a foundation Brecht's dramatic theory also attempted to counteract.

Every character in Aristotle's conceptualization is capable of goodness, which is not a single principle but, rather, a "system of analogies in which every creature, animal or human, can participate at his level" (Else 1957, 457). Vernant described this kind of hierarchical system as a harmonic one, each type proportionately good, according to its *capacity* for goodness. According to Else, besides the character of the hero, tragedy "presents us with other people of all ranks and conditions—wives, cousins, friends, slaves—and Aristotle's prescription of goodness is meant to cover them also, each according to his kind" (457). This proportional distribution of goodness results in "classes," and characters can express goodness only if it is appropriate to their class, argues Aristotle: "[Good character] can exist in every class [of person]; for a woman can be good, and a slave can, although the first of these [classes] may be inferior and the second wholly worthless" (1987, 19).

The proportion of goodness in this way determines what is appropriate behavior for each class, and the tragic poet's ability to express truth has to do with how well he is able to express the appropriate goodness for which each class has the capacity, capacities that are immanent in the structure of the cosmos, or the universe in its order.

The capacity for goodness thus establishes a hierarchy, with goodness coming to mean something like the capacity for subjectivity. The appropriate portion of goodness for a man is, of course, greater than that for a woman or a slave, and only the character who has a great capacity for goodness can appropriately express bravery, or *activity*. It would be *in*appropriate, says Aristotle, in the only example he gives as evidence of what he means by appropriateness, that a female character be manly or clever—active.

The male character (the citizen, not the male slave) has the capacity for activity, and the appropriate attributes of male and female characters in the *Poetics* prove to be identical to the appropriate characteristics of the male and female of human, animal, and plant species in *Generation of Animals*. An unabashedly biological description based on Aristotle's perception of generation (reproduction) determines the male protagonist's right to the active plot space, which is based on one privileged *act*: the act of creating, forming, and discharging semen: "the semen from the male," says Aristotle, "is the cause of the offspring." The semen is "that which acts and makes, while that which is made and receives the form is female. . . . The female, as female, is passive, and the male, as male, is active, and the principle of movement comes from him" (1984, 1132).

In character portrayals, as well as in this interpretation of biology, the enforcement of separation, the resistance to mixture, is of primary importance. The active must be separated from the passive, the masculine from the feminine; the active assigned to the male, the passive to the female. The *Poetics* and *Generation of Animals* come together for a moment, which has not ended:

> But since the male and female are the first principles of [classes of men and animals and plants], they will exist in those things that possess them for the sake of generation. Again, as the first efficient or moving cause, to which belong the definition and the form, is better and more divine in its nature than the material on which it works, it is better that the superior principle should be separated from the inferior. Therefore, wherever it is possible and so far as it is possible, the male is separated from the female. For the first principle of the movement, whereby that which comes into being is male, is better and more divine, and the female is the matter. (Aristotle 1984, 1136)

These male and female principles, which exist "for the sake of generation" and which define "life," are a part of an order that cannot be changed: "The order of the cosmos is eternal, beyond the reach of change" (Else 1957, 468).

This biological division comes to be represented by other oppositions, such as open/closed, light/dark, visible/invisible, as the transition
from an agricultural society to a centralized urban one resulted in the
divisions between the agora and the private domestic places of female
activity. Women and slaves moved into isolated, enclosed living spaces
that were dark and unsanitary, in contrast to the open, sun-drenched site
of public debate. Work done in the isolated, or invisible, places was
devalorized along with those who did the work.

Simultaneously, technical advances intensify the division. As the
provision of water was improved, for example, those who had formerly
gathered at the water source located out in public lost that opportunity
to meet others like them, and, as a man's economic position within this
urban organization improved, the more likely his wife was to be
confined and isolated within the domestic space, while her slaves went
out in the open to perform errands and, coincidentally, to meet with
other women outside the family unit. The greater the improvements of
the domestic space, the greater the isolation of those who occupied it.
This will lead us, eventually, to a phenomenon the heroine of *The
Women of Trachis* experiences, exile within the space that, for men, is
marked as a haven and retreat.

The Cultural Contract

The characters who are appropriate for the active plot space in dramatic
plot (and for participation in the polis)—men—are also the participants
in marriage as Benveniste described it. The history of marriage is, thus,
a history of the cultural construction and use of a particular "biological"
male/female unit, the mediating force of its institutionalization:

> One can speak of a break between archaic marriage and that in
> Athenian democracy at the end of the sixth century. After
> Clisthenes, matrimonial unions no longer had as their object the
> establishment of power relations or mutual services between great
> sovereign families, but their object was instead to perpetuate those
> houses, the domestic units that constituted the City. That is, they
> were to assure by a more strict regulation of marriage the perma-
> nence of the City itself, its constant reproduction. (Vernant 1974,
> 62–63; my translation)

The need to reproduce a particular form of culture *precedes* the definition
of biological reproduction. But it is actually the city of men that is
reproducing, giving birth to itself. As Pierre Bourdieu argues:

> Matrimonial strategies . . . belong to the system of reproductive
> strategies, defined as the sum total of the strategies through which
> individuals or groups objectively tend to reproduce the relations of
> production . . . by striving to reproduce or improve their position
> in the social structure. (1977, 81)

The clarity of the "natural" male/female unit, which "produces"
children who make possible the continuation of the city, is presumed to
be obvious; at this twentieth-century moment the *American Heritage* dictionary defines the *family* as "the most instinctive, fundamental social or
mating group in man and animal, especially the union of man and
woman through marriage and their offspring." The "social or mating
group" is thus still defined as "instinctual"; it has to do with the natural
characteristics of male and female; and it has a clear teleology: offspring.

But in spite of the fact that the definition of marriage refers to it as
a male/female reproductive unit, the word *marriage* does not describe a
relation between male and female. This natural "instinctive social or
mating group" nowhere includes the relation between male and female
in the etymology or the history of the word and the concept. Because
the polis is an organization of male citizens and marriage is a thoroughly
masculine concept, the city and its symbolic system "give birth" to an
offspring, but it is not a child. It is, instead, a very particular model of
biology, procreation, and representation.

Centaurs and Amazons

The city's reproduction of itself relied on both endogamy and exogamy.
The rule of exogamy, the exchange of women *outside* the blood family,
organizes marriage and establishes culture by defining appropriate sexual
partners. The prohibition to men of sexual relations with certain women
within the family (however weakly that prohibition may be enforced) is
simultaneously an injunction to exchange those women with other males
as the men of a group agree to exchange their daughters and sisters
instead of keeping them for themselves; through the incest taboo they

cement alliances with other men "like" them, sealing the contractual unit in networks of gifts and debts sealed by the bodies of women.

According to Lévi-Strauss, this exchange of women also founded the principle of reciprocity within society: "It is no exaggeration, then, to say that exogamy is the archetype of all other manifestations based upon reciprocity, and that it provides the fundamental and immutable rule ensuring the existence of the group as a group."[4] The blindness that makes possible this ironic nonreciprocal reciprocity is still stunning. Reciprocity will thus be possible only among men who are like, as it structures the prestigious fictions of the duet, the dialogue, the marriage, and the scholarly communication.

Many males in Greek society did not have the right to exchange Greek women; though male, they were "unlike" in certain ways, i.e., they were either non-Greek slaves or they were *metics,* who were either freed slaves or Greeks born free in other cities but without Athenian citizenship. Those who were like, "We," were distinguished from everyone else, "They," in a strict dichotomy that was absolute and exclusive: "It began as the aristocrats' view of society and reflects the idea of the gulf between themselves and 'others.' In the minds of a comparatively small and close-knit group like the Greek aristocracy, there are only two kinds of people, 'we' and 'they'" (Else 1959, 75).

Because of this dichotomy, the rule of exogamy, having to do with the immediate family, was overlaid with a larger rule of endogamy, or the rule that required the exchange of women among the group constituted as We. A man had to exchange the women of his immediate family but only with men who were like him, members of the political family of Greek citizens, which established race and status limits. Oedipus' problem was that he chose a sexual partner from within his immediate family; in *The Women of Trachis,* however, Herakles's problem is his choice of a sexual partner from outside Greece.[5]

The importance of the marriage exchange in defining a society can be illustrated by the use of myths of the Amazons and Centaurs in classical Athens, these myths that made it possible to conceptualize the social unit's use of marriage. Because they were stories of male and female creatures who lived outside of civilized, patrilineal marriage, they provided examples of difference by means of which the boundaries of culture and marriage were strengthened, as Page duBois argues, marking "the farthest boundary within which the community could inscribe itself" (duBois 1982, 96).

Centaurs, who were doubly virile because they were part male horse and part man, were outside the circle of equals that made up the polis. Their exclusion, like the exclusion of other beasts, helped define the circle of equals; i.e., the beast that Oedipus unwittingly became reinforced the definition of his opposite, the civilized citizen who did not engage in bestial behavior. Centaurs were characterized by their disorderliness, their chaotic behavior, and especially by their hostility to the orderly exchange of women. They simply abducted what they needed for mating; civilized biological reproduction, as distinguished from uncivilized mating, did not occur in myths about them. Amazons, too, were hostile to the exchange of women that joined men together. They, too, kidnapped men for mating once a year and then got rid of them. Hostile to marriage, they were obviously hostile to reproduction, and, in the familiar collapse of biological mating into cultural reproduction, that meant they were hostile to civilization. Neither the Centaurs nor the Amazons reproduced the family as a contractual unit that would reproduce culture.

The relationship of the Amazons to marriage, however, was not the same as that of the Centaurs. The hostility of the Amazons to marriage could be rectified if they were abducted by a hero, as Hippolyta was by Theseus. Amazons could be "cured" of their hostility to marriage, but there are no examples of a Centaur being kidnapped to cure his hostility to marriage.

Border Problems

There are contradictions in a conceptual system based on clear boundaries between an Inside, the hero, and an Outside, the Amazon. The discursive and logical structures of fifth-century Greece can be represented by a circle, with Man at the center as the common element. Those groups analogically related to each other because of their status as not-Man are then arranged in relation to the center "like the spokes radiating from the hub of a wheel" (duBois 1982, 129). The Inside is Man's place, within the circle of equals; its occupants are mobile. The outside is static and motionless. The center is both mobile and firm; its outside is immobile but also infirm and chaotic.

Women, however, are both Outside and Inside in this circular system. Associated isomorphically with barbarians and beasts as not-Man, women also occupy a place on the Inside of the city, their bodies the

necessary means by which men reproduce themselves and their culture. The immobility and chaos that marked the Outside and its monsters were associated with women, who threatened to import them into the midst of the family, the center of culture, making the clear binaries no longer adequate for marking difference. *The Women of Trachis* is a tragedy about classification problems that arise in the transition from an analogical circle of equals based on binary oppositions to a more efficient hierarchical way of arranging difference in order to take into account the inner disruptions introduced by women and slaves.

The instability of the system of binary oppositions was, in part, a result of the effects of the Peloponnesian War (431–404 B.C.), a conflict among the city-states themselves, rather than a war against Outsiders. Greeks fought Greeks, upsetting a carefully constructed Greek/Other conceptual system, and "the violence and aggression once reserved for barbarians were continually enacted against fellow Hellenes" (duBois 1982, 130).

Another factor that led to instability was the presence of slaves introduced into Athens from other Hellenic areas; they were not differentiated by *appearance,* an important factor in their potential for interior disruption.[6] If they were born of Greek slaves or if they had learned Greek, they were indistinguishable from Greek citizens, unlike the case of Greek women or, later, Africans enslaved in North America, who could always be distinguished by sight. Freed slaves became *metics,* freed men who were noncitizens; *metics* were also free citizens from cities other than Athens. Insiders in some ways, they were nevertheless not legitimate Insiders: "There was no action or belief or institution in Greco-Roman antiquity that was not one way or another affected by the possibility that someone involved *might* be a slave" (Finley 1980, 65).

The slave, a border character like the woman, was positioned between nature and culture, man and animal,[7] occupying a double position as human being and exchanged object, as M. I. Finley argues: "The fact that a slave is a human being has no relevance to the question whether or not he is also property; it merely reveals that he is a peculiar property, Aristotle's 'property with a soul'" (73). He was closer to his body within the signifying system because his body is the *site* of his exchange as commodity, and he was answerable with his body and unrestrictedly available in sexual relations (94). Another absence appears here in Finley's analysis, and that is the status of the being closest to the body in this system, the slave woman, who does not show up in any of Aristotle's categories.

The possible internal disruption that slaves introduce into clearly articulated We/They oppositions produces certain "inscriptions" of bodies: "If a slave is a property with a soul, a non-person and yet indubitably a biological human being, institutional procedures are to be expected that will degrade and undermine his humanity and so distinguish him from human beings who are not property."[8] The institution of slavery, like the institution of marriage, requires that human beings be identifiable; if they are not, it makes them so. The relationship between the status of slaves and the status of women is important, but the equivalence is not exact. They are compared here in order to discuss the analogies that associate them as Inside Outsiders, but there are very specific historical differences in their circumstances.

For Aristotle slavery was a natural institution that was "good and just," but this natural slavery, or urban "classical slavery," was already secondary to a more primary slavery found in agrarian households:

> The sharp rise in demand for urban labour, driven by a great increase in the standard of living, in the new hunger for luxuries of every kind, prostitutes, fine public and private buildings, fine jewelry and metalwork, and so on, led to the emergence of the classical form of slavery, distinct from the "personal" slavery found in pastoral agrarian households. (1980, 37)

In a familiar pattern Finley's analysis of slavery stumbles over the family. In explaining the difference between classical slavery and personal slavery he makes a fundamental distinction between labor for oneself and labor for others. But in order to make the distinction and keep his categories neat, he must erase female labor:

> "Oneself" is to be understood not in a narrow individualistic sense but as embracing the family, nuclear or extended as the case may

be in any particular society. That is to say, the work of the women and children within the family, no matter how authoritarian and patriarchal its structure, is not subsumed under this category of labour for others.[9]

Echo reappears, to add *labor, others,* and *oneself* to the long list of ironic terms whose use excludes women.

Classical slavery disrupted the Inside/Outside opposition because it made the judgment of likeness difficult, a judgment that also presumed activity. The male citizen was like other male citizens in his capacity to penetrate; females had the capacity to be penetrated. As Michel Foucault argues, "the Greek ethics of pleasure is linked to a virile society, to dyssymmetry, exclusion of the other, an obsession with penetration, and a kind of threat of being dispossessed of your own energy."[10]

Because of this hierarchy, sexuality presumes an active/passive distinction that is upset when Greek males are on both sides of the opposition in homosexuality: "A woman, a slave, could be passive: such was their nature, their status. All this reflection, philosophizing about the love of boys—with always the same conclusion: please don't treat a boy as a woman."[11] The boy was not to be treated as a woman, but neither was he to be allowed to be active: "[The Greeks] couldn't even imagine reciprocity of pleasure between a boy and a man." The strict binary opposition could not account for different levels of activity; what was required was Aristotle's concept of appropriateness.

Aristotle's hierarchical categories arose out of "a particular moment of stress in Greek culture when social conflicts within the city, the recognition of difference within made it imperative that order be defined strictly in terms of mastery."[12] As Aristotle says:

> Authority and subordination are conditions not only inevitable but expedient; in some cases things are marked out from the moment of birth to rule or be ruled . . . because in every composite thing, where a plurality of parts, whether continuous or discrete, is combined to make a single common whole, there is always found a ruling and a subject factor, and this characteristic of living things is present in them as outcome of the whole of nature. (Aristotle, quoted in duBois 1982, 144)

The Women of Trachis

A reading of Sophocles' *The Women of Trachis* can show how subordination is organized to work both as description and prescription, the unreliable male/female binary opposition organized, or administered, through the institution of marriage. On the one hand, Sophocles describes the cost of excluding women from subjectivity in a profoundly beautiful tragedy. *The Women of Trachis*, however, also serves as a safety valve for the hostility women might feel toward civilization. It presents a woman, Deianeira, as the representative of the forgiveness and sensitivity that could tame the frontier savagery of a hero like Herakles and make the world more civilized; she could turn him into a civilized man, a citizen. Here Sophocles' portrayal of Deianeira becomes prescription, what women's behavior—normal femininity—should be if savagery is to be overcome. The fate of civilization lies with her.

A presupposition that structures the play is that Greek civilization is difficult and dangerous, but it is all there is. And its price, ultimately, even sadly, must be paid. It is the lesson of Freud's *Civilization and Its Discontents* and Hegel's tracing of the history of Spirit, perhaps even Barthes's sadness over the bad faith of knowledge, a sad shrug of the shoulders at the inevitability of the price of men's contract, that price the disappearance of the female subject. And since women were probably not to be found in the audience of Greek tragedy, the lesson must have been one for husbands about what to expect, or demand, from their wives.

It is tempting to compare the situation of Greek women in *The Women of Trachis* to the situation of Greek women in general, but there are very different kinds of heroines in Greek tragedy. In discussing the strong ones such as Medea and Antigone, Page duBois suggests that strong women characters on stage, like the myths of a powerful matriarchy, operated according to the binary principle of inversion. In establishing a system of differences by which the male subject affirms his position in contrast to what he is not, his strength may seem greater if the opponent he has defeated has been portrayed as strong. The stronger the Amazon or Medea, the stronger the force that can subdue them. Their tragedies simply allow men to investigate the not-Woman, Man.[13]

But Deianeira is another kind of heroine, the Amazon who is changed into a wife. *The Women of Trachis* shows what that change requires, both aesthetically and politically, though, in *The Poetics*, these appear to be the same.

The basic plot text, as we have been following it, organizes the active/passive opposition in the interests of the reproduction of a contractual polis. For the polis to hold together Oedipus' encounter with Laius proved the necessity of a legal process of substitution rather than a violent one.[14] The plot text concerned a public problem—the plague that threatened the city of Thebes, though the plague was caused by an intimate act within a particular family. Oedipus' deliberations occurred out in front of the palace before a chorus of Theban citizens, and the entire tragedy takes place in public, with the audience never seeing the private chamber of Jocasta.

Two-thirds of the action of *The Women of Trachis,* on the other hand, occurs inside the palace of Herakles, which was a difficult site to represent in the enormous open-air Greek theater, whose architectural design suited it to the representation of public matters. Intimate and private incidents depending on nuance and the subtlety of the individual actor were difficult to stage because tragedy, by definition, was not concerned with particular individuals. The design of the tragic stage, like the *Poetics,* privileged the public over the private and the universal over the particular.

Hidden Guilt

The story of *The Women of Trachis* is straightforward. Deianeira, the wife of Herakles, waits at home for news of his return from wars abroad. When she finally gets word from a messenger that his ship has landed and he has paused to offer thanks to the gods, she and the women with her rejoice. But the rejoicing is interrupted by the entry of a train of captured women who are Herakles' booty. One in particular, Iole, has been selected as a replacement for Deianeira, though Deianeira does not yet know it.

A second messenger tells her the truth, and in order to reincite Herakles' passion for her she sends him a gift—a cloak dipped in a special potion given to her years ago by the Centaur, Nessos, who was then killed by Herakles. The potion, however, poisons Herakles when it touches his flesh. Before he dies he curses Deianeira, gives Iole to his son Hyllos, and instructs Hyllos to kill him by burning him alive on a funeral pyre. The pyre was originally to have burned his offering of thanksgiving to the gods for his safe return.

The title of the tragedy, *The Women of Trachis,* takes its name from the young women who make up the chorus; in *Oedipus* the chorus was made up of elders of the polis. Because the story is about Deianeira, it is tempting to interpret it as her tragedy, but the drama is more likely the city's tragedy, a tragedy of a form of civilization which must rest somewhat tenuously on women's influence in taming the epic hero, in limiting his freedom and his use of force to subdue the world. The city whose strength had depended on colonizers like Herakles at a later historical moment cannot allow his disruptive possibilities into the city. Man must learn discipline in order to be an urban citizen subject to law, but in this process the city's *dependence* on the wife—on simultaneously marginalizing and appropriating her—shows how vulnerable that law and discipline might be.

This tragedy also continues to arrange the city's definitions of male and female. Deianeira is not a woman, but a Woman, a narrative image: the wife/mother whose body, like Jocasta's, can provide the closure the tragedy needs. That body is all the city needs from her; it does not need her voice or her knowledge. But if her body is contaminated, it threatens the city's contract and its calculable reproduction. In a rearrangement of cause and effect which we will follow in detail Deianeira's body becomes the *passive cause* of the death of Herakles. A woman in her particularity, Deianeira, must be purged from inside the city so that other men will not be endangered, but Woman's place inside must be reinscribed and reinforced.

The tragedy is structured so that two-thirds of it is devoted to Deianeira in her private domestic space. The remainder concerns Herakles, who is out in the open, on the very edge of Trachis, where his ship has just docked. He is the frontier colonizer who has subdued the lands on the edges of the city but who now must learn how to subdue his own violence and desires in a contract with other men. He gets no further into the city than the beach at its outskirts.

Deianeira and Herakles are connected only by the words of three people: Lichas, a news bearer; another messenger who reveals that Lichas was lying to Deianeira in order to protect her from the truth about Iole; and Hyllos, the son of Deianeira and Herakles. Originally, the same actor may have played both Deianeira and Herakles, perhaps technically explaining why they never speak to each other. But their separation also represents the marriage: two separate spaces in search of a connection. So far the male actor as norm links the spaces, and the demands of plot reflect the mediating force.

Deianeira's character foregrounds the contradictions that the wife/
mother faces in tragedy. She does what is appropriate to her, and she is
a very sympathetic character—sensitive to Iole; forgiving, understanding, tolerant of Herakles' treatment of her; saddened by the fate of the
slave women he has brought home as booty. But she has learned her
lesson too well, and her timidity and passivity, characteristics related to
those Aristotle interpreted as positive ones for a woman, are cloying.
The nurse, who, as a woman of lower status, is allowed a measure of
unfeminine activity so she can do more work, has to prod Deianeira to
send her son to find out if Herakles is on his way home; Deianeira stands
indecisively trying to get someone to tell her what to do.

She is a good wife, obedient and docile, having learned the lesson
of femininity well: "No sensible woman should let herself give way to
rage," she says.[15] She continues:

> I am not a woman who tries to be—and may
> I never learn to be—bad and bold.
> I hate women who are.
> But if somehow by these charms
> these spells I lay on Herakles, I can defeat
> the girl—well, the move is made, unless you think
> I am acting rashly.
> If so, I shall stop.
>
> (299)

This hesitant, deferential behavior will, by the end of the tragedy, be
subtly transformed by Herakles and Sophocles into what they will call
"power." The contrast is striking between this timid, sensitive woman
and the fear and hatred she will be said to "cause," as active and passive, subject and object, cause and effect, are intricately refined and
redefined.

Her role, as we would expect, is to *wait,* and she does so within a
specific radius of her "husbandless bed," the center of the domestic part
of the play. The center of Herakles' part of the play, the public part, is
Herakles. Deianeira's two-thirds of the tragedy is controlled by his absence: the empty bed, his delay in returning, the promises of his arrival,
then further delay.

Tragedians of the fifth century selected their subject matter from extant legends; Sophocles took the Deianeira of legend and radically transformed her. She is important as a prize in the tragedy, the "bed" Herakles and the river god Achelous fight over ("they come together then in the middle desiring her bed" [297]). In the legend she was a secondary prize; the real prize of the encounter was the Horn of Amalthea, a magic cornucopia carried away by the victor, Herakles.

Her background has been carefully narrowed by Sophocles for use in the tragedy. In the legend she was a member of a warlike and violent Aetolian family, but Sophocles changed her home to Pleuron, which has no such violent connotations. Timid and relatively passive in this play, her name marks her as an Amazon; it means "Fighter-with-men," "Hostile-to-men," or "Man-killer." In legend she was a woman who "drove a chariot and practiced the acts of war" (Dickerson and Williams, introduction to Sophocles 1978a, 6). The Amazon who constituted the boundary, or limit, of the definitions of male and female is transformed by Sophocles into the passive woman whose bed will reproduce the polis, the compliant wife. This presents an aesthetic problem that makes this tragedy awkward in ways *Oedipus the King* was not. In *Oedipus the King* the ambiguity centered on Oedipus is symmetrical and perfectly balanced; his happiness changes to unhappiness in proportion to the degree the unhappiness of Thebes changes to happiness. The balance is perfect and beautiful.

The Women of Trachis, however, is assymmetrical from the beginning. A character like Deianeira who has learned the Woman's cultural lesson of submissiveness and good behavior is a character difficult to present in any interesting way. To be interesting she must *not* be a good wife, as Medea was not. Or like Antigone, she must not be a wife at all. Amazons and strong women lend themselves to tragedy, but deferential Women make better wives.

There may be a partial solution to this problem in the character of Iole, the concubine Herakles brings home as booty from the war, intending to replace Deianeira with her. Iole is good and obedient, but unlike Deianeira, her submissiveness does not mark her as uninteresting because of two factors: she is silent, and she is young and beautiful. The aesthetic problem finds one solution: the enigma. If the image of the normal "civilized" female does not make for an aesthetically pleasing story because she plays her wife/mother role too well, the enigmatic, silent one enlivens the plot. She, too, obediently conducts herself as she should for the needs of civilization and its reproduction, but she brings interest, mystery, danger, and eroticism to her domestication.

Deianeira is the Woman who is being taught to be silent like Iole; her mistake is that she tries to be active, behaving rashly and impetuously in a moment of desperation. She, like Iole, had been brought to Trachis as an Outsider. (In matrilineal succession the son left his family; in patrilineal succession the daughter leaves.) Herakles is an Insider, but the boundaries of the Inside have not yet been clearly enough established by regulated marriage exchange. He is the son of Zeus; therefore, his kingdom is both everywhere in the unlimited world of the epic hero (not the citizen) and nowhere. He is in Trachis only because he has been exiled as punishment for his violence. We are not told from where he has been exiled, but it must be from the center of the world, Greece.

Herakles had abducted Deianeira from her father, Oeneus, who, understandably, would not permit Herakles to marry her because Herakles had killed his last wife, Megara, and all their children. Herakles simply stole Deianeira, such an abduction a serious insult to his host. But Oeneus had also been duplicitous; he had first promised Deianeira to Herakles then insulted his guest by reneging on the promise. The relationship between Deianeira and Herakles is thus marked from the beginning by lying and abduction, which introduce contamination into the Inside of Trachis. Marriage based on theft rather than on reciprocal exchange proves to be risky for the city.

As Herakles flees with Deianeira, he allows Nessos, a Centaur, to carry her across a river, but Nessos also contaminates her: "When I was halfway across / his hands touched me lustfully" (299). The metaphor of hands here and at the end of the tragedy function as a metaphor for sexual contact. Herakles, however, knows only that Nessos has threatened Deianeira, and kills the Centaur with an arrow dipped in the poison of the Hydra's blood. There are several ways Deianeira will carry the Outside into the Inside: she is a barbarian, or not-Greek; she is female, or not-Man; and she has been violated by the Centaur, who is part beast and monster, also not-Man.

Each Inside/Outside opposition can be divided again into male and female. When two Outsiders are in opposition—for example, Deianeira and Nessos—the male/female asymmetry means that Nessos will be dominant because Deianeira is female. She is as much at risk of abduction or violation around Nessos as she is near Herakles. The active space belongs to the male, whether he is of the dominant group or not.

Passive Causality

In an earlier look at the Insider/Outsider opposition it appeared that the private sphere was the sphere of women. In *The Women of Trachis,* however, the private is shown to be another place dominated by masculinity. What we thought was the sphere of women is, instead, the sphere of Woman, already marked by the doubly virile Centaur. The private bed does not belong to Deianeira; it is the site of the struggle between the Centaur and Herakles, and it is also the prize.

Deianeira does import pollution and contamination to the Inside, but it is as a receptacle, a carrier for the real contamination, which comes from Nessos, who exacted his revenge by means of her body. Deianeira carried with her to Trachis a gift from Nessos—the charm given to her in Nessos' dying moments. It is a *pharmakon* taken from his blood mixed with the Hydra's poison.

Deianeira is the *cause* of the poisoning of Herakles because she has been violated; the cause is actually the effect of something done to her by Nessos, the representative of virility. Without being the agent, her body transfers or carries danger. She believed the Centaur when he advised her to use the substance as a love potion if she needed it to recapture Herakles' passion after she had grown older, after Herakles had turned to younger women, whom he characterized as "blossoms" instead of "flowers."[16] Her threat to Herakles is associated with love. But Nessos instructed her to make sure that the robe "should touch the skin of no man before it touches his, nor should the light of the sun look upon it" (300). What he transferred to Herakles was the danger that lies behind the taboo of virginity; this taboo will be followed later.

Deianeira's body has the potential of carrying into the Greek Inside not only poison but a hybrid offspring, part Greek, part non-Greek, as a result of the Centaur's violation. At a time in Greek history when distinguishing Greeks from non-Greeks was problematic, hybrid offspring presented a threat to the heredity of property and name. To avoid questions of loyalty and genealogy women were isolated, marriage functioning as a form of regulation that assured "the permanence of the City itself, its constant reproduction," as Vernant argues. Nessos' potion, too, required isolation; it was not to be exposed to the light of day. It had to be kept, like Deianeira herself as wife, "always deep in the house where no warm ray of light may touch it" (303), and Nessos, in a sense, seduces Deianeira into taking the gift. The effect of light upon the potion was hideous and ominous. Having dipped Herakles' robe into the liquid, Deianeira sent it to him, only to notice too late what happened to a piece of wool saturated with it and left in the sunlight: "This piece has disappeared, devoured by nothing in the house but destroyed by itself, eaten away and crumbled completely to dust" (303). In a similar way Herakles' body will rot and suppurate when he puts on the cloak.

Deianeira's *act* of sending the robe appears to be the *cause* of the threat to Herakles; she momentarily becomes an active, bold, rash woman who breaks out of her normal passive feminine role. But her act is both her act and something else; it has already been appropriated by Nessos. She had hidden his potion safely away in the dark, private sphere, incubating the kernel of his virile and savage world inside the domestic space where she had tried to find security and unwittingly carrying forward the very savagery she had hoped to escape. She will unintentionally but inevitably reproduce virility, just as the wife/mother of the oedipal contract will reproduce phallocentrism.

Deianeira commits an "act" inspired by passion and associated with duplicity, contamination, and poison. One of the most disturbing consequences of her act within the tragedy is that it means that the son of Zeus has been "done to" by a woman. This mixture of what should have been kept distinct, the categories of activity and passivity, masculinity and femininity, almost immediately produces corruption, rot, suppuration. When Herakles puts on the robe as he prepares to sacrifice bulls in thanksgiving for his return home, he feels it meld to his body. The robe becomes a metaphor of his own lust, its heat causing it to eat into his flesh, and he cries out in horror, as he is made passive to her activity: "Now in my misery I am discovered a woman" (317).

Having acted, Deianeira is guilty, but because she is a woman, guilt does not carry the same kind of meaning as does responsibility. There are two levels of activity here, each appropriate to the actor. When a man acts in this tragedy, he is *responsible* for the results of his act, but when a woman acts, she is *guilty;* her act is rash, "manly," inappropriate. What we called guilt in *Oedipus the King* has here been divided into two—guilt and responsibility—then distributed according to gender.

The two characters in this tragedy who are assigned guilt, Deianeira and Iole, are paradoxically referred to as powerful. Herakles says of Deianeira: "A woman, a female, in no way like a man / she alone without even a sword has brought me down" (316). There are two ways we could read Herakles' words: as proof of the power of Woman or as a way to free Herakles of the guilt of his own savagery.

Hyllos. too, assigns blame to Deianeira:

> Mother, this is what you have planned and done to my father,
> and you are caught. For this, Justice who punishes
> and the Fury will requite you. If it is right
> for a son, I curse you, and it is right since you
> have given me the right by killing the best of all men
> on earth, such as you shall never see again.
>
> (307)

She has given him the right because it is true that she killed Herakles, the best of all men on earth.

But, of course, she also did *not* kill him; Nessos and the Hydra did. Deianeira was simply the carrier of the poison she innocently uses; she was innocently guilty, an oxymoron which, in Oedipus' case, made him a tragic hero and which makes very awkward Sophocles' determination to bring this tragedy back around to a focus on Herakles. It was Herakles himself who originally dipped the arrow in the poison that finally infects him. He had also killed the Hydra and the Centaur, indirectly causing his own death, and on his deathbed he insists that the responsibility for his own death be recognized. Any active role by Deianeira in his death must be limited, while her guilt, paradoxically, is to be firmly established. The plot sets up a situation in which the effects of Nessos' poison will be purged, freeing the male characters of the debilitation of guilt for what they may have done. Purgation will take two forms: death for the character Deianeira and for Herakles, who trusts too much in physical force and passion in terms of the plot; and the symbolic assignment of guilt to characters in the passive plot space rather than the active one.

To dilute Deianeira's activity and assign her guilt, Herakles orders Hyllos to burn him alive so that it will be Hyllos who takes responsibility for his death, not Deianeira. In this way Herakles' power, which began the cycle of violence that led to his poisoning, will pass directly from father to son, breaking the connections with both the Centaur and Deianeira. The possibility that his power will go astray and pass into the wrong hands can be minimized if Herakles can make sure Hyllos will do as he is ordered.

Deianeira, too, assigns guilt to woman in this description of Herakles' desire for Iole, which led to war: "Her own beauty has destroyed her life"; and "Against her will, this unfortunate girl has sacked and enslaved the world of her fathers" (296). Like Deianeira's act of murdering Herakles, those active verbs mock the sentences that contain them. The "actors," the supposed subjects of the active verbs with direct objects receiving that action, were themselves acted upon in the earlier active/passive opposition we have followed for so long. Their passive situation, the "condition" Benveniste described, has now, in the form of these sentences, been described as an act that causes death, contamination, destruction. Herakles will die on his funeral pyre, "damning the mismating in your wretched bed" (307). A verbal and symbolic scapegoating frees father and son, and the like members of their contractual group, to proceed with the work of the city; Woman, as the site of guilt, is the necessary sacrifice. The arrangement of events in the dramatic plot has thus made it possible to say that Deianeira, Iole, Woman, are more powerful than Herakles, for it is true that the strongest, ablest hero of all time, Herakles, the son of Zeus, has been brought down by the power of a woman in a highly ironized form of activity.

The female characters in the drama have at last been encircled as devices of passive causality. That is, they are assigned power *because* they have no power. Excluded from the position of agency, as tragic poets, philosophers, or citizens, women could not themselves assign guilt; it is, as a result, assigned to Woman because women cannot assign it. And because there is only one site of agency, the passive partner becomes the passive cause by default. Herakles can then acknowledge Woman's power:

> Neither the spear of battle, nor the army of
> the earth-born Giants, nor the violence of beasts,
> nor Greece, nor any place of barbarous tongue, not all
> the lands I came to purify could ever do this.
> A woman, a female, in no way like a man,
> she alone without even a sword has brought me down.
>
> (316)

From Stammering to Silence

Organizing activity also organizes the capacity for speech. The tragedy opened with a group of very talkative young maidens, who do not speak wisely, unlike the chorus of elders in *Oedipus the King*. Instead, their words are idealistic, naive, and hopeful, while they try to maintain illusions that can comfort Deianeira and themselves as they await news of Herakles' return. Deianeira has all along been moved more by determination than hope, her own illusions long gone. The maidens, unlike the chorus of elders, do not attempt to *know*; instead, they are concerned with giving Deianeira advice on the way to *be* while awaiting the one who knows.

The maidens are clearly distinguished from the married women, the group of women divided by the significance of the marked hymen: "When King Herakles set off from home on his / last journey, he left an old tablet in the house, on which some signs had been inscribed."[17] Deianeira recognizes this division within the group of women and addresses the maidens:

> May you never learn
> by your own suffering how my heart is torn.
> You do not know now. So the young thing
> grows in her own places; the heat of the sun-god
> does not confound her, nor does the rain, nor any wind.
> Pleasurably she enjoys an untroubled life
> until the time she is no longer called a maiden
> but woman, and takes her share of worry in the night,
> fearful for her husband or for her children,
> by looking at her own experience, she comes
> to understand the troubles with which I am weighed down.
>
> (284)

The young girl who grew "in her own places" has been confounded by the "heat of the sun-god," and, as a result, she is now the wife/mother, listening fatalistically to the youthful, unrealistic, but sympathetic advice of the young maidens, who do not yet know what is in store for them. She never follows their advice but, instead, listens to the nurse, whose passage in and out of the private space gives her a certain clarity about what must be done. Deianeira, exiled in the private space, attempts to speak and act only with her help. As in *Oedipus the King,* it takes two women to take action, to do what one good man might.

Deianeira listens to the nurse, the maidens, and the messengers, and she grows progressively more silent. The speech/silence opposition becomes clearer when the group of women are noisily rejoicing over the first news of Herakles' return, and they are interrupted by the entrance of Iole and the captured slave women, "the trophies and first-fruits of victory" (305).

Iole is obviously more than a concubine—she is a replacement wife who appears on stage in absolute silence. She has no lines in the tragedy. She, not Deianeira, is the wife the young maidens are to emulate—mysterious but docile and, above all, silent. Once Deianeira recognizes this and learns that her love gift has destroyed Herakles, her speech will be gradually reduced from a hesitant stammer to silence, a silence that is complete because *whatever* she might say would reveal her guilt. But it is not only her speech that reveals guilt. As the chorus warns her when she leaves the stage: "Why do you go off in silence? Surely you see / that by silence you join your accuser and accuse / yourself?" (307). Speech and silence amount to the same thing.

Deianeira's last words are delivered to the bed behind closed doors and reported to the audience by the nurse. In her final moments Deianeira has arranged the bed, then climbed on it to kill herself there with a sword. She *is* the bed in the isomorphic mytholgical system in which men's reason located Woman. Though suicide was considered a cowardly act, she at least kills herself with a manly sword, which penetrates and kills her:

> O my bed, O my bridal chamber, farewell
> now forever, for never again will you take me
> to be as a wife between these sheets of yours . . .
>
> (311)

This death, says the nurse, was a last "motionless journey," but it was brought about actively by Deianeira: "She herself by herself set her hand to it" (310). Her only possible autoaffection—"she herself . . . set her hand to it"—leads to death rather than transcendence, occurring within the plot space of immobility. (In one of the most influential contemporary attempts to play with this kind of narrative, the movie *Thelma and Louise,* the two main characters were trying to break out of a very similar plot. But even in 1991, no ending was available, at least in Hollywood, that went beyond Kate Chopin's *The Awakening* and its heroine's suicide. And so Thelma and Louise went flying over the edge of a canyon to their deaths.) Herakles will leave a copy of himself when he dies; Deianeira's line ends.

Deianeira's relationship to Iole might have led to a different kind of copy, which could have threatened the institution of marriage. The bar between wives and maidens divides a group at large: women, as marriage relies on a vertical power structure, man over woman, which breaks up horizontal affinities, woman to woman. The man's penetration, his signature of ownership, distinguishes Deianeira from the other women, turning her into Man's Woman. And ideally, it will keep the other women separated by fomenting competition among them for Man's favor. Deianeira recognizes the way the vertical relation disrupts the horizontal one and the way both she and Iole must now compete for the passive plot space:

> For here I have taken on a girl—no,
> I can think that no longer—a married woman, as
> a ship's master takes on cargo, goods that outrage my heart.
> So now the two of us lie under the sheet
> waiting for his embrace. This is the gift my brave
> and faithful Herakles sends home to his dear wife
> to compensate for his long absence.
>
> (298)

Deianeira's sympathy with Iole, both of whom were abducted brides, introduces a danger into the domestic space when she looks sideways at Iole, constituting a horizontal relationship instead of a competitive one that corresponds to the vertical hierarchy with Man at the top.

Iole comes onstage in a *mourning* procession, which continues the threat to likeness. Mourning had been associated with a predemocratic period when aristocratic families competed with each other by financing extravagant shows of wealth at funerals. These excesses belied the still fragile, democratic concept of likeness, which depended on at least some limitations on competition. This expression of grief had consequently been limited by law, but its temptations remained recent and strong.

Deianeira's identification with Iole presents another problem. The Greeks rarely represented current history onstage, carrying out "an injunction against showing the present directly in the tragic ampitheater" (duBois 1982, 82). One reason was to ensure that the tragic actor represented a Greek rather than a tribal hero—tribal loyalties, like extravagant funerals and excessive wealth, threatening the fragile circle of equals. An injunction against representing current enemies onstage may also have limited the possibilities of sympathy for the enemy.

Excluding women from representing themselves similarly limited indentification with or sympathy for them, though men could freely identify with males dressed as females. For even Herakles had once dressed as a female after being enslaved by Omphale for a year.[18] But he was able to accomplish heroic tasks during this time, proving that the change of costume was superficial and that he had not been "infected" by passivity during that period. His activity was never threatened, and he emerged from the period in which he dressed like a woman strengthened in his masculinity, an initiation model that bears some resemblance to later theoretical moves like those of Nietzsche, Artaud, and Derrida, who appropriate the concept of textuality as feminized then emerge from that feminized space all the stronger because of their capacity to theorize it, or, as Kristeva argues, to make capital of it, even if only cultural capital.

The Privilege of the Patriarch

This tragedy divides the problem of women into two parts. First, women have the potential of carrying the mark of an Outsider like Nessos into the hero's family. And second, they may bring hostility and resentment against their abductors into the most intimate situation, marriage. That hostility has something to do with Herakles' final command to his son to marry Iole, his second wife, and to sacrifice Herakles himself, this sacrifice bringing about the symbolic patrilineal substitution of father by son. The replacement of Deianeira by Iole will be a last step in another kind of substitution, Woman for women, which is the function of the patrilineal form of marriage (and of plot), as the substitution of Iole for Deianeira symbolically arranges the form of monogamous marriage.

Though neither Iole nor Deianeira was a virgin, there is a difference between the relation of each to the state of virginity, and that difference has to do with an old custom Freud describes in an essay, "The Taboo of Virginity." The nineteenth-century valorization of virginity affects his view, as he acknowledges: "The demand that a girl shall not bring to her marriage with a particular man any memory of sexual relations with another is, indeed, nothing other than a logical continuation of the right to exclusive possession of a woman, which forms the essence of monogamy, the extension of this monopoly to cover the past" (Freud 1957b, 193). The first man who breaks the hymen, he continues, "creates a state of bondage in the woman which guarantees that possession of her shall continue undisturbed and makes her able to resist new impressions and enticements from outside" (193). The Centaur made this first mark upon Deianeira. As an agent of the Outside, he was there first, his mark or signature preceding that of Herakles, the Insider. The Centaur entered, penetrated, the center of the property of Greek society, its "pro-pre," in this way marking the very intimacy of its hero's privacy.[19] As Outsider, the Centaur has already preceded Herakles in marking the private and unique thing that it is Herakles' right to have to himself as husband.

There are here several kinds of Insiders and Outsiders. Freud posits an Inside that is ostensibly constituted by the marriage unit made up of the man and the woman whose body the man has a right to. Outside that unit "new impressions and enticements are possible." But the Centaur has preceded the husband, having already formed his own Inside made up of Deianeira's body and his mark on it. But there is another element to Freud's story of this development of man's access to a woman's body, one that links the forced one to the forcer, what he calls bondage:

> [Bondage is] the phenomenon of a person's acquiring an unusually high degree of dependence and lack of self-reliance in relation to another person with whom he has a sexual relationship. This bondage can on occasion extend very far, as far as the loss of all independent will and as far as causing a person to suffer the greatest sacrifices of his own interests. (193)

How does this self-erasure come about and what does it have to do with Deianeira? In his descriptions of gender, which share many similarities with Aristotle's, Freud suggests that in the past this bondage may have been influenced not just by emotions but also by "other motives and inducements." Whatever the reason, the result is useful: "Some such measure of sexual bondage is, indeed, indispensable to the maintenance of civilized marriage and to holding at bay the polygamous tendencies

which threaten it, and in our social communities this factor is regularly
reckoned upon" (194). Though the dictionary definition of *polygamy* is
"the practice of having more than one wife, husband, or mate at a single
time," Freud was talking about men having many mates. The word
polygamy comes from the generic "he," from the Greek *gameo,* used only
of men in the active voice. The temptation of men to engage in polygamy could be limited, as this argument goes, if one woman could be
bonded to each tempted male.

The valorization of virginity is related to the development of this
bondage. But what about the opposite of the valorization of virginity—
the taboo of virginity which *refused* the husband the right to a virgin
bride? In some groups this taboo of virginity was observed by ensuring
that the hymen be broken by something or someone other than the
husband. Frequently, according to Freud, this occurred at puberty or
before marriage by means of an instrument wielded by others, but it
was also done through penetration by other men besides the bridegroom:
strangers, professional deflowerers, priests. The word *groomsmen* originally meant those whose function it was to break the hymen. All of these
men were substitutes for the bride's father, who in some cases still
performed that function himself. His was the privilege of the patriarch.

The taboo of virginity has several possible explanations, according
to Freud. A fear of blood, especially menstrual blood, may have had
something to do with it—menstrual blood being associated in some
cultures with an ancestral spirit related to the tribe in an animistic, isomorphic connection with blood in general. Menstrual blood is sometimes interpreted as proof of women's intercourse with that animal spirit
or with having been bitten by that spirit, making women the carriers of
that animal Outsider we have traced; the Centaur's bestiality may be
linked to this animal spirit.

Freud, however, says the taboo cannot be wholly attributed to the
fear of menstrual blood. Other possible reasons might be man's fear of
first occurrences or a taboo on intercourse or even on women themselves
because of their potential to *infect* others with their femininity, like a
disease or a pollutant:

> The man is afraid of being weakened by the woman, infected with
> her femininity and of then showing himself incapable. The effect
> which coitus has of discharging tensions and causing flaccidity may
> be the prototype of what the man fears; and realization of the

influence which the woman gains over him through sexual intercourse, the consideration she thereby forces from him, may justify
his extension of this fear. In all this there is nothing obsolete, nothing that is not with us today. (199)

But these are still not the main reasons behind the taboo. There is
something else, he says, that can help explain "what underlies the narcissistic rejection of women by men, which is so much mixed up with
despising them," a force that "opposes love by rejecting women as
strange and hostile" (200). Behind the taboo of virginity is the desire to
spare the husband from something related to the first sexual act: "The
first act of intercourse stands out as a danger of particular intensity"
(199). The danger and enmity associated with it paradoxically arise
where the most intimate and affectionate relation might be expected: in
marriage.

Defloration risks drawing the bride's hostility onto the person most
likely to receive it, her husband, who has already, because of the mechanism of projection, perceived hostility on her part: "The minor differences in people who are otherwise alike . . . form the basis of feelings of
strangeness and hostility between them" (199). Projection from the direction of the male, in this version, intensifies the hostility he feels toward the woman and magnifies his assessment of her hostility. And since
the female subject is nowhere to be found in Freud's writing, we only
hear about this hostility from man's perspective: as taboo and projection.
Whatever remained of her activity has now been intensely controlled to
satisfy civilization's needs: "The first act of intercourse mobilizes a number of impulses [in the woman] which are out of place in the desired
feminine attitude" (202). These "impulses," which presumably have
something to do with activity, are overwritten by male needs. It is
important to note the gap available for female agency here, however—"a
number of impulses" which precede the male's reproductive need of her.
As Deianeira said, "the young girl grows in all her own places." But the
needs of the male, "the heat of the sun-god," intrudes, and those female
impulses are forced to give way to masculine needs.[20]

The violent subtext of this "natural" subjugation that occurs in the
"spontaneous" establishment of the family is based on something resembling the Aristotelian concept of appropriateness. There are two kinds
of activity described by Freud, the activity of the female and the activity
of the male, but because of the needs of calculable reproduction, one of

those kinds of activity is more appropriate, or privileged; it may even legitimately require force to overcome female impulses in order to translate its activity into reality, which means its activity coincides with the needs of society constituted by alliances, or bonding, among males. We have already seen that reproduction is valorized retroactively from the direction of the city, according to the needs of civilization, as the Family of Man.

The taboo of virginity seems to involve an act that the male group performs for its members in order to protect them from the women whose bodies they need and whose activity they must control. As in Benveniste's etymological study, the activity of the bride is nowhere to be found other than those impulses, unless she might be said to have "caused" the husband to lose control of himself. A trace of agency may also, paradoxically, live on in her guilt, associated in psychoanalysis with aggression turned inward.[21]

Marriage is a defeat for the bride, but it may be a *secondary* defeat. The initial defeat occurred at the hands of other men who were substitutes for the first man, the patriarch, in Freud's description of the workings of tribal organization. This privilege has to do with the patriarch's desire for and right to his daughters. Ordinarily, when Freud speaks of the incest taboo and analyzes its significance he refers to the son's desire for the mother and, in particular, the necessity for the father and his representatives to separate mother and son. But the other side of the incest taboo is the taboo of virginity, and it seems to mean the opposite of what the incest taboo means. While the taboo of virginity *requires* that the patriarch, or one of his substitutes, penetrate the daughter, the incest taboo *prohibits* the mother to the son. What would appear to be the father's right to the daughter is covered over in psychoanalytic and political theory by a great silence, which has left largely unquestioned the violence of fathers and their rights to the bodies of the women within their families.[22]

In Freud's theory the needs of civilization unequivocally coincide with the needs of heterosexual men, and he takes from Sándor Ferenczi a short narrative that describes the way copulation became an act that produced hostility in women. As in many cases when Freud openly speculates, he then pretends to take it back:

In a palaeo-biological speculation, Ferenczi has traced back this hostility of women—I do not know if he is the first to do so—to a period in time when the sexes became differentiated. At first, in his opinion, copulation took place between two similar individuals, one of which, however, developed into the stronger and forced the weaker one to sexual union. The feelings of bitterness arising from this subjection still persist in the present-day disposition of women. I do not think there is any harm in employing such speculations, so long as one avoids setting too much value on them.

Freud suggests another reason for the woman's hostility: "After this enumeration of motives for the paradoxical reaction of women to defloration, traces of which persist in frigidity, we may sum up by saying that a woman's immature sexuality is discharged onto the man who first makes her acquainted with the sexual act" (206). We now find in Freud's description not only a stronger male but also an older one. The description of the two sexes has slipped to a description that might apply to father and daughter, the relationship in which the taboo ostensibly originated.

Because Freud takes his oedipal paradigm from Greece (or a particular historical received version of Greece), it helps to refer to Greek marriage itself. Marriage was of primary importance to genealogy and property in Athens, the optimum time for marriage being when the woman was healthiest and in her childbearing prime. It was her body that was needed. It was believed that she reached her prime when she was very young; thus, the average age of marriage for women was fourteen, for men thirty. Aristotle preferred that women be somewhat older because very young wives tended to have, he thought, more female babies and were more likely to die in childbirth; the optimum age for marriage, he suggested, was "eighteen for women, thirty-seven for men" (Pomeroy 1975, 51).

The female's archaic hostility resulting from being forced into sexual relations with an older man could be dangerous to her husband unless that hostility was defanged; Freud compared it to the way snake charmers caused a snake to bite a cloth and expel its venom. After being defanged the snake could be handled with safety. In spite of the husband's best efforts the wife's "archaic reaction" of hostility could live on and become a factor in frigidity and rebellion: "analysis of disturbed marriages teaches us that the motives which seek to drive a woman to take vengeance for her defloration are not completely extinguished even in the mental life of civilized women" (206).

The woman's hostility has, however, been put to very efficient use. According to Freud, the greater the resistance to the patriarch or his substitutes, the greater the bondage when that resistance is overcome. One is reminded of the silence/speech situation Deianeira found herself in; one option was just about as bad as the other. Here we find that the more the daughter resists, the greater will be her bondage. The more the Amazon fought, the greater her "cure" when she was rescued by a hero.

The transition from the right of the patriarch to the right of the husband can be seen in Lévi-Strauss's description of the contradiction women introduce into the marriage exchange because they are both person and sign, rather like Aristotle's "property with a soul." The woman, in this contractual system, is "seen under two incompatible aspects: on the one hand, as the object of personal desire, thus exciting sexual and proprietorial instincts; and, on the other, as the subject of the desire of others, and seen as such, i.e., as the means of binding others through alliance with them" (Lévi-Strauss 1969, 496). In a patrilineal system this can refer only to the father.

The patriarchal tribal system, in which the daughter could be the object of the patriarch's desire, developed into the city dependent on exchange, in which the daughter became the object of the desire of others, the means of binding the group together. The exchange transferred the daughter's hostility toward the patriarch onto her husband. In Sophocles' text, of course, even the daughter's *hostility* is not hers; the Centaur uses it to get his own revenge. Deianeira's act merely transfers the Centaur's violence to Herakles, as her function is to be the medium of this masculine competition.

The daughter's hostility, like her activity, is encircled and controlled. When Herakles replaces Deianeira with Iole, the daughter's place is finally eliminated. Iole, the silent wife/mother, takes over from Deianeira, the stammering, rash wife/daughter, and the oedipal dramatis personae are in place: father, son, silent wife/mother.

That Deianeira represented another threat to Herakles is illustrated in Hyllos' response to her death, once he learns that she had not intended to kill Herakles but had inadvertently poisoned the robe. His response is dangerous because of its overdetermined threat of mixture; it involves sympathy, mourning, and the link between mother and son, the disputed ownership of that bed whose private ownership defines the male:

Then the miserable boy abandoned himself utterly
to sobs and mourning for his mother; he threw himself
upon her lips and there, pressing his die to hers,
he lay and groaned over and over that he
had struck her thoughtlessly with a cruel accusation,
weeping because at one moment he was doubly
orphaned for all his life, losing his father and her.

(312)

The relation to the mother is, as Freud says in another essay, a relation of particular threat because, unlike other possibly duplicitous ones, it is based on "an event [birth] that is not open to any doubt and cannot be repeated" (Freud 1957a, 168), unlike fatherhood, which is always open to doubt. The mother and son attraction, which is described to us by the nurse, who throws open the doors to the inner room where Deianeira lies on that familiar bed with Hyllos lying beside her body, is an attraction that must be broken by the father's prohibition. Herakles had hoped to bring Deianeira onstage and torture her so that Hyllos would have to choose which parent's suffering disturbed him the most. Deianeira, by killing herself, deprives him of that chance. But Hyllos' link with her must be completely severed: "Discover yourself the finest rule—obedience to your father" (320), which means carrying out his wishes: "O my son, now truly be my true-born son and do not pay more respect to the name of mother" (316).

Obedience also means that Hyllos must follow Herakles' commands: to place him, while still alive, on a funeral pyre, and to take Iole as his wife. As a result, two things will be accomplished. The influence of Nessos would be counteracted by being mediated, since Hyllos, not an Outsider, would have the power to cause Herakles' death. And Hyllos would be spared the guilt of it, "as long as I don't touch it with my own hands" (322). The autoaffection will be abstract. Similarly, Iole must not be touched by anyone outside the father and son pair, which will found the circle of culture: "No other man but you must have her who has lain with me at my side" (323). Deianeira owns the guilt, Hyllos the responsibility, for the father's death, and Woman is split in two: the pure one and the carnal one.

Hyllos has himself been forced into a situation not of his own choosing. He has now become the citizen, trapped in the ambiguity that is tragic, civilized man's fate. He is also trapped as an eternal substitute for

Iole's father: at least in the oedipal version of the story, the husband is
never the right man; the wife always desires her father.[23]

Hyllos is trapped in marriage. As he says, it would be "better for
me, too, to die than live with my own worst enemy" (323), this "fatal
bride" who is Iole. His marriage to Iole will set the paradigm, unhappy
as it sounds, for marriage itself as the bedrock of the cultural contract,
an ambiguous victory for man but an unambiguous defeat for woman.
She is "fatal" because of passive causality—her place in the plot line
showing her to be immobile, capable only of waiting in a place where
Herakles might find her, be overcome by her beauty, and abduct her.
In a different kind of tragic irony, she would "cause" his death. The
vertical contract between father and son, sealed by the gift of a domesticated Iole, will ensure that the resistance of the daughter is encircled and
controlled because of the archaic hostility unleashed by defloration, but
this unhappy structure also has the "one, civilized consequence of binding the woman lastingly to the man" (Freud 1957b, 208). This civilized
consequence introduces another irony, as it sounds remarkably like a
description of the psychology of abused women.

Herakles' command that Hyllos sacrifice him has another effect.
Herakles was defeated, in part, because he had not disciplined his physical nature and his sexuality, which was especially susceptible to the
corruption and infection that Deianeira and Iole caused. He gave instructions that his body be burned alive in the sacrifical pyre, while his spirit
was to be passed on to Hyllos. The fire of the sacrifice to Zeus will purify
him of the physical weakness the fire of his body represents, as its
uncontrollable nature, its carnality, had allowed Deianeira and the Centaur to infect him. What the Greek citizen must do that the hero,
Herakles, did not was control and discipline himself and his sexuality.

His order to Hyllos means that, besides abstracting his power
through sacrifice and gaining control over the physical nature of the
body, he will leave behind a son who is like himself. By proving that
he is like Herakles—i.e., that he will do Herakles' bidding as Herakles
would do that of Zeus—Hyllos will make it possible for Herakles to die
knowing that he has given birth to a son like himself. He will have
symbolically given birth to himself, as Zeus has to Herakles, in a circular
self-reproduction of fathers. But because Hyllos must now join the
democratic circle of equal sons, a circle that cannot support Herakles as
tyrannical father, the father's place is abstracted and idealized, and the
son becomes the main character.

When Hyllos obeys his father's command he completes another turn of the circle of fathers in a vertical substitution. His obedience also seals the horizontal circle of men by distributing privacy (what it is Man's right to have) among each of the equal men—each is entitled to his own private family. Herakles tells Hyllos that he must separate from his mother and from his father and "cleave to his wife." Hierarchical marriage is established, its power dynamic organized, its reproductive possibilities assured. The attention will have shifted from the father's desire for the women in his family to the son's desire for the mother/woman in his.

Coincidental to the establishment of the father's power in the family is the abstraction of that power into symbolic power. The father, who is now Hyllos, will already have removed himself from his family, located in the private space, to become a citizen of the public space, his real Family. Thus, the father will be *absent* from the very place that his power is symbolically strongest, his right to power within the private family strongest in a culture in which he is absent from that family space most of the time. As Deianeira said about Herakles:

We have had children now, whom he sees at times,
Like a farmer working an outlying field,
Who sees it only when he sows and when he reaps.

(280)

The body is sacrificed to the spirit, the son's desire for the mother is prohibited by being shifted onto the wife, the violent right of the father to the daughter is memorialized, kept alive but silenced, and the symbolic, abstract Name of the Father is established. The wife's bondage is assured, her hostility defanged and bargained away, and in order to keep the family intact she is turned into an erotic, silent threat, titillating but controlled, the enigma that excites masculine desire but is encircled within the proper space of the family. Deianeira, associated with the beauty, passion, and poison that the daughter threatens, is eliminated, while Iole as the enigmatic second wife keeps silenced, domesticated women interesting because they are mysterious. This enigma helps keep the family, as ideal, intact.

Herakles' sacrifice has also reclaimed pathos for the male characters. Rather than being defeated by a woman, Herakles dies by Hyllos' hands, a death that carries out a command from Zeus. As a result, Herakles is not being "done to," finally, by Deianeira but, rather, by the only force greater than he, Zeus.

All of this extensive cultural organization occurs in the last one-third of the tragedy, which seems awkwardly to try to reign in the longer earlier section. Part of this reestablishment of control rests on the fact that it is the maidens who have observed the last scene between Herakles and Hyllos who prove to be the object of this dramatic lesson. Hyllos turns to one of them at the end:

> Maiden, come from the house with us.
> You have seen a terrible death
> and agonies, many and strange, and there is
> nothing here which is not Zeus.

(325)

Chapter 3

Relearning Language: A Clean Break or the Mess of Coagulation

One can learn how our sense of ordinary reality is produced by examining something that is easier to become conscious of, namely, how reality is mimicked and/or how it is faked.

—Erving Goffman

But man only asks (himself) questions that he can already answer, using the supply of instruments he has available to assimilate even the disasters in his history.

—Luce Irigaray

The Women of Trachis provides an important look at the structuration of meaning that underlies centuries of writing on aesthetics and drama in Western culture, where gender and subjectivity are interpreted not as discursive effects of the system within which they are articulated but as meanings lying outside language or discourse, waiting to be discovered in reality. This version of meaning in *The Women of Trachis* might be said to be organized and given its coherence through a particular cultural logic, with *cultural logic* defined as a systematic form of organization that provides guiding principles and offers explanations that link cause and effect. As Claude Lévi-Strauss suggests, a cultural logic has no other purpose than to ensure the survival of a particular cultural group: "The prime role of culture is to ensure the group's existence as a group, and consequently, in this domain, as in all others, to replace chance by organization" (quoted in Silverman 1983, 179). A cultural logic is, in fact, a *socio-logic*.

Stuart Hall makes a distinction in a discussion of racist logic that also applies here. He distinguishes between *overt racism* and *inferential* racism, the former explicitly racist, the latter having to do with "those apparently naturalized representations of events and situations relating to race, whether 'factual' or 'fictional,' which have racist premises and propositions inscribed in them as a set of unquestioned assumptions" (quoted in Omi 1989, 113). The effects of inferential racism are, in fact, more insidious because this kind of racism "is largely *invisible* even to those who formulate the world in its terms." The cultural logic that structures inferential misogyny and links *The Women of Trachis* to familiar stories in Hollywood movies and experimental twentieth-century novels is equally invisible and powerful because of that invisibility. Julia Kristeva extends Lévi-Strauss's definition of a cultural logic to include the logic of the construction of individual subjectivity within the group whose survival is at issue. A cultural logic, in her revision of the concept, thus has another goal as well: the survival of the individual subject (or those who are defined as proper subjects), whose psychic development and "normality" depend on a certain position within the larger cultural group.

In spite of all the historical differences, the cultural logic traced in *The Women of Trachis* shares a number of similarities with that of the late twentieth century: a hierarchy of power in which the male is dominant because he is the active, public partner; and a "biological norm" of heterosexuality within the family in the interests of calculable reproduction. This logic is also marked by a feature that takes on great significance in nationalist movements of the twentieth century: the family as the site of a cultural organization within monotheistic religious traditions that privileges purity and Oneness: One privileged gender, One form of sexual orientation, One race, One nation.

Thus, a structural description of a certain family arrangement, the institution of the family based on one privileged kind of family whose broad structural similarities are not seriously disturbed by its historical differences, brings together classical Athens and the postmodern West through issues of cultural politics, signification, and subjectivity. For it is the family whose discourse establishes symbolic positions within language, grammatical positions that precede the individual and are available to be activated by individual subjects born into that family and that discourse. But family discourse works retroactively: its requirements are written backwards from the direction of the cultural contract that needs subjects, and as Judith Butler argues, "one needs to read the drama of the Symbolic, of desire, of the institution of sexual difference as a self-supporting signifying economy that wields power in the marking off of what can and cannot be thought within the terms of cultural intelligibility" (1990, 78).

Before developing this notion of family discourse and its role in the construction of gender through language, it helps to set out Kristeva's specific use of the term *language*. Her work has involved an extended criticism of what she calls an "idealist" linguistics whose analyses of language and grammar have left both of those in their most abstracted form, separated from the conditions of their enunciation and their performance by embodied subjects. Her description of the logic of signifying practices is dialectical in its insistence on a constant movement, or process, back and forth between the physical conditions of embodiment and symbolic representations, though it also depends on a critique of the abstraction of the Hegelian concept of a symmetrical dialectic of opposites. In Kristeva's reading Hegel's most radical insights into theorizing heterogeneity and materiality are compromised by his reproduction of a purifying Christian logic, one that constrains the very heterogeneity his notion of negativity attempted to articulate. She offers a more radical kind of negativity, one not driven by the repudiation of the feminine that underlies the history of metaphysics within Western monotheism.

Along with a rereading of the philosophical tradition, Kristeva also attempts to join her heterogeneous linguistic analysis to materialist theories of culture, in particular through trying to conceptualize work prior to its representation in exchange. Oswald Ducrot and Tzvetan Todorov describe her work in this way:

In the face of formal logic—a logic of the homogeneous (as a logic of expression)—the "logic of the *production* of signifying systems" can only be a logic of contradiction . . . understood, above all, through a passage to that which ultimately determines the signifying practices as a necessary linkage of meaning to that which is heterogeneous in relation to it; it is further understood that this heterogeneity, in the perspective in which meaning (and with it the subject and understanding) is grounded, is to be sought on the one hand in the body and in death (above and beyond the unconscious of psychoanalysis), on the other hand—and principally—in history (as it is governed by the class struggle); thus in the last analysis, that a dialectic posits the laws of production of meaning, precisely insofar as meaning emerges from (and in) *matter*. (1979, 365)

This expanded logic of signifying practices can help broaden and even politicize Benveniste's notion of *discourse,* for discourse now becomes the place where the enunciation of subjectivity occurs through the medium of embodied discursive subjects. In heterogeneous discourse the positing of a subject position takes place in a performative, enunciative space that momentarily joins together both materiality and symbol, body and language—the performative space of the body in a discourse where, as Benveniste argued, "the foundation of subjectivity . . . is determined by the linguistic status of 'person' " (quoted in Silverman 1983, 1). Historically, of course, the "speaking subject" has been constructed logically and structurally as the generic masculine, its place made available and ready for it by the historical workings of the symbolic system. This presumption of a historically legitimate form of subjectivity that marks every use of language—i.e., a sentence must have a subject—means that *every* text will always already have to do with gender. Rather than being some sort of "special interest," a gender analysis is required from the beginning.

But because women actively use language and theory all the time from bodies not inscribed as masculine, yet claiming to be human, language, theory, the very discourse of subjectivity has not yet caught up with the echoing history of speaking women in female bodies. It is here that "this apparent blockage at the level of theory," as Mary Ann Doane calls it (1987, 7), still troubles feminist theory. One of the main strategies for attempting to describe or theorize the doubleness constituted by the absence of women in theoretical and discursive structures alongside their presence in the world has been theatricality, a theoretical approach that can simultaneously claim both absence and presence yet work to rearrange and reconstruct symbolic possibilities for representing female agency. The concept of theatricality here first of all acknowledges, as do theories of performance, that the conditions of enunciation, the mode of production of the subject, must always be a part of the analysis, these different conditions and different kinds of bodies complicating Foucault's notion of discourse because, at least for now, it *does* matter who speaks, who listens, and upon what stage the subject is "spoken."[1]

Acknowledging that the subject is neither unified nor autonomous but is produced in and by discourse, we can nevertheless use a theatrical notion of the subject as performance to describe the specificity of particular historical situations, particular kinds of bodies, and particular conditions of possibility—what we might call specific symbolic capacities, with *capacity* referring to differential access to power. That is, a part of this project will be to "demystify the *community* of language as a universal and unifying tool, one which totalizes and equalizes. In order to bring out—along with the *singularity* of each person and, even more, along with the multiplicity of every person's possible identifications (with atoms, e.g., stretching from the family to the stars)—the *relativity of his/her symbolic as well as biological existence,* according to the variation in his/her specific symbolic capacities" (Kristeva 1982c, 35).

A strategy of theatricality has to take into account two levels of meaning. The first level is the construction of the logic of the *socius,* or, as Lacan refers to it, the "Symbolic"—the larger, symbolic structures into which we are all inserted, the system of signs that organizes naming, syntax, semantics, denotations that historically precede us. The Symbolic consists of structures and meanings determined both by the exchange of symbols linked to an economic system and to language as an exchange of symbols that succeeded the exchange of women in the sex/gender system. The second level of this two-part simultaneous analysis is the construction of the speaking subject, the individual instance of enunciation. Thus, the study has to be double-handed in order to include: (1) the larger cultural organization of representation, the Symbolic; and (2) the individual, or specific, originality of a subject "subjected" within that social group. Each of these levels of organization is, however, incommensurate with the real, though it is inextricably and heterogeneously mixed up with it.

Foregrounding this doubleness and connecting it to language may make possible a kind of poetics whose resources are historicized forms of representation as those are linked to particular forms of social organization, or *ideologemes,* that "define the specificity of different textual arrangements by placing them within the general text (culture) of which they are part and which is, in turn, part of them" (Kristeva 1980, 36). It may also provide a way to trace historical forms of subjectivity so that two things can be described simultaneously: the process of heterogeneous materiality that always disrupts meaning; and the social forces and their specific figurative forms that attempt to constrain the field of interpretation and argument so that a certain meaning cannot be too seriously disrupted. Kristeva's work on the relation between the mode of production and signifying practices provides a way to begin to analyze this complicated overdetermination:

We shall call the signifying practice the setting in place and the cutting through or traversing of a system of signs. The setting in place, or constituting, of a system of signs requires the identity of a speaking subject in a social institution which the subject recognises as the support of its identity. The traversing of the system takes place when the speaking subject is put in process and cuts across, at an angle as it were, the social institutions in which it had previously recognised itself. [This traversing] thus coincides with the moments of social rupture, renovation and revolution. Signifying practice is therefore not a superstructure overlaid . . . on a given mode of production [economic system. It is rather] that through which the [economic system] signifies its stabilisation and its (self) expenditure—the condition of its renewal . . .

"Signifying practice and mode of production," therefore, does not at all imply an initial separation of the two which has then to be reconciled, but the intrinsic belonging of a mode of sign-production to the mode of production of the socio-economic ensemble. The specific terrain on which this relation of intrinsic belonging is played out is that of the speaking subject and, more concretely, the relationship set up within this subject between unity (foundation of the signifying and social ensemble) and the process which precedes and exceeds it. (1976, 64)

What she describes is a constant interaction or imbrication of the individual embodied speaking subject and the symbolic structure as it is related to an economic and political system. Unity and process are here always in some kind of mixture. It is this notion of mixture, on which, at different historical moments, there are different emphases—at one time on unity, at another on interruption—that might be useful to a theory that looks at subjectivity as a series of performances. Such a theory might be able to describe a kind of performed subjectivity that can keep in play both a constant deconstruction of identity (or identities) and a constant reconstruction of them.

But in the case of the female subject whose activity has not been theorized, the performance may have to originate from an "elsewhere," like the performances of the agents of naive history on the way to re-structuring the Symbolic.[2] This elsewhere proves not to be the mysterious, repressed place of the Other, nor is it closer to the real or to Nature or to the fullness of Being. It is, instead, an untheorized semiotic position within a network of signifiers—a *conceptual* absence. Judith Butler suggests a way of thinking about what it might mean to articulate this absence: "The task here is not to celebrate each and every new possibility *qua* possibility, but to redescribe those possibilities that *already* exist, but which exist within cultural domains designated as culturally unintelligible and impossible" (148).

Discourse and the Family: How to Become
a Proper Subject

Developing connections between language, female agency, the effects of the mode of production, and the construction of subjectivity as theatricality inevitably involves a return to the family, the supposedly coherent, mythical unit that, however, is almost never coherent. It is within the historically variable representations of the "discourse of the family" that the major cultural division of human life, sexual difference, takes place, and it is this feature of the family—or families—which explains the intense religious and political attempts to guarantee that this division works in particular ways.

Jacques Lacan's description of the workings of the Symbolic order helps make connections between this family discourse and culture as well as revealing a relationship among Lacanian psychoanalysis, tragedy, and religion. As Butler argues, Lacan's theory works like a religious tragedy that seems, like the pathos of Greek tragedy, to "be a romanticization or, indeed, a religious idealization of 'failure,' humility and limitation before the Law." Its failure, of course, is a tease because what never fails is the masculinity of the Law. Lacan's version, like Aristotle's, reveals itself to be a description of a status quo which refuses to question fate and, indeed, insists on a theory of Symbolic Law that is both impossible to perform or to reform.[3] It is situated squarely within the realm of tragedy's ritualized submission to the fate of law and language, and, argues Butler: "This structure of religious tragedy in Lacanian theory effectively undermines any strategy of cultural politics to configure an alternative imaginary for the play of desires" (56).

But describing the historicity, or particularity, of this supposed universality makes it possible to isolate those points along the way where the oedipal organization of meaning proves to be remarkably vulnerable and even phobic in its recognition of that vulnerability. As Erving Goffman writes, "The study of how to uncover deception is also by and large the study of how to build up fabrications" (1974, 251). If the privileged masculine subject is a social construction, perhaps theorizing female agency involves learning how that fabrication works on a symbolic level then using that knowledge to theorize specifically female subject positions. This also involves, of course, the simultaneous cultural work of changing material conditions that have to do with the mode of production and the sites of knowledge production.

Lacan argues that all subjects are alienated from their organic being because of a "linguistic structure which does not in any way address [their] being, but which determines [their] whole cultural existence" (Silverman 1983, 166). The loss that this kind of signification imposes, the separation of the phenomenal from the Symbolic, is experienced by men as well as by women and results from a primordial "lack," or, as Kristeva describes it, "want," which all subjects experience as they are interpellated in language. Entry into language, in this version, means gaining access to meaning, but this access will always rest on loss: on the difference between the word and the thing. Even if we can never definitively separate the signifier from the signified (that is, we cannot perceive a table as a table without some sort of cultural pattern or signifier that helps us pick it out as a table), nevertheless we still know that the word *table* is not the same thing as the table. The lack that separates the Symbolic from the phenomenal arises out of a gap, or fissure, that underlies all symbolicity, and it is a gap that cannot be traversed. This lack institutes an Outside—language itself—that founds culture, language, and subjectivity, all of which might be seen as processes of interpretation whose stimulus is an ongoing, impossible, but inevitable attempt to traverse the gap between word and thing.

The split that separates symbolicity and physicality upon the entry into language also institutes the unconscious, which comes into existence at this entry and is organized around the spatialization of unsignifiable loss. But while Lacan seems to claim that the form of the unconscious he describes is universal, Kristeva attempts to historicize it by arguing that some form of unconscious is, in fact, universally a part of the makeup of human subjectivity, yet the specific *mode* of coming-to-Being in language is specific to the historical organization that accompanies monotheism in the West. She suggests, in fact, that the unconscious is specifically different in its structuration according to the forms and grammar of the language within which the subject comes to be subjected. The particular form of metaphysical argument that, like Lacan's, arrives at the notion of Being in language is traceable first in the Old Testament and then through the cultural logic of the New Testament, to which I return later in this chapter. Though language *as* site of the Other may be universal, different languages and cultural logics organize the relation to the Other differently. In the West the blame for the gap or the incompleteness in language is blamed on Others—on women and people of color—rather than on the very workings of language itself.

In this process where subjectivity is the pivot point that intimately brings together bodies and language, all subjects suffer loss, as signification divides the stream that is "reality" into readable units, or articulates it. Articulation, differentiation, occurs: at birth; at the prelinguistic territorialization of the body by the mother's care, which begins to organize sexual difference and erotogenic zones; and at the time of the entry into language. It is at these moments that the discourse of the family is ready at hand to supply the representations from the symbolic resources, whose very effects *are* the subject as well as the medium in which the subjects can perceive their "loss," on the one hand, their gain of symbolicity on the other.

The son in this family discourse recognizes that he cannot be the father and internalizes the father's image along with an internalization of what he can desire to be. That produces the superego as well as the ego ideal. The representations provided within the family discourse make possible a different kind of loss for the girl. She, like the boy, can never be the parent of the same sex, though she can identify with the mother. But unlike the son, she cannot identify legitimately with the possessor of the phallus, the father. Her loss, if things work out right for the system, is double his. She loses an unmediated relationship to her organic being as does he, and she also loses a representation that, for him, assuages the loss of organic being through identification with the father as stand-in for the phallus and through the ritualization of pathos, whether tragic, Romantic, deconstructive, etc.

The subject, in the Lacanian schema, is "the product of signifying activities which are both culturally specific and generally unconscious" (Silverman 1983, 130). Even the subject's desires are culturally determined and collective because the unconscious is a signifying network organized by the society in which the subject finds itself. The unconscious of the subject, its desires, are said to be the discourse of the Other, what it has had to repress to become a subject—the matter that constitutes its body, its drives (which become not drives or instincts but, rather, culturally mediated desires constructed in historically specific ways), the system of articulations that constitutes language, the other sex. Heterosexual reproduction thus symbolically structures a narrative of the subject which leads its subject toward a genital stage organized at puberty, one "which stands in opposition to the 'polymorphous perversity' and auto-erotism of infantile sexuality" and is organized around genitality, or the primacy of the penis and the vagina; that is, it is organized around a teleology of procreation. The boy, as subject, will learn to desire a woman like his mother; the girl will, upon realizing she cannot "have" the phallus of the father, supposedly desire a baby as a substitute for it, or she will desire to "be" it.

The duality of male and female within this structure proves to work as a structural opposition (very similar to Aristotle's "biological" one), which is then subsumed by the larger symbolic order for which subjects have been engendered. These initial dualities, or *structural oppositions,* "function at the level of thought and are constantly affirmed in all the hierarchies that are operational in everyday life, mythic thought, and established values," as Dean MacCannell argues (1984, 33). A second principle that organizes those structural oppositions, he argues, is that of *embedded organizations subject to administration.* The discourse of the family produces structural oppositions, which are then managed in Western industrial societies by bureaucracies.

The *incitement to a discourse of the family* in the West establishes the division between boys and girls that rests on the desire of the mother for the phallus, a desire essential to the process that establishes sexual identity but one that also introduces into social organization an element that marks its extreme vulnerability, the mother's desire. The son ideally learns to desire to have the phallus to satisfy the mother, such a process ensuring that sons will desire to succeed fathers and that Oedipus will be reproduced. The boy will internalize the imago of the father, who, as the representative of culture, carries out his function of prohibiting the mother and the sister to the son, and, by doing so, he institutes the prohibition of incest as a negative rule that simultaneously involves a positive command requiring exogamy and heterosexuality. Exogamy, in this structure, is paradoxically a racial and class endogamy: marry a woman outside the immediate family but inside the race and class.

The agency of the Oedipus complex, besides constructing the difference between boys and girls, also produces a girl who ideally is antifeminine, another way of defining penis envy. She accepts her castration and identifies with the mother, but she simultaneously learns to be hostile to the mother, whose fault it is that she lacks a penis, which symbolizes access to power—a lack also symbolized by the fact that the mother herself has no penis to match the symbolic phallus. Penis envy is thus not a desire for an actual penis so much as a desire for power in a culture that produces the name of the father, not the mother, as a signifier with a closer relation to other privileged signifiers, such as law, money, power, and knowledge, as Silverman suggests.

The mother is thus defined in opposition to all these things (law, money, power, knowledge) as well as in opposition to the father. As a result, since the Oedipus complex produces an internalization by the boy and the girl of the ideal imago of the parent of the same sex, the girl's internalization of the image of the mother may be an internalization of inferiority and of hostility to women and even of hostility to herself, which probably helps define Freud's description of women as masochistic. This cultural logic might almost be said to require self-hatred and masochism on the part of "normal" women. When the Oedipus complex works well it separates women from each other as competitors for the father's favor.

At the moment of the father's proscription the male child can identify himself as having a penis and the female child as lacking one—the famous scene of the authoritative male vision, the little boy's recognition that the girl lacks a penis, a retroactive reading. The boy understands lack only *after* he understands the culture's valorization of fathers over mothers, after he has understood the father's threat in relation to his own body, which has a penis susceptible to castration. This threat ends his Oedipus complex, differentiating him from the female child as he identifies with the father. The girl, however, only begins her complex when she identifies with the mother and accepts the "fact" of her castration as part of the supposedly inevitable and universal phallocentric nature of civilization.

Subjectivity as a Metaphoric Event in a Field of Differences

But what does the discourse of the family have to do with the workings of discourse in general? And what does it have to do with the fact that signifiers are the mark of the subject's radical alienation from the real: where the signifier is, the subject's organic being is not? Signification, which includes ritual, gesture, illness, dress, etc., as well as linguistic signification, operates in a closed world in which signifiers mark not referents but relations; that is, signifiers can only mean something in a network of differential relations with other signifiers. Though constantly interrupted by the phenomenal, unsignifiable world, signifers are, nevertheless, separated from it, that separation producing, in fact, what might be called a reality effect.

This characteristic of signifiers as operating within a system of differences is the very basis of discourse, for words in a language work as symbols, or "nonrepresentative representations." They represent, but what they represent are not referents or the real so much as other words, or signifiers; they are indexical elements that refer only to other words within the system and to the system itself.[4] Certain other forms of signification, like photography or mirror images, might be said to be iconic, as they are thought to retain some kind of resemblance to what they represent. Though iconic signifiers such as a photo might seem to be "motivated" (connected to reality or to something outside the system of signifiers) in a specific sense because they resemble what they signify, they, too, are ultimately related only to other elements in their particular system of visual differences. The history of perspective in Western art shows how historical any notion of "resemblance" is. As Victor Burgin argues in relation to the visual, what we see and the way we see it, or the way we assess resemblance, has a history. It, like everything else, is a product of representations, whose effects come to be "seen" as natural (Burgin 1990, 104–23).

This notion of systems of differences also affects the way we have to think about individual subjectivity, which, because of its discursive nature, also can only make sense within such a system. The human subject has experience of its identity only as a complex, overdetermined poetic matrix, not as an inert, separate, pure identity to be discovered by tearing away, like the heart of an onion, all the outside layers imposed by culture. My "I" is a signifier for another signifier. In this construction of subjectivity, nothing is the subject's "own," its "proper" self, its property—not even its "instincts" or drives, which have been culturally inscribed as desires. The signification or meaning of everything comes to it from the cultural order, the discourse of an already constituted social order. Each instantiation, or activation, of discourse, however, is specific to the particular subject's enunciating body, whose lack of fit engages in constant interruption of those cultural definitions and representations.

And Lacan links the very structure of language to marriage strategies of a particular kind:

> The Oedipus complex—insofar as we continue to recognize it as covering the whole field of our experience with its signification—may be said, in this connexion, to mark the limits that our discipline assigns to subjectivity: namely, what the subject can know of his unconscious participation in the movement of the complex structures of marriage ties, by verifying the symbolic effects in his individual existence of the tangential movement towards incest that has manifested itself ever since the coming of a universal community.
>
> The primordial Law is therefore that which in regulating marriage ties superimposes the kingdom of culture on that of a nature abandoned to the law of mating. The prohibition of incest is merely its subjective pivot, revealed by the modern tendency to reduce to the mother and the sister the objects forbidden to the subject's choice, although full license outside of these is not yet entirely open.
>
> This law, then, is revealed clearly enough as identical with an order of language. For without kinship nominations, no power is capable of instituting the order of preferences and taboos that bind and weave the yarn of lineage through succeeding generations. And it is indeed the confusion of generations which, in the Bible as in all traditional laws, is accused as being the abomination of the Word (*verbe*) and the desolation of the sinner. (Lacan 1977, 66)

These signifiers of the discourse of the family are activated only when family members identify with them: "The discourse of the family—a discourse which is absolutely central to the perpetuation of the present, phallocentric symbolic order—needs subjects" (Silverman 1983, 182). The signifiers that are available for activation constitute the dramatis personae of the oedipal drama of sexual difference, signification, and subjectivity, which are remarkably unchanged from those described by Aristotle. As Lacan says: "Only this division [the sexual division] . . . makes necessary what was first revealed by analytic experience, namely, that the ways of what one must do as man or as woman are entirely abandoned to the drama, to the scenario, which is placed in the field of the Other—which, strictly speaking, is the Oedipus complex" (1977, 154).

In tragic oedipal discourse the phallus, or transcendental signifier that adjudicates meaning, has become the central nonrepresentative representation, the organizing signifier or site of judgment. Because it has no connection with the real, according to Lacan, because of the nature of signification as a system of differences in which signifiers refer only to other signifiers, the relation between the penis and the phallus is one of "irreducible disequivalence." But as Silverman says, "the inevitable failure of the actual father to correspond to the symbolic father, or the penis to embody the phallus in no way jeopardizes the existing cultural order" (1983, 184), that disequivalence requiring symbolic violence to enforce itself. The penis and the phallus are further related by what the phallus connotes: the privileges that accrue to males; and the penis, the "pound of flesh," whose possession and mortgage activate those symbolic privileges. A third meaning of the phallus is the supposed fullness of Woman when she "is" the phallus, when she comes to represent plenitude and fullness, usually as the phallic mother.

The success of the phallus in the Symbolic is itself highly dependent on the success of a linguistic category, the *paternal metaphor,* which condenses the Symbolic paternal into the site of the father of the individual family. If the child identifies with the father, or, in the case of the girl, determines to "be" the phallus of that father, a "metaphoric event" will have been successful, the child's identity "properly" structured in relation to the phallus as transcendental, organizing signifier. The child will be identified metaphorically as "he" or "she" in a particular way and will have learned to desire having (if he is a son) or being (if she is the daughter) the phallus that satisfies the mother's desire. Psychosis, in this normative version, will occur if either the mother's or the child's desire fails, and, at a larger level, the perpetuation of the symbolic order will be threatened if the mother's or the child's desire continually defaults. The metaphors must be inscribed in the child's identity and on its body.

But because this particular discourse of the family finds few perfect families to reproduce oedipal definitions of sexual difference or to enforce the clean certainty of this metaphoric event, proper identity rests on a site of extreme vulnerability and metonymic slippage. And because it is founded on a "correct" reading of the *desire of the mother,* the importance of this site of vulnerability begins to reveal the phobic nature of compulsory heterosexuality as a procreative logic of purity. For what if the desire of the mother is not for Dad? What if her desire is multiple, bisexual, queer, interracial? What does this phobic oedipal structure mean for the increasing numbers of daughters and mothers who have escaped "normal femininity" by not having passed successfully through the Oedipus complex, who have not acceded to psychoanalysis' description of femininity but who are also not psychotic, supposedly the other possibility for those who are not successfully "identified" in the Oedipus complex? What if the entry into signification and the fictional status of identity were not read as *tragic* or if the separation between signifier and signified were not seen as proof that subjects are condemned to separation from the real and isolation from each other? The inevitability of signification and the split subject might instead be interpreted as the very proof not of tragic isolation but, instead, of sociality, intersubjectivity, in short, of community, as proof of the *impossibility* of solitude, rather than the condemnation to it.

The impossibility of enforceable identity might just as reasonably be read as *proof* of materiality, *proof* of the real, a real that reveals itself as interruption. In such a reading, the interruption of the subject's identity means that the subject is still alive, that history is still in process. The question to be asked is: How did such evidence of intersubjectivity and community and evidence of the real, come to be read *negatively* as tragic—as signs of solitude, on the one hand, and the complete alienation from the real, on the other? In what ways is that reading specifically and thoroughly gendered? And what ways are there to talk differently about connectedness, materiality, and women, who are still very much "subjected" within phallocentric culture, which assigns them a certain linguistic status but for whom that status, as Ursula LeGuin says, "doesn't exactly seem to fit very well lately" (1985b, 27)?

The Productive Poverty of Prohibition: The Cultural Logic of Purity

A discussion of several forms of theatricality as strategies of resistance requires an initial look at the effects of the coding of the female body on women's attempt to participate in discourse. For in contemporary critical discussions theories of the cultural construction of gender have been so effective that it is increasingly difficult, within the space of such discussions, to talk about the ways the performances of certain bodies, culturally constructed as they are as feminine, are specifically different from the performances of other equally constructed bodies that are masculine. One effect of the impossible project of division into clean gender categories weighs very heavily on attempts to theorize female agency.

Besides not being included in the theoretical space of the subject, the woman who tries to become a subject takes on the symbolic connotations of abjection that are produced by what Kristeva calls the "poverty of prohibition."

What escapes the classification rules is a woman speaking—not simply "what is called a woman" but "what is called a woman," in one kind of body, in the place of "what is called a man," in another kind of body, constructed as both those bodies are. This is a classification system that is itself constructed to produce the purified place of the speaking subject as masculine; no matter how resistant and how complex his resistance strategies, he still finds himself located in The Body, the idealized, abstracted one whose very construction depended on the repudiation of the feminine. As a result, as I hope to show, Man and men coexist in the space of the performance of theory and the theory of performance in a way that Woman and women do not, in spite of a disabling equation between those two kinds of contructedness in much poststructuralist theory.

A woman in the place of agency never enacts a "simple reversal," in spite of what has come to be a red herring, the threat of the repetition of the Same that will supposedly be the inevitable result of naming female agency. She wears as her body, speaks in her voice, the remainders and debris that went into constructing the masculine speaking subject and his kind of Body. "She" is simultaneously the filth, the debris, the improper *excess* speaking from the place organized for the clean and proper body. She is not simply symptom but also speaking subject *and* the residue of the "dispositions of the place-body and the more elaborate speech-logic of differences," in Kristeva's terms (1982a, 92).

Because masculinity and femininity are not ultimately separable, prohibition always, inevitably, fails, and the phobic insistence on such separation results in an ambiguous, threatening, tantalizing category of mixture. In trying to set out the complexities of abjection and its relationship to theorizing female agency, I use *phobia* here to describe an important structural effect of this oedipal family organization. Freud, in his analysis of Little Hans's fear of horses, concluded that phobias are not caused by an "independent pathological process" (Laplanche and Pontalis 1973, 38). He proposed an analogy between a phobic neurosis and anxiety-hysteria, in which a psychic conflict is transposed to a somatic symptom (usually a paralysis, anesthesia, or pain). These two are linked by a structural analogy that suggests that both are part of an

analysand's attempt to separate *affect* from *idea*. In anxiety-hysteria libidinal resources are set free as a kind of free-floating anxiety, unlike conversion hysteria, where freed libidinal resources are converted into somatic
symptoms. But a phobic neurosis differs from either of these in that it
emerges through a displacement of anxiety *onto a phobic object*: "The
formation of phobic symptoms comes about because 'from the outset
in anxiety-hysteria the mind is constantly at work in the direction of
once more psychically binding the anxiety which has become liberated'"
(Laplanche and Pontalis 1973, 38).

Through this displacement of anxiety the oedipal organization thus
not only censors the daughter in representation; it also *abjects* her, displacing anxiety onto the defiled femininity, not of an object, as Freud
suggested, but onto the "abject," to use Kristeva's terminology. As I
will argue more extensively, defiled maternal femininity becomes associated with the signifiers of death, disease, and contamination. It also
arouses fascinated desire as a shadowy, unsignifiable, simultaneously
repulsive and tantalizing femininity. These significations of the maternal
are written on the symbolic construct called a female body, and they
cause problems for the daughter that the son, in his differently socially
constructed body, will not encounter. For female bodies as visual symbols will signify *before* women's speech does, just as "blackness" will
anticipate the African-American subject who speaks words that otherwise are indistinguishable from the words of a white subject. These
gendered and raced bodies signify the abject; one can read on them a
script of body language, the terms of the desire of man in the "disgrace
and shame with which he charges those he wants to exclude."[5] This
bodily script will have been read prior to any performative analysis of
their speech; its effects must be read with as much specificity as possible.

The workings of this cultural logic need to be set out in order to
provide a basis for reading the specificity of ways the abject marks
women's bodies differently from men's. The cultural logic that organizes
the division of the sexes and the construction of the abject works to insist
on the purity of its categories, but this insistence on purity is productive.
It simultaneously and crucially *ensures* that the purity it ostensibly insists
on will fail, and it is this very failure that legitimates its claim to power
based on the need to enforce the requirements and the divisions based
on the privilege of purity. Divisions can only be enforced within signifying networks if there are margins that limit the meaning of each of the
elements of the division, margins that hold a place between those divi-

sions, and, paradoxically, these margins are the result of the weakness of the "imperative act of excluding" (Kristeva 1982a, 64), an imperative act that cannot enforce itself in a system of differences. Taboos, according to Kristeva, are placeholders that enforce *definition,* or the determination of outline, extent, or limits. As an example, George Bataille isolates the taboo on excrement as a margin so fundamental to the organization of primitive societies that it is never even expressed, but it holds a place between the two elements divided: human and animal. The object to which the taboo refers excites horror and disgust, which then helps enforce the limit.

This organization and production of margins can be seen as part of a historical symbolic organization I call a cultural logic of purity. Kristeva's description of this cultural logic traces it through two monotheisms, Judaism and Christianity. The two traditions ultimately feed into the consolidation of state power in nineteenth-century Europe, a state power that functions only as a "representative of capitalist relations that determine it, exceed it, and tend more and more to usurp it: [state power] is a fetish power" (Kristeva 1976, 69). These monotheistic logics valorize two things: the relationship between agency and masculinity; and the dominant place of language in the constitution of Being. These are, thus, historical developments, not universal ones. Kristeva argues, by relying on the implications of Mary Douglas's *Purity and Danger,* that the biblical project is "a history of confrontation with the feminine and the way in which societies code themselves in order to accompany as far as possible the speaking subject on that journey" (1982a, 58). That had to do with the gradual and progressive ordering of the clean and proper body through rituals of pollution and defilement, the historical construction of an embodied subject who could speak to his God—this clean and proper, purified, active masculine space of the speaking subject the result of a historically developed form of "subjection." This "riting" of the body is on its way to becoming the "writing" of it.

Kristeva argues that the Judaic cultural logic moved through a series of topological orderings of social space by means first of sacrifice then of taboo, in order spatially to exclude certain substances, then certain kinds of persons who came to be associated with those substances from the place where one spoke to God. Related to hygiene as well as to the sacred, the logic of purity developed through a process of separations, always inadequate and incomplete. The link between symbolic and subjective levels allows a tracing of this process in the development of a subject as it distinguishes itself from what come to be seen as its objects, its inside and its outside.[6]

This ordering process is a logic of purification. What was purified was masculinity and the identity of a certain chosen group, that chosenness reflected now as masculinity, race, and the access of "clean and proper" subjects to property. Thus, through a series of developing categories in the Old Testament (i.e., certain kinds of flesh as food, certain excluded substances) one arrives at the marking of femininity in its relationship to the materiality of the body and to blood, which itself constitutes a strange, mixed category of life/death, birth/death. The speaking subject gradually developed as one who had access to the space of the temple; that is, the act of speaking and the possibility of agency are linked to the boundaries of the masculine body. As Kristeva says, the historically developing form of the subject arises out of "the dispositions of the place-body and the more elaborate speech-logic of differences" (1982a, 92).

The topology is, in the New Testament, developed into a logic; the move is from topologic ordering to logical ordering. It is no longer the spatial distinction that is foregrounded but a classification system based on a taxonomy of morals. And in ways that require a kind of Foucauldian bracketing of notions of progress, the New Testament succeeded in feminizing its God through the incarnation of God in Man in Christ. Thus, those things formerly associated with the feminine, with the body, with corporeality and matter, are now incorporated by and within the masculine God made human, his crucifixion symbolizing a violated body, his feminized humanness then surpassed. Abomination, the repulsion at the physicality of the body, is interiorized and transcended. One has to look very carefully at this model, in particular in terms of what appear to be other similar developments in the history of Western thought: Nietzsche's radical notions of ambiguity and difference incorporated by a feminized philosopher-womb, haunted by mixtures marked as disease; Artaud's return to the corporeal, feminized body but only by going through its repulsiveness in order to transcend it by annihilating, purifying it into a "body without organs." In other words, it is a double pattern: the recognition of femininity that looks like progress; and an appropriation of femininity by means of the sufferings of a feminized, masculine Christian man-God. The suffering Romantic hero, Nietzsche's birth-giving philosopher, Artaud's recorporealized masculine body, Lacan's sad empathy with excluded women, Barthes's sigh about the sad fate of interpretation, share at least some of these same characteristics, as did Herakles' initiation, in which he had to spend time with Omphale dressed as a woman in order to reemerge stronger into the world of men.

The inevitable failure of the phallus, the demarcating imperative in this logic whose purpose is to separate in a system of differences—the failure of the agency that separates the inseparable, the masculine from the feminine, the spiritual from the material, the unconscious from language, etc.—must *produce* a border to keep apart these categories and provide a place for itself, as we have seen. It requires a border whose ambiguous nature produces more and more paranoid attempts at enforcing separation. Kristeva calls that border the abject, the remainder of an inevitable improper separation, what marks the unsignifiable but disruptive permeability of boundaries, eventually associated with filth, waste, interiorized abomination, that which has had to be simultaneously excluded and incorporated: corporeality and what corporeality has been linked to over thousands of years—femininity. The coding of corporeality is ultimately the remainder of the defiled maternal, the female body from which the speaking subject has had to separate himself in this long biblical project. The abject, the filthy, the loathsome is not an essence in and of itself but, rather, the product of a classification system; it is "that which disobeys classification rules peculiar to the given symbolic system" (Kristeva 1982a, 92). It also grounds that classification system, making the economy of its categories possible.

It is not only women who are related to the abject produced by this logic of the purification of masculinity. Other groups are categorized as feminine, in historically different ways, and marked by this relationship to the repudiated defiled maternal. Though these groups cannot simply be collapsed into one another, we can trace connections among them related to the logic of purity based on the organization of the boundaries of the purified masculine body. The logic of separation always fails, and what is striking in the discourses of racism, fascism, the rhetoric of anticommunism, homophobia, and misogyny is the frequency of images of filth, of fluidity, both of these related to the mixture of categories in a logic of purity based on separation.

Menstrual blood, childbirth, fertility, and the female body itself were, in this logic, inscribed as unclean, as signifiers of a contaminated Outside from which the pure Inside, the male members of the community, were to be separated. In Kristeva's analysis the division between pure and impure is theoretically held in place by the *sème* of blood, which marks a border that both defines and disrupts categories that can never be definitively, completely separated because they achieve meaning in a system of differences. Blood comes to mark inseparability, borders, mixture, as motherhood and birth are situated precisely at this ambiguous, dangerous site.

The symbolic danger of female fertility, represented by the ambiguous nature of blood, which simultaneously signifies life and vitality, death and contamination, is concentrated in the connotations of birth, which is both hopeful and terrifying. The speaking subject's individual task of separation from the mother and from femininity can be compared to culture's task of separating the paternal from the maternal, as culture, through the paternal metaphor, the Word, "must continually thrust aside [femininity and death] in order to live" (Kristeva 1982a, 110). Though at times the semiotic, which is also related to artistic experiments, can function in the interests of resistance or renewal, or heterogeneous contradictions that disrupt culturally legitimate symbolic forms, it is also intimately productive of another relation to heterogeneity as Otherness: "the fascination with the wandering and elusive other, who attracts, repels, puts one literally beside oneself. . . . And it arouses the paranoid rage to dominate those objects, to transform them, to exterminate them" (Kristeva 1982b, 91). Fascism as well as revolution, artistic activity, and religion also arise in this space.

Kristeva's concept of the "speaking subject" seems initially to be another version of "Oedipus in germ," but her slow, careful ongoing analysis of that subject is still very much in process. In fact her work is an ongoing retheorizing of subjectivity in such a way as to describe not only the historical forms and structures of subjectivity but the material it is made of. At least an opening can be found in her essay "Stabat Mater," part of *Tales of Love*:

What an inconceivable ambition it is to aspire to singularity [for a woman], it is not natural, hence it is inhuman; the mania smitten with Oneness ("There is only One woman" [the Virgin Mary]) can only impugn it by condemning it as "masculine." . . . Within this strange feminine see-saw that makes "me" swing from the unnameable community of women over to the war of individual singularities, it is unsettling to say "I." The languages of the great formerly matriarchal civilizations must avoid, do avoid, personal pronouns: they leave to the context the burden of distinguishing protagonists

and take refuge in tones to recover an underwater, transverbal communication between bodies. It is a music from which so-called oriental civility tears away suddenly through violence, murder, blood
baths. A woman's discourse, would that be it? . . . (1987b, 258–59)

She posits at least obliquely an ethics she calls "herethics" based not on
death but on undeath, or love, itself based on the inevitable intersubjectivity of discourse. Yet this is not intersubjectivity in identity but in
difference; she also distances from the reinstitution of any reified representation, phallic or female. For this version of *herethics* and the possibility of reading all language as poetic language is more nearly modeled
on the way music signifies in both bodily and symbolic ways, as it
"swallows up the goddesses and removes their necessity" (263).

The Maternal and Its Dangers

Kristeva's description of the effects of the maternal body helps make the
notion of fluidity more specific, but her description of the fluid effects
that accompany signification has been misinterpreted, it seems to me,
to suggest that she sets up an opposition between the *semiotic,* or the
traces of the effects of the relation with the maternal body, and the
Symbolic, the organized system of symbolic meaning which unites
speakers of a language. What often falls out of discussions of her work
is its context in Continental philosophy and its concern with the relation
between metaphysics and idealist linguistics. In particular, she is engaged
in a dissection of dialectical oppositions; the semiotic and Symbolic are
not so much involved in a Hegelian or Marxist dialectical opposition or
Freudian dialectic of repression as they are in an inextricable mixture
that does not privilege concept over matter, or vice versa. She insists
that neither semiotic nor Symbolic could exist alone, though their relationship can be traced historically according to the predominance of one
or the other.

   Kristeva thus reconceptualizes Hegel's idealized negativity, Marx's
concept of materiality, Freud's concept of negation, and Husserl's intending consciousness of phenomenology, all of which rely indirectly
on one of the fundamental concepts of Western metaphysics, the *chora*
described by Plato in his story of the creation of the cosmos, the *Timaeus.*
Plato's *chora* is the space or womb within which intelligibility, Being,
reason, takes place. Because it is solely a mediating space, it has no form

of its own but is simply there to be used by consciousness. Kristeva slowly provides a theory for that space, reconceptualizing it as rhetorical spacing that can be traced as historically specific typologies of signification. Her theory of negativity attempts to account for what is simultaneously necessary to and in heterogeneous mixture with language: the body (or bodies), the unconscious, the drives and their ordering, death. She thus expands the notion of textuality so that it cannot be separated from politics and the real.

Because the semiotic and the Symbolic are not oppositions, she can also propose a theory of the speaking position, the *thetic* (drawn from Husserl then extended by a poststructuralist dissection of its implied subject). The thetic subject position is momentarily enunciated then dissolved, this enunciation of an "I" proving to work like a poetic word, constantly shifting in its meaning according to context and intersubjectivity. Any enunciation, of necessity, requires a grammatical position and a claim to identity, but, because it cannot enforce that identity, it can only enact it as a thetic subject in process/on trial. Thus, Kristeva's theory does not have to privilege human nature over Nature, even as it posits the necessity of a momentary subject position, or concept.

Her *chora,* or spacing, unlike Plato's amorphous motility, or space, has to do with constant motility that is *already* constrained according to historical factors, though it is not yet readable as language. The infant's body, prior to the mirror stage and the insertion into language, has already been organized in particular ways associated with the specific activities of care with touch, smell, sound, sight, and rhythm. From birth the infant's drives encounter stases and movement, which produce markings that are, however, not yet language: "Discrete quantities of energy move through the body of the subject who is not yet constituted as such and, in the course of its development, [these quantities of energy] are arranged according to the various constraints imposed on this body—always already involved in a semiotic process—by family and social structures" (Kristeva 1984, 25). It is already regulated, its vocal and gestural organization subject to what she calls an objective ordering, not a symbolic Law, "established through the objective constraints of biological (including sexual) differences and concrete, historical family structures" (29). In this way the drives, "which are '*energy*' charges as well as '*psychical*' marks, articulate what we call a *chora*: a nonexpressive totality formed by the drives and their stases in a motility that is as full of movement as it is regulated" (25).

This theory of the historically variable mixture of the semiotic and Symbolic has the potential to ground a theory of performance by providing a semiotic methodology for more finely articulated descriptions of the ways bodies come to be lodged—as they are constructed—in symbolization, an articulation that traces a relationship, a mixed economy, between two limits: the specificity of the preparation of the body for its entry into the Symbolic (preparation always mediated retroactively by the Symbolic); and the constraints and historical variations of the Symbolic system that preexists the subject's insertion into it. This is ultimately an aesthetic (or politically poetic) relation between bodies and symbols based on *anaclisis,* the propping of signification on bodies which that signification also simultaneously constructs.[7] Tracing infantile language acquisition means learning to read memories of bodily contact, warmth, and nourishment, vocal and muscular contractions, spasms of the glottis and motor system, gestures, and voice, which are meaning functions eventually endowed with linguistic functions.

This also opens up possibilities of reading the *originality* of each subject rather than its *origin,* as Kristeva argues. These traces are "undoubtedly significant for the acquisition of language, which will soon be articulated along the same vehicle" (1980, 282). Language acquisition happens in and on a body that is already a site of the motility of drives and their stases. And though these traces are prelinguistic, they are not precultural or prehistorical, unless we are willing to claim that the interaction with mothers is not a part of culture, as I think some readings of Kristeva's semiotic as essentialist imply.

Kristeva also radically revises the dramatis personae of psychoanalysis by constructing a different allegory of interpretation, an analytic situation theorized according to a model of love involving transferences and countertransferences between an analyst as mother/child and the analysand as child/analyzer. She bases this model of analysis on what she calls maternal attentiveness, and a recent article expands this model to include other levels of transference that expand the boundaries of analysis: "Is analysis grandmotherly or adolescent? Perhaps, after all, it is never the one without the other—if we wish to remain attentive to an open structure" (Kristeva 1990, 11). Her description of the logic of purification means that the female as speaking subject, or Oedipus, will be wearing the symbolic evidence of the not-Oedipus. As female speaking subject, this subject, or "female Oedipus," female Man, will not only have to abject the maternal in the formation of "its" own subjectivity, but its body will also signify what has been abjected by male subjects. In the as yet untheorized space of female desire, however, it can at least be established that "rarely does a woman [unlike a man] tie her desire and her sexual life to that abjection" (Kristeva 1982a, 54). The male subject, Oedipus, on the other hand, will abject the defiled maternal, and it will construct his sexual life. But he will not *signify* it. Kristeva's theory allows us to follow her concept of the semiotic in attempting to describe the difference between the enunciative sites of these two subjects and the effects of those bodies on the enunciation.

Though it is very clear that the risks to women of being reappropriated into cultural representations that equate women with mother, particularly in a contemporary baby boom whose oppressiveness seems to lie principally in the exploitation of an unrealistic model of motherhood by advertising, which has always located the nuclear family as the most highly prized target of a market economy, it nevertheless seems that Kristeva's theory is misread as essentialist. This highly volatile issue in feminist theory pits women trying to grapple with their exclusion from society because they are responsible for the invisible maternal and domestic labor that reproductive labor involves against other women who are trying to untangle themselves from the most restrictive biological codings of their bodies in relation to compulsory heterosexuality. This is a tense and intimate collision that can only be approached again and again in an attempt to make it possible for these two different ways of reacting to the maternal to negotiate with each other. A study of the history of Kristeva reception might isolate places where the internalization of misogyny and repudiation of the mother shows up in discussions of the maternal, even in the work of feminist theorists, for her discussions of motherhood have become the site of fixing blame, but the terms used are remarkably gendered: she is essentialist, reactionary; she spends too much time on motherhood rather than dealing with politics. Such arguments, however, have to be simultaneously countered by a critical analysis of places in her work where heterosexism, at best, homophobia, at worst, disrupt her more radical insights. An old familiar story keeps constructing the impasses in this discussion.

Separation, Rhetoric, Coagulation

Kristeva's reading is also important because she looks more closely at the connection between language and the paternal metaphor, which in Freud enforces the alienation of the child's organic being in her or his accession to symbolization in primary narcissism, the separation of being and desire and the constitution of that separation as absolute. She finds, as did Freud in "On Narcissism," that the gap that marks the distance between the preconscious and the unconscious, like the bar between the signifier and signified, is sustained by difference. But her analysis focuses on the psychic terrain *prior* to the constitution of ego and objects, that is, the effects of the infant's relationship with the preoedipal mother—the history of what "is not yet an ego and what is not yet an object, [a relation] between the *infans* and the abject" (Chase 1984, 197). This analysis thus displaces the concept of the "gap" of absolute separation in a discourse that can only be activated by bodies in the *process* of signification, a discourse that maintains "the heterogeneity of the signifying process against its reduction to symbolization." Cynthia Chase calls what Kristeva proposes "coagulation": "the inscription (not the image) of the archaic mother as productive dissolution" (Chase 1990, 128). Yet Freud concludes that this coagulation is covered over by a direct and immediate identification with the father. Why?

Kristeva suggests that Freud's description of the "immediate" identification with the father as object of the mother's desire might be explained both by the rhetorical nature of language and by Freud's historical position, this theoretical insight coming soon after his own father's death and during his own years of fathering children—perhaps also his own incestuous desires in relation to those children.[8] At this point Freud laid down the rhetorical system of the oedipal male child in which, says Chase, "The imagination of the primary identification with the *gap* as an identification with the *father* is an anthropomorphism, entailing . . . the personification of a proper name (the name of the father), the conflation of an inscription and a person" (1984, 199). What should be defined as a transference like any other is picked out as being of universal significance; transference and displacement seem to become indistinguishable. Metaphor overwrites metonymy—a particular form of signification (the father) overwrites difference (inscription, coagulation)—in a retroactive reading by an adult male. Kristeva suggests that such an identification conflicts with other parts of Freud's theory because this special kind of identification with the father (whose image here is anachronistically the ego ideal) occurs chronologically prior to any possibility of an ideal ego in the child, prior to the infant's recognition of any special significance on the part of the father, prior to the formation of an ego that might allow for a recognizable object.

What thus might be seen as *temporal* juxtaposition—that is, recognition by the infant of the mother's desire for something else followed by the image of an actual father—is *figured*, or troped, in Freud's discourse by the image of the father, that figure then enforced by Law. A personification takes place, which is "the consolidation, as an agency or power, of that violence that inscribes displacement as a sign" (Chase 1984, 198). The anthropomorphic identification of the father is thus specifically connected to the larger cultural order to legitimate it by implying an inevitable connection between male authority in society as a whole and a linguistic Law that requires the third term, the generic *he,* to establish a universal language. (In Kristeva's maternally attentive analytic situation the third term is love, or an intersubjective transference and countertransference: "Love replaces narcissism in a third person that is external to the act of discursive communication" [1980, 279].)

The origin of subjectivity in Freud's description of the infant proves to *be* the transference. Since a transference implies a repetition, this originary transference repeats the structure of writing, functioning like an originary spacing. Kristeva suggests that this means that the language of rhetoric is "the precise terminology, the most rigorous referent, for descriptions of the very accession to the possibility of signification" (Chase 1984, 199). Freud's Oedipus is thus the product of a rhetorical process, a polemics that is "lucidly presented to support the inevitability of the symbolic and/or social code" (Kristeva 1980, 274). This oedipal son is thus "Freud's error," part of an anthropomorphic rhetoric of mourning for the father, assuaging the guilt of the son who replaces his father—inevitably, in this system, as in the stories in which an oracle legitimated the inevitability of parricide—by interpreting that replacement as unavoidable, enforced as it is by a linguistic and anthropological Law he finds to be universal. The universality of Oedipus is the negative of the "guilt experienced by the son who is *forced by the signifier to take his father's place*" (Chase 1984, 200). A historical situation is thus "troped," overwritten by the claim to universality of the oedipal son, the reading by Freud as son/father. And Kristeva goes further to suggest that, because this process is cultural, social, historical, this particular form of the emergence of symbolization through paternal prohibition is "a possible variant within rather than . . . the foundation of, the signifying process" (Chase 1984, 200).

There is another trope as well that is intimately involved in this misreading and continues to hamper the conceptualization of the maternal, and that is the *fantasy* of motherhood "that is nurtured by the adult, man or woman, of a lost territory." For this fantasy again involves troping what is, in fact, a relationship: "it involves less an idealized archaic mother than the idealization of the relationship that binds us to her, one that cannot be localized—an idealization of primary narcisissm" (Kristeva 1987b, 254).

What the trope of the father and the archaic mother cover over is the coagulation or productive dissolution that is the remainder of the desire of the mother—that is, the recognition by the infant that the infant does not represent plenitude for the mother, that there is, as well, something else. That "something else" is thus historically variable; it very well might not be for the father or even for a person but, rather, it is the effect of the process of signification itself. This coagulation finds its *sème* in blood, which is connected not only to death but also to birth. The importance of analyzing this extremely intimate *sème* in its relation to questions of violence and of race is increasingly evident, and this coagulation of the mother and her desire is, perhaps, constitutive of the very heterogeneity a materialist theory or performance looks for. It is here that we might find a different space for organizing difference, "provided we hear in language—and not in the other, nor in the other sex—the gouged-out eye, the wound, the basic incompleteness that conditions the indefinite quest of signifying concatenations" (Kristeva 1982a, 113). Yet masculine theorists have resisted this coagulation by subsuming the possibilities of difference into threat alone, collapsing two kinds of bodies into one and collapsing the connotations of blood and nature into death and regression alone, with threat located in closeness. This resistance, on the part of masculine theorists, becomes identifiable formally and thematically as an ideologeme of threatening, seductive engulfment and threatened boundaries. The resistance to this fluidity that threatens to overrun unenforceable boundaries is, at bottom, a resistance to nonidentity. A feminine subject position, however, might much more likely be constructed around a resistance to separation, not to closeness.[9]

A gendered reading of the abject might isolate differences. A mother, says Kristeva—using *mother* allegorically, as the maternal, not the genetrix—"protects herself from the borderline that severs her body and expatriates it from her child" (1987b, 254). Here the abject is resisted because it *brings* separation, not because it threatens it with the flood of engulfment. It has been precisely this maternal attentiveness to an Other, not necessarily a real mother/child relationship so much as an allegorical one, which has provided what Kristeva calls the excess/access to difference. But it also just as easily *might* be an actual mother/child situation, this model "recognizing the merely natural nature of maternal care and its supersession by the child's [later] identification with an Imaginary Father, or a patriarchal imagination" (Chase 1990, 134). The resistance here is to the singularity of the ego, to the expulsion of the Other, the child or the loved one, outward. This is very different from the threat to the masculinized, "autonomous" ego, which insists on singularity and which perceives the threat as coming from the outside, from the Other. There is here a productive, radical site of knowledge production in an intersubjectivity, an analysis of transference, allegorically modeled on a relation between mother and child, where language encounters biology. As Chase argues, "The relation between mother and infant as conceived by Kristeva [the allegorical model of an analytic situation based on maternal attentiveness] becomes a figure for the relation between figure and grammar or the cognitive and performative dimensions of language" (1989, 81n). This allegory of mother and child deserves more investigation, for, to repeat Kristeva's claim: "Where life and discourse come together, that is where the destiny of subjectivity is caught up in the claims of civilization. Today, the pill and the Pope know this indeed" (1980, 272).

Mimicry

The disciplinary discourse of the family incites desires and identifications, which it is organized to gratify, as Mark Seltzer argued about discourses of power in general. By means of its organization of what is "normal" the family also reproduces itself: the more normal males and females there are, the more normal families there will be. The more normal families, the more normal males and females, etc. The structural opposition organized in the family in the twentieth century is managed or administered at a wider level through a discourse of reform as the rational, enlightened human subject tries to reproduce itself by first producing certain subjects as Other then, secondarily, including those Others in the category of "person." (All men are created equal. But all Others must become men in order to be treated as equals.) The discourse that attempts to reproduce itself by means of Others is colonial discourse, and both Third World people and females are colonized, though very differently, by the phallocentric discourse of purity.

Colonial discourse does not operate according to a dialectic of negation that simply excludes certain subjects; historically, it is a product of liberalism as a political philosophy in the nineteenth century. Rather than simply relying on an opposition between subject and object, or male and female, colonial discourse attempts to *produce* the Other in its own image. This Other might be called the "reformed Other." For example, British schooling trained Africans and Indians to perform Britishness as they took over local rule. Similarly, women are required to perform like men within the general category of subject called "human," whose logical requirements are very specifically masculine. What is presumed in both cases is a supposedly neutral category—person, subject, human being—which is not differentiated according to race or sexual identity. (Race and gender are thus attributes of people of color and women. They are not attributes of the human, the neuter privileged category unmarked by race or gender.) Those individuals who will be equal are those who can act like "persons"; those who can be equal will be equal, as we reencounter Aristotle and tragedy.

The subject/object model that had made sense in an earlier period was refined in part because of a particular tension that made it inadequate for power's needs, a form of this tension already present when Greece was a colonial power. As Edward Said describes it, this is "the tension between the synchronic panoptical vision of domination—the demand for identity, stasis—and the counterpressure of the diachrony of history—change, difference . . . " (quoted in Bhabha 1984, 126).

Colonial mimicry emerges as a compromise between the two opposing needs of power: stasis and increase. The Other is allowed to become a subject in order to reproduce the symbolic system in its particular capitalist form. Its subject status occurs in a double articulation: (1) it is the *sign of reform* of the Other, an Other reformed to be more like the One. It is also the sign of discipline, regulation, and appropriation. But the Other's status is also (2) the *sign of the inappropriate,* the copy, difference. Like metaphor, colonized subjects authorize and legitimate whatever they try to copy by their desire to copy. But they also differ from and defer the original, which always risks losing control of its copies.

Homi Bhaba's work on colonial relations between England and India in the nineteenth century has to do with *colonial mimicry,* though it makes no distinction between male and female subjects. I want to use his concept of colonial mimicry, however, to discuss the democratic rhetoric of equality that ostensibly attempts to reform the inequality between males and females by including females in the category of "mankind," or subject. This does not mean that the experience of colonized or postcolonial subjects (any more than the experience of slaves) is the same as the experience of all women; they each require a specific analysis. But they are structurally linked as results of the organization of phallocentric political systems. Bhabha's description of the disciplinary nature of dominance is helpful in showing how various kinds of Others become partial subjects.

Democratic or Liberal rhetoric organizes its claims that all persons are equal in a discourse of liberty while at the same time establishing a norm of eligibility for that liberty. One must be a person to qualify. The contradiction between liberty and normalization, like the contradiction between stability and increase, means that mimicry, "acting like a speaking subject," rests on very tenuous and tense ground.

The colonial normalization of subjects—Anglicizing them in one case, "individualizing" them as persons under the sign of the generic subject, on the other—rests on that ambivalence. The Other is produced as a partial subject; that is, the colonized subject or the woman, who is a subject, or a person, is always simultaneously marked, because of the symbolic writing of her objectified and abjected body, as the Otherness that presence has disavowed. Nonwhite subjects, in this logic, are partial subjects, carrying on their bodies the visual evidence that they are *inappropriate* subjects. The white male could not be engaging in reform if the female and nonwhite, as Other, did not differentially make his position possible in the field of signifiers. This is a situation in which the denial of any difference among subjects ("all people are created equal") only makes sense if differences are in place—if there are subjects who are not equal.

Robert Stoller argues that the assignment of sexual identity, like identity in general, has far more to do with an *interpretation* of appearance than with biology. It is the parents' socially inscribed response to the appearance of the child's body that establishes sexual identity. He cites examples of children who, because of underdeveloped genitals, were "misdiagnosed" in terms of sexual identification and who developed all the psychological traits of the sex their parents believed them to be (1967, 394). Biology establishes a certain appearance, which is then so-

cially interpreted, and that interpretation writes the body. Society's response to a member of a nonwhite family similarly bases itself on appearance. As Frantz Fanon says, "a normal child raised in a normal family
will be a normal man. A normal Negro child . . . having grown up with
a normal family, will become abnormal on the slightest contact with the
white world" (1967, 142). A normal Negro female child will find that
appearance makes the contradictions double those that confront Fanon's
male child.

The rhetoric of equality and reform, which depends on inequality,
also constitutes the Other as a partial but virtual subject who poses a
certain threat. The Other might very well take the claims of equality
seriously. The promise of equality or normality—that there is no difference between subjects—is violently contradicted by the workings of
culture, which enforces differences.

Mimicry, acting like a speaking subject, is not based on representation as copy or imitation but, rather, on mimesis, because there is no
essence or identity behind the mask of the father to imitate. It is the
repetition of an origin which is a nonrepresentative representation, a
signifier. This mimicry is a matter of camouflage, as Lacan says. In a
field of subjects who are social constructs a subject imitates by acting
like a social construct:

> Mimicry reveals something insofar as it is distinct from what might
> be called an itself that is behind. The effect of mimicry is cam-
> ouflage. . . . It is not a question of harmonizing with the background,
> but against a mottled background, of becoming mottled—exactly
> like the technique of camouflage practised in human warfare. (Lacan,
> quoted in Bhabha 1984, 125)

The look of surveillance, which is a metaphor for the authoritative
vision of power, is reflected back by the mimic. Were the occupant of
the panopticon's tower to make himself visible, the prisoner's imitation
would not give back to the occupant a specular reflection, a mirror
image. Instead, since the mimic, or former object, is now a partial sub-
ject/partial object who can gaze back at the occupant of the tower, she
or he reflects back only a *partial* mirror image. The gaze of surveillance
is returned as "the displacing gaze of the disciplined" (Bhabha 1984,
129). The partial vision of presence is repeated as a metonymy that
menaces the narcissistic, specular demand of metaphoric presence.

The double message of normality and mimicry can be read in its two effects: reproduction of culture when normal blacks and/or normal females act like persons; and the menace that results when they try to claim the privileges of persons, who, by definition, are white and male: "The ambivalence of colonial authority [or, in my usage, a colonized subject] repeatedly turns from *mimicry*—a difference that is almost nothing but not quite—to *menace* —a difference that is almost total but not quite" (Bhabha 1984, 136). According to Bhabha, colonial discourse and its reproduction of partial subjects alternates between narcissism and a demand for metaphor and specular reflection by Others and phobia, a reaction to the production of partial subjects as metonymic part objects of presence which threaten the "phobic myth of the undifferentiated whole white body" (133).

Masquerade

Bhabha's description of mimicry in colonial discourse did not differentiate between the experiences of male and female subjects or acknowledge the fact that the phobic myth of the undifferentiated white body revolves around a white male body. Subjects of mimicry, too, are expected to be genderless, abstracted individuals, persons. A different form of acting, the masquerade, specifically concerns women. Rather than mimic the masculine subject, Oedipus, the woman here "acts like" a Woman.

Joan Rivière's "Womanliness as a Masquerade" has been very influential in feminist theory, though studies of it have overlooked its particular structuration in terms of race. It is a case study of an intellectual woman who tries to compete with the father by becoming an active subject, hiding her activity through a kind of masquerade. She is an educated white American woman whose analysis almost immediately brings up an effect of the cultural logic which produces a horizontal division among women of different races and classes, an effect few commentators on Rivière's work take seriously enough. At one point in the case Rivière's patient describes one of her fantasies: a Negro man attacks her, and her response to this attack is to seduce him and turn him over to the authorities. Such a fantasy was familiar to Frantz Fanon, who isolated just this feature of a cultural unconscious as one of the most frequent manifestations of the racism that is constructed simultaneously in a logic of purity along with misogyny. This evidence of racist fantasies in the unconscious of white women suggests the importance of analyzing the historical intersection of racial purity in the construction of white female subjectivity as well as simultaneously dissecting the misogyny in the unconscious of men of color. The intimacy of these connections can more nearly be accounted for by seeing the similarity of their structuration within this logic of purity, which is also a logic of white supremacy.

Rivière's analysis focuses on female activity, which she refers to as "the wish for masculinity." This might be redefined simply as the wish for activity, a rebellion against being acted upon in the cultural equation between femininity and passivity. Placing oneself in an active position that has been traditionally masculine may be dangerous to women, and Rivière attempts to "show that women who wish for masculinity may put on a mask of womanliness to avert anxiety and the retribution feared from men" (1929, 303).

The subtleties of this masked behavior are many. In order to be able to continue her activity without danger Rivière's female active subject acknowledges the way the Symbolic is structured around normality. She disguises herself as the normal passive mother/woman, the object the oedipal complex should produce if it worked correctly. This disguise allows her to play the available roles against themselves in a kind of theatrical performance, such a performance itself a proof of her capacity to be active, to have the capacity to *act* by grabbing the symbolic resources available to represent that activity. What is available is Man and Woman; she can either act as a mimic Man or as a Woman, and in this instance she chooses the latter, a role that quite obviously does not fit. So, initially, as one form of resistance, she tries to manipulate that role yet stay beyond it in some "elsewhere." The threat to Oedipus may be significant because it is in her most womanly submission to the oedipal requirements for her that she may always be playing. Because the very possibility of a successful Oedipus depends on her fulfillment of the role of mother/woman, the danger represented by this womanly playing may be very great.

This playacting sets off a certain confusion, as Rivière says. Because such a woman fulfills both female and male roles as well as the average woman and the average man, "it is really a puzzle to know how to classify this type psychologically" (304). The dividing lines are blurred because there is no conceptual place for the active woman, the masquerade theoretically has to come from the elsewhere, which Michèle Montrelay describes as the censored, not repressed, place of woman.

This early superwoman, who could succeed as both male and female, experienced a particular anxiety and required reassurances from various father figures, some of whom had no real influence over her chances of success. Her need for reassurance took two forms: a need for recognition and compliments on her masculine performance; and a reassurance that she was sexually desirable, successful in her feminine performance: "Obviously, it was a step towards propitiating the avenger to endeavour to offer herself to him sexually . . . to make sure of safety by masquerading as guiltless and innocent" (Rivière 1929, 306). As an active subject, she takes herself in hand and offers herself as passive object, an offer that has a passive *aim* but is itself active. She had also disguised the aggressiveness of her behavior (and *any* activity on a woman's part is, by definition, aggressive) by frequently joking about her success in the male world, as if it were not something to be taken seriously, in spite of the fact that she pursued it with great intensity: "She has to treat the situation of displaying her masculinity to men as a 'game,' something not real, a joke" (305).

In the dreams of Rivière's patient people saved themselves from disaster by donning disguises; they were dreams filled with masks: "Womanliness therefore could be assumed and worn as a mask, both to hide the possession of masculinity and to avert the reprisals expected if she was found to possess it" (306). This womanliness proved to be more a device for avoiding anxiety than it was her primary mode of sexual enjoyment. She was "abnormal," says Rivière, because, though she was heterosexual in her relationships, she was homosexual in her fantasies. But here the rhetoric of normality inadvertently isolates a productive excess, for something about this role playing is situated on what would seem to be an absence. But again this is a performance from the space of a conceptual absence, providing a way to "read" an embodied enunciation of that theoretical absence.

Rivière argues that this patient was motivated by the desire to placate the father, whose position as an active subject she is taking (just as a son would). But the father's threat to her was never as great as her mother's, for whom the entire performance had been staged. This rivalry with her father was, in fact, an attempt to placate her mother in a form she assumed would satisfy her. She attempted to read her mother's desire and to become what she presumes would have satisfied the desire she thinks she has read.

But the analysand's difficulty with this masquerade stemmed from her need for recognition, which made her continually look for approval from father figures as agents of the Symbolic. That need matched the historical situation in which she found herself; in spite of her own ability, she nevertheless had to answer to those people who had power over her, all of whom were men. The need for recognition was not so much a need for recognition of her ability as it was, says Rivière, a "need for absolution." And though the mother's power was at first denied, while also feared, even disparaged, the guilt over the daughter's triumph could only be absolved by the father, for a very good reason: "By giving her recognition, he *gives* her the penis and to her instead of to the mother, a *double* victory over father and mother. Little as he may know it, to her the man has admitted his defeat" (312). This victory over her father, her ability to exact an admission of defeat, is then offered as a gift to her mother.

The analysand thus has turned the cultural logic's assignment of guilt to Woman into a defeat for the father. For by absolving her, the father shows that *he,* too, is role playing the act of the omniscient Father. He is not omniscient; if he were, he would not have been fooled. The father figure, by acting out his power as father, shows that he, too, is a mimic, that he, too, cannot possess the phallus. As a result, his recognition of her paradoxically acknowledges that the father's eye can be blinded if one knows how to play with its desires.

This masquerade rests, says Rivière, on a base of sadism, on the female aggression against the father that the oedipal complex attempts to dissipate. The normal Woman would have maneuvered around that sadistic stage by renouncing sadistic wishes: "I must not take, I must not even ask; it must be *given* me" (313). If a woman accepts castration in the normal way, that acceptance would ideally bring about humility and the admiration of men. If it does not work normally (and when does it?), it brings masquerade and a difficulty in attaining "normal" heterosexuality, whose structuration might be called the production of a mother/Woman who will be there waiting to be impregnated by a heterosexual Man. The aggression that marks the masquerading woman produces, rather than a normal Woman, a woman who is either lesbian, bisexual, or differently heterosexual. That is, she finds herself able to play both the active and passive roles.

The analysand *makes* the father give the penis, or power, to her in this active playing of her passive role. Rather than waiting, in the normal oedipal fashion, she causes it all to happen. Here the concept of passive causality isolated in *The Woman of Trachis* takes on a new form: it is now active passive causality, the manipulation of forms from whose production she was excluded.

This theatrical masquerade of womanliness has another effect. One of the results of the oedipal cultural logic was the production of a distance between the image of Man and the real, whereas Woman, in this classification system, appears to be closer to nature and further from reason and the abstract. Man is related to the universal, Woman to the particular; he to distance from the real, she to proximity; he to historical agency, she to matter.[10] Linking Woman to the real makes it especially easy to explain discriminations against women as a result of their presumed biological and physical limitations. Closer to the body, they are also more limited by it, more suitable for mindless, low-wage labor in this view in which women are easily confused with Woman. Man is abstracted and coded as rational, the agent who exchanges Woman as cultural and linguistic currency. He can generalize and manipulate the discrete units of signification because he is not so intensively inscribed as one of the units to be manipulated.

Masquerade suggests a way for a woman to gain some control over the cultural imagery of Woman. By acting like a Woman, perceiving as well as introducing a gap in that image between women and the image of Woman, she makes it easier to manipulate it without being wholly caught in it. Actively playing passivity at some moments, activity at others, allows for the manipulation of both passive and active signification. Mimicry involved playing the master, or subject, but masquerade allows her to play both subject *and* object, playing and complicating both parts:

> Womanliness therefore could be assumed and worn as a mask, both to hide the possession of masculinity and to avert the reprisals expected if she was found to possess it—much as a thief will turn out his pockets and ask to be searched to prove that he has not the stolen goods.
>
> The reader may now ask how I define womanliness or where I draw the line between genuine womanliness and the "masquerade." My suggestion is not, however, that there is any such difference; whether radical or superficial, they are the same thing. (306)

The masquerade separates the object of desire which the Oedipus complex structures as natural, from actual women, doubling representation and revealing the difference between women and Woman as well as suggesting a way of reading this womanliness as part of compulsory heterosexuality's masking of homosexuality. The body uses itself as its own disguise in an enactment that defamiliarizes female iconography in a masquerade that is more transparent to other women than it is to men, as Rivière points out. A subculture more easily recognizes the theatricality of its members.[11]

Judith Butler argues that in this case study, which she suggests is autobiographical and related to Rivière's circumstances as an intellectual woman within a male-dominated institution, the rivalry with the father concerns not the desire of the mother but, rather, a rivalry for the place of the speaker, "the desire to relinquish the status of woman-as-sign in order to appear as a subject within language" (1990, 51). (I would argue that Butler's formulation here depends on an oversight of the mother's desire; that is, Butler does not consider that the desire of the mother might *also* have been the desire to appear as a subject.)

She suggests that Rivière's description of the masquerade produces its own defense against the lesbian sexuality described within it—that is, that "the woman who 'wishes for masculinity' is homosexual only in terms of sustaining a masculine identification, but not in terms of sexual orientation or desire." Instead, Rivière constructs an explanation that suggests "a 'defence' against homosexuality as *sexuality*," a defense that functions as an asexual construct even though her fantasies are homosexual. As Butler argues, "there is no clear way to read this description of a female homosexual that is not about a sexual desire for women ... What is hidden is not sexuality but rage" (52; Butler's italics).

Butler's primary question about Rivière's analysis, then, is: "What is masked by masquerade?" Perhaps, she suggests, the masquerade covers "the melancholic and negative narcissism that results from the psychic inculcation of compulsory heterosexuality" (53). That is, what is masked may be masculine identification that is "dominated and re-solved" in a mask that proves to be the figuration of two simultaneous things: a refusal of female homosexuality and the incorporation "of that female Other who is refused," a kind of double relationship to the oedipal logic's repudiation of the feminine, in both its lesbian and its maternal components.

Rivière's analysis, Butler suggests, is still locked within the model of sexuality in which all libido is masculine, all subjectivity male, where all desire is structured in relation to the normalizing phallus. Yet this structurally limited analysis, which finds a homosexual without homosexuality, can be explained, argues Butler, by looking at the discursive space of the analysis itself, a lecture space within a primarily masculine institution and a mostly male audience, the discursive space of Echo. This discursive space has itself already prohibited the possibility of the enunciation of sexuality as homosexuality, the conditions of production for its performance not yet available.

Rivière's discussion has, nevertheless, been the occasion for a number of classic studies in feminist theory. Sue-Ellen Case's review of their work and her own revision of the theory of masquerade suggests that it has to be contextualized so that its use as a concept does not flatten out history and ironize very specific historical circumstances and contexts. In particular, she argues that "the lesbian subject of feminist theory will have to come out of the closet, the basic discourse or style of camp for the lesbian butch-femme positions will have to be clarified, and an understanding of the function of roles in the homosexual lifestyle will need to be developed, particularly in relation to the historical class and racial relations embedded in such a project" (1988–89, 70). A broad, undifferentiated notion of masquerade elides the specific history of lesbian strategies of disguise within compulsorily heterosexual society.

Case's important development of the Rivière case history for lesbian theory generalized to feminist theory suggests that the masquerading subject Rivière describes is enacted in the doubled, split subject position occupied by the butch-femme couple. Where the heterosexual analysand of the case history does not claim the possession of the penis but, rather, constructs reaction-formations, Case argues that "homosexual women openly display their possession of the penis and count on males' recognition of defeat." Butch-femme roles thus escape the concept of "the female body" altogether, playing out roles in "signs themselves and not in ontologies" (Case 1988–89, 78). For the butch-femme couple "the female body, the male gaze, and the structures of realism are only sex toys" (70). The couple reclaims agency and playfully inhabits "the camp space of irony and wit, free from biological determinism, elitist essentialism, and the heterosexist cleavage of sexual difference" (71), playing, even doubling, the masquerade—the butch displaying the penis, the femme playing the "compensatory masquerade of womanliness." In this theatricalized situation, says Case, the "women play *on* the phallic economy rather than to it" (64).

Parody as Corporeal Style / Style as Writing

The notion of masquerade, at least in Butler's analysis, suggests that
even such a theory as Case's still locates itself within a concept of identity—in this case, lesbian identity. In another context Butler's resistance
to a "return of the real" argues against "a necessary relationship between
the homosexual point of view and that of figurative language, as if to
be a homosexual is to contest the compulsory syntax and semantics that
construct the real." Theorizing masquerade, for Butler, leads to the
concept of parody rather than masquerade, a resistance strategy that both
acknowledges and manipulates the way gender functions within discourse. Like Bhabha's notion of mimicry, the parodic imitation Butler
suggests is not an imitation of an origin but, rather, "the parody is *of* the
very notion of an original." She continues:

> Just as the psychoanalytic notion of gender identification is consti-
> tuted by a fantasy of a fantasy, the transfiguration of an Other who
> is always already a "figure" in that double sense, so gender parody
> reveals that the original identity after which gender fashions itself
> is an imitation without an origin. To be more precise, it is a produc-
> tion which, in effect—that is, in its effect—postures as an imitation.
> This perpetual displacement constitutes a fluidity of identities that
> suggests an openness to resignification and recontextualization; pa-
> rodic proliferation deprives hegemonic culture and its critics of the
> claim to naturalized or essentialist gender identities. (139)

This parody is itself a "fleshly" one, what she calls "a corporeal
style," an act, in which each style proves to have a history, which limits
and constrains the possibilities of its act. And these acts are based on the
importance of repetition; they may, in fact, be rhetorical acts upon the
very site Kristeva isolated as part of the polemics that produces a figure
to cover over a gap that is the "origin" of signification. The parodic
repetition of gender, as in camp or drag or "Vogueing" or womanliness,
is "at once a reenactment and reexperiencing of a set of meanings already
socially established; and it is the mundane and ritualized form of their
legitimation." Gender itself, as Butler argues, is therefore the history of
an "identity tenuously constituted in time, instituted in an exterior space
[on the surfaces of bodies, though these identities come to be lived as
"interior substance," or depth] through a *stylized repetition of acts*" (140;

Butler's italics). Gender is thus "produced through the stylization of the body and, hence, must be understood as the mundane way in which bodily gestures, movements, and style of various kinds constitute the illusion of an abiding gendered self." She continues at a later point: "Genders can be neither true nor false, neither real nor apparent, neither original nor derived. As credible bearers of those attributes, however, genders can also be rendered thoroughly and radically *incredible* " (141).

This repetition of gender as originary imitation connects with Kristeva's isolation of the figure of the father and the archaic mother as anachronistic anthropomorphisms, figured retroactively as figures covering a gap. A subject position, a discursive "I" dependent on a "you," is constituted within an intersubjectivity whose analogy is transference in the analytical situation. It imitates originary repetition, or the repetition of originary spacing which marks the very structure of signification. Its act repeats an "I" in relation to a "you." Both the artistic repetition and the analytic repetition are temporary, deictic, contextually and discursively determined, and both are acts that also simultaneously repeat the cultural figurations of the characters involved in the discursive intersubjective situation. This acting, however, both continually reinstates (repeats) while also undercutting and displacing (deferring) what Kristeva called "the conflation of an inscription and a person." This instantiation of a subject position through an act depends on an originary aesthetic troping, which is both an effect of the process of signification and a thetic reinstatement of an identity that will immediately be undercut in the next moment: this is the subject in process.

Butler's notion of parody, as it might be juxtaposed to Kristeva's notion of the thetic subject, locates us in the discursive field of the play of signifiers, and it means that from here on the analysis will presume that location. But once we have located ourselves in this conceptual terrain there is a need to stay vigilant to the continuing influence of the repudiation of the feminine, as that applies to the maternal, even on strategies of resistance. This might suggest a way to find intersections between Butler's notion of corporeal style and what Kristeva calls "the effervescence of passion and language we call style" (1982a, 206). For Butler argues that "the postulations of a true gender would be revealed as a regulatory fiction" (1990, 141).

The repudiation of femininity, however, may still be at work in a too-quick understanding of the "free play" of signifiers, both in masculinist appropriations of that free play in a textualized femininity that proves to find no place for women as speakers or writers or for studies of legal discourse or of the arrangements of working conditions for women that find that the argument that gender is constructed can potentially, though not necessarily, reinforce a model of organization based on requirements whose ideal subject is male. In those circumstances the notion of gender constructedness can itself provide a "regulatory fiction" that requires that the different kinds of physical requirements for living in men's and women's bodies not be taken seriously because they suggest biologism or essentialism. Such a regulatory fiction of gender constructedness can, then, reinforce the oppression of women in the workplace because it overlooks their reproductive needs or the continuing difference, or doubleness, in Symbolic *capacity* that results from the simultaneous symbolic coding of women's bodies as abject.

For as Kristeva's concept of the abject suggests, women are coded doubly, simultaneously the filth, the debris, the improper *excess* speaking from the place organized for the clean and proper body—residue *and* speaking subject, in a specifically different way from the act of the parodying masculine body. The community of discourse must be demystified; men acting or performing gender signify differently than women acting or performing gender, even as these acts undercut that very difference. But to jump too quickly to equating the two acts is a dangerous move.

There are thus still at least *two* regulatory fictions to be disentangled here. In this study I will continue to focus on the repudiation of the feminine that results in the denial of the specificity of the maternal, but there must be many models for theorizing gender constructedness, and Butler's is perhaps at the moment the definitive study of the specificity of the repudiation of femininity as it applies to lesbian sexuality.

The "We" in Process

Bertolt Brecht described the task facing the dramatist interested in a political theater of change: "The difficulty is that it is hard to work on the first stage (new subjects) when one is already thinking about the second (humanity's new mutual relationships)." Changing the form of drama also involves exploring "humanity's new mutual relationships . . . via the exploration of new subject-matter. (Marriage, disease, money, war, etc.). The first thing is to comprehend the new subject-matter, the second to shape the new relations." And comprehending the new subject matter requires a new dramatic and theatrical form: "Can we speak of money in the form of iambics?" (1988, 29–30). In terms of this study, however, the question to be asked is: Can we any longer speak of subjectivity in the form of tragedy?

In the next chapters the plays of three playwrights, Adrienne Kennedy, Marsha Norman, and Rosario Castellanos, suggest various ways of reconceptualizing subjectivity and, as a result, concepts of connectedness or community. A model for thinking about those concepts is suggested by bell hooks, in a chapter entitled "Postmodern Blackness" from her book *Yearning: Race, Gender, and Cultural Politics*. She takes on two projects in this essay, one task the revalorization of intellectual work for women—and, in particular, African-American women—the other the description of possibilities of community suggested by postmodern or poststructuralist ways of conceptualizing meaning. For, she says, "postmodern culture with its decentered subject can be the space where ties are severed *or it can provide the occasion for new and varied forms of bonding*" (hooks 1990, 31; my italics). By this she suggests that the disintegration of unitary forms or privileged meanings opens up gaps, fractures, ruptures, surfaces, contextualities that allow intellectuals to escape the narrowness or even the isolation that formerly marked scholarly work.

The resonant concept in her book is "yearning," for desire here has more to do with the desire for community than for isolated *jouissance,* and this makes itself visible in an increasingly diffuse relationship between "high" culture and popular culture: "Much postmodern engagement with culture emerges from the yearning to do intellectual work that connects with habits of being, forms of artistic expression, and aesthetics," for it is not only intellectuals but also people interested in popular music, rap, melodrama, television, and other forms of popular culture who are concerned with aesthetics. "On the terrain of culture, one can participate in critical dialogue with the uneducated poor, the black underclass who are thinking about aesthetics" (hooks 1990, 31). This intellectual opening out, she argues, can provide a new space for critical exchange in which there are many kinds of "experts," no longer simply academic specialists, and in which there is greater connection to the everyday. The critical intellectual might be increasingly found both in and outside the university.

The discovery that identity is not static is not a tragic discovery. It does not have to lead to the sad sigh of the intellectual trapped within himself—in spite of himself. Rather, hooks refuses that tragic sigh in an interpretation of postmodernism from a perspective that recognizes both the economic decimations of a postmodern economy as well as the possibilities to be found in its fragmented culture. In the next chapter other nontragic possibilities of connection will be considered, all of them motivated, like hooks's work, by a yearning for a "we" that is, nevertheless, always in process.

Chapter 4

Theatrical Subjects: The Plays of Adrienne Kennedy

In the theater, the body recovers its authoritative role.
—Geneviève Fabre

Everybody said I was "so sweet." Sometimes I longed to be bad like Mildred Pierce's daughter.
—Adrienne Kennedy

the sun is now myself
dismembered in darkness
my blood my dismembered
self at sundown on the moon

—Adrienne Kennedy

Adrienne Kennedy is one of the most original talents of twentieth-century North American theater. Herbert Blau, who suggests that she and Sam Shepard are among the finest playwrights of the modern stage, describes her as "surely the most original black dramatist of her generation and, along with Shepard, the most original" (1987, 55). While everyone recognizes Shepard, whose work has produced a veritable industry of criticism, fewer people have studied Kennedy's work, though interest in her plays is growing.

Kennedy's plays reveal a smoldering anger that first exploded when she left the racially and ethnically mixed public schools of Cleveland to attend Ohio State University. Much of the rage in her plays can be linked to this particular encounter with racism; the other passionate center of these plays grew out of her experiences with a miscarriage and childbirth during a period when she was trying to write. Her work has been performed in Europe; she has received an Obie award in 1964 for *Funnyhouse of a Negro*; she was a protégé of Edward Albee and Joseph Papp;

and she received Guggenheim and Rockefeller grants—yet her work is still rarely performed. As a result, the plays are not given the wide critical discussion that might make it possible for them to reach a larger audience and to be included in discussions of the history of North American theater. These short but highly complicated plays introduce students of drama to experiments in dramatic form, decentered subjects, and postmodern fragmentation that unfailingly indict the Symbolic workings of racism and misogyny. Kennedy's plays experiment with what Fredric Jameson calls the "omnipresence of culture," in which the economy and the culture have collapsed into each other, these experiments producing a kind of drama in which the links between politics and aesthetic form are simply unavoidable. Their mesmerizing complexity, horror, and grotesque beauty works like Möbius strips that keep turning inside out to show what goes on in the ambiguous, troubled process called acculturation. There are few North American playwrights who have brought together a study of the symbolic construction of racism and sexism so powerfully.

Kennedy was born in Pittsburgh and grew up in Cleveland, the daughter of a middle-class couple. Her father was a well-known businessman who spent much of his time raising money for community projects, and her mother was a schoolteacher. In Cleveland she went to school with first-generation immigrant children:

> It just so happened that I was very lucky. Cleveland was at that time almost by accident one of the most democratic cities in the United States. It was truly a melting pot for first generation Blacks from the south. It has excellent public schools. . . . I loved to read; I read every book in the school library. Yes, I was really very well read by the time I was a child! There was a lot of competition in our elementary school. We had first generation Italians, kids from Poland, all European countries, plus Blacks. There was a lot of competition, and so people tended to be well-read. (quoted in Binder 1985, 101)

This passage might suggest a discussion of literacy in terms of colonization and the liberal goals of the Enlightenment as they "normalize" the Other, or it might elicit an analysis based on Pierre Bourdieu's description of petit bourgeois aspirations toward the "distinctions" of the bourgeoisie, but those arguments, while important, also risk covering over the way class and literacy very specifically intersect with race and gender.

Kennedy's culturally mixed education and environment provide a wide range of material for both her plays and her autobiography, the latter joining bits of family lore, popular culture, and heroes in the black community, such as this collection from one page: Charlotte Brontë, spirituals, Paul Robeson, Freddy Jamison, "the boy I fell in love with at eight," Jesus, white people, Dr. Benjamin Mays. On the next page we find Mr. Kuzamano, zombies, mummies, and the Cat Woman, then Lowell Thomas, Marian Anderson, Mary Bethune, Billie Holiday, and Snow White. This fragmentation of bits of memory becomes more somber as the autobiography progresses through high school, marriage, motherhood, her experiences of traveling to England and Africa; these memory fragments always circle around a very tense relationship between her mother and her father. Her own childhood nuclear family, whose tensions and contradictions are supposed to remain hidden according to middle-class mythology, becomes more and more the site for aesthetically reworking situations in her later life. The autobiography, like her plays, has a structure that can only be described as fragmented and metonymic; it is organized like the logic of the dreamwork in that it does not sift or sort or order categories according to a privileged signifier that will impose linearity but, instead, lays out the bits and pieces of memory in all their heterogeneity. Both the plays and the autobiography suggest that received identity is better described as identities.

And though Herbert Blau recognizes Kennedy's brilliance, he nevertheless misreads her work in a serious way to argue that her plays are concerned less with African roots than with the "romance of white history, the interminable bastardizing of the dream" (1987, 61). He argues that she writes from a colonized psyche, "formed by white culture which she finds not contemptible but beautiful, more maybe than black is beautiful, the poetry, the fictions, the achievements in music and art" (58). Yet his diagnosis seems to come out of the structure of tragedy, for he posits an either/or impasse: the plays are about the primacy of *either* African roots *or* the archaic romance of a white Western tradition.

But the originality of Kennedy's work lies precisely in its staging of the phobic nature of such binary logic and its costs. The plays are obsessively, unwaveringly about the impossibility of any kind of definitive separation of African culture from the "romance of the Western tradition," though Blau's reading still seems to rest on a nostalgia for the wholeness of each of these identities. The logical result of his tragic nostalgia would be that the violence and despair that lead at least one character to commit suicide is caused by a lament that the subject is not white, not "cleanly" identifiable. Yet for Kennedy this privileging of wholeness (the focus on whiteness here is countered in other critics by an insistence on a black essence) is itself the problem because it symbolically inscribes mixtures as degraded and polluting. That this inscription of mixture as degraded occurs in a North American culture whose very heritage is one of ethnic intermingling would seem paradoxical if it were not for the cultural logic of purity which helps explain how such an obvious feature of a multicultural society can be so phobically denied. The cultural logic of purity, in fact, depends on differences. In Kennedy's work it is not mixture that leads to death but its phobic devaluation by groups with the power to enforce their own meaning through violence, shame, humiliation, and appropriation.

Within this white supremacist logic Kennedy's work connects with that of Frantz Fanon, specifically in relation to a particular characteristic of his work, as described by Homi Bhabha. Fanon, Bhabha argues, draws on a "painful re-membering, a pulling together of a dismembered art to make sense of the trauma of the present." Kennedy, like Fanon, refuses to romanticize or cover over "the phobic image of the Negro, the native, the colonized [which is] deeply woven into the psychic pattern of the West." Such an image, argues Bhabha, offers to blacks and whites, colonized and colonizer, "a deeper reflection of their interpositions, as well as the hope of a difficult, even dangerous, freedom." Neither Fanon nor Kennedy sees the image of the self as grounded in "an originary past or an ideal future"; they, instead, investigate its cultural production (Bhabha 1989, 146).

The subject proves to be deconstructed in Kennedy's plays in a way that historically locates it in the specific cultural struggles of the United States, but it is also a deconstruction that provides the most tantalizing though dangerous promise of another way of living as subjects, one not caught up in the phobic insistence on purity and its cleanly separated categories, unities, and singular identity. Reading her autobiography means getting caught up in her joy, amazement, and curiosity, as she darts here and there to find and sensuously remember the cultural productions with which she identified, mixed as they are in terms of high art and popular culture, black political and middle-class life, ethnic friends and white movie celebrities, African history and Christian religious imagery. This aspect of her work may, in fact, provide one way to draw on poststructuralist theory while also trying to describe the specificity of her experiments. Cornel West argues that the relationship between black culture and postmodernism requires investigating high culture along with popular culture because of the latter's wider exposure and influence, in order to make possible "critical positions for blacks both in and around popular culture [and to investigate] the ways in which these positions can be viewed as sites of a potentially enabling yet resisting postmodernism" (West 1989, 96).

This kind of enabling and resisting aesthetic strategy on Kennedy's part, its staging of a decentered political poetics, might also fit bell hooks's conclusion about the relevance of postmodernism to black culture, even though, "given a pervasive politics of white supremacy which seeks to prevent the formation of radical black subjectivity, we cannot cavalierly dismiss a concern with identity politics." Yet there "is a radical difference between a repudiation of the idea that there is a black 'essence' and recognition of the way black identity has been specifically constituted in the experience of exile and struggle" (hooks 1989, 26).

Cultural Logics and Symbolic Denominators

The initial clash of contradictions in Kennedy's plays is set up by the juxtaposition of symbolic logics, one historically linked to African culture, the other an outgrowth of the Greek and Judeo-Christian logic traced in the first three chapters of this study, with the result that, as Henry Louis Gates argues, the black tradition is from the very outset double voiced. But within this double logic Kennedy very specifically focuses on splits within each of those logics—in particular, the feminized residue of the contemporary relationship between the black tradition and what Ian Angus and Sut Jhally call the present stage of capitalism, the stage of mass-mediated culture, or the mode of information. That residue, or unconceptualized leftover, is related to something Kristeva calls a *symbolic denominator:*

[A symbolic denominatory] is the cultural and religious memory forged by the interweaving of history and geography. . . . The variants of this memory produce social territories which then redistribute the cutting up into political parties which [are] still in use but

losing strength. At the same time, this memory or symbolic denominator, common to them all, reveals beyond economic globali-
zation and/or uniformization certain characteristics transcending the
nation that sometimes embrace an entire continent. A new social
ensemble superior to the nation has thus been constituted, within
which the nation, far from losing its own traits, rediscovers and
accentuates them in a strange temporality, in a kind of "future perfect," where the most deeply repressed past gives a distinctive character to a logical and sociological distribution of the most modern
type. For this memory or symbolic common denominator concerns
the response that human groupings, united in space and time, have
given not to the problems of the *production* of material goods (i.e.,
the domain of the economy and of the human relationships it implies, politics, etc.) but, rather, to those of *reproduction,* survival of
the species, life and death, the body, sex and symbol. (1982c, 13)

An African symbolic denominator that informs African-American
culture, argues Paul Carter Harrison, arises out of a "memory that
reflects certain aspects of African ceremony while dealing with the
specificity of experience culture dictates." Plays that draw on this symbolic denominator "share in common a peculiarly native resonance"
(Harrison 1974, 10). Harrison here refers to the effects of an African
memory on African-American culture as a part of "the African continuum," a ceremonial, collective narrativizing structure that works very
differently from the linear, binary, logical structure that underlies Aristotelian tragedy. This ceremonial structure depends far more on cyclical
and circular patterns of organization than on linear ones. Brecht's analyses of the influences of the humanist and capitalist notion of the individual in theater in the Aristotelian tradition are also important to the deconstruction of that individual, but Brecht's critique still depends on a dialectics that remains far too binary and depends on both the privileged
subject of the productive sphere and on an instrumental relationship to
nature, which justifies an idealistic belief in the positive effects of technology. Kennedy's plays avoid both these difficulties, for the most part
because they are grounded in a very different African-American cultural
context and turn for their primary structuration toward what goes on
in the sphere of reproduction, both cultural and biological. By so doing,
another strict division of categories becomes untenable—the clear split
between the public and the domestic, between the productive and the

reproductive. These spheres prove to be every bit as intimately imbricated and inseparable as do complete, or "clean," separations that supposedly separate black and white or literate culture and popular culture.

Harrison describes the ceremonial nature of African theater that underlies African-American drama and is a characteristic of other forms of black culture, such as the black Baptist church, Caribbean carnival, and the musical structuration of the blues. This ceremonial history results in art forms that depend on participation, distinguishing them from the tradition of passive spectatorship which has informed Western theater in the modern period. African-American dramatic form is best described, says Harrison, as "secular ritual," in which the "formal ritualistic style of the black church [serves as a] paradigm for African-American dramaturgy" (1989, xv). Experimental dramatists who draw on the tradition Harrison describes, what he calls Kuntu drama, are also influenced by a specifically African concept of the word that distinguishes it from the logocentric concept of the word. Within the Kuntu tradition, a ritualistically repeated, performed word might activate the soul both of the cosmos and the community, but this notion of the ritual word, paradoxically, does not locate the promise of plenitude or full meaning in some idealized full, complete moment of presence represented by the act of speaking that word. (This romanticized view of performance and ritual often disables performance theory; it is a view that deconstructive readings of the full plenitude and presence of the act and the event have attempted to dissect.)[1]

Instead, unlike the logocentric word in the Western metaphysical tradition, whose history involves separating body from spirit, this African notion of the performed word of secular ritual *insists* on the materiality of the signifiers: sounds and rhythms are repeated in such a way that it is not simply semantics that make meaning but also the repeated sounds and their syntactic arrangement. This insistence on materiality, however, does not fall into the logocentric temptation to reify an origin in something "outside" signification, whether that origin be ideas or matter; in the logocentric tradition, such an origin is posited, like Lacan's longed-for plenitude, as something that can only be approached through signification, which is always tragically fated to fail, leaving us only with a poor substitute for the missing plenitude we long for.

Unlike the West's metaphysical tradition based on the complete separation of materiality and ideas or symbolization, such as the one Lacan reifies, separation does not propel this version of the African word. Instead, this notion of ritual which grew out of Dogon and Akan traditions depends on and insists on the intermingling of sensuality and intellection. Participation in a secular ritual also functions to reconcile past historical knowledge and present circumstances in a continuing, constantly changing repetition of cultural forms that help construct a collective historical memory.

According to Harrison, performance of the ritual word in this African tradition still rests, of course, on the gap between signifier and signified, but it does not attempt to fill that gap with the presence of its performance as a kind of plenitude. Instead, he argues, this antirealistic African-American aesthetic models itself on the way African-American music works; it bears "witness to what's left out of our concept of reality, or if not exactly what, to the fact that something *is* left out," what is called a "phantom limb" (xxi). This is a concept of performance that is, from the very beginning *about* incompleteness and nonidentity, but it differs from the Lacanian model that posits that incompleteness as an originary lack. In the Kuntu tradition the fact that something is left out is one element among many. Lack, or absence, does not predominate because what is equally important is what is *present:* an audience, a sensuous, embodied gathering of people. The importance of the participating presence of the audience can be seen in the witnessing testimony in the black church and its call-and-response structure.

Harrison, however, like Barthes, Vernant, and Finley, proves to be insufficiently self-reflective about gender in his description of African-American drama. In particular, in his introduction to a collection of plays entitled *Totem Voices: Plays from the Black World Repertory,* he discusses the ritual word, or Mother/Word, as if such a concept had nothing to do with women, and the best examples of dramatists who rely on such a Mother/Word prove to be men. He also draws on Wilson Harris's *The Womb of Space,* again without comment on the irony of the use of a metaphor of the womb that needs no women; in so doing, he replicates at least one feature of Western metaphysics in which birth imagery is used to describe the collaborative cultural productions of men. And finally, Harrison devotes some of the very few disparaging comments he makes about any African-American artist to women, arguing that Whoopi Goldberg and Oprah Winfrey "trivialize, even profane, the integrity of the soul: one can easily conclude that Oprah Winfrey's mammyism and Whoopi Goldberg's piccaninnyism are arrested states of negroidness, a *pigment* of the dominant culture's imagination" (xli).

The misogyny of this passage provides an example of the cultural unconscious of black masculinity that finds its objects of ridicule and trivialization located close to home.

So, while Harrison's description of the influence of African tradition is very important in establishing the context and characteristics of the secular ritual of African-American theater, it takes Kennedy's plays to draw attention to the costs of misogyny both in those traditions and in the cultural logic of purity.

Repetition, Revision, Signifyin(g)

Because one of the most striking features of Kennedy's dramatic structure is her use of repetition, Henry Louis Gates's description of a very particular form of repetition that characterizes the blackness of black literature is especially helpful. He calls this form of repetition "Signifyin(g)," a neologism coined to name a striking intersection between black culture and white culture in the United States. Literary criticism has been interested in questions of signification since the work of Saussure was imported from France, yet the use of the word *Signification* (which Gates capitalizes to keep its specific use in the black vernacular) has been used prominently in black culture for two centuries to talk about meaning making. It refers to an identifying feature of black culture, which is talking about talk, and it is evident in such practices as "the dozens," a kind of one-upmanship that very specifically depends on verbal complexity in which one is able to achieve a victory over an opponent through talk.

The fascinating near-homology between the two words, *signification/Signification,* provides an insight into culturally constructed meaning and the possibilities for resistance inherent in that very notion of constructedness. For as Gates describes it, Signification, or Signifyin(g), allows for the reading of a double-voicedness in the analysis of black literature as this signification/Signification relationship brings together black vernacular and critical discourse in the use of the same signifier for radically different signifieds. One signified refers to poststructuralist and "high" theoretical notions of the construction of meaning through systems of differences; the other refers to the long history of black vernacular in which Signification is a strategy used both to be "in" white culture, an unavoidable fact, and to rework the meaning of that culture from the perspective of the African-American experience, another fact.

This overdetermination sets up a confrontation between two parallel discursive universes: black and white: "Two separate and distinct yet profoundly—even inextricably—related orders of meaning dependent precisely as much for their confrontations or relations of identity manifested in the signifier as on their relations of difference, manifested at the level of the signified." The "different similarity" of the meanings of *signification/Signification* produces "a homonymic pun of the profoundest sort" (Gates, 47). Signifyin(g) depends on vacating the signifier then substituting a signified that does not stand for a semantic content but, instead, stands "for the system of rhetorical strategies peculiar to their own vernacular tradition." There is, then, in *Signifyin(g)* a semantic content, a "literal" meaning—that it is a rhetorical troping. Paraphrasing Roger D. Abraham, Gates says, "one does not signify something; rather, one signifies in *some way*" (54). This concept of Signifyin(g) is literally a making or doing that involves "inserting a new semantic orientation into a word which already has—and retains—its own orientation" (50), a "repetition with a signal difference" (51). To rename and to revise proves to be the very meaning of the infinitive *to signify*.

In signifyin(g) a rhetorical performance is doubled, the old form continuing to "speak," while a different semantic content or signified is added, which also and simultaneously speaks. Gates argues that this double-voicedness is quite different from a mere colonizing of the white term because it insists on directing attention from the semantic content to the rhetorical nature of all meaning. It is a "repetition with a signal difference," and that difference is a resonating linkage between the black vernacular and the literary tradition, perhaps even an inextricable mixture.

Funnyhouse of a Negro

Funnyhouse of a Negro opens with a carnival that brings to mind the Bakhtinian concept of carnival where time is stopped, held open, while hierarchies are momentarily collapsed, rearranged, and challenged in a heterogeneous moment of freedom. Caribbean carnival often makes use of that kind of inversion and mixture of categories and ranks, but in *Funnyhouse* the site of the carnival in the opening scene sets up grotesque, exaggerated carnival imagery that is nightmarish. It produces an image of the carnivalesque that is threatening to the most vulnerable members of society, as if, in this model of carnival, it is not the weak who are freed to invert hierarchies but, instead, the powerful are released from their constraints, no longer held in check by civilization or inhibition but freer to do whatever they wish. Jacques Rossaud describes analogous situations in medieval France where releasing constraints frequently released only those who had some measure of power, men, and led to collective rape as a "veritable rite of initiation or virilization for neighborhood bands." This behavior was, for many, "the expression of even deeper impulses and aspirations; it was a denial of the established order" (Rossaud 1978, 12); for others it represented even greater vulnerability.

Such an image of a denial of the established order by the strong more nearly describes the terrifying carnival imagery in Kennedy's play, which reproduces grotesque effects of the paranoid or phobic nature of civilization itself. The play is filled with images of bestiality, evil, deformity, and horror, which Bhabha might explain as white culture's projections: "Black skin splits under the racist gaze, displaced onto signs of bestiality, genitalia, grotesquerie which reveal the phobic myth of the undifferentiated white body" (1989, 132).

Two white characters, a landlady and a Jewish male poet, are transformed into the white faces of bitterly laughing and mocking characters in this Funnyhouse. Just as in Rivière's case study, in which the white woman's racist fantasies almost immediately showed up, and in Harrison's narrative, where misogyny explodes, here in Kennedy's play another result of a logic of purity finds a different form of culturally structured racism. The Jewish intellectual here momentarily seems to symbolize white male oppression in general. But though Kennedy seems to fall into a too-ready anti-Semitism here, another of her works, *A Rat's Mass,* investigates the relationship between fascism's murder of Jews with violence against African-Americans and women.

The main character, Sarah, is played simultaneously by different actors, these character(s) sometimes speaking the same lines but never in unison and never in dialogue where each might hear or understand the other. These simultaneous monologues work with great complexity to set up many narratives, each one linked to a particular figure or identification within the character Sarah. The narratives continually weave in and out of the stage space, united in what may be called a dense, overdetermined matrix tenuously united by the name Sarah. The name, in fact, seems to work much more as the economy of a vector. A *vector,* in mathematics, is defined as a quantity whose specifications (what constitutes an element by which to count) depend on its magnitude and direction. *Magnitude,* in this formulation, refers to the differential relationships among members of the same set; it works, like signification, to assign value according to the location of an element within a system of differences. The Latin root of *vector* means "to carry" which might allow us to link it back to rhetoric or metaphor, the trope that "carries" a figuration that straddles a gap. Conceptualizing subjectivity as something locatable only as mobile, temporary points of difference along a vector gives subjectivity both a momentary identity and a linkage to the cultural set within which it is made intelligible, or acquires magnitude.

This strange notion of name and character as vector proves troubling to grammar, or cultural history sedimented into formal and syntactical order. It is grammar that first reveals the breakdown of the coherent subject, for the character Sarah "are" multiple.

Initially, Sarah appears to be a young woman living in a brownstone in New York City, an English major whose friends and lover, the poet, are white. Her tastes are reflected in the decorous room she occupies: European antiques, photographs of Roman ruins, walls of books, a piano, oriental carpets, and a white glass table. Pierre Bourdieu's notion of "taste" as a marker of a differential nonessence that nevertheless identifies authentic members of a privileged class describes this particular form of mimicry. The petit bourgeois, or newly arrived member of the middle class, is marked as a newcomer to that class precisely by her overimitation. That is, she proves that he is not a "natural" member of the middle class by her insistence on knowing and enacting its codes very well, but the code she can never learn and embody is that of taste, of doing what comes naturally, because the natural is not an authentic origin at all but, instead, the result of the training of mind and body from the very first day of life in a particular milieu, or *habitus.* Such intimate training of the body cannot be "learned" by outsiders.[2] It is a cultural construction that can only be mimicked by a mimicry that marks its actor as always already outside the charmed circle of those who were born with taste.

Kennedy describes the structure of this play as a "growth of images," and the kind of repetition of the ritual, secular word that Harrison described works here through images, whose growth begins to establish a shimmering layering. As Kennedy says about this almost eerie repetition: "the images remain" (Lehman 1977, 46). Sarah in no way suggests a self-identical, closed, autonomous subject or character. Instead, it is a proper name that, with great difficulty, must hold past and present together in a space of character which finds its organization to be circular and repeating, rather than linear and distributive. What Jurij Lotman called the mythological nature that keeps interfering with the clarity of logical organization has, by now, become the poetic nature of the proper name. Here the signifieds of the word *Sarah* only have in common the word *Sarah,* their "Sarahness," its function only to provide a space of overlapping and crisscrossing. Gates suggests that (re)naming with the same name is a part of the rhetoric of Signifyin(g) in which the names are repeated, but they are revised by that repetition. What is challenged by such a repetition is the meaning of meaning.

The "Selves" of Sarah are here metonymically, not metaphorically, arranged; they are then brought together in an enactment that provides a kind of definition for theatrical character in general. As Anne Ubersfeld argues, theatrical character functions vertically as a lexeme, or a word, and more particularly as a poetic word. This notion of theatrical character draws on Jakobson's theory of the poetic function: "This is what allows the unification of dispersed simultaneous signs. The character figures in this textual space as the most exact crossing point of the overlapping [rabattement] of the paradigm upon the syntagma. *It is the proper place of the poetic* " (1978, 124; my translation; Ubersfeld's italics).

Each of Sarah's many identities is played by a separate actor, some men and some women, and some of them wear white masks that appear petrified. Those wearing white masks have kinky black hair sticking out from beneath their hairpieces as a kind of defect, or excess, that immediately identifies the mimics who attempt to imitate the reified white image.

Other characters who float within a vector marked as Sarah are: the Duchess of Hapsburg, who is "One of Herselves," as Kennedy describes her; Queen Victoria, also One of Herselves; Jesus, a yellow, dwarfish One of Herselves; and Patrice Lumumba, who appears with his head bloodied and split in two by an axe. The use of masks was originally influenced by the work of Picasso, as Kennedy has said, but after a stay in Accra, West Africa, and her encounter with African masks there, the fixed and haunting appearance of character masks took shape (Kennedy 1987, 121).

In a politically poetic way Kennedy's notion of dramatic form brings together two traditions: Eurocentric poststructuralism, which foregrounds the implications of interpreting formal textual and dramatic features through the influence of Jakobson, Lacanian connections between language and subjectivity, and Freud's description of dreamwork; and Afrocentric dramatic form that depends on context and on arrangements of meaning according to circularity, contiguity, and layering. Such arrangements constitute other kinds of logics that fall outside the logical categories of distribution, for it is the logic of distribution which has come to be called, for all its partiality and cultural specificity, logic itself. This intersection suggests a curious link back to Aristotle's *Poetics*. For Kennedy's political dramatic poetics show how impossible it is, particularly in terms of a necessarily decentered notion of character, to separate aesthetics from politics, just as Aristotle's theory of aesthetic practice showed how the protagonists in Greek tragedy functioned as a site where the relation between aesthetics and politics found its figurations. Kennedy's anti-Aristotelian theater winds up showing how to use Aristotelian concepts such as the intimacy of aesthetics and politics against themselves. It may be that, in this anti-Aristotelian rebellion based on Afrocentric ritual forms, she paradoxically reads Aristotle better than his champions. By doing so, however, she inexorably undermines the very structure of the Aristotelian stage and its tragic protagonist.

Conceptualizing this notion of character as lexeme, or word, makes the relationship between the discursive "I" and the difficulty of speaking it show how this speaking is both a grammatical and a political problem, foregrounding the cultural construction of identity. For as George Yudice argues, "Identity, then, is not a given but a *practice, a deployment* across the institutionalized terrain of a social formation" (Yudice 1990, 137). This discursive notion of character also requires a linkage to the physical body of the actor and the cultural inscriptions that she wears onstage as a body. As social construct, the body is transformed onstage into a *scenic* sign that unites the visual, the grammatical, and the codings of materiality. Sarah thus proves to be a materialized trope, or figuration of the practice called identity.

In many of the plays, including this one, part of Sarah's life is spent in an enclosed room; this is quite different from the spaces of many black plays located in the open street. But the enclosed rooms that are found in Kennedy's plays are often claustrophobic, private, marked as the interior spaces of the nuclear family in the United States. Enforcing the separateness of this privatized space, like other kinds of enforced separation, requires constant vigilance and rigidity. This kind of claustrophobia and tension is uneasily poised over what might be called the African antecedents of African-American tradition, where the nuclear family is quite artificial. In many non-Western cultures, as well as within ethnic communities within industrialized societies (for example, in many African-American communities, in Appalachia, in Native American communities, in Hispanic communities), the family as extended kinship system is itself a network that often makes resistance to hegemonic culture possible. Within this network the role of women as organizers and builders of alliances is central. The family as an oppressive nuclear structure is here contrasted to the family as a kinship system that resists the dominant culture, "an extended family of kinsmen related chiefly through children but also through marriage and friendship, who align to provide domestic functions . . . fluctuations in individual household composition do not significantly affect cooperative arrangements."[3] Though these arrangements need not be romanticized because such arrangements are often still patriarchal in spite of the possibilities women may find within them to work together, within these groups "kinship ties (which may or may not be blood ties) take precedence over civic obligations and introduce children to resistance strategies" (Caulfield 1974, 83).

But for the character(s) Sarah, the family space or spaces have had to be so rigidly enforced in such impossible ways that they have turned into a grotesque funnyhouse. The impossibility and absurdity of oedipal requirements are here, as an outcome of these mimic middle-class, tortured family encounters, almost obsessively, nightmarishly reenacted in spite of their impossibility. And in some ways Sarah's search for a father whose place in the cultural system leads to devastating contradictions is central to this impossibility.

Sarah describes her Selves in this way:

The characters are myself: the Duchess of Hapsburg, Queen Victoria Regina, Jesus, Patrice Lumumba. The rooms are my rooms; a Hapsburg Chamber, a chamber in a Victoria castle, the hotel where I killed my father, the jungle. There are places myselves exist in. I know no places. That is I cannot believe in places. To believe in places is to know hope and to know the emotion of hope is to know beauty. It links us across a horizon and connects us to the world. I find there are no places, only my funnyhouse. Streets are rooms, cities are rooms, eternal rooms. I try to create a space for myself in cities. New York, the midwest, a southern town but it becomes a lie. I try to give myselves a logical relation but that too is a lie. For relationships was one of my last religions. I clung loyally to the lie of relationships, again and again seeking to establish a connection between my characters. Jesus is Victoria's son. Mother loved my father before her hair fell out. A loving relationship exists between myself and Jesus but these are lies. You will assume I am trifling with you, teasing your intellect, dealing in subtleties, denying connections then suddenly at a point reveal a startling heartbreaking connection. You are wrong. For the days are past when there are places and characters with connections with themes . . .

Too, there is no theme. No statements. I might borrow a statement . . . refusing to accept the fact that a statement has to come from an ordered force. I might try to join horizontal elements such as dots on a horizontal line, or create a centrifugal force, or create causes and effects so that they would equal a quantity but it would be a lie. For the statement is the characters and the characters are myself. (Kennedy 1971, 195)

In a revised version of the play, published in the collection *In One Act,* Kennedy leaves out the second paragraph, which connects the lack of a logical relationship to the impossibility of making statements. All further references to the play will be drawn from the revision.

The play opens with a version of the interlude, or dumb show, that allegorizes the collection of images that is to come. A woman wanders across the stage as if in a trance, carrying a bald skull. She appears to have no face and wears a yellowish-white mask with no eyes. Her hair is black, wild, and straight, falling to her waist. After she has left the stage one curtain opens to show another one behind it made of cheap white satin that looks like the lining of inexpensive caskets, stained, frayed, and gnawed by rats. The play's structure then begins to unfold, not only as a growth of images but also as collections of events "that unfold through episodes which lend rhythm to the action like the beats of a drum," in Geneviève Fabre's description (1983, 204).

Hair takes on importance throughout the play, its progressive loss equated with the loss of African-American identity. In folklore hair often symbolizes fertility or power over the person whose enemy might shear it. In this play, which begins with a bald head, various characters lose their hair, which slowly and nightmarishly falls out around them. Kinky black hair sticks out from the headpieces of all the European Selves, while the long, straight black hair that continually falls out is associated with the Sarah of mixed blood who tries to be as white as possible. In terms of white culture's imagery the further away from blackness one gets, the further away from evil and disease, but in this play the further away one gets from blackness, the more the hair falls out—the whiter the character, the balder. Sarah finds herself caught in the middle with patches of bald scalp and patches of long black hair: "But if I had not wavered in my opinion of myself, then my hair would never have fallen out. And if my hair hadn't fallen out, I wouldn't have bludgeoned my father's head with an ebony mask" (6). The landlady says of her, "She's suffering so till her hair has fallen out" (8).

The characters the Duchess of Hapsburg and Queen Victoria enlarge the concept of character as materialized trope because of the weight of their historical figurations. As Kennedy said of Victoria in an interview, "It always seemed to amaze me that one person could have a whole era named after them" (Lehman 1977, 46). As a historical character, Victoria is a trope of history itself, lending her name to the era of English capitalism's greatest colonial epoch and its participation in rearranging cultural logics all over the globe. The Duchess of Hapsburg, too, signifies a family whose intrigues were generalized to the level of world history in the Holy Roman Empire; in these intrigues marriage strategies were used politically on a grand scale to amass an empire.[4]

Yet Kennedy's refusal to separate categories finds that these tropes also include Hollywood and mass culture, for the Duchess of Hapsburg connects history to the movies. Kennedy, who loved movies as a child and hid movie magazines under her mattress to hide them from her mother, draws on another Duchess of Hapsburg here: Bette Davis (who is also a very important character in another of her plays, *A Movie Star Has to Star in Black and White*), from the Hollywood film *Juarez*, which also appropriates or capitalizes on while collapsing the complex layerings of Mexican history. Some time before writing *Funnyhouse* Kennedy visited Chapultepec Palace in Mexico City and bought postcards of the Duchess of Hapsburg, who became, she says, "one of my character's most sympathetic alter egos or selves. At the time in Mexico there seemed something amiss about European royalty living amid the Aztec culture. European royalty in an alien landscape. Soon my duchess of Hapsburg would exist in an alien persona, that of the character of the Negro writer" (1987, 96).

The fragmentation and reconstruction of all these selves is held

together by name, of course, but also by the haunting repetition of a
continual knocking in the scenes where there are different characters
onstage simultaneously but separately. Though the characters cannot be
linked in any relationship with one another—they appear in heterogeneous, contiguous spaces—this repeated knocking intrudes into the separate spaces, linking them obliquely through their separate relationships
to its knocking. This linkage proves to return obsessively to the family
space, for the knock proves to be that of the black father. Jesus describes
this knocking in words that mingle with the words of other characters
as they wander about, speaking the same lines, in the metaphoric space
of the tendrilled, wild, savage jungle. The "Dark Continent," however,
is shown in a garish light that emphasizes the constructedness of this
coding from the direction of white culture:

> In the jungle, RED SUN, FLYING THINGS, wild black grass.
> The effect of the jungle is that it, unlike the other scenes, is over the
> entire stage. In time this is the longest scene in the play and is played
> the slowest, as the slow, almost standstill stages of a dream. By
> lighting the desired effect would be—suddenly the jungle has over-
> grown the chambers and all the other places with a violence and a
> dark brightness, a grim yellowness.
>
> JESUS is the first to appear in the center of the jungle darkness.
> Unlike in previous scenes, he has a nimbus above his head. As they
> each successively appear, they all too have nimbuses atop their heads
> in a manner to suggest that they are saviours.
>
> JESUS: I always believed my father to be God.
> (Suddenly they all appear in various parts of the jungle, PATRICE
> LUMUMBA, the DUCHESS, VICTORIA, wandering about
> speaking at once. Their speeches are mixed and repeated by one
> another:)
> JESUS: I always believed my father to be God.
> All: He never tires of the journey, he who is the darkest one, the
>   darkest one of them all. My mother looked like a white woman,
>   hair as straight as any white woman's. I am yellow but he is black,
>   the darkest one of us all. How I hoped he was dead, yet he never
>   tires of the journey. It was because of him that my mother died
>   because she let a black man put his hands on her. Why does he

keep returning? He keeps returning forever, keeps returning and returning and he is my father. He is a black Negro. I am tied to a black Negro. They told me my Father was God but my father is black. He is my father. I am tied to a black Negro. He returned when I lived in the south back in the twenties, when I was a child, he returned. Before I was born at the turn of the century, he haunted my conception, diseased my birth . . . killed my mother. He killed the light. My mother was the lightest one. I am bound to him unless, of course, he should die.

But he is dead.

And he keeps returning. Then he is not dead.

Then he is not dead.

Yet, he is dead, but dead he comes knocking at my door.

(20–21)

Her father returns, knocking, to prove to her that she is black, while simultaneously revealing the gap between himself and the culturally legitimate space of a father. As a young man, he had spent time in Africa as a Christian missionary, "dedicating his life to the erection of a Christian mission in the middle of the jungle" (9). He signifies both jungle and attempts to order that jungle in the interests of Christianity. The cultural condensation increases, as Jesus' identity, too, is stacked onto this site of the father: "He wrote her from Africa where he is creating his Christian center in the jungle"; and

My father . . . his mother from the beginning in the kerosene lamp of their dark rooms in Georgia said: I want you to be Jesus, to walk in Genesis and save the race, return to Africa, find revelation in the midst of golden savannas, nim and white frankopenny trees, white stallions roaming under a blue sky, you must walk with a white dove and heal the race, heal the misery, takes us off the cross. . . . At dawn he watched her rise, kill a hen for him to eat at breakfast, then go to work down at the big house till dusk, till she died. (14)

His father, however, "told him his race was no damn good" (14).

Repetition, in this case, the repetition of the knock as well as of the various phrases characters speak, was one of the characteristics of Kuntu drama Harrison identified, marking its African resonance. This repetition of phrases or sounds in drama might also be related to the vernacular traditions of African drama and the rhythmic backgrounds of African music fitted to the beats of drums. The regularity provided a way of translating tonal languages that were difficult to transcribe phonetically, so that the drum became a "cultural matrix through which all messages pass," as Geneviève Fabre suggests (1983, 207).

This rhythmic articulation sets up a kind of mystical effect, which also draws on something whose ground is Europe and Hollywood and West Africa. Kennedy's mother, she tells us, read the psalms to her in the kitchen on winter evenings (after listening to "Stella Dallas"). Later the effects of actresses speaking monologues from *Funnyhouse* and *The Owl Answers* suggested to her the kind of trancelike effect she felt while listening to warm, intimate readings of the psalms in her mother's kitchen and sharing troubles in women's talk around the kitchen table. After traveling to Africa the power of such rhythmic articulations took on another dimension through her encounter with African culture, which gave it "a new power, a fierce cadence."

Rhythm also suggests a way of reorienting attention from the signified to the signifier and defining what is meant by the materiality of the signifier, its thingness, as Gates argues. That is, the sense of the syntactical ordering or the semantic meaning may become secondary to the meaning making of the repeated sounds; in this way a move that "redirects attention from the semantic to the rhetorical" focuses on words as things and allows an opening for "the meanings that lie in wait along the paradigmatic axis of discourse" to bear more strongly on the syntagmatic axis (Gates 1988, 58).

The black father who had ostensibly gone to Africa to teach Christianity and to carry out the wishes of his mother brings into relief the role Christianity plays in Sarah's confusion. Her mother had aligned herself with Mary in a Christian family when she gave birth to a son, but the Christian Holy Family is modeled on a virgin birth with a son whose father is God. Conceiving a black son by a black father reveals the contradiction: the black father/Father/God homology is impossible in white culture. A black man in white culture created in the image of God would ostensibly have to be white; the jarring dissonance of this impossible conflation shows up in Fanon's description: "a normal child raised in a normal family will be a normal man. . . . A normal Negro child having grown up within a normal family will become abnormal on the slightest contact with the white world" (Fanon 1967, 142).

Sarah's father, like Sarah herself, is a highly complex border character. Though he has been charged with enacting the redemption story of
white Christianity for his black people in Africa, another part of his
image stands for the evil Christianity attempts to purge. Connected to
abjection and pollution, the coding of blackness has been fundamental
to the symbolic privileging of whiteness. Because of the very coding of
his body, a kind of "uniform" of race he wears, her father can never *be*
Christ but only a mimic Christ, the slave in the master's clothes: the
yellow Jesus. (This impossibility of *being*, of course, can also be seen
positively as an element in strategies of resistance that emphasize the
theatricality, the naïveté of any notion of identity.) He can only mimic
Christ as a mimic Man, the slave in the master's clothing.

Another part of his image is that of the black father as savage,
threatening, violent. In the play he is never visible himself but, instead,
is described by the characters and heard in the repeated knocking. After
the repetitions of his knock, all rush around in the tall grass then stop
and speak in a chant:

I see him. The black ugly thing is sitting in his hallway, surrounded
by his ebony masks, surrounded by the blackness of himself. My
mother comes into the room. He is there with his hand out to me,
groveling, saying—Forgiveness, Sarah, is it that you will never forgive me for being black.
Forgiveness, Sarah, I know you are a nigger of torment.
Why? Christ would not rape anyone.
You will never forgive me for being black.
Wild beast. Why did you rape my mother? Black beast, Christ
would not rape anyone.
He is in grief from that black anguished face of his. Then at once
the room will grow bright and my mother will come toward me
smiling while I stand before his face and bludgeon him with an
ebony head.
Forgiveness, Sarah, I know you are a nigger of torment. (21–22)

The black father has been inscribed as grotesque and horrible, the
very personification of disease and evil, and this coding shows up in the
place where the white father, created in the image of God, ideally *should*
have been. But in Kennedy's universe the black father is also partially
inscribed with white culture's imagery of black men as rapists, a part of

white supremacy's cultural unconscious that makes it difficult to analyze aggression by men within black families. The father takes on the cultural shame assigned to blackness and begs Sarah for forgiveness in a guilt that circulates freely among abject subjects. She, too, had wanted forgiveness for bludgeoning him with an ebony mask. But for both of them the only place from which absolution can be given is the place where their guilt was assigned, the site of the White Father.

These Sarah characters thus find neither absolution nor coherence, partially because the father has none but also because the mother's place is highly ambiguous, for it is she who is symbolically powerful, in one sense, because she is associated with the light and is closer to whiteness, or racial normality. But her lightness is a result of passive causality, whatever privilege she might have largely a result of the history of the sexual exploitation of slave women by white masters, who had the power not only to exploit the labor of female slaves but their bodies as well. As bell hooks argues, the story of African-American women has to do with the "psychosexual history of slavery that explores the meaning of white male sexual exploitation of black woman [and] the politics of sexuality." Her argument is part of a broader look at the way histories of resistance in the African-American community have largely told only about men's resistance: "There is no discussion of sexual sadomasochism, of the master who forced his wife to sleep on the floor as he nightly raped a black woman in bed" (hooks 1989, 57). This history of white men's use of black women's bodies also shows up the cultural logic of purity for what it is, a phobic nostalgia for a "purity" that never was.

Sarah's mother had died in an asylum, after she went crazy and lost all her hair following her stay in Africa and her rape there by Sarah's father, all of these events presented as phantasmatic, nightmarish situations with no guide to reading what "really" happened ("Then in Africa he started to drink and came home drunk one night and raped my mother. The child from the union is me"[14]). Before her death Sarah's mother had spent her time walking through the night and talking only to owls, the totem animal of women in many cultures and, in particular, in many African cultures. A totem animal functions to unite members of a particular social group by means of ritual relationships; a totem could unite a tribe, a clan, or other groups whose members believe they are descended from a totem ancestor. The totem itself works as a group symbol and a symbolic protector of the members of the group. The totem owl here ambiguously begins to take shape as a totem of women.

But the relationship among women is fraught with tension and contradictions. As Sarah turns from her father to her mother, she finds that she has been rejected by her mother because her mother blames her for trapping her in her blackness. That is, as a dark child, she proved her mother's lightness to be a lie, though, as Sarah says, "her straight hair and fair skin and grey eyes [are] so identical to mine" (14). As the MAN carrying a mask says, "in my sleep I have been visited by my bald crazy mother who comes to me crying, calling me to her bedside. . . . She comes to me, the bald skull shining. Black diseases, Sarah, she says. Black diseases. I run. She follows me, her bald skull shining. That is the beginning" (11–12).

The part of Sarah who is the yellow Christ discovers a feature of Christian logic, that is, that Christ's "raging apocalypses tried to escape being black." This shrunken yellow Jesus later kills Patrice Lumumba with an axe blow to the head when this Jesus discovers that his father is black; in this murder the biblical logic of the Apocalypse as final purgation intersects with imperialism's logic of ridding Africa of its militant leaders.

The longest scene in this montage of scenes takes place in the jungle, and by this time the color white has come to be associated, in the masks of the characters and in the lighting, with a deathly pallor and fixation. It is the color white, associated with leprosy and sterility, that produces the reified cultural imagery that kills. This deathly white is reinforced by the huge plaster statue of Queen Victoria that looms over scenes that take place in her room, "a thing of astonishing whiteness," and, as Raymond has told her, "it is a thing of terror, possessing the quality of nightmares, suggesting large and probable deaths. And of course he is right." Victoria, says the NEGRO, "wants me to tell her of whiteness. She wants me to tell her of a royal world where everything and everyone is white and there are no unfortunate black ones. For as we of royal blood know, black is evil and has been from the beginning. Even before my mother's hair started to fall out. Before she was raped by a wild black beast. Black was evil" (5).

As a daughter, Sarah proves to be doubly contaminated because she is both black and female. As she tries to gain some agency from this position, she can only attempt to kill her father by bludgeoning him with an ebony mask in order to avenge and placate her mother. The real effect of this murder, however, is her own suicide, for in killing her father for his blackness and rejecting her mother as part white and female, she also kills and rejects herself. She finally hangs herself in her room to the noise of knocking, as "her FATHER'S black figure with bludgeoned hands rushes upon her, the LIGHT GOES BLACK and we see her hanging in the room" (22).

The landlady, who with garishly loud laughter has played her role as the carnival gatekeeper at the entrance to the Funnyhouse, tells the poet Raymond, Sarah's lover, that Sarah hanged herself in despair over her father's suicide in his Harlem hotel room after learning of Patrice Lumumba's murder in Africa. But her father, like everything else, may not exist except in his ebony masks:

RAYMOND: She was a funny little liar.

LANDLADY: Her father hung himself in a Harlem hotel when Patrice Lumumba died.

RAYMOND: Her father never hung himself in a Harlem hotel when Patrice Lumumba was murdered. I know the man. He is a doctor, married to a white whore. He lives in the city in a room with European antiques, photographs of Roman ruins, walls of books and oriental carpets. Her father is a nigger who eats his meals on a white glass table. (23)

Sarah, whose ancestors are all out of place, found herself in a kind of limbo, unable even to "stay in her place" because there was not one for her. This limbo has to do with owls as ancestors, a theme Kennedy suggests in this play and develops more fully in *The Owl Answers*. The excess here locates an untheorized absent presence of a "speechless" African-American woman, and, by so doing, the play points to the importance of theater in analyzing the conditions that make discourse possible. For, says Anne Ubersfeld, theater is the privileged place for bodies to speak and to expose the relationship between bodies and symbols, materiality and grammar, like the theatrical performance that links Sarah's death to her inability to speak: "Theater speaks not so much words as how one can or cannot speak" (Ubersfeld 1978, 253).

The Owl Answers

Another of Kennedy's one-act plays, from a collection entitled *Cities in Bezique,* is *The Owl Answers.* It was first presented at the New York Shakespeare Festival Public Theater in January 1969 and produced by

Joseph Papp. Bezique (from the French *bésigue*) is the name of a card game in which a player can win by coupling the Queen of Spades and the Jack of Diamonds. The cities of the title are not real cities, though real cities are important to this play—Savannah, New York, and London. New York is represented by an enclosed subway car with slamming metal doors and London by the Tower of London with clanging gates.

The fragmentation of character is at issue in this play, too:

> The characters change slowly back and forth into and out of themselves, leaving some garment from their previous selves upon them always to remind us of the nature of She who is Clara Passmore who is the Virgin Mary who is the Bastard who is the Owl's world. (25)

The play returns to the family space, but this time the mother is black; she is the Bastard's Black Mother who is the Reverend's Wife who is Anne Boleyn. The father (or at least one of them) is white; he is Goddam Father who is the Richest White Man in the Town who is the Dead White Father. These white fathers fade into the Reverend Passmore, who is black. The other characters are a White Bird who is Reverend Passmore's Canary who is God's Dove, and there are the Negro Man, Shakespeare, Chaucer, and William the Conqueror.

Kennedy's plays almost always include a woman caught in a family relationship where there are tensions and hostilities that circle around the question of mixed race and the conflict between light and dark skin. The theme of the mulatto in African-American literature has its own repertory of stereotypes which come out of the way black women have been portrayed in novels and drama by both black and other writers. Sherley Anne Williams describes the limited range of images for black women:

> On the one hand, the ham-fisted matriarch, strong and loyal in the defense of the white family she serves (but unable to control or protect her own family without the guidance of some white person), and, on the other, the amoral, instinctual slut. Between these two stereotypes stood the tragic mulatto: too refined and sensitive to live under the repressive conditions endured by ordinary blacks and too colored to enter the white world. (1978, vii)

The mulatto has also been used to mark the danger of importing subversion into the pure heart of the white family. This danger shows up with particular virulence in D. W. Griffiths's coded mulatto and the freed slave in *Birth of a Nation*.

Throughout Kennedy's play, She Who Is tries frantically to bring some sort of order to the pages of writing that constitute the chaotic stacks of notebooks she always has with her. While pages continually fall all around her like leaves, these notebooks remain in a jumble no matter what order she tries to give them. She frequently glances intensely at a page then drops it, distracted, before returning to it later with a repetitive, desperate gesture. The notebooks contain letters to her father, the Goddam Father, the Richest White Man in Town, the Dead White Father. They are, she says, "communications, God, communications, letters to my father. I am making it into my thesis. I write my father every day of the year" (42).

These papers are not simply communications *to* the father but communications about getting him a proper burial in the soul of England, St. Paul's Chapel. The chapel is located in St. Paul's Cathedral in London and, according to tradition, stands on a hilltop, Ludgate Hill, where a Roman temple once stood. Rome plays an important role in Kennedy's work; here the symbolic weight of the dominant European culture links that culture with both England and Rome, with its historical legal and imperial connotations as well as its link to the Catholic church. But Rome also suggests her own love of reading stories of Caesar and of tracing the etchings from Dante's *Purgatory*. She also describes her enjoyment of sitting in her Latin classroom at school surrounded by drawings of ancient Rome on the walls. As an adult, she visited Rome and the places she had studied, these "ruins" of Rome a part of her history, like the ruins of England.

If the writing of She Who Is can bring about her father's burial, it will establish his legitimacy by proving his whiteness. Again in this play whiteness is initially equated with authenticity; if her father is white, he is an Englishman, not an Anglicized copy. And here whiteness implies a connection to an origin, someone original, someone who could be buried in St. Paul's Chapel as an equal of Shakespeare, Chaucer, and William the Conqueror, who represent the fathers of English culture. If she can prove that link, she can also legitimate her own connection to this cultural tradition.

Her relation to her father is complicated by her mulatto bastard birth, though, as a daughter, even her status as bastard is questionable, for there is no female term for a bastard. Clara is the educated spinster schoolteacher daughter of the Richest White Man in Town and the Bastard's Black Mother, "who cooked for somebody," her character indelibly marked by kinky hair. Ignored by the town as the illegitimate mulatto child of the cook and the master, Christianity emerges again in this play when she is recognized and named only upon her adoption by the Reverend Passmore and his pallid wife, their last name marking them as mimics. Within her border space she is referred to as Mary, her new legal name, positioning her in the family space that Christianity has marked out, the one reserved in symbolic imagery for the Virgin Mary.

This play returns again to the costs exacted by comparing families to the white Christian Holy Family, a model that constituted a backward step for women in the history of development, industrialization, and the growth of capitalism. In the Third World women were able to participate more fully in their communities before they were taught by missionaires and schoolteachers that their role was to be subservient in their individual relationships with men and before their economic role in agricultural economies was diminished with the introduction of market economies and wage labor that privileged the productive work done by men.

The name Mary seems to mark her out for special difficulty, as she is warned by the Reverend's Wife, who shows her a vial of blood: "These are the fruits of my maidenhead, owl blood Clara who is the Bastard Clara Passmore to whom we gave our name, see the Owl blood, that is why I cry when I see Marys, cry for their deaths, Owl Mary Passmore" (30–31). She explains what she means by reminding Clara that, as a wife, she herself accepted the biblical advice to imitate and identify with the Virgin Mary as a model of womanhood. But something did not work out, for the reverend came to her, obviously not understanding what Mary's duties were, not understanding that she was a Virgin: "Does he not know I am Mary, Christ's bride? What does he think? Does he think I am like your black mother who was the biggest whore in town? He must know I'm Mary. Only Mary would marry the Reverend Passmore of the church on the top of the Holy Hill. . . . We adopted you, took you from your bastard birth, Owl" (41). (There are three Holy Hills involved in the play: the hill in the small town, the hill in London upon which St. Paul's is built, and the hill upon where St. Peter's is located, the dome of St. Peter's in Rome framing the final scene.)

The training in womanhood that the reverend's wife had received prepared her to be Christ's bride, not man's. She could not do what the reverend wanted her to do if she did what Christ wanted. The Virgin Mary as a model for women counters the internal threat to that social group posed by female sexuality, but it may also produce a woman who takes Christ's message seriously and prefers virginity: "The Reverend took my maidenhead and that is why I am not a Virgin anymore and that is why you must be Mary, always be Mary, Clara" (37). At this point the reverend's wife and the Bastard's Black Mother merge into one.

The Virgin and the Whore coexist in Clara, whose character, now thirty-four and a teacher in Savannah, exists at another level as She, a mulatto who spends her time in Harlem picking up black men on the subway and taking them to a hotel room. They accuse her of lying about being the ancestor of her white father, using She's relationship with black men as proof that she cannot have a white father: "If you are his ancestor, what are you doing on the subway at night looking for men? What are you doing looking for men to take to a hotel room in Harlem? Negro men? Negro men, Clara Passmore?" (33).

She replies, "I am Clara Passmore. I am not His ancestor. I ride, look for men to take to a Harlem hotel room, to love, dress them as my father, beg to take me" (37–38). A "great dark bed" has meanwhile been dragged onto the stage by the Bastard's Black Mother, who is gradually becoming feathered like an owl, but throughout the rest of the play, as Mary/Clara/She talks, a White Bird laughs and mocks her speech. Clara has taken these black men to her hotel room to find love, but, as she says, "something always happens" to prevent it.

The religious difficulty of reserving oneself to be Christ's bride, Christianity's model of monogamous marriage based on the son's love for the mother, again mingles cultural and racial meanings. First of all, She has sought to prove that she is her White Father's ancestor. To be his ancestor, while she is at the same time his descendent, means that, in order to have conceived Christ (who is also her bridegroom and her father), she would have had to be Mary as Virgin. In other words, as the character of She/Clara/Mary is telescoped into a tense homology, so is Christ/Husband/White Father/God the Father.

To be her father's ancestor means that She would have to be either the Virgin Mary or a white son. A son gives birth to his father, as Herakles did to Zeus, for a father cannot be a father without a son, who legitimates him by turning him into a father. Through this legitimation of the father, the son becomes the father of the father—the ancestor. (Freud's logic, reinforcing that centrality, depends, as well, on the importance of the son as ancestor. Freud, the son, gives birth to the father, who legitimates Freud the son as well as the institution of psychoanalysis.) The daughter, however, cannot be either her father's ancestor or his descendent because she interrupts, rather than continues, his self-reproduction.

Besides the fact that she is female, She is also the mulatto daughter of the White Father, whose ancestors and descendents must all be white. Were She to prove to be his descendent, she might also prove to be his ancestor, but such a discovery would mark a very serious danger for him because it would mean that somewhere in his own white lineage, there had been black blood. The imaginary closed circle of pure white blood, like the closed circle of father and son, must enforce itself, dependent as it is on purity and sameness, even though the obvious fact that slaveowners' rights to slave women's bodies makes that purity impossible from the start. The phobic insistence on the myth of purity has to be all the stronger, the more impossible it is.

These complications in the father-son relationship also prevent a relationship between a man and a woman, the love She/Clara is looking for in all those Harlem hotel rooms. Her dream of love depends on finding the father, but, strangely, when she calls the White Father her communication always goes astray and is answered not by the father but by the owl. This strange totem marker of excess interrupts her attempts at communication:

> I call God and the Owl answers. It haunts my Tower calling, its feathers are blowing against the cell wall, speckled in the garden on the fig-tree, it comes, feathered, great hollow-eyed with yellow skin and yellow eyes, the flying bastard. From my Tower I keep calling and the only answer is the Owl, God. I am only yearning for our kingdom, God. (43)

As in *Funnyhouse,* the owl is associated with women, here with the Bastard's Black Mother and with border figures, the mulatto Clara and the female in the cultural universe of William Shakespeare and Geoffrey Chaucer: "Now they, my Black Mother and my Goddam Father who pretend to be Chaucer, Shakespeare and Eliot and all my beloved En-

glish, come to my cell and stare and I can see they despise me and I
despise them" (43). The owl connects the two women to the night and
to camouflage because of the owl's ability to be invisible during the day
and powerful when it is harder to see at night. The owl also suggests the
women's African antecedents and their horizontal, totemic relation to
each other. When the plea addressed to the father goes unanswered the
Owl answers from the darkness.

Kennedy began working with the image of a bird during the period
she spent in Accra in West Africa, where she bought an African mask
of a woman with a bird flying through her forehead. This same period
also brought together the linkage in her plays between being African,
having a female body, and the costs those two exact. In particular,
childbirth and blood come to be associated with owls, as in her description of an experience in West Africa:

> The owls in the trees outside the Achimota Guest House were close,
> and at night, because we slept under gigantic mosquito nets, I felt
> enclosed in their sound. In the mornings I would try to find the
> owls in the trees but could never see them. Yet, at night in the
> shuttered room, under the huge white canopied nets, the owls
> sounded as if they were in the very center of the room.
>
> I was pregnant again. And there were difficulties. I had to stay in
> bed for a week, as I bled. I listened to the owl sounds, afraid.
> (121–22)

In the play the mother has built a huge altar upon the stage, a High
Altar of owl feathers; she tells Mary/Clara/She that there is only one
way out of owldom, one way to St. Paul's Chapel. That way is death,
and at this point the mother kills herself with a butcher knife, "now part
the black mother and part the REVEREND'S WIFE in a white dress,
wild kinky hair, part feathered" (43).

She Who Is desperately calls upon God to recognize her, as a subway screeches, the music of Haydn is heard in the background, and a
black man tries to pin her down on the bed/altar:

> God, say "You know I love you, Mary, yes, I love you. That love
> is the oldest, purest testament in my heart." Say, "Mary, it was a
> testament imprinted on my soul long before the world began. I pray
> to you, Mary." God, say, "Mary, I pray to you. Darling, come to

my kingdom. Mary, leave owldom—come to my kingdom. I am awaiting you." (44)

As she begs Him to recognize her, the sentences begin to reveal an unsettling ambiguity in her request, for it is impossible to tell whether she still prays to God or whether she tries to get God to pray to Mary. Her calls to God begin to turn into calls to Mary/God: "I call god and the Owl answers . . . from the Tower I keep calling and the Owl answers" (43).

The black man, understanding nothing of her confusion, confused and frightened himself at her actions, tries to help her but cannot. The final scene assigns the last action to the White Father, whose breath ends the play. She Who Is ends, however, by speaking not His language but the owl's:

> Suddenly she breaks away, withdraws the butcher knife, still with the blood and feathers upon it, and very quickly tries to attack him, holds the knife up, aiming it at him, but then dropping it just as suddenly in a gesture of wild weariness. He backs farther. She falls down onto the side of the burning bed. The NEGRO MAN backs farther out through the gate. SHE, fallen at the side of the Altar burning, her head bowed, both hands conceal her face, feathers fly, green lights are strong, Altar burning, WHITE BIRD laughs from the Dome. SHE WHO IS Clara who is the Bastard who is the Virgin Mary suddenly looks like an owl, and lifts her bowed head, stares into space and speaks: Ow . . . oww. *(FATHER rises and slowly blows out candles on bed)*. (44–45)

Not finding any recognition from Him, she turns horizontally, obliquely toward owldom, to black women, to the memory of Africa, for even Mary's virginity could not keep her pure enough to be His ancestor. Owl blood has to be shed now, the fruits of her maidenhead; bloodied red rice will be tossed at her to mark her marriage. Her mother had pecked at the bloodied rice like a bird, marking both the female reproductive body as site of sacrifice in this sacrificial contract and an owl excess to it.

The lesson she learns near the burning bed, the High Altar to owldom, is obscure and double. The burning bed may mean both the sacrifice of women on it, or it may mean the sacrifice of the bed itself.

Owldom itself proves to be double. On the one hand, it stands for the loss of her maidenhead to representatives of the father and the association between animals and women produced by an oedipal logic's organization. But on the other, her mother's earlier question seemed clear: "Why be confused? The Owl was your beginning, Mary" (35).

Two possibilities have been laid out with great complexity. One presents the entry of She Who Is into the Dead Father's world: "Yes, my Mary, you are coming into my world. You are filled with dreams of my world. I sense it all" (34). Entry into that world inscribes her into his whiteness, with the father's breath reasserting its dominance, though by way of a mask; earlier, even though he was dead, he was still ambiguously powerful: "The DEAD FATHER removes his hair, takes off his white face, from the chair he takes a white church robe and puts it on. Beneath his white hair is dark Negro hair" (28).

That may be one reading of the ending. An equally possible reading finds the owl "voice" pointing obliquely to the speech that comes from the present absence of the missing conceptual space, a kind of speech not yet codified or quite interpretable but disruptive and resistant. What may appear negative from Christianity's perspective and from that of the cultural logic of purity—her contamination by her blackness and her femaleness—proves to be highly overdetermined with different possibilities for agency, for it is also the site of her linkage to owldom and to Africa.

A Lesson in Dead Language

The relationship between owldom, blood, and femininity is very important in the universe of Kennedy's other plays. In *A Lesson in Dead Language,* a short, dizzyingly concentrated work, her multilevel associations center on blood, the *sème* Kristeva isolates as the marker of borders, overdetermined because of its connections to both violence and intimacy, to life and death.

The lesson of the play's title is double; it seems to refer indirectly, on the one hand, to the site and space of lessons and, because the play takes place in a schoolroom with artifacts and pictures dealing with Roman history, to Latin as the representative of the language and Law, through its religious, legislative, and imperial history. On the other hand, the lesson of the title refers to the lesson women must learn about their entry into civilization, and on this level the dead language may refer to the language of the mother. The Symbolic is built upon the writing of the body from the earliest days of caregiving and on the constant propping of signification on that written body.

In *Funnyhouse* the dead language was the Symbolic, the reified words and images that kill and petrify subjects through the Father's agency and His power to "subject" subjects. In *The Owl Answers* a move was made toward a different language whose enunciation ambiguously and dangerously, even eerily, seems to "double" or haunt phallocentric language. In *A Lesson in Dead Language* language is more directly connected to bodily inscription. The play takes place in one of the centers of the reproduction of culture, the classroom, where a great white dog sits at the front of the room. An actress plays this role costumed from the waist up as a dog in a begging position, the audience unable to see any personal expression because of an immobile white dog mask, the mask of the mimic. As she speaks the lesson aloud to her young female pupils (the stage directions do not specify their race), they write the lesson "in unison with their arms on imaginary tablets. What they write they speak aloud" (48). Their lesson consists of this basic sentence which they must continually, obsessively repeat and write: "I bleed, Teacher. I bleed. I am bleeding, Mother" (48).

The character called the WHITE DOG with her white mask may be a white bitch, and she has as her white female task to teach the young pupils in white organdy dresses their lesson; it is a lesson in what civilization will require of them, the white dog serving as civilization's stand-in. The young girls repeat after the teacher dully and in confusion, occasionally breaking off the recitation to call out to their mothers or to ask why they must learn the lesson, but the lesson goes on repetitively, like the dead father's knocking in *Funnyhouse*.

The schoolroom has walls topped by a ridge upon which rests larger than life-size statues of Jesus, Mary, Joseph, two wise men, and a shepherd. The imagery is dreamlike, as the religious figures coexist side by side with the young girls' reminiscences of a pet white dog they played with in the grass. Eventually, we learn that Jesus, Mary, and Joseph, like the little dog, were "friends of childhood" and that they all died at about the same time, when the bleeding started. That was also a time when Caesar, the sun, and, by extension, the Father died. When no one will come forward to admit having killed the white dog, the sun, and Caesar, all the little girls have to bleed as punishment for their deaths. In the structure of passive causality the murder of Caesar, or the Father, whose responsibility Freud attributes to the sons, is assigned as guilt to the little girls, who must atone for it in their bodies.

The assignment of female guilt here is structurally similar to black guilt and Jewish guilt in the cultural logic of purity. In another of Kennedy's plays, *A Rat's Mass,* two black children, one male and one female, are assigned blood guilt by a privileged white playmate named Rosemary, and this blood guilt is compared to the blood guilt the Nazis are punishing in Europe. Here on the playground the female who left blood on the slide must also be punished, as all three—blacks, Jews, women— are metaphorized as rats: "Now there will always be rat blood on the rat walls of our rat house just like the blood that came onto the slide." All rats are eligible: "Everywhere I go I step in your blood" (62).

As these hallucinatory images float about in the almost trancelike scene of the lesson, circles of blood begin to grow on the backs of the girls' white dresses, as they become more and more subdued. The beginning of their menstruation is also the beginning of their domestication, for disciplined reproduction replaces the powerful generativity whose control Kristeva saw as part of the history of Western logic. Here reproduction is put to the use of civilization as the menstrual period marks the girl's suitability for sexuality, which is constrained in the interests of reproduction. In Kennedy's work blood is also ominously and frighteningly connected to the dangers of miscarriage and to the bleeding that occurs with childbirth.

But the other lesson menstrual blood might have taught the girls in an owl logic is that "menstrual flow ignores the distinction virgin/ deflowered," as Luce Irigaray writes (1977, 211; my translation). In this configuration blood marks woman as woman without the need for penetration, blood that does not come from a wound made by man but of its own accord, comes from the woman, with or without penetration. The phrase "Lesson I Bleed" may also suggest relief at the sight of menstrual blood, which means a woman is not pregnant.[5]

The White Dog dictates the lesson again and again until the girls have mastered it: "I killed the white dog and that is why I must bleed" (49). The White Dog as mimic teaches the pupils to accept their guilt, like that assigned by Herakles to women. The reproduction of the father/ son lesson taught by Herakles to Hyllos is here circulated through the words of the white bitch, a woman herself. In European folklore the white dog was often an embodiment of the spirit of the harvest or generativity, which lurked in the field until all the corn was harvested.

The person who cut the last sheaf of corn was said to "kill the dog." This kind of conquest of generativity may be part of the lesson the girls learn. In the Thargelian ritual of Greece in Sophocles' time, the ritual that was underway at the opening of Oedipus the King, the spirit of generativity had already been "killed" or culturally located as part of phallic power which required the fertility of women, land, and animals as its medium.[6] The girls are, in some measure, marked in this lesson as the field upon which the crop will be planted, rather than part of the power that makes the crop possible.

The teacher as White Dog, or white teacher, had long ago been domesticated. In the final scene the White Dog becomes an expressionless human being with a "bland human face," an undifferentiated white human mask, and the religious statues change into Roman statues. Religion and Law legislate sexual difference, and the girls repeat Calpurnia's words in what seemed to be concern over the death of Caesar: "Calpurnia dreamed a pinnacle was tumbling down" (51). At the end of the play, however, the pinnacle that was Caesar proves to be the pinnacle that was the girls: "I bleed. I bleed. Ever since I became a woman. I bleed. Like Caesar will I bleed away and die? Since I became a woman blood comes out of me. I am a pinnacle tumbled down" (52). The blood spots have been growing grotesquely, brightly, threateningly, as the pupils stand with their heads hung, ashamed, their fertility now completely reinscribed through this mark of horror and shame. The blood of reproductive bodies has now become the sign of defilement.

The girls speak of a game of lemons they played in the sun on the green grass; by now this story has come to suggest an old, popular use of lemons for contraception and, in the related shame, the use of lemons to lighten the skin. The pupils, by the end of the lesson, simply repeat the teacher's words "as if translating," haltingly, numbly, but with finality. The WHITE DOG "turns slowly about a full circle, revealing a blank human face. . . . 'And what is the answer? Translate what I read'" (53). One of the students raises her hand, is recognized with a nod, and answers after a long pause: "Calpurnia dreamed a pinnacle was tumbling down" (53).

There are two dead languages here, that of the Law, powerful in its hollow deathliness, and the language of the young girls that is being written over and translated. This lesson in blood, corporeality, and shame has also all along kept sexuality and violence in close proximity. The blood stands not only for fertility but, as Geneviève Fabre argues, for "the sign of sexual games that end in death. [In this play] all the images of birth are conveyed with visions of death, and every game leads to an inevitable fall" (1983, 121).

A Movie Star Has to Star in Black and White

Another of Kennedy's plays moves directly to the specificity of the female reproductive body and the way it disrupts what might be called a universal aesthetic disposition like the one that has marked the history of dramatic criticism. In poststructuralism the universal aesthetic disposition has been dissected and shown to be an effect not only of discourse but also of the material conditions of existence that are, among other things, "rarest because most freed from economic necessity,"as Pierre Bourdieu argues. The partiality or specificity of those rarest conditions most often passes unnoticed, even though these conditions are, paradoxically, so obvious: "The most 'classifying' privilege thus has the privilege of appearing to be the most natural one" (Bourdieu 1984, 56).

But it is not only economic privilege that makes itself invisible. An aesthetic disposition in poststructuralism still often means that the privilege of indifference is available to critics for whom gender remains a marker of femininity, not masculinity, and race a marker of the non-white, not the white. This aesthetic disposition allows a critic to forget his or her dialectical relationship to necessity and his or her own historical possibilities of distance from it, which may be quite different from that available to other kinds of subjects.

In particular, this aesthetic nostalgia is elicited in the face of questions about the specificity of the female reproductive body, questions that are linked in very intimate ways to racism. Discussions of David Lynch's films or those of Brian de Palma, for example, often depend on intricate aesthetic descriptions of the way each director foregrounds the devices and strategems of representation, though their films eerily mirror representations that are much too familiar from their regular occurrence in far less experimental films and in life, generally depending on violence against women. But there is a presumption that pointing out constructedness by repeating the constructions, only this time at an ironic remove, is somehow enough. The response to criticism of that irony, however, is that representation, like gender, is constructed. Yet, strangely, once we have all stopped believing in the biological truth of gender, its effects in terms of constructing the site of knowledge production are presumed to have gone away. It is here that a curious "blurring," a strange effacement of the theorist's subject position, links back up with Bourdieu's description of the main characteristic of the aesthetic disposition, its "privilege of indifference" to legitimacy.[7]

Kennedy disrupts this legitimacy by her insistence on the female specificity of birth, but, in order to situate her play *A Movie Star Has to Star in Black and White* in relation to a cultural refusal of female specificity, I first want to make a provisional horizontal comparison among several cultural discourses where that specificity is, at the moment, being refused, as we find ourselves in a continuation of what Susan Jeffords calls "the remasculinization of America." This comparison might help foreground a broad structural feature that still constrains the poststructuralist study of differences. The elements of these discourses include: (1) the fact that on cable television, there is a channel called the Family Channel, where the shows one can watch on weekends are those old "family" standbys: "Bonanza,"[8] "Wagon Train," "The Rifleman," "Gunsmoke," and "The Big Valley." The most striking thing about the Family Channel is that these families, for the most part, have been cleaned up of women. These are basically families made up of white men who are busy taming the West—cleaning it up in the interests of the middle-class white, Christian, decent Body;[9] (2) the fact that the Gulf war, the supposed origin of a "New World Order," planned and executed by men, was billed as the "Mother of All Wars," and the spectacular celebration of it, the "Mother of All Parades"; and (3) the way many deconstructive or Foucauldian arguments show how the constructedness of masculine identity is destabilized by a reliance on a form of femininity that as often as not does not require women, a structure that in many ways appropriates femininity for its own project.

There seems to be a troubling risk of remasculinization in an increasingly overt but paradoxically invisible reliance on the specificity of the *masculine* body. As one example, the latest star on the poststructuralist horizon, Slavoj Žižek, offers as his figurative model of interpretation a "phallus" experience in which the radical exteriority of the body is figured by a phallus, the transcendental signifer with its "pulsation between 'all' and 'nothing.'" To explain the paradox of interpretation Žižek gives two examples. One has to do with the impossibility of control. That is, he says, referring to St. Augustine, "Someone with a strong enough will can starve to death in the middle of a room full of delicious food, but if a naked virgin passes his way, the erection of his phallus is in no way dependent on the strength of his will." And to show the opposite side of this riddle, he tells this joke: "What is the lightest object on earth?—The phallus, because it is the only one that can be elevated by mere thought" (1989, 223). There is here a striking instance of theoretical amnesia. No longer is any attempt made to distinguish between organ and figuration, even though, in the earlier days of La-canian theory, much ink was spilled attempting to do just that, to show that men really don't have "it" either.[10] Now it looks like they do. This overtly masculine figuration whose partiality founds the oxymoronic irony of poststructuralism (the point of coincidence between omnipo-tence and total impotence) serves, as did the earlier aesthetic model, as a universal model for interpretation and guarantees an indifference to le-gitimacy. But its partiality can be foregrounded by looking at the figura-tion of birth, for it is in and around discussions of birth and the maternal body, those places where the label of essentialism is most often pinned, that the most intense resistance to female specificity can be found.

Though this discussion of Kennedy and birth depends, in part, on a revisionary reading of psychoanalysis, Wayne Koestenbaum warns in *Double Talk: The Erotics of Male Literary Collaboration* that the origins of psychoanalysis, the discourse within which the paradoxical invisible but obvious relationship between phallus and penis gets organized, circle around an appropriation of femininity and, in particular, of birth by men: "By collaborating with Breuer, Freud sought to fuse male bonding and scientific labor, and to appropriate the power of female reproduc-tion" by way of a woman's hysterical birth giving, that of Anna O., or Bertha Pappenheim, who was to become a feminist activist. In that collaboration, argues Koestenbaum, the fantasized, or hysterical child-birth experienced by Anna O. and interpreted by Freud, "loses texture as a woman's experience, and becomes, within the history of psycho-analysis, a possession prized by a chain of male mentors and their dis-ciples" (Koestenbaum 1989, 18). Thus, Anna O.'s uterus figuratively becomes an anus, as Freud "erases the maternal and feminine origin of his science at the same moment as he stresses it." Anna O. is passed on as "male property, a representation of male intercourse" and of the "pleasure-giving, child-delivering hole in men" (14).

The abstraction and circulation of metaphors of birth here organizes a crucial intersection between symbolicity and bodies, and it is in the textualization and appropriations of birth where aesthetics and politics meet. The risks for feminism of talking about birth may, at this historical

moment, have to be taken, in order to dissect the masculinist appropriations of birth which accompany what is too often unambiguously called
"femininity."

These femininities, like these "births," are still to be disentangled.

The Political Economy of Spectacle: Hiding the Mess
from View

Life and discourse, or the destiny of subjectivity caught up in the claims
of civilization, are at the moment intensely focused on race and the
intimate control of women's sexuality. Adrienne Kennedy commented
almost twenty years ago on these intersections in *A Movie Star Has to
Star in Black and White,* first performed at the New York Shakespeare
Festival in 1976, directed by Joseph Chaikin. Like the plays of Lorraine
Hansberry, it long ago raised the kinds of questions about middle-class
African Americans that Spike Lee's movies are only now addressing
twenty years later. A feminist in a period of masculinist black nationalism, she was also a postmodern experimentalist in a period of realist
political drama and a woman writing very specifically about the consequences of the physicality of blackness and the bleeding, pregnant female
body when theoretical discourse could not account for those differences;
it still cannot. In this play what is available is, on the one hand, bloody
miscarriage and the complete responsibility for pregnancy and blood on
the part of the woman, even if she is a middle-class, African-American
intellectual who possesses some measure of cultural capital; and, on the
other hand, brain-damaged, military-related paralysis for her brother in
a white supremacist cultural logic.

The play stages the way photography and film insist on constructing
a family, within a site organized and coded by public culture within
what might now be described as the mode of information.[11] That is, as
Ian Angus and Sut Jhally argue, we are currently within a third stage of
capitalist formation in which the economic and the cultural are indistinguishable, the result of two earlier stages: *class* culture, from the beginning of industrial capitalist society in the seventeenth century, divided
into high culture and popular culture; from the turn of the century to the
1960s, *mass* culture, with homogeneous cultural products for mass consumption; and since the 1960s, *mass-mediated* culture of the mode of
information, accompanying "the explosion of electronic media, the shift
from print literacy to images, and the penetration of the commodity

form throughout all cultural production" (1989, 5). In this latest period of postmodernity, they argue, the construction of social identity is centered on a politics of images which produces staged differences, differences that are overlaid on the homogenized mass culture produced in the earlier cultural formation. These staged differences are, in some measure, differences without much difference, as their real inequalities lie hidden behind a screen of consumer goods. It is the implications of these differences without much difference, the way they show up in discourses that would ostensibly seem to be quite different, that need to be considered.

And within this mode of information it is spectacle that determines possibilities for representation and performs the move of abstraction away from materiality, where, as Guy Debord argues, "the tangible world is replaced by a selection of images which exist above it, and which simultaneously impose themselves as the tangible [itself] . . . . The spectacle consists in taking up all that existed in human activity [in order to] possess it in a congealed state as things which have become the exclusive value by their formulation in negative of lived value." Here "we recognize our old enemy, the commodity, who knows so well how to seem at first glance something trivial and obvious, while on the contrary it is so complex and so full of metaphysical subtleties" (Debord 1983, passage 35). As political economy circles back around to postmodern possibilities of representation, we find that this abstract spectacle, with its differences without much difference that unite the economic and the cultural to produce what Fredric Jameson calls the "omnipresence of culture," increasingly rests on a global opposition between an active, masculinized North and a feminized South, whose resource often is the cheap labor of nonwhite, female workers.[12] The majority of female workers who work to produce the chips for the mode of information are young women who must retire by the time they are twenty-five, after their eyesight has been ruined by the close work. They leave the work force, according to what Jennifer Wicke calls the employers' "beneficient fiction" that they will marry, a fiction that provides a justification for using them up and discarding them.

The mode of information makes possible a new elite, not of manufacturers or those who invest in production so much as those who invest in and work with information, what Robert Reich calls "symbolic analysts": management consultants, lawyers, software and design engineers, research scientists, corporate executives, financial advisers, advertising

executives, television and movie producers—and academics, poststructuralist critics as well as nuclear physicists or professors of finance (1991).
Within this cultural formation the mode of information's symbolic common denominator is its feminized debris.

Interrupting the Sanitized
Spectacle/Disgusting Bodies

Cultural reproduction and the reproduction of a culture thus both prove
to rest on while they displace the female reproductive body. *A Movie
Star* interrupts three classic Hollywood black and white movies—*Now,
Voyager* (1942), *Viva Zapata!* (1952), and *A Place in the Sun* (1951)—by
situating an African-American family within scenes from those movies
to draw attention to what is left over from the sanitized spectacle. This
dramatic use of cinematic imagery points to the ambiguous nature of the
relationship between technological reproduction and drama. On the one
hand, as Timothy Murray argues, the history of technology and technological reproduction, within which cinematic images are available to us,
is a continuation of the constraints imposed by the Western metaphysical
privileging of visibility, its ideology of vision, of the eye, the gaze. There
is, he argues, a complex relationship between the camera, transcendental
philosophy, and drama, a relationship that is a part of "theatre's institutional indebtedness to the technological tradition of monocular vision."[13]

Yet drama has its own specificity. Unlike film, it has to do with the
"presentational fact of the body," which both repeats and interrupts
historically produced images,[14] a "presentational" body that is not, however, simply an "empirically privileged place lying outside of the pene-
trating gaze performed daily by the mechanical production of film and
television" (Murray 1985, 117). Instead, there is much at stake in the
relationship between drama and cinema, what Murray calls "the character of a cinematic memory, a memory of corporal fragility in an age
where technology increases both the stakes and the potential of he-
gemonism" (118). No spectator at a dramatic performance, no actor
either, comes to a play without bringing along a cinematic memory, and
at the center of this cinematic memory is the "image of a living, breathing, but always fractured filmic body" (121). This is a body that is
always simultaneously corporeal and symbolic, reified and material, its
bodily/cinematic memory working through the senses. As Fredric
Jameson argues, it is "the senses that remember, and not the 'person' or

personal identity" (1990, 2). Though in film, especially, the privileged sense is vision—the obsessive insistence of the visual image, its repetition, functioning as the mark of this doubled colonization of the imagination—the intrusion of a very specific kind of coded body may prove to unsettle that visual privilege, to cause it discomfort and even disgust.

Kennedy's play consists of three scenes, each divided into a kind of double shared space. The characters are very specifically represented as mixtures, or, rather, sites that constantly and relentlessly metamorphose to bring together technologically available images and presentational bodies, as the presentational bodies of actors are brought into relationship with characters whose figurations layer several other kinds of cultural reproduction. Clara, the female lead, who is, however, called a bit player, comes from another Kennedy play, *The Owl Answers;* in that play her identity, like that of all Kennedy's female characters, is already multiple.

These metamorphoses make any enforcement of a separation between the public and private spheres impossible to enforce. Family characters who are grieving over the injured son lying in a hospital bed in a coma or the pregnant woman worrying about the bloody effects of pregnancy are characters who would normally be located in domestic and interior spaces reified here by static photos of the family. The family members find themselves, however, part of several scenes from the most public space of all in American culture, film. Their individual identities are thus immediately fragmented as they are inserted into and compared to the symbolic places publically provided for them by the films. This insertion sets up a shimmering, wavering movement between sites of subjectivity which simply do not match up, which will not fit. The jarring interruption—and insistence—of the cultural reproduction of "public personal" identities is achieved by having the leading roles played by "actors who look exactly like: Bette Davis, Paul Henreid, Jean Peters, Marlon Brando, Montgomery Clift, Shelley Winters. (They all look exactly like their movie roles)" (80). The supporting roles are played by an African-American family, "the mother, the father, the husband (They all look like photographs Clara keeps of them except when they're in the hospital)." The cinematic and photographic images of the characters are thus eerily located onstage alongside the bodies of the actors in a direct staging of filmic bodies. (Kennedy herself was named after an actress, Adrienne Ames, whose movie her mother saw while she was pregnant [Kennedy 1987, 10].) The personal or subjective, whatever might be called individuality or specificity, shimmers within the "omnipresence of culture" alongside very particular family identities. And hovering over Kennedy's investigation of cinematic memory is the transcendental figure who alternately metamorphoses into Clara then exists singly and symbolically: the Columbia Pictures Lady.

The opening scene of the play, staged like all the scenes in shades of black and white, includes movie music that "throughout is romantic" and plays whenever Clara is not thinking aloud. The scene brings together a hospital lobby and the ship's deck from *Now, Voyager,* directed by Irving Rapper.[15] Characters are the Columbia Pictures Lady, Bette Davis, and Paul Henreid. Wandering into the scene are the mother, the father, and the husband, who are African-American, or Negro, as Kennedy calls them because of the period in which she follows them, the 1950s in Cleveland, for the most part. Bette Davis alternately speaks as if she were a member of the family talking about segregation in Georgia and racism in Cleveland then as if she were a character, Clara, a character from *The Owl Answers,* who most often introduces autobiographical elements into the plays. Clara is partially based on a girl, Sarah Clara, who lived in the neighborhood near Kennedy's grandmother's house, her beauty envied by all the other girls. The overdetermined site of this character layers identifications with different people and different variations of female beauty, drawing on idealizations and inevitable failures of ordinary women to live up to them. That difficulty is multiply complicated by issues of lightness and darkness within the African-American community itself, an issue that haunts this as well as every other Kennedy play and is part of her relationship to her mother.

Now, Voyager has had a special appeal to North American movie audiences, perhaps especially women. Bette Davis plays a homely, supposedly mentally disturbed spinster who escapes from her rich, domineering mother, undergoes therapy with a fatherly psychologist,[16] meets a man on a cruise, and metamorphoses into a fascinating, independent woman, who heroically takes care of everyone and steals the movie by her very presence—the presentational intrusion of Bette Davis as actress into the narrative of the film. The character in Kennedy's play does not use the name of the character in the movie, Charlotte; instead, she uses the name of the actress, Bette Davis. At the end of the film Davis's character makes a female sacrifice that, in effect, removes the sexualized female body from the movie. Because of her love for Paul Henreid, she agrees not to consummate their love but, instead, to serve as a pure,

abstracted mother *figure* to his teenage daughter. No birth, no vagina
need intrude.

The history of that movie is also layered. Taken from a popular
novel by Olive Higgins Prouty, the screenplay changed important features of the novel: the mother was made meaner, the supportive
influence of the sisters was changed to emphasize their pettiness, and the
male lead was changed from someone who was himself also a mental
patient to someone perfectly sane, a kind of substitute for the real father
figure of the movie, the psychiatrist. Dana Polan argues that the psychiatrist's position works to guarantee Bette Davis a star image in a "kind
of self-promotion of cinema," over and above the narrative of the film.
It is through his mediation that Charlotte's metamorphosis can coincide
"with the emergence on the screen of that Bette Davis that audiences
have come to the film to see; without [his] intercession, Charlotte would
have remained an inadequate Davis, not at all the image that she is
supposed to have in the Hollywood mythology" (1986, 168). It is the
mythology of Bette Davis that Kennedy cites.

Scene 1 then finds Bette Davis talking to Paul Henreid on the ship's
deck, but she is talking about an event linked to Kennedy's past: "June,
1955. When I have the baby I wonder will I turn into a river of blood
and die?" (83). Suddenly and quite unexpectedly, given the movie's
detour away from the bloody consequences of sexuality, the fear and
anxiety of giving birth is inserted into the play, the "giving" of birth
torn from its idyllic, abstracted connotations. Though in the movie Bette
Davis agrees to give birth cleanly and purely, the play's pregnant Negro
woman is involved with the liquids and blood of female reproductive
functions and the fear that this blood may represent for the woman
herself. One female figure has been cleaned up; the other, more closely
associated with the bleeding specificity of female bodies (whether the
blood has to do with pregnancy or menstruation), has not. Yet the
identities of the characters unpredictably and unsettlingly hover between
the two.

Onto the deck walks the Negro family as they looked in 1929 in
Atlanta, forerunners of Spike Lee's middle-class African Americans.
They are well dressed, attractive, the father wearing a Morehouse
sweater. Their discussion, as the only people of color on the ship deck
of the black and white movie, centers pointedly on the WHITE and
COLORED signs that were posted all around Cincinnati. The meaning
of such signs is evident here, though the signs themselves are invisible.

The dialogue does not work in any kind of traditional way but, rather, proceeds in additive layers, using one temporal stage moment as a node to join together a number of moments from other contexts and times, like condensation in the logic of dreamwork. One point of reference is the relation between the bleeding, pregnant body and July 1955, when Clara's husband returns after serving in the military in Korea. She is again pregnant, after having suffered a miscarriage alone: "When I lost the baby he was thousands of miles away. All that bleeding. I'll never forgive him. I was a virgin when we married. A virgin who was to bleed and bleed" (87). Soon after these violent images of blood and birth come passages borrowed from another Kennedy play, *The Owl Answers,* which draws on grotesque, frightening images: references to the burial of a white father and to a flying bastard owl, "Its feathers are blowing against the cell wall, speckled in the garden on the fig tree, it comes, feathered, great hollow-eyed with yellow skin and yellow eyes, the flying bastard" (89). Bastard imagery always refers, in Kennedy's plays, to Clara's self-representation as the child of a light-skinned, beautiful, educated mother and a dark Southern father, and the owl is a profoundly disturbing, camouflaged totem figure that links some sort of un-signifiable signification to mothers, night, childbirth, and Africa.

At this point in the play the conversations and metamorphoses then begin to refer to Clara's divorce, juxtaposed to Jean Peters's reference on her wedding night in *Zapata,* to *Lesson in Dead Language,* in *In One Act,* the play that frighteningly showed what the onset of menstruation means to young female students. The lesson they must learn is limitation, restriction, being left behind while husbands advance their careers, as was Kennedy. These girls reveal a growing numbed catatonia at the recognition that they are what is to be sacrificed in this sacrificial logic, as menstrual blood becomes the marker of the guilt and shame assigned to young girls the moment their bodies are capable not of beauty or ironic masquerade but, instead, reproduction. This lesson is condensed into the nuptial bed, the bed that begins to signify bleeding and Clara's divorce.

Then Bette Davis, standing at the *Now Voyager* railing, tells of her father's attempt to commit suicide by trying to jump off a roof and, instead, falling onto a scaffold. This happened on the afternoon after he had been presented an award by the mayor of Cleveland for his work raising money for a New Settlement building, which was to function as the center of the Negro community in Cleveland, his suicide attempt a jarring glimpse into the crevices of middle-class Negro respectability. Clara then displaces Davis and arrives back at the hospital room, where her brother Wally, a veteran who had been stationed in Germany, lies paralyzed long after something mysterious had happened to him there, resulting in his court martial, imprisonment, and subsequent psychological and physical destruction.[17] On his return he divorced his wife, returned to live with his mother, and spent much of his time in despair, driving the streets and drinking.

Scene 2 joins his hospital room to a scene from *Viva, Zapata!*: "There is no real separation from the hospital room and *Viva, Zapata!* and the ship lights as there should have been none in *Now, Voyager.* Simultaneously brighter lights come up stage center. Wedding night scene in *Viva Zapata*. Yet it is still the stateroom within the ship" (90). The film, directed by Elia Kazan and written by John Steinbeck, also has a history and a seductive appeal. Ultimately an anticommunist film with a message about the dangers of politics, its site of evil is a devilish, anachronistic Stalinist who abuses the power of literacy to manipulate the peasants. No Gringo capitalists are ever mentioned in this story of the Mexican revolution, and Steinbeck introduces a mystical element at the end of the story, a white horse, which was suggested to him by the socialist Diego Rivera's mural, showing Zapata with a white horse.[18] The peasants in Kazan's film learn to avoid anybody who claims to be a political organizer, and they learn, conveniently, to refuse power because it corrupts. That, later, many people came away from their first viewing of this film equating its mythical Zapata and his white horse with Che Guevara, however, shows the unpredictability of the reception of film, one of Kennedy's points.

On their wedding night Marlon Brando as Zapata, wearing brown makeup to look like a Mexican campesino, asks Jean Peters to teach him to read by using a Bible: "Teach me now. Get a book. . . . Begin." They both then sit chastely on the nuptial bed that seems to have been completely purified of all female sexuality; she reads, then he repeats after her: "In the beginning God created the heavens and the earth." Christianity, literacy and, finally, homosocial relations among men essentially organize and displace the specificity of female sexuality, for Brando has just spent much of his time at the window on their wedding night staring longingly out at Anthony Quinn, who plays his brother, and his revolutionary *compañeros* in the dusty street. Jean Peters now circulates in and out of the character of Clara and tells of standing by her brother's hospital bed, as he lies in a coma, then of losing her baby and being pregnant again: "MARLON BRANDO listens. They kiss tenderly. She stands up. She is bleeding. She falls back on her bed. BRANDO pulls a sheet out from under her. The sheets are black. Movie music. JEAN PETERS: The doctor says I have to stay in bed when I'm not at the hospital" (95–96).

The center of the movie scene, which Kennedy uses obsessively later in the play, is this bed with white sheets which organizes the movie shot, the bed whose sheets turn black in the play. The bed also sets up a comparison between two types of injury, or "wound," Clara's and her brother Wallace's, both of their wounds psychic as well as physical. The hospital bed of the returned, destroyed Negro veteran is symbolically linked to the bed in which the blood of miscarriage appears. And as Brando and Peters reenact the "teach me to read" scene in this play of many lessons, Clara's mother is teaching Peters another lesson by confronting Clara with the question of the guilty mother, a question related to the shame the girls had learned was signified by their bleeding bodies: "What did I do?" Here Clara's mother attempts to take the blame for Clara's divorce, for Wally's despair, for everything: "I don't know what I did to make my children so unhappy" (92). The hostile, almost violent, fragmented, obsessive family discussions that, throughout the play, continue to increase in tension have all circled around not only birth and miscarriage, accidents and injury, but also around the raging animosities, the near hatreds among members of the family, as the veneer of Family gets peeled away.

Scene 3 telescopes and condenses more overdetermined cultural sites. Jean Peters and Marlon Brando sit in the *Viva, Zapata !* scene. The static family photos rest above what has now become the bed in Clara's childhood room, which the ship lights from *Now, Voyager* illuminate. Then a small dark boat enters the stage from near the brother's darkened room on the edge. In it are Montgomery Clift and Shelley Winters from *A Place in the Sun*. This third movie tells the story of a working-class young man, Montgomery Clift, who dates a working-class girl, Shelley Winters, both of them lonely outsiders who live in depressing, drab rooming houses. She becomes pregnant, but Clift must get rid of her because, in the meantime, a beautiful, rich young heiress, Elizabeth Taylor, has fallen in love with him. He is portrayed as a sad, doomed lover, who finally takes Winters out in a rowboat, curiously leaving all kinds of clues and essentially letting her drown when she falls in the water. He does not directly cause her death, though he has set up the circumstances and then does nothing to help her.

The scene onstage reconnects the difficulties of being a woman artist constrained from every side by her family and then by her pregnancies; as Eddie says, "I have enough money for us to live well with my teaching. We could all be so happy." But from the boat Clara speaks, "Eddie says I've become shy and secretive and I can't accept the passage of time, and that my diaries consume me and that my diaries make me a spectator watching my life like watching a black and white movie. He thinks sometimes . . . to me my life is one of my black and white movies that I love so . . . with me playing a bit part" (99). While Eddie is critical of her for playing one kind of bit part, he wants her to play another.

Then in the boat Clara is displaced by Shelley Winters, who has obsessively returned to the family hostilities, this time those between Clara's mother and father in Cleveland: "He and my mother got in a fight and my mother started laughing. She just kept saying see I can laugh ha ha nothing can hurt me anymore. Nothing you can ever do, Wallace, will ever hurt me again, no one can hurt me since my baby is lying out there in that Hospital and nobody knows whether he's going to live or die. . . . My father said how goddamn crazy she was and they started pushing each other. I begged them to stop. My father looked about crazily" (100). This is part of a devil's pact, her son's injury the only thing that could provide her with the strength to resist her husband. A few lines later Shelley Winters tries to get Montgomery Clift to listen to her tell how her father came to her with whiskey on his breath to explain his behavior: "Now, your mother has always thought she was better than me. You know Mr. Harrison raised her like a white girl, and your mother, mark my word, thinks she's better than me" (101).

The lights then shift back to Jean Peters and Marlon Brando, as Jean Peters tells of Wally's gradual defeat, after being a track star in high school to moving from college to college then finally to the army, along the way "learning" his own lesson, to think of himself as a failure: "After he left the army he worked nights as an orderly in hospitals; he liked the mental wards. For a few years every fall he started to school but dropped out after a few months. He and his wife married right before he was sent to Germany. He met her at Western Reserve and she graduated cum laude while he was a prisoner in the stockade" (102).

Then the dark boat reappears, with Shelley Winters and Clara, who is crying; Montgomery Clift rows. Jean Peters, who, with Brando, is still obsessively changing the black sheets, says, "I am bleeding." Then, "quite suddenly SHELLEY WINTERS stands up and falls 'into the water.' She is in the water, only her head is visible, calling silently. MONTGOMERY CLIFT stares at her. She continues to call silently as for help, but MONTGOMERY CLIFT only stares at her. Movie music." As Winters calls "silently as for help," Clara speaks, telling of the doctor's conclusion that her brother will be brain damaged and paralyzed: "After he told us, my mother cried in my arms outside the hospital. We were standing on the steps, and she shook so that I thought both of us were going to fall headlong down the steps" (103). The last thing we see in the play is this: "SHELLEY WINTERS drowns. Light goes down on MONTGOMERY CLIFT as he stares at SHELLEY WINTERS drowning. Lights on CLARA. Movie music. Darkness. Brief dazzling image of COLUMBIA PICTURES LADY" (103).

The slow, sure inevitability of her drowning, her brother's paralysis, and her mother's loss are sealed by a transcendental, pure, white female figure.

The Signifying Economy of Purity: Coagulation or the Mirror Stage?

Something happens by way of these liquids involved in drowning and bleeding. Cinematic memory was based on the privilege of the visual, as Jameson argued; that is, he says, if an ontology of the present were still possible, "it would have to be an ontology of the visual, of being as the visible first and foremost, with the other senses draining off it" (1990, 1). Modernity, then postmodernity, transformed human nature into "this single protean sense." But something else is at work here in relation to the visual, as Kennedy dredges up other senses, the *sème* of blood perhaps most significantly trying to remind us of those senses. Blood simultaneously and eerily has to do with *both* life and death, its fluidity an unstable but vital margin. Because the fractured filmic body is always simultaneously propped between life and death, and corporeality and symbolicity, the ambiguous nature of blood's semiotic codings is intimately important. In attempting to describe Kennedy's interruption of the visual by the introduction of signs of blood, I want to turn to Julia Kristeva's concept of the *chora* and the related though not identical concept of the abject. Though the *Tel Quel* group with which Kristeva was associated has, in some measure, come to seem outdated in its insistence on the usefulness of avant-garde subversions of hegemony, the possibilities inherent in the work of the only woman member of that group still has much to say about the dissection of the predominance of the visual, which overwrites the relationship of the other senses to the maternal body. This is the question with which Kennedy is also concerned.

In particular, the mode of information and its spectacles seem to require such a Kennedy/Kristevan reading, or, as Kristeva argues, "It seems to me that the role of what is usually called 'aesthetic practices' must increase not only to counterbalance the storage and uniformity of information by present-day mass media, data-bank systems, and in particular, modern communications technology, but also to demystify the identity of the symbolic bond itself" (1982c, 35).

It is perhaps here that Jameson's "protean sense" might find its own critique, though he overlooks it. To repeat his claim about memory and film: "it is the senses that remember." Theorizing this sensual memory that chronologically predates yet discursively coexists with the effects of the mirror stage requires more than a theory of the gap between bodies and symbols, or the parodic ironizing of the forms of constructed representations. Instead, it requires reading more specifically the mixture of symbols and bodies, their inscription or coagulation, to use Cynthia Chase's term for "the inscription (not the image) of the archaic mother as productive dissolution" (1990, 128). And as Burgin says, "the abject can no longer be banished beyond some charmed, perfectly Euclidean circle" (1990, 119). It must be read.

Kennedy's pregnant female body and its continuing, frightening relationship to blood and hemorrhaging within the cinematic image conjures up that remainder of the maternal and draws on the memory of the other senses which the visual has covered over, this play perhaps serving as an allegory of the way movies are actually watched, both with the eyes and with the body. It may be that a theory of cinematic memory based only on the image has already bypassed most of the resources of memory that are drawn from interaction with the specificity of the spectator's body and its relation to the specifically female maternal body. There is, in Kristeva's theory, a kind of sight that precedes the mirror stage, a reduplication prior to the specular identification that takes place in the mirror stage, when in the child is first "imaged" in the Symbolic's mirror, the Imaginary. Prior to the Imaginary, however, is a prior sight, argues Kristeva, "a gaze in addition to sight [that asserts] itself as a

privileged universe, unfathomable as to desire." Its referent is "the outposts of our unstable identities, blurred by a drive that nothing could
defer, deny, or signify" (1989, 246).

As Heiner Müller writes about photographic images, though without recognizing the maternal connection: "Language is memory and
images are not. Images are too abstract. That's their danger: you blot
out memory with these kinds of images." And in another place he continues this resistance to the image: "The horrifying thing for me in this
is the occupation of the imagination by clichés and images which will
never go away; the use of images to prevent experiences, to prevent the
having of experiences" (1984, 79).

Birth, Mass Culture, and Mass-Mediated Aesthetics

The spectacle that Kennedy disrupts by a strategy of leakage is a sanitized
one from which a certain kind of femininity is cleaned up, a spectacle
sealed by the Columbia Pictures Lady as the *figure* of the abstracted, pure
femininity that covers over and displaces the messy, corporeal, dirty
kind, trying to remove it from view. Kennedy's insertion and display
of the intimate and private bleeding of the female reproductive body to
displace the purified figure of femininity can be situated centrally in
order to comment on a number of disparate discourses that are united
around some kind of figuration of birth in a logic of purity, or white
supremacy. Thus, this seemingly isolated and ostensibly banal question
of the pregnant Clara is related to the implications of what is called birth
in quite another context, D. W. Griffiths's *Birth of a Nation*. Following
this relationship might help show why a reading of the structures of
misogyny and a reading that attempts to specify the structures of racism
simply cannot be separated.

The cinematic memory that haunts Clara is traced by Michael
Rogin, in *Ronald Reagan: The Movie and Other Essays in Political Demonology,* where he investigates the genealogy of the spectacular phenomenon
of a president who has *no other* memory than a cinematic one. But even
Rogin could not have predicted the Gulf war as a media event staged as
a public relations campaign to raise the president's ratings, the spectacle
of a rebirth of a nation that required a war. The blood of humiliated,
feminized, dark Third World bodies was as unimportant as the blood of
the pregnant female. Misogyny, racism, and militarism circle around
this deceptively innocent question of birth and the bleeding female body.

In Kennedy's play the Columbia Pictures Lady cannot help but blur into the Statue of Liberty.

This national rescue whose hero, the Klan, saved the South, the North, and the Union from Reconstruction—symbolized by greedy Northerners, barbaric, ignorant blacks, scheming mulattoes, and vulnerable, wilting white women—codifying a resistance to the disorder and chaos represented by freed slaves and emerging women's movements. Tracing race and gender samenesses within periods that are historically very different helps foreground a kind of full circle from one birth of a nation to the current rebirth of white supremacy achieved through a spectacular war against a nonwhite people, this war perhaps part of a phobic reaction to internal differences introduced by feminism, the struggles of minorities, and gay and lesbian activism. Thomas Byrne Edsall and Mary D. Edsall, in the *Atlantic Monthly* in May 1991, argue that political rhetoric and imagery are again based on an opposition to disorder, and, again, disorder is symbolized by race: "When the official subject is presidential politics, taxes, welfare, crime, rights, or values, the real subject is race."[19] The structure of this logic of purity ensures that the sense of chaos and threat, the uncertainties of modernity and the ravages of Reagonomics, will be blamed not only on people of color but also, simultaneously, on feminists and gays, lesbians, and bisexuals, all of whom threaten the "values" of the decent white middle-class Body. Not so coincidentally in a cultural logic whose privileged term is *purity,* economic disruption is immediately blamed on Jews.

Part of *Birth of a Nation's* black and white coloration came from white actors in blackface playing the dangerous black or mulatto characters, while the more obscure people in the crowds were played by people of color. Griffiths admitted color into this film as a kind of disguise, something that could be cleaned up after the filming was over. And whatever "birth" he could picture had to do with white men in white sheets, dresses almost, giving birth cleanly to a nation of white men. This birth purified his version of "the nation" of two things: women and blackness.

But while Griffiths could use *birth* as a concept to refer to something that was abstracted away from women, blackness, and bleeding bodies, birth as a metaphor in Kennedy's world could only refer to those things as they circle around bloody femininity, which has historically had to be disguised, hidden by a masquerade, or covered over by a pure female figuration. The play's conclusion obsessively returns to Jean

Peter's bleeding body, bleeding from what is more likely a miscarriage than a birth; it is neither abstracted nor idealized but is bloody and messy, the sheets not white but black.

By this time what Kennedy has staged are not the black and white negatives of color photos or films within what Murray called the "technological tradition of monocular vision." Instead, she has shown why these films simply will not develop.

Bodies and Spectacles: What's Birth Got to Do with It?

The play has been about what was left out of the spectacular staged differences without much difference of postmodern culture—the conditions of enunciation as those are affected by specific kinds of bodies. Images, like commodities, never circulate without bringing human bodies into play. It is not only, as Marx saw, that the materiality of masculine human bodies is abstracted out of *production;* capital results from the abstraction of human labor. But there are human bodies still involved in circulation, consumption, reception—and, perhaps most significantly, in *reproduction* in both its senses: cultural repetition and the reproduction of the species.

Birth of a Nation and the Gulf war rebirth circle back around to the family story that has so relentlessly grounded Kennedy's play. For the Family Channel (with its "family" movies without mothers—"Bonanza," "Wagon Train," "Gunsmoke," "The Rifleman") and the Gulf war rebirth of the nation tell a story that includes the same characters we saw in Griffith's film. This is a story told by, about, and for families made up of white men—the Willie Horton ads, the Helms Senate campaign, the Supreme Court gag rule on abortion counseling. It is, as well, a public relations, or marketing, "reconstruction" of political rhetoric "cleaned up" of race, gender, and sexuality, so that every progressive idea is coded negatively as reverse discrimination, racial preference, or political correctness.

And central to this rebirth is a form of femininity—the Mother who figures all battles, the war a spectacular, ostensibly surgical, sanitized operation. The celebration of this war, says Jean Baudrillard, who has similarly overlooked the misogyny of his own poststructuralist theory, was a "celebration of a colossal representation" in which the dead bodies are the least real of all (1991, 19). And it is the people who are most "feminized," in the dirty sense, those of dirty countries and dirty parts of this country who are increasingly in the mode of information simply abandoned as waste or residue, in what Robert Reich calls the secession of the successful. Their further humiliation, Baudrillard argues, is fundamental to the circuit of entertainment where what is constructed went far beyond the spectacle of "Ronald Reagan the Movie" to the construction of war as entertainment and campaign publicity. In a similar structural way the mutilation of women's bodies and their humiliation is fundamental to the circuit of Hollywood entertainment, even when the Hollywood entertainer is part of a filmic avant-garde. The humiliation of feminized dirty peoples is the necessary material for the production of the spectacle of a femininity so clean it is virile: the Mother of all wars—the missing term always clear. This was a mother*fucker* of a war —with one kind of mother absent from the Family Channel, the other becoming the symbol of war, misogyny, and nation.

And perhaps this Mother of all battles, where decisions and agency almost entirely excluded women and people of color, inadvertently but structurally does intersect with some strains of poststructuralist theory that determinedly refuse to theorize the prelinguistic, the pre-Imaginary, or the historical and gendered specificity of birth, as a central organizing node of postmodernity, and may be unwittingly involved in this larger structure called by Susan Jeffords the remasculinization of America. For the continued abstractions that remove birth from any connection to women's bodies selects out only half of the *sème* of blood—its coding in relation to death, not life, as well as rewriting *life* by means of technological reproduction to free it from maternal influence.

The sanctioned ignorance of female specificity brings us back to the issue of the privilege of the indifference to legitimacy, a legitimacy that comes from living in one kind of body and not another. For as we might have learned from Kennedy, while there are decentered subjects and spectacles, there are no disembodied ones.

Chapter 5

In the Shadow of the Polis: Mothers, Daughters, Marsha Norman

We haven't the words—we haven't the words. . . . Behind the eyes;
not on the lips; that's all.

—Virginia Woolf

Mais t'ai-je jamais connue autrement que partie?

—Luce Irigaray

Stylistic awkwardness would be the discourse of dulled pain.

—Julia Kristeva

During the early years of twentieth-century North American feminism white middle- and upper-class concerns about the oppressive nature of the nuclear family, and, even more specifically, the suburban white nuclear family dominated much academic feminist study. But work on the very different experiences of women in other classes, races, and ethnic groups began to enrich feminist theory, making it impossible to talk about Woman as a homogeneous category. It is, nevertheless, still important to look at a relatively invisible group of women: lower middle-class women who either work in the home or hold low-paying noncareer jobs outside the home and identify more strongly in relation to the home than to work. In particular, at this historical moment, which finds many women attracted to right-wing, conservative politics as they emphatically distance themselves from feminism—or, at least, feminism as defined by their pastors or the media—issues of housework and domestic life must still be conceptualized with care.

I need the help of an anecdote at this point to show in what way the invisibility of this group of women seems to function at the moment. A class I recently taught on postmodernism brought together theories of signification with discussions of economic and political structures. It was a senior-level humanities class made up of highly motivated and thoughtful students, two-thirds of them men, from a number of disciplines, among them film, philosophy, psychology, architecture, as well as English. Their discussions of the theoretical works were impressive as was their ability to dissect structures of representation in literature and media texts. What took me completely by surprise, however, was their reaction to a segment of "Oprah Winfrey" we watched after reading articles by Paolo Carpignano and Elayne Rapping on television talk shows, what Carpignano calls "Chatter in the Age of Electronic Reproduction" (1990). One need not romanticize talk shows to conclude that they must be studied to try to understand their appeal, but I was completely unprepared for the contempt directed at this show by these smart, progressive, politically minded students. Their comments were aimed primarily at the people who watched the show, most of them women, even though they seemed genuinely surprised when reminded of that. Oprah Winfrey was not dismissed so much because of her race as because of her gender, and one of these young, feminist men even opened the discussion by talking about her weight. The men were, in fact, almost rude in their aggressive comments about the show, whereas in all our other discussions they had politely shared the discussion space. They also characterized our classroom discussion of the show as mimetic of the show itself: unfocused, hysterical, circular, not sticking to the subject—though my own interpretation of the discussion was that it was one of the most intense and involved we had had, with some of the women speaking up for the first time all term. It was not only I but the women students in the class who were caught off guard by these reactions, in particular because of the feminist sentiments these young men had expressed throughout the term. Many of the women spontaneously formed an angry group standing around after class to talk about it.

This kind of reaction, though not so heated, is not unusual even among many leftist critics who are far more interested in studying the avant-garde in popular culture (i.e., MTV [Music Television] and Madonna) than they are in talking about daytime talk shows, sitcoms, and soap operas—for example, "Roseanne," or "Days of Our Lives." These latter shows are more likely to be watched by a demographic cross-section of women considered to be uninteresting, boring, not so highly educated, relatively invisible, than they are by potential masqueraders or mimics; they constitute a faceless, perhaps older, undifferentiated mass of nondescript women. Lynn Joyrich argues that television's dismissal by many cultural critics is related to the way it "feminizes" its audience; that is, television supposedly makes audiences passive, easily influenced by emotional appeals, malleable, incapable of critical analysis of commodity fetishism—just like women. She argues that to compensate for the threat of being feminized, what she calls "hypermasculinity," has begun to mark television programming, reassuring the masculine targeted viewer (and the media critic) that he is not like all those passive, faceless women who were television's earlier prime audience. Thus, the male audience and the male critic may believe that they are not really television watchers at all but are, rather, sports fans or scholars of popular culture who are capable of the critical distance necessary to avoid being taken in by, "seduced" by, TV. This introduces into the discussions of popular culture a very predictable, very familiar gendered distinction between high and low, the avant-garde and the common, though represented by two female celebrities, Madonna and Roseanne. One woman's resistant art is "too good," really, for the degraded medium of television; the other's is seen as tainted by its sitcom format and its sentimental, banal, domestic subject matter.

There are connections between the invisibility of certain women, this division in readings of popular culture and reactions to Marsha Norman's play, 'night, Mother. A male critic reviewing it found that "the circumstances strike me as alien, pat, and unlikely" (Watt 1983, 334). Another male critic asked if it could even be called drama, a recurring question reviewers also initially asked about Kennedy's work. As the second critic says of Norman's play, nothing along the way makes us compassionate about these women, primarily because they "have led plain, unlyric lives" (Kissel 1983, 336) and because the playwright does not seem to want to poeticize or aggrandize them. The characters are "not true enough," he says explicitly, but he implicitly suggests something else: these lives do not provide the stuff of drama. And he is right. They are not the stuff of drama analyzed according to the criteria of tragedy and its characters.

Jill Dolan's study of Norman's play argues that the reception of 'night, Mother by mainstream male critics has had two effects. On the one hand, the play was dismissed as banal and boring, and, on the other, its radical questioning of the subject matter of drama was neutralized by an insistence on the play's "universality" (Dolan 1988). Dolan argues

that, when Robert Brustein, in particular, valorized the play by arguing
that it did indeed satisfy Aristotle's requirements for tragic drama, he in
fact recuperated it to a masculine definition of universality, defined as
the ability to speak to a generic spectator. Thus, both the dismissal of
the play and its valorization depended on erasing its specificity as a play
about women and, more specifically, about certain kinds of women.

Another feminist critic, however, Jenny Spencer, argued that what
such a generic reading overlooks is that the performance of the play
achieves its power, in fact, precisely because of its different positioning
of men and women as spectators:

> If we accept the psychoanalytic premise that given the specific pres-
> sures, complications, and resolutions offered the female child within
> the Oedipal situation, the process whereby men and women gain
> their sexual identity is not identical, then it stands to reason that a
> literary work in which such issues are represented should provide
> for the audience of each sex a different *kind* of experience. [This
> play] . . . both self-consciously addresses a female audience and sub-
> consciously works upon the female psyche in powerful ways, posi-
> tioning male and female viewers differently in the process. Indeed,
> because of the way in which the text foregrounds issues of female
> identity and feminine autonomy, focuses on the mother-daughter
> relationship, and controls the narrative movement; the relatively
> detached position available (however tentatively) to male viewers
> simply cannot (without great risk) be taken up by women. (Spencer
> 1987, 375)[1]

Interpretations of this ostensibly simple play have been varied and
the complexities of those interpretations are not easily resolved. It has
been described as a "kitchen drama" that deals with the banal concerns
of mother and daughter, making it different from the weightier "domestic drama," which also deals with fathers and sons in the domestic space
and is particularly beloved of Marxist critics, who trace there the rise of
the bourgeois individual and the construction of the notion of privacy,
often overlooking the fact that it is *his* privacy. But feminist critics have
also claimed the play for various interpretations, some insisting that it
is a quintessential middle-class liberal drama that has no political edge,
others interpeting it primarily from the space of the daughter and finding
the mother trivial and absurd, yet others angry that the daughter doubly

punishes the mother both by killing herself but, prior to that, by setting up a second chance for the mother to fail to save her.

John Winkler's description of the audience of Greek tragedy should be referred to again as a reminder of the way tragedy's requirements continue to constrain the reception of dramas like Norman's. Winkler's argument, discussed in the introduction, makes clear that the ideal audience for tragedy was the *ephebate,* the group of young male citizens who were in military training, the origins of Greek tragedy not to be found in Dionysian ritual but, rather, in a kind of initiation into knowledge that was intimately connected to military training. The *ephebate* was the "still center," the perspective symbolized by the chorus: "the events and characters portrayed in tragedy are meant to be contemplated as lessons by young citizens (or rather by the entire polis from the vantage point of the young citizen) . . . the watchful scrutiny of the chorus [is therefore] structurally important as a still center from which the tragic turbulence is surveyed and evaluated." Tragedy served to initiate young men into adulthood and, in particular, into military and civic responsibility through social ritual; the identifying characteristic of this audience was its virility: "the entire audience is organized in a way that demonstrates its corporate manliness as a *polis* to be reckoned with" (Winkler 1985, 32).

The "stuff of tragedy," in relation to this history, obviously had little to do with women as spectators or with the domestic arrangements that have become the province of women; the context within which women's lives most often must be considered is a family context, even when women do not spend all their time there (Papanek 1985). It is little wonder, then, that in the twentieth century other men of the polis and many women can view a play about the occupants of the domestic space and conclude that nothing of importance happens there or react with contempt when women talk about relationships, problems with children, or domestic problems.

In the twentieth century women speaking on their own behalf are still considered to be illegitimate—or worse, boring. Pointing to this gendered reception, Alisa Solomon, in the *Village Voice,* inaugurated a competition for the "Dickies, the National Sexist Theater Critics Award," a race, she says, that "will be stiff indeed":

Gloria Foster plays a black matriarch of tragic stature in Bill Gunn's *The Forbidden City* and reviews describe her character as "a mon-

ster," "a dragon," and the "Wicked Witch of the West." Cassandra
Medley examines three generations of mothers and daughters, and
the *Times,* complaining that *Ma Rose* should have been a one-act,
says the play shows "stretch marks." Meanwhile, hardly an issue
of *New York* goes by without John Simon passing judgment on a
woman's anatomy. Maria Irene Fornes, one of America's greatest
playwrights, has been alternately ignored and trashed by the mainstream male critics. (Solomon 1990, 4)

Connecting this particular aesthetic problem to politics also inevitably connects grammar and politics, for this aesthetic dismissal is related
to the absence of a female speaking subject and to the invisibility of
women's labor in society in general. Invisible (present but absent) subjects are responsible for invisible (present but absent) labor in a way that
helps provide a materialist foundation for the present/absent female subjects who shadow aesthetic theory.

But looking at the question of women's work means that a too-
simple division between the public and the private spheres must first be
analyzed. Nancy Fraser's "Rethinking the Public Sphere" sets out both
Jürgen Habermas's concept of the public and the private spheres before
pulling it apart in order to offer her own theory of a possible postbour-
geois model of the public sphere. Habermas's description of the public
sphere is initially very important because of the way it breaks apart the
public sphere into constituent parts too often collapsed solely into the
"public." He argues that the public sphere is multiple, consisting of: the
state; the official economy of paid employment (workplaces, markets,
credit systems, etc.); and arenas of public discourse. In his conceptualization of the liberal bourgeois state there is a utopian potential contained
within this third category, but it is a potential that has never been developed, though it might provide a site for democratic theories about the
transformation of the capitalist state.

But Fraser, drawing on the work of Joan Lands, Mary Ryan, and
Geoff Eley, argues that the history of this public arena of discourse
upon which Habermas models his utopian, or ideal, speech situation
was made possible because it *depended* on the stigmatization of women's
culture and that this opposition produced a "new, austere style of
public speech and behavior . . . a style deemed 'rational,' 'virtuous,'
'manly.' . . . Masculinist gender constructs were built into the very concepts of the republican public sphere" (Fraser 1990a, 59); the very style

of reasoned deliberation thus has a history. Similarly, these gender norms were built into the definition of the emerging bourgeois class, and they were norms that exacerbated sexism by enforcing a sharp distinction between what is defined as public and private spheres, relegating certain women (and not others) to that domestic sphere and representing bourgeois women as ornaments to enforce the respectability of an emerging class engaged in a process of differentiating itself from other classes (Fraser 1990a, 60).

Fraser argues, then, that Habermas's notion of a public sphere of discourse depends on an unanalyzed definition that overlooks other publics in order to define itself as *the* arena of public discourse. In particular, in describing the rise of the public discursive space of the bourgeoisie, Habermas overlooks alternative women-only voluntary associations, public activities by nonwhite groups, class protest activities, street protests and parades, and women's rights advocates who used the public space to contest "women's exclusion from the official public sphere and the privatization of gender politics" (Fraser 1990a, 61).

Habermas's ideal public sphere thus gained its validity, in part, through gender distinctions it then erased. Though he argues that the public sphere of discourse might ideally provide a place where differences could be bracketed so that communication could take place among various unequal groups and interests, this free space under erasure sounds remarkably like the duet and the linguistic etymologies described in the first chapters of this study, where bracketing differences that are the result of a differential access to power, in actuality, structurally reinforces that very inequality.[2]

Fraser's insistence on countering the division into a too-simple notion of public and private by conceptualizing the multiplicity of public arenas, or what she calls "subaltern counterpublics," helps adjust feminism's reliance on a similar binary division, which she argues has replicated "the bourgeois public's claim to be *the* public."[3] Such a division repeats the ideology that helped relegate women to the domestic sphere in the first place. Like the force of the phobic myth of purity that is all the stronger the more mixture there actually is, so is the myth of women's unsuitability for public tasks all the stronger the less true it is.

Fraser suggests that the term *subaltern counterpublics* might be useful in conceptualizing differences according to style. That is, different *styles* of speaking are not equally *heard* in the articulation of political discourses. Grammar and politics in this project of articulating a political

poetics of drama come into play here, for, though Fraser's suggestion
comes out of an entirely different kind of analytical discourse, it joins
Kristeva's description of language as the place where the Symbolic and
subjective, the mode of production and discourse, come together and
where speakers who use the same language have different *symbolic capacities,* or different styles that can be read as marking different kinds of
access to power. The way they speak and the coding they wear as bodies
ensures that they will be heard differently.

Complicating the split between public and private or between public and domestic is important to feminist dramatic criticism, just as it is
also important to studies of the domestic dramas of, for example, Ibsen,
Strindberg, and Miller, in order to complicate theories of the construction and disciplining of privacy in capitalist culture. It may be that the
term *kitchen drama* needs to be revalorized for two reasons. One, the
kitchen and the living room often prove to be gendered, with one the
female space, the other the place men are found within the home. But
the kitchen is also the site of hired domestic workers, a space available
for their conversation and socializing; when they walk out of the kitchen
and into the other rooms of the house, they are "out of place."

The Invaluable Worthlessness of Women's Work

Women's invisible labor is priceless, that is, it is something without
which nothing in men's lives or their civilization could continue to function, just as male narratives would go nowhere if there were not female
subjectless spaces through which they could advance. Yet this priceless-
ness undergoes intense symbolic reworking; it is turned into something
worthless.

Housework as real work can help connect the symbolic and grammatical absence of females to their social and political absence. Hannah
Papanek's materialist analysis isolates two separate structures within
which the family functions: the industrial, or capitalist, structure; and
the familial, or patriarchal, one, though the family may be patriarchal
and still provide possibilities for resistance to the cultural values of the
dominant system, as Mina Davis Caulfield showed. This double structure helps account for the difficulty in theorizing women's labor and
women's place in Marxist theory; domestic labor exists in a different
system of reference from waged labor, though it contributes to that
system and is marked by the fact that it is work performed but not

named: "Both women and men may not refer to particular activities as 'work' at the same time that the family's strategies for survival (or class mobility) clearly rely on the performance of these activities to achieve certain goals in production as well as consumption" (Papanek 1984, 141).

But the primary function of women's labor in the family becomes clearer if we break down the family unit from an assumed couple of two equals identified by their same *class* into a comparison of the economic position of each member of the couple. Their positions are not the same, and the labor within the family is performed not only for society but also for the comfort of an individual male in what might be seen as a serf relation within the domestic mode of production. This is labor that is not exchangeable for remuneration; in fact, the only time similar tasks are remunerated is when they are not done for the woman's individual family, though another woman may be hired to do that work for her. The housewife's labor is unpaid, but the worker gets her maintenance. Even that maintenance, however, depends on the goodwill and the wealth of the male and is directly related to her responsibility for child-care. It has very little to do with the quality of the actual labor performed, and it is different from other labor, too, in that sexuality is mixed in with this economic relationship.

As Katha Pollitt argues, work traditionally performed by women—housework, childcare, sex—when performed "within marriage, for no pay . . . are slathered with sentimentality and declared beyond price, the cornerstone of female self-worth, family happiness and civilization itself," by society as well as often by women with resources who can pay for someone else to do those tasks. Yet when they are done for pay they "become disreputable work performed by suspect, marginal people" (Pollitt 1990, 825). Childbirth, too, functions that way, as Pollitt points out in her article about surrogate mothering in the case of Baby M, "When Is a Mother Not a Mother?"

This situation is defined as dependence, even when the houseworker has a job outside the home; that is, it is usually her wage that pays for another woman's housekeeping or childcare labor, the job she would otherwise do for free. The dependence within the family is reinforced backwards by the capitalist economy's discrimination against women in the marketplace, though the situation for women whose husbands occupy different class positions is obviously different. At a certain economic level family status production becomes even more important than actual wages: "Women's contributions to status enhancement [unpaid support activities for men's paid work and children's schoolwork as well as the performance of ritual and information gathering] may have far more value than small contributions to family income that may also entail status loss" (Papanek 1984, 134).

This double system of reference unsettles the categories of class. In most class descriptions, if women do not have a second job, one added to their domestic job, they are classified according to their husband's or father's class. If they do have another job, it is sometimes used to classify them in terms of class, which is generally lower than their husband's. Thus women without a second job are assigned the *same* class position as their husband as if their dependent economic situation were not an independent economic factor; as Christine Delphy argues, "it is not treated as an economic situation" (1984, 36). Instead, that dependence is considered sufficient reason to attribute to them someone else's class, even though the relationship to the mode of production is, in fact, quite different for the husband than it is for the wife.

The lack of a separate occupational category other than that of houseworker means that the classification system defines a woman according to marriage, rather than work, her place determined by the male she is linked to, even if she is not dependent upon him for financial support. Men, on the other hand, are not classified according to marriage, even when they are unemployed and married. This mediated relationship of women to the mode of production is then equated with a direct relation to it because marriage has already been legally defined as a contract between two equal partners. But it is only as dependents, or wives, that most women have entered the class of their husbands. In a familiar ironic reversal they become "equal" because they are unequal.

What has occurred in this confusing categorical egalitarianism is revealing. The assignment of people to a particular class bases that classification on the structure of capitalism, while their assignment to a class based on marriage is a classification based on the patriarchal system and its exchange of women who take the name and class of the husband. As Delphy points out, this particular equation of two individuals reveals the way the patriarchal system overrides the capitalist one while effacing that move: "[Economic classification] roots its analyses in the specific antagonistic relations of production between husbands and wives, and then not only denies this relationship, but transforms it into its very opposite: a relationship between equals" (1984, 39).

Considering the heterosexual couple as a unit thus presumes what it denies, the inequality of women and men, and commits "the major sin of considering the very place—the household—where certain class relations are exercised . . . as the place where they are annulled" (Delphy 1984, 42). Benveniste's tracing of the very different relationship men and women have to the word *marriage* illuminated this "unit." Delphy writes, "As a group which is subject to this [domestic] relation of production, [women] constitute a class; as a category of human beings who are destined by birth to become members of the class, they constitute a caste" (1984, 71).

The invisibility and worthlessness of women's domestic work is crucial to every system, capitalist or otherwise, and the invisible subject position Delphy describes is reflected in an aesthetic exclusion, for those who are aesthetically appropriate characters either engage in public activity or mediate the experiences of a public figure. Marriage is thus certainly not the duet of Lévi-Strauss's description; it is, rather, the "institution by which unpaid work is extracted from a particular category of the population, women-wives" (Delphy 1984, 54). The legality of that extraction of free work is enforced backwards by the marketplace in which women are at an economic disadvantage, which constitutes a pressure that drives women into marriage and keeps them there:

> We are confronted with a paradox: on the one hand marriage is the (institutional) situation where women are exploited; and on the other hand, precisely because of this, the potential market situation for women's labor (which is that of all women, not just those who are actually married) is such that marriage still offers them the best career, economically speaking. (Delphy 1984, 97)

Susan Faludi's study of the situation of married women in *Backlash: The Undeclared War against American Women* suggests that the women's movement has undercut this characterization of marriage as the best economic place for women, and it has set off a backlash against women that attempts to reverse that progress and enforce women's participation in marriage. "The more women are paid in the workforce, the less eager they are to marry," she argues in her investigation of the scare heralded by *Time* and *Newsweek* that career women stood as much chance of being married as of being hit by a falling satellite, finding that this was a manufactured scare belied by more extensive studies that found that marriage was no longer the focus of the lives of single women and that they were, in fact, dodging it. Reinvestigating a number of cultural myths about marriage, Faludi quotes Charles Westoff, a Princeton demographer in the *Wall Street Journal* in 1986: "What is going to happen to marriage and childrearing in a society in which women really have equality?" (1991, 16). Her research finds that it is men, not women, who benefit from marriage. "Being married is about twice as advantageous to men as to women in terms of continued survival," argues Paul Glick, a government demographer (quoted in Faludi 1991, 16). In fact, men's health is made worse by divorce, women's by marriage.

In a chapter entitled "Blame It on Feminism" Faludi also looks again at statistics that claim that the living standards of women whose divorces were made easier by no-fault divorce laws go down precipitously (73 percent) while those of men go up (42 percent). An influential study by Lenore Weitzman made this claim and has been quoted extensively to argue that the women's movement made things worse for women. But Faludi shows that Weitzman's study is seriously flawed, as attempts to verify it by an economist from the University of Delaware, Saul Hoffman, and a social scientist from the University of Michigan, Greg Duncan, found instead that women suffer a 30 percent decline, men a 10-15 percent improvement, yet that decline proved to be temporary; after five years the average woman's living standard was higher than it had been when she lived with her husband because of her participation in the work force, suggesting that the best way to remedy this disparity is to correct the inequality between men's and women's wages at work. (After several years, however, many of the women had also remarried, a point Faludi overlooks.) Weitzman's study also failed to include control studies to see what happened to women under traditional divorce laws, and it omitted the fact that the no-fault divorce laws were instituted by panels made up mostly of men, not members of the women's movement. And finally, it failed to note that, because of the women's movement, there has been at least some access to better jobs, and the increased participation of women in the work force helped save many women from the economic results heralded by those eager to blame women's poverty on the women's movement.

In fact, Weitzman acknowledges, in a phrase that was not widely quoted by those arguing against feminism, that "judicial antagonism to feminism was aggravating the rough treatment of contemporary divorced women" (Faludi 1991, 25). Thus, argues Faludi, "the real problems of divorced women's woes can be found not in the fine print of divorce legislation but in the behavior of ex-husbands and judges" (24), as economic abandonment, especially of children, functions as a threat by which divorced men may exert control. As Arlie Hochschild argues: "The 'new' oppression outside marriage thus creates a tacit threat to women inside marriage. Patriarchy has not disappeared; it has changed form" (quoted in Faludi 1991, 25).

On the Margins of Theater

Norman's *'night, Mother* stages the space of women's worthless domestic work and its aesthetic invisibility, initially foregrounding the spatial organizational role of architecture in a set representing an isolated middle-class or lower middle-class house in the United States. It is purposely not identified as regional, and it represents what appears to be the homogeneity of much of American life, though its specificity will later be developed. One of the most intimate and private places, the home, at first appears to be one of the most general, its rooms filled with similar consumer products, magazines, television programs, by way of its new hearth. The mythical "uniqueness" of the American notion of individuality is, at least in the marketing of individuality, paradoxically very homogeneous.

It is in this living room that the Family and the family overlap in a key link in the organization of the social contract, the site of the intersection of the industrial and the domestic modes of production. The privacy Oedipus looks for in the Family is what it is Man's right to have, and in economic terms, not coincidentally, the health of the housing industry, which is built on the concept of the single-family house and the idealization of that form of privacy, is crucial to the health of the national economy as a whole. The development of the American housing market flourished following the First World War, accompanied by very specific historical influences: the desire of whites to flee crowded cities occupied increasingly by immigrants and nonwhites and high unemployment among men, which led to their need for jobs held by women. As the National Association of Home Builders said, "What was good for housing was good for the country" (Hayden 1984, 38).

The propping of the national economy on the housing market supported by the image of home and mother has been centered indirectly on those women who are eligible to participate in this metaphor of Woman: white, middle-class women, but usually only as those women were attached to a male with an income. The male of choice, whose income can most likely qualify for a loan to buy a house, is white.[4] As Delphy's analysis of class stratification shows, relatively few white women would be in the middle class were they not linked to a man. A social ordering accompanies the phenomenon of the single-family home and partially determines the activities to be performed inside it, as it becomes a fundamental reproducer of the sexual division of labor as well as of capitalist values and consumption. It also further orders society in the use of the long-term mortgage, which reinforces the stability of long-term workers.

Not so coincidentally, "the rapid development of the advertising industry in the 1920s was influential because advertisers promoted the private suburban dwelling as a setting for all other purchases."[5] As De-lores Hayden argues, the American dream house, rather than the ideal city, which was seen to have a kind of utopian possibility around the turn of the century, became the spatial representation of the hopes for individual freedom, expression, and privacy. The mythologized concept of home as haven presupposed a place to be a haven from, based on men's needs to recuperate from the public world of work. Because women who work outside the home and women who work in it see the home as, among other things, a site of domestic labor, they were left without the haven men have long idealized.

Norman's play takes place in an organized space whose differential nature is important; it is private and domestic because it is not public, its isolation no accident. The small, bland kitchen and living room, the gaping bedroom door, are private spaces, represented in a public forum, the theater. Like the kitchen whose keeper is not there in Susan Glaspell's *Trifles,* when the sheriff and other men enter it there is something almost embarrassingly too private, almost naked about this space, as if it had not been "picked up" before visitors entered. The set makes strikingly evident the division of lived space and the banishment of children and certain kinds of women from some places in order to concentrate them in other less visible ones. The theatrical set also raises a question: "Who fits the image this room imposes on anybody who must use it?"[6]

The two women who live in Norman's play are women for whom the ruses of the masquerade have been irrelevant; they are not attractive and educated women who might assert their activity through a manipu-lation of female imagery. Instead, they are quite ordinary, lacking the skills or resources that might allow them to be mimics or masquerades.

Within the norm of Woman is another norm, or range of acceptability. Ugliness, age, disabilities are the taboos that predetermine, according to male rules, who can and cannot play the game of the masquerade. One of the characters in the play is old, the other handicapped by epilepsy, though this "crippling" might be overdone in the light of Ntozake Shange's description of the training of middle-class white women as "culturally condoned incompetence."

Norman chooses as characters two white, lower middle-class women and investigates their relation to one another as well as their relation to the home, as it partially defines them. Delphy argues that valorizing domestic labor can easily become a celebration of masochism because most women are not doing this work by choice but are, instead, economically and culturally pressured into it. But because doing housework is a specific experience that defines many women's lives, it might be approached in a double way that attributes worth to it as physical and emotional expenditure, while simultaneously analyzing its social nature in relation to freely chosen work. Feminist discussions of domestic work have, very importantly, shifted in the last few years to analyses of women who must go outside their own families to do the domestic labor in someone else's house, but, because I am especially interested in looking at why many lower middle-class and middle-class women are not drawn to feminism but turn, instead, to religion or conservative politics, my focus here will be on those women who work as housewives in their homes.

The play's nondescript house built out on a country road (though the exterior is never visible) is not exactly rural, nor is it suburban; it is ordinary, drained of uniqueness—not stylish but not quite dowdy either. Depending on the way the play is staged, the room can be either antiseptic or dowdy and well-worn; either choice results in different comments on the domestic space. The room may, in fact, be marked by its blandness, and, because the *bland* and the *banal* are such negatively coded words, they are most likely also gendered and show up as adjectives to describe activities engaged in by women. Blandness also usually has to do with the erasure of specific differences and uniqueness in mass production, K Mart the usual metaphor of choice for insulting someone for having no "taste." This kind of accusation again falls into Aristotelian tautology: capitalism rests on a class structure, which means that many people can have consumer goods but their class will be reflected in the consumer goods they can afford to buy. Thus, though their purchases at K Mart generally reflect their lack of money, those purchases circle back around to mark them as somehow inferior and more materialistic than those with either more capital or more cultural capital, including those on the Left. And because women are often the ones who must shop for children's clothing, food, and household supplies, they are, in this familiar Aristotelian tautology, targeted as the most materialistic of all society's consumers. Assigned by patriarchal and capitalistic structures to be responsible for domestic work and consumer purchases, even when they work outside the home, women are found inferior because, to no one's surprise, they spend their time on domestic work and consumer purchases.

This particular home is not bland in the sense of its being impersonal; its rooms are marked by handmade articles like crocheted doilies, skilled needlework, well-used objects individuated from other identical mass-produced copies by *use*. They carry the signs of human hands upon them as distinctions among individuals marked by style, in the sense that both Fraser and Kristeva use that term to refer to different styles of subjectivity. In Kristeva's terms *style* is the mark not of the *origin* of any kind of uniqueness but, rather, of *originality*. This refers both to the specificity of the way a subject has been subjected by the Symbolic as well as the way she also resists it.

Style can also be used to trace a poetics of the ordinary, or of the traces of hands on mass-produced objects, which may be another version of the traces to be found and read in what are recognized as more artistic cultural products: handcrafted objects like pottery or weavings or in the specificity of formal features in the works of different writers. The traces or differences in the use of ordinary objects may make visible the unexpected ways in which subjects rebel against commodity culture, whose ravages and conversion of all value into market value does deep violence to subjective experience. Rainier Maria Rilke described one way a theory of style in relation to the use of consumer products might find its artistry and a history of specificity in which originality takes precedence over sameness: "Take a couple of schoolboys: one buys a pocket knife, and the same day his friend buys another exactly like it. And after a week they compare knives, and it turns out that there is now just a very distant resemblance between them—so differently have they developed in different hands" (1985, 24).

That these products and their use is considered to be trivial might also be revalorized by looking again at definitions of the banal, in order to talk about the clichéd, mass-produced object that eliminates historical difference and characterizes the deadening effects of mass production. John Berger suggests that "banality" denotes a site of shared, intersubjective experience within which a desire for community might once have been located and that it might be retrieved as a kind of utopian spark. He describes the way such a moment of banality functions to overcome, for just an instant, the mystery of Otherness, its strangeness, in a moment of recognizing the joint situatedness in subjectivity. Berger's discussion of banality concerns the bridging of Otherness momentarily in the banality of the loved one as he distinguishes between the "nude" in the history of art, the image of women that marks her as surveyed possession, from the "naked," the picture of the unclothed woman that reveals her to be the loved one whose subjectivity the lover shares.

Though he grounds his discussion, finally, in a kind of biological notion of sex, it seems to me that this intersubjectivity, as he describes it, might instead be located *in language*. The concept of banality could then be used to refer to a shared location within the space of signification in general, as it promises to disclose something recognizable, familiar even though still strange, uncanny because it is located in language.[7] But this familiar/strange recognition might then be "grounded" in the common space of language, where we are all subjected: "The loss of mystery occurs simultaneously with the offering of the means for creating a shared mystery. The sequence is: subjective – objective = subjectivity to the power of 2" (Berger 1977, 108).

In these intersubjective moments or, at least, in the possibility of such moments of shared discursive subjectivity there might be recognitions of something held in common or moments of community, though it is quite clear that an unanalyzed, romanticized notion of community can just as easily describe David Duke crowds, with their concerns for sameness in sameness, as it can rallies for the Rainbow Coalition, concerned with sameness in difference.[8] The etymology of *banal,* in fact, suggests a history of usage based on something shared but shared problematically, as is all language. Banal comes out of an identity, something held in common, as defined by a feudal jurisdiction, but the other side of that shared identity was the fact that the "ban" that defined it was a summons to military service. Other forms of shared identity existed but were perhaps not "heard" the same way as was one originating from the direction of feudal lords. An ironic echo also turns up here in this etymology that finds that the word *banality* developed out of a completely masculine category of the "ban." In the late twentieth century, on the other hand, the word *banality* is most often found in descriptions of activities that have to do with women.

But it might be that, within this space of banality, what is banal and trivial from the top down may be conceptualized because it is personal and irreplaceable from a different perspective, like the basket made of the most stereotyped Hallmark cards sewn together with yarn by a child for her mother—a priceless, worthless object wrested out of its sameness. It is, perhaps, in the residue, the trivial, the detail that resistances are to be read. This domestic, banal place of nondescript and seemingly trivial traditions might be connected to Walter Benjamin's admonition to "seize hold of a memory as it flashes up in a moment of danger" in order to recognize it before it is lost. For Benjamin tradition, especially as he watched the rise of fascism, was a very ambiguous concept; it marked sites of struggle, where utopian desires were intermingled with other dangerous impulses: "In every era the attempt must be made anew to wrest tradition away from the conformism that is about to overpower it." The danger to that tradition "affects both the content of the tradition and its receivers. The same threat hangs over both: that of becoming a tool of the ruling classes" (1976, 255). Benjamin wrote about what were recognized as political issues, and the questions feminism asks about "the family" circle around this notion of tradition to suggest the political importance of rethinking this bland domestic space in terms not only of its oppressiveness but also its utopian memories.

In *'night, Mother* ordinary, bland, but personally marked objects are strewn around this living room: magazines, needlework catalogs, ashtrays, candy dishes. The homemade articles are, however, mostly the widowed mother's; this is her house, her home ownership mediated by her link to a man who died.

Orienting the play's trajectory is a bedroom door, which stands ajar and opens onto blackness, gapes open to that blackness: "It is the open door that opens onto absolute nothingness." This door, which ideally would open onto the symbol of femininity which makes readability and narrative closure possible—the bed—does not here hide one; the bedroom's center is thus empty of the organizing point in the oedipal narrative that arranges the significance of femininity. All we are able to tell about the door is that it is a threshold, a path between here and there, between light and dark; something changes when that threshold is crossed, which occurs only once and from only one direction. The sheltering but, at times, claustrophobic kitchen and living room may perhaps be escaped by going through the bedroom door, though we know from earlier chapters that going through a marital bedroom door usually leads instead *to* the kitchen and living room, as woman's place within man's place.

On the set are clocks, which are set with the actual time in which this long one-act play is performed without intermission. The passage of time is thus silently noted both onstage and as the audience's real time; its passage structures the intensity of the dialogues between the two women. The relationship to the present, which this notation of time suggests, marks a difference between certain masculine experiences and others more common to the activities culturally allotted to women. The passage of time forward in this play in a very stark sense means loss, as it does in everyone's life, as aging leads to death. But in the public space careers more frequently involve attempts to move forward from the kind of originary loss Lacan described in a movement from one position to a higher one, an investment in time, progress marked by keeping score and adding things up, quantifying accomplishments, increasing notations on a vita, higher wages, speculation. In the private space of the home, however, time moves toward progressive loss—loss of the woman's youth, which marked her worth in Western culture and which essentially ends with the beginning of the marriage that produced the family; loss of her individuality, as she often erases herself for her children or her husband; and the devastating knowledge that the passage of time, the increase of years, brings closer not a culmination of accomplishment but, instead, separation from those very children, tearing away a part of herself in their loss.

Relationships with children are at the center of some women's different relation to time, as children represent randomness in literally disrupting any linear arrangement of time that depends on predictability and order; it is certainly no accident that children are excluded from the polis. As Alexander Kluge and Oskar Negt argue, "One of the most effective ways of exposing the true nature of any public sphere is when it is interrupted, as a kind of alienation effect by children" (1990, 28). Children present another challenge, too, to social organization, in this case the organization of time. Looking forward, sacrificing the present for the future, for an abstraction, brings rewards in the world of work, just as investing one's money for future increase rather than spending it brings profit. But in the world of children, sacrificing the present means an irrecoverable loss, a hole in history; they are not the same from day to day or week to week; time lost cannot be made up. People associated with children are often accused of *spending* or *wasting* time as they order their working lives around them, both inside and outside the home, in contrast to a more masculine arrangement of time that *saves,* "maximizes," invests it, by rigidly enforcing the separation from children, delaying instant gratification for later profit.

The gaze of the male of the family is most likely forward, as he tries to act on the future, control it, turn the present into future gain, though it is significant that, in this play, the father was himself more feminine in his approach to time. A failure in the world of men, he is made known to us only through anecdotes told by the women about a passive, tired, "big old faded blue man in the chair," going off alone and pretending to fish while he made endless stick figures out of pipe cleaners, "wasting" time. He is the absent weak father, or the gentle male who also has few representations in the Symbolic system.

Separation, of course, is also part of the very nature of language, involved in the introduction of an articulated network of differences which makes "the real" available to be interpreted on condition that the subject be separated from it. But as many feminist theorists have argued, because male and female children enter systems of representation differently, women and men often experience the separation that institutes symbolization very differently. This cultural phenomenon has nothing to do with any kind of essential nature of either men or women; it has to do instead with acculturation: "Certain biofamilial conditions and relationships cause women (and notably hysterics) to deny this separation and the language which ensues from it, whereas men (notably obsessionals) magnify both and, terrified, attempt to master them," as Kristeva argues.[9]

In this play structured by the suicide of her daughter Jessie, Thelma Cates, a woman in her sixties, spends time fighting separation, gathering together memorabilia as registers of those moments lost—photos of children, relatives and friends, letters, remembrances, objects given to her, even when those objects may appear very superficial to others and especially to the audience. A part of the order she keeps in the house is thus an order of memories that would otherwise disappear in a speeded-up historical time. She literally recollects, focusing backwards in the present in order to carry this archive with her and actively rebelling against being made an object by the Symbolic's sacrificial contract. This kind of rebellion, however, may not express itself as a heroic refusal in terms of masculine behavior. A heroic rebellion—a choice to leave—would most likely repeat with only slight differences the sacrificial contract, for, without any rearrangement of the structure of the family, a woman's heroic rebellion might simply mean that children would be the sacrifice, not women. Jessie's rebellion is not heroic but, rather, resistant, drawing on the activity of popular ingenuity, which "uses whatever little there is at hand to preserve experience, to recreate an aura of 'timelessness,' to insist upon the permanent" (Berger and Mohr 1982, 108). This recollection, the popular ingenuity whose materials in advanced capitalism may be plastic and polyester, is paradoxically a battle against the ephemeral, against the passage of time without its being remarked, against the loss of people without notice.

Thelma's time inside the house and the identity for her that the house partially determines are oriented to the present and to immediate responses that make long-range goals almost irrelevant. Part of her role is to be available to react to immediate situations along the way. As Thelma (Mama to Jessie) says, "Things happen. You do what you can about them and you see what happens next" (58). In a discussion about how disappointed her husband was with her ("How could I love him Jessie. I didn't have a thing he wanted" [46]), she says, "Well, I wasn't here for his entertainment and I'm not here for yours either, Jessie. I don't know what I'm here for, but I don't think about it" (49). When Jessie tries to calm her mother by telling her she still has plenty of time left to live, Thelma says, "I forget what for, right now" (78).

The ordinariness of the scene and of the ostensible superficiality of the things they talk about sets up the contrast between the residue of these lives, its trivia, its topics based on the merits of various consumer goods, its insignificances, and the real subjects at issue in the relationship between them—what does a life like this mean, what difficulty in meaning drives a daughter to suicide, what is the cost of this culturally enforced dependency, what distance exists between mothers and daughters? What does this have to do with the oedipal narrative? The communication will ride along *between* words, not on their surface but, instead, in gestures, sideways looks, what Norman calls the "shorthand" of people who have lived together a long time and of women who have learned the lesson of language that excludes them: "[People] said conversation was to keep people from knowing what you are thinking" (Norman 1984, 1). What those who are not in a dominant position listen for are not the words but the edges.

The words they do exchange will be place markers, noise, as they hide what is actually going on, which is too subtle, tenuous, dangerous, in its possibilities of loss to be articulated. It could only be articulated in another language, and they do not yet have the words. If the most important, deepest things are said and the suicide takes place anyway, the effect of the loss will multiply exponentially; there will be no way for Thelma to survive it, no word that can pull her back together afterward. Like the metaphors that shelter us from fear, the words between them assume an intensity, a solidity, that has nothing to do with their outward meaning—banal words like, "I think I'll stay here. All they've got is Sanka," words spoken by the mother after learning of her daughter's carefully worked-out plan for her that night after her suicide, words whose banality becomes a form of protection.

The ordinariness of those words are their mask and their mark, hiding a dogged attempt on the mother's part to grasp words as concrete objects and to use them as instruments to stop the time that is moving toward such a loss, instruments to cover over, erase her daughter's words, as if in that way to deny the very possibility of Jessie's carrying out her plan. She stuffs them like rags in the chinks between the minutes to try to stop their movement. The rebellious and desperate attempt to preserve ordinariness is what is going on in this subtle mother-daughter conversation, and positions change by a hair's width in an understanding that is already so deep only the most minute changes can occur.

From the mother's point of view preserving ordinariness would mean saving her daughter's life, keeping the days one just like the last without this hideous disruption for which her daughter has collected old towels, the cushion of a lawnchair, and plastic garbage bags to keep the mess down. When the mother automatically, but unwittingly, says, "Don't go making a big mess," in the mechanical, banal phrase of the nagging mother, its resonance is intensified by her growing despair at what that mess will mean, her inability to say anything else but those automatic words. But it simultaneously adds life backwards to the way the phrase had been used before, extracting a moment with the living child and re-membering it. The resonance is intensified by the contrast between the bloody scene to come and the endless, childish messes this same daughter once made. These words ensure, like a cipher, a particular shared understanding, both of what it is like to have children and of what it is like to face their loss, a generalizable uniqueness as a shared experience. At another point Thelma, frantically, can say only: "You can't use my towels! They're my towels. I've had them for a long time. I like my towels" (19). With no words to say what she means she yanks out ordinary language like towels to stop a hemorrhage. This life is not lyrical or poetic, and neither are its words.

For the daughter, however, preserving ordinariness would prolong her own living death, her stranded position as an aging daughter serving as mother to her mother, a mother who really is healthier than she is and who still retains indirect control of her house, watched over from an invisible, outside, public vantage point by the son, Dawson. Jessie is a transient in terms of the oedipal narrative, having failed at being a mother and at being a wife. Now, as the mothering daughter, she will disrupt the temporal sequence and die before her mother. She is a highly dignified woman, and these humiliations have led her to take a certain control: "This life is all I really have that belongs to me and I'm going to say what happens to it" (36). Norman, however, uncomfortably exploits the image of the epileptic as "cripple," even though the play's power does not require it.

The striking difference here between the daughter who is the mother of the mother and the son who, like Hyllos, fathers the father centers on mastery. Jessie's accession to a position in which she mothers her mother is just that—mothering—and, in a sense, it is a complete loss of control, as she is smothered by the mother/Woman image, the role driving out the woman. It is more a loss of control than is the decision to take her own life. In spite of the costs of motherhood, however, there may be another side that escapes, an excess, a minute overlap of loss and shared subjectivity of a mother with her mother, a residue, a receptiveness to another human being in a careful way, rather than a dominating one. There is the Symbolic's requirement for mothers, but there is, besides, the caring or receptivity to the Other that may have also been constructed in women's acculturation, a kind of care giving men are able to learn as well. Mothering is not only an institution that exploits women; it has another aspect, "impelled also by a nonsymbolic, nonpaternal causality" (Kristeva 1980, 239). It can (but does not necessarily) suggest a way of conceptualizing an ethics of care.

Jessie, the daughter, is a woman in her late thirties, early forties, pale and normally taciturn, but on this evening she is very talkative. The easy familiarity between her and her mother suggests an affection that finds its expression in their physical relation to each other onstage. Their conversation, paradoxically, articulates what women have long used with one another to deal with a language and a coded world that is not theirs, a language of the glance, the touch, quick flashes of comprehension that may escape men but are signs of an underground, oblique language among women as a dominated group.

Thelma likes to talk, using words in ways that suit the moment: "She believes that things are what she says they are." They may be, as long as she thinks she has a child around to whom she means what she says and who, she thinks, reflects her back to herself. She has a strong sense of humor and tells fanciful stories about a crazy friend named Agnes who keeps her house filled with birds; in fact, she says, Agnes is still making payments on the parrot. When this proves to be false—Agnes has only two birds—she says, "I only told you to make you laugh. Things don't have to be true to talk about 'em, you know" (48). Language is not used to mean; it is used to do what the situation requires, to make people laugh, to persuade them, or to console them. It is often small talk, pasting sounds over silences, diverting dangerous confrontations, maneuvering, a kind of diplomatic domestic rhetoric.

Jessie goes about her very carefully planned operation, following a linear organization of time that looks forward and schedules everything she must get done that evening, even planning the time the actual suicide should occur (before her brother Dawson and his wife have gone to bed, so her mother will not be alone too long waiting for them to get dressed and come over). Thelma does not at first understand what is happening as she settles down with the *TV Guide* for a regular Saturday night at home. She even gives Jessie the mother's tired criticism that she watches too much television; that would obviously, on an ordinary day, be the only way to account for the fact that she is looking for her father's gun, having determined to protect herself against the kind of violence she sees on television. But Jessie is determined to kill herself with her father's gun and has tricked her brother into buying the bullets for her; in case she could not locate her father's gun, she had her husband's, Cecil's, gun at hand. This lineup of male accomplices in her death constitutes an active determination to take control of their influence over her. Her mother laughs at what Jessie wants the gun for, "protection," and says, "We don't have anything anybody'd want, Jessie. I mean, I don't even want what we got, Jessie" (10). This description of that idealized American home and simultaneously those idealized wife/mother occupants of it is telling.

Jessie's reference to the gun she needs for protection brings up her son, Ricky, who, as she says, is the only criminal they know; he has been arrested several times and has even stolen from her; she could have prevented that had she been able to keep him a baby, to stop those minutes. He is like her: "We look at the world and see the same thing: Not Fair. And the only difference between us is Ricky's out there trying to get even. . . . He walks around like there's loose boards in the floor, and you know who laid the floor, I did" (60). He becomes a metaphor for the jumbled mismatch of her marriage: "Ricky is the two of us together for all time in too small a space." Like the attempt to measure up to what is required of women by a culture that always finds them lacking, she was not enough, either for Ricky or for her husband, "I never was what he wanted to see, so it was better when he wasn't looking at me all the time." To her mother's lament that her husband should have taken her with him when he left, she says, "Mama, you don't pack your garbage when you move" (61).

Jessie's "fits," as her mother calls them, have marked her, over and above her femininity, as abject, terrifying, disgusting. Thelma's best friend, Agnes, will not visit them anymore because she has once witnessed one of Jessie's seizures. One of Jessie's most painful reasons for suicide is that she has been seen in this state of absolute loss of control that horrifies everyone. In particular, her brother, the son, has gained an extra power over her by his arrogant, humiliating care of her after she wet herself during one of these fits. Jessie's relation to Dawson is never shown to us directly; he is never onstage but functions, instead, as an absent magnet. Jessie at these moments of helplessness enacts perhaps most intensely the ideal of the mother, which she struggles against, for these moments of absolute self-forgetfulness make her absolutely vulnerable.

The very difficult relationship between a mother and daughter which underlies Jessie's busy arrangement of her mother's house has to do with the oedipal contract, whose circularity makes it no accident that females are thrown into conflict with each other. In order to be normal the girl must learn to reject this mother, who is so much like her, in essence rejecting herself in order to replace the mother with the father as her love object; "in patriarchy, the revival of relations between mother and daughter always creates conflict" (Irigaray 1985, 118). Conflict between the two women forestalls conflict with men.

The mother has no real stake in helping a symbolic contract that has been so damaging to her and which will be damaging to her daughter; she may not be able to encourage the girl to make the break with her that the daughter must make in order to change love objects: "Why and in the name of what dubious symbolic benefit would she want to make this detachment so as to conform to a symbolic system which remains foreign to her?" (Kristeva 1982c, 29). The mother's *gift*, the child as part of her, is turned into an *obligation* by the Symbolic, and it is no surprise that she resists making such an obligatory separation. What is left in the relation between mother and daughter is a magnetic field of attraction and rejection, as they are drawn to each other and pushed apart by the Symbolic, which drops down between them to teach the little girl that women are, in fact, degraded and inferior, driving a wedge of abjectness and even of hatred between them. If Jessie's mother is repulsive and weak in the eyes of society, what does that make Jessie—her mother's very image? What happens as she grows older and meets her mother again and again in the mirror?

Danger arises here, however, because of closeness. The refusal of separation can also mean that family members smother each other, as multiple subject positions present a dilemma: How can a subject be both multiple and specific? The two women maneuver to distinguish themselves from each other without sacrificing either one of them, but language does not provide the words to separate them with care, carefully, from their location within the same symbolic image, the Woman/mother. Because of the failure of language, the daughter's decision to kill herself is not susceptible to rational argument and can only be approached by the desperation of the mother, who is willing to try anything—her own submissiveness, offering the neck, insults, humor, pleading.

The symbolic contract's sacrificial nature is nowhere more dissonant than in this doubleness of the female image; encouraged to be her mother, the daughter is thus encouraged to be society's leftovers and to hate her femaleness. The Woman/mother idealized by the oedipal contract is admirable only in the abstract; she is none other than the domestic worker and the housewife disparaged or ignored by both the men and the mimic men—or childless career women, or reformed Others—of that contract. She is Thelma busily counting the supply of cupcakes and Jessie spending her last minutes explaining to Thelma that she should not forget to empty the lint filter on the dryer and warning her not to dry her house shoes because the soles might melt. This is society's message, its glue, that simultaneously provides it with free labor and gives it subjects of ridicule and objects for its jokes. The daughter's closest friend and love object, her mother, is reflected back to her as ridiculous and dependent. Brought up to expect the freedom of a little boy, she must, like Fanon, face the fact that, when she goes out into the world, she always already wears a uniform, and it is the uniform of the mother.

The Costs of Stopped Time

Jessie and Thelma re-collect moments and attempt to slow down time, but it has its price; their own time is in many ways stopped and emptied, rather than being valued in moments of full time. The sense of presentness, the unplanned responsiveness to interruptions which family life requires, fragment time and rob it of value. As Thelma suggests to Jessie that she stick around so that they can have another discussion as good as this one, Jessie says, "It's this next part that's made the last part so good" (75). The end point, as Freud and Oedipus knew all along, defines retroactively the moments along the way, giving them worth; they can only become "moments" leading up to some culmination or other if the culmination is known and valued ahead of time. The ideal role of the Woman/mother is not to move toward an endpoint but, rather, to be available in order to make it possible for males to move forward. For the woman, however, stopped time may be simply empty, waiting time: "Whatever else you find to do, you're still mainly waiting. The waiting's the worst part of it. The waiting's what you pay somebody else to do, if you can" (22).

In terms of what that means to the individual woman whose life consists precisely of waiting, of being on call to the demands of others whose time is more valuable than hers, Jessie has this to say: "Well, I can get off right now, if I want to, because even if I ride fifty more years and get off them, it's the same place when I step down to it" (33). It all comes to the same thing: "Once I started remembering, I could see what it added up to" (68). Repetition, the incompleteness of disconnected moments, the dependence enforced by culture—all turn into rage directed inward, or, as Freud ingeniously concluded, women are naturally masochistic; "patient labor at instinctual self-destruction. Ceaseless 'activity' of mortification," says Irigaray (1981, 127). Thelma claims that, if Jessie has the courage to kill herself, she certainly must have the courage to stay alive; Jessie's response is to agree: "It's really a matter of where I'd rather be."

There will be another variation on the manipulation of time at the end of the play. Jessie has carefully made sure that her mother prepared cocoa for the two of them to share as they talk, the cocoa used to sweeten the taste of milk, in a kind of metaphor for sweetening the inevitability of turning into a mother. Cocoa serves several purposes: it sweetens, and it creates a tradition, though not a particularly pleasant one. The milk curdles, as it always did, and neither of them likes it, sharing the same complaints about it they have shared for years. You can always taste the film of the curdle beneath the sugary chocolate taste, the skin on top of the milk, claims Jessie, like the skin on milk which has no real identity of its own but whose own consistency is eerie, abject, disgusting, tantalizing. It is not milk, but it is not "not milk" either. For Kristeva the skin on milk is an appropriate metaphor for the abject, a kind of repulsive and fascinating trace of a kind of "swarming" border that is in some inarticulated way associated with the relationship to the mother's body and to corporeality itself, which can never be completely bounded or given rigid borders.

The other purpose of the cocoa is, finally, to produce a messy pan, such banalities proving to be very serious. That messy pan will be Thelma's only support after Jessie has escaped into her room: "You wash that pan till you hear the doorbell ring and I don't care if it's an hour, you keep washing that pan" (83). The dirty pan, sticky and crusted with curdled milk and hardened chocolate, will be what Thelma holds onto for dear life as she phones Dawson when the shot is fired. A dirty cocoa pan turns into something that protects her, as did her banal words. For many women like Thelma the image of mother may be an anchor in a world that as yet has not articulated the relationship between women and mothers, a subtle and risky point Kristeva makes in her discussion of the image of the Virgin Mary in Catholicism. Abruptly rejecting or abandoning the women whose identity depended on that image for lack of another one leaves them placeless, abandoned even by other women. The separation of the symbolic Mother from the mother has to be done slowly and carefully, or the only beneficiaries will be the pope, Randall Terry, and Jesse Helms.

The empty spaces in Jessie's narrative are both origin and tele-ology as she faces a future indistinguishable from the present. This empty future is the result of an origin that proves retroactively to have been a misinterpretation. There is a difference between Jessie at present and Jessie in an old baby picture of "who I started out and this is what's left." She continues: "I am what became of your child. [. . .] I'm what was worth waiting for and I didn't make it. Me . . . who might have made a difference to me. . . . I'm not going to show up, so there's no reason to stay, except to keep you company, and that's . . . not rea-son enough because I'm not . . . very good company. . . . Am I" (76). The photograph, the saved moment, was valuable because of the future it assumed, but, when that future did not materialize, the back-ward look at the photograph shows that the baby and the adult are two completely different people. The origin was misread; it was the origin of the human subject as homologous to the male. Found out, revealed to be female, her connection to that origin and teleology is severed.

Castration on Oedipus' terms has intervened, severing the promise of the baby in the photograph when the little girl became a woman without origin or teleology, at the same moment Dawson was turned into an adult with both; the oedipal triangle has spaces only for mother/wife, father, and son. This photograph and its distance from Jessie, the distance between the early Jessie and the late one, portray what mascu-line culture calls castration, the choice of one kind of body to be "hu-man" rather than another; her castration, Freud would say, is a "fact," while his is symbolic and abstract. Hers is the body that is linguistically and culturally separated from the category "human," the lesson the girls in Kennedy's play also learned.

The relation with Dawson is central, while absent here. Jessie's instructions to her mother are to make sure that, at the end, it is the police who find her body first, *not Dawson*. The brother's eye, the eye of the son, had already defined her and cut her to pieces: "He just calls me Jess like he knows who he's talking to" (23). He has been able to name her and to enforce his name for her, as he pulls down into place the deadly image culture gives her. His name smothers her, *his* name for her, leaving no place for her contribution to its meaning. The brother's gaze is the eye of the son, the perspective from which judgments are made that mark the different paths sons and daughters take if Oedipus has his way. This is the eye of the brother, the chosen One, who decides, according to his own famous vision, who is good enough and who is crippled, castrated.[10]

Brother and sister share a certain equality before their passage through the oedipal complex, perhaps potentially the most equal male/ female relationship we can image in this symbolic organization. But this shred of equality is destroyed and turned into hatred by that social selection. The proper name, Dawson's name for Jessie, is, nevertheless, also the unstable and shifting place of semiotic disruption. The earliest memories of the infant have to do with light, the mother's face, and sound, essentially an experience or memory of space, as yet unnamed, unmarked, by language but marked by laughter before language. Entry into language marks the separation from this space, a first victory over the mother by syntax, but her influence is never totally covered and eliminated. Its disruptiveness and unreliability remains alive as "the dynamic and semantic ambiguity of proper names, their lack of precision as to the notion of identity, and their impact within unconscious and imaginary constructs" (Kristeva 1980, 290). Dawson's attempt at forceful elimination of that ambiguity through his act of knowing her is Adam naming Eve.

Dawson is part of the Oedipal family that knows you before you are ready:

> They know things about you, and they learned it before you had a chance to say whether you wanted them to know it or not. They were there when it happened and it don't belong to them; it belongs to you, only they got it. (23)

The family provides a situation in which women can know each other closely, while it can also mean stifling confinement and the theft of identity. Thelma is a kind of survivor of all this, getting along because she has an indirect link to the future in her children but suspecting the problems: "Family is just accident, Jessie. It's nothing personal, hon. They don't mean to get on your nerves. They don't even mean to be your family. They just are" (23). Her response to life is to survive it: "I will stay here until they make me go, until they drag me screaming and I mean screeching into my grave, and you're real smart to get away before then because, I mean, honey, you've never heard noise like that in your life" (78).

Jessie and Thelma spend this evening in a different kind of privacy, not the privacy that is man's right but, rather, a privacy between women without men. This is the way Jessie has arranged things: "It's private. Tonight is private, yours and mine, and I don't want anybody else to have any of it" (53). Specifically, this I/you dialogue between two women is not to be interrupted, judged, or observed by the third person, the "he" of universal grammar, the generic subject represented by Dawson. The oedipal requirements of language will still unavoidably intrude and cause difficulties, but the fundamental condition of this dialogue is enforced: no men. They settle down for their last talk, though much of it, of course, is not talk at all but shorthand in a second language, an idiolect inside their native, misnamed "mother" tongue.

The competition between the two of them for the father's favor in the past is painfully brought up. The father chose to talk to his daughter rather than his wife; even on his deathbed he had nothing to say to Thelma: "It was his last chance not to talk to me and he took full advantage of it" (48). Thelma tries at this last moment to learn from Jessie what he was like, since here only the daughter can carry to her the words the father rarely addressed to her directly.

Jessie pulls out lists of reminders for her mother as she cares for her in these last moments—lists that indirectly cite housewifely lists that gather together and organize not concepts or ideas or public matters but, instead, masking tape, lightbulbs, batteries, the contents of all the drawers, whom to call to deliver the groceries, who can be depended on not to put the fudge in the bottom of the bag where it will be smashed. She has drawn up a list of Christmas presents for her mother for the next twenty years, a list to be given to Dawson, and has also prepared a cardboard box of presents "for whenever you need one," trivial things like a sample tube of toothpaste and other objects like her grandmother's ring. These two remembrances, ostensibly of different monetary value, from two different paradigms, are evened out and intensified in significance because they will be fundamentally revalued as bits of Jessie at each moment her mother chooses an object from the box. They will be contiguously arranged in a new paradigm: reminders of Jessie.

The grandmother as absent presence slips into the place a father might occupy if the mythical oedipal triangle worked smoothly. The grandmother's presence begins to hover as third term between mother and daughter, keeping that moment a private one among women. But the ring also introduces ambiguity; it is the grandmother's *wedding* ring, the mark of her entry into the oedipal marriage requirements. Jessie has specifically rebelled against her mother's assumption that what she really needed to make her happy were grandchildren, the predictable fruits of a calculable, reproductive marriage: "It always comes to the same thing." The circle of the ring, an unbroken but nonlinear connection between the mother and daughter, is still not an adequate expression of their connection, but it works for the moment, even as it edges precariously close to oedipal requirements. It is, however, excessive: even this wedding ring of the third woman subverts the daughter's required desire for the father by sealing a pact between mother and daughter.

What has been going on quietly beneath these exchanges of information and humor ("Why does suicide appeal to you? Because it's dark and quiet. So's the back yard, Jessie!") is a minute and gentle attempt to separate what is daughter from what is mother, without cruelty or blame for either. The conflation between mother and daughter produced by the oedipal narrative eliminated any distance between the two that might allow their mutual but separate existence. The daughter's teleology is only to become mother, while the son can become man, then father, the daughter thus retroactively erased. One of the women can exist only at the expense of the other: "When the one of [them] comes into the world, the other goes underground. When the one carries life, the other dies," writes Luce Irigaray (1981, 66).

Irigaray helps articulate this problem of closeness without distance that mother and daughter face as they maneuver around the image of one Woman that assures narrative closure and structures readability by fixing her place. Conflated into an idealized narrative image are a daughter who may or may not be a mother and a woman who is not only a mother but always also a separate individual, a daughter: "Each of us lacks her own image; her own face, the animation of her own body is missing. And the one mourns the other" (Irigaray 1981, 67). This mourning, unlike the son's mourning the missing mother, has no mastery to assuage it, to be sublimated and memorialized as a rewriting of the past.

The daughter's words to the mother in Irigaray's double-vision lyric piece let us see the conflict: "I look like you, you look like me. I look at myself in you, you look at yourself in me. . . . But always distracted, you turn away. Furtively, you verify your continued existence in the mirror" (1981, 67). That mirror is the Imaginary, the oedipal specular reflector; it might become "you/I exchanging selves endlessly and each staying herself," in the other mirror, the "speculum" of the other woman.

Thelma is caught in a mirror as she watches Jessie prepare to kill herself: "Everything you do has to do with me, Jessie. You can't do *anything*, wash your face or cut your finger, without doing it to me. That's right! You might as well kill me as you, Jessie, it's the same thing. This has to do with me, Jessie" (74). The doubled bodies, each feeling the other's pain in her own body, suggests an intersubjectivity that is specifically different.

Irigaray's voice responds: "You look at yourself in the mirror. And already you see your own mother there. And soon your daughter, a mother. Between the two, what are you? What space is yours alone? ... And how to let your face show through, beyond all the masks?" Mother and daughter resemble one of Virginia Woolf's female characters who has befriended a gay man, whom she describes as "the lip reader, her semblable, her conspirator, a seeker like her after hidden faces" (Woolf 1941, 205). Irigaray continues:

> It's evening. As you're alone, as you've no more image to maintain or impose, you strip off your disguises. You take off your face of a mother's daughter, of a daughter's mother. You lose your mirror reflection. You thaw. You melt. You flow out of yourself.
>
> But no one is there to gather you up, and nothing stops this overflow. Before day's end you'll no longer exist if this hemorrhaging continues. Not even a photographer's remembrance as a mark of your passage between your mother and your daughter. And, maybe, nothing at all. Your function remains faceless. (1981, 67)

It is a function with no figure. The *sème* of blood reappears, and the edges, the threshold, the border, prove to be all there is. That *sème* means differently from the direction of the female subject whose words never took form. For the male blood marks the unenforceable edges that leak as he tries to impose meaning, but for the female the blood marks her position as edge; she *is* the leak.

The problem is to avoid getting flattened between the two images of mother and daughter, one of which will be erased to make a place for the other. But not getting caught can also mean not being there, hemorrhaging, remaining form-less and disappearing without a word to hold oneself together. The daughter cannot be helped by the mother, who was herself once a daughter who didn't know her own face either: "You wanted me to grow up, to walk, to run in order to vanquish your own infirmity" (Irigaray 1981, 64). The mother who is looking for her reflection in her daughter may only find there nothing, transparency. There can hardly be a reflection, a figure, of face*less*ness, particularly by a faceless daughter, an unfigured subject.

"And if I leave, you no longer find yourself [says the daughter]. Was I not the bail to keep you from disappearing, the stand-in for your absence? The guardian of your nonexistence?" In finding no reflection Thelma pours herself more and more into her daughter to "maintain the memory of [herself]" (Irigaray 1981, 65). The child can be used to sustain the adult: "I'd snatch you up and walk the floor. Hold you pressed in my arms against my heart like a shield. Needing you much more than you needed me" (Wideman 1984, 26). The mother's loneliness and isolation can make her dependent on the child.

What has happened is that each of the females has tried to find her reflection in the other one, who has already entered into someone else's gaze, the gaze of the male eye, the male I: "I received from you only your obliviousness of self so that with my physical appearance I redoubled the lack of your presence" (Irigaray 1981, 67). The daughter, repeating the mother, functions as a "foyer" for her disappearance, a threshold without a chance to capture that sliding into each other that occurs as they face each other: "But have I ever known you other than gone?"

The empty mirror the women find provides a double *want* of presence, a power-less absence in the mirror. The double invisibility of Oedipus, however, works as *point de fuite*, the absent point of perspective that Foucault analyzes in his discussion of the painting *Las Meninas*. There the absence was that of the observer for whom the painting was painted; it was oedipal absence as redoubled *presence*, the missing face of the humanist subject that orients everything toward himself.

What the Symbolic phobically pushed away in order to produce this destructive empty mirror is an identification between mother and child prior to the mirror stage, and Kristeva refers to that identification as *reduplication*, even a "jammed repetition," whose jamming is the consequence of its retroactive interruption by the privilege of the mirror. This reduplication occurs on "the far or near side of sight" as "the masochistic joissance of the couple who preceded" the specular mirror stage or the Imaginary, a couple made of the mother and child. Accessible only through the chronologically later Symbolic, this moment of reduplication produces "a gaze in addition to sight" and "refers to the outposts of our unstable identities, blurred by a drive that nothing could defer, deny, or signify" (1989, 246).

Thelma has desperately tried to cling to the two of them, to Jessie and to herself through Jessie. At the moment of Jessie's shot, after Thelma has wildly tried to prevent her from going into the bedroom, from going over the one-way threshold, pushing the *sème* of blood to its conclusion, she slumps to the floor: "Jessie, Jessie, child. . . . Forgive me. I thought you were mine" (89). Or I thought you were me. Intersubjectivity can also be fatal. She, rather than Oedipus, assumes the guilt for the suicide, once again revealing her worthlessness. By definition, unworthy of authority because she is a woman, when she does assert authority as a mother and when things go wrong, she is doubly guilty. She had no business asserting authority.

Hers is the familiar guilt of the woman, the mother who blames herself in an assumption of guilt which matches society's blame of her for giving too much love or for not giving enough. Passive causality has never been far away. A part of Thelma's puzzlement has been trying to figure out what she has done wrong, so she could at least survive by assuming the blame and saving Jessie's life. Hyllos, we remember, was able to live because Deianeira had absorbed the blame. If Thelma can absorb blame here, perhaps she can save Jessie: "I don't know what I did, but I did it, I know." "Maybe I did drop you. . . . Maybe I fed you the wrong thing. Maybe you had a fever sometime and I didn't know it soon enough. Maybe it's punishment" (72). When asked what it is a punishment for, she says, "I don't know. Because of how I felt about your father. Because I didn't want any more children. Because I smoked too much or didn't eat right when I was carrying you. It has to be something I did" (71). But she is doubly at fault now, with a *second* chance to stop the suicide and a second failure: "How can I get up every day knowing you had to kill yourself to make it stop hurting and I was here all the time and I never even saw it. And then you gave me this chance to make it better, convince you to stay alive, and I couldn't do it. How can I live with myself after this, Jessie?" (72). Having failed once, she is given another chance and fails again. For Jessie this last encounter has not been orchestrated to blame her mother but, instead, to explain her choice and to say good-bye: "I didn't want you to save me. I just wanted you to know." All their speech is difficult: "You're real far back there, Jessie. How could I know you were so alone?" (73).

Norman's play is so spare and simple that it works like a balancing scale to show every imbalance, every shift of power, between the mother and daughter. The most subtle change in dynamics between actresses changes the effect of their encounter. A stronger actress playing Thelma smothers Jessie; a stronger actress playing Jessie turns Thelma into a clinging simpleton. But occasionally, both Norman and Irigaray fall into the pattern lying there waiting—blaming the mother. Feminist discourse may itself be unbalanced because mostly daughters have determined its course, yet Kristeva's articulation of the relationship between motherhood and discourse brings mother/daughter to bear precisely on the mother's body. For her motherhood, pregnancy itself, can be a rebellion against Oedipus, a rebellion whose meaning and experience has been almost completely stolen from women, not only by masculine culture itself but also by what that culture has done to determine the categories of thinking about motherhood that still, even in feminist attempts to articulate the relation between women and mothers, structure the debate. Though attempting to theorize pregnancy remains difficult and risky, it is necessary in order to refuse the equation of women's bodies with men's, an equation that elides the specificity of women's bodies, socially constructed as that specificity is. Otherwise, the visible invisibility of the masculine body as norm simply proves to underlie every theory, only with much more subtlety. Overlooking pregnancy also plays into assumptions that "pregnancy is a trivial, empty experience with nothing positive about it except the end product, the genetically connected baby," as Katha Pollitt argues in a discussion of surrogate motherhood. These assumptions cover over the fact that "the long months of pregnancy and the intense struggle of childbirth are part of forming a relationship with the child-to-be, part of the social and emotional task of parenthood" (1990, 825).

Pregnancy in Kristeva's version constitutes an instant of the splitting of cells in which two are one without presence or hierarchy, but this can be true *only* when that pregnancy is her choice. This pleasant description of the two in one which pregnancy constitutes would make little sense if a woman were forced to bear a child because of oedipal constraints or because of violence: "Within the body, growing as a graft, indomitable, there is an other. . . . Pregnancy seems to be experienced as the radical ordeal of the splitting of the subject: redoubling up of the body, separation and coexistence of the self and of an other, of nature and consciousness, of physiology and speech" (Kristeva 1980, 237). The real stake in such a discourse, argues Kristeva, is the possibility that, if we do not retheorize the maternal in relation to language, the cycle of fetishizing the mother in religion is simply reinforced. For it is often only in religion (and perhaps advertising) that women find motherhood to be a subject taken seriously, though for all the wrong reasons.

Though the father gives that Other a sign, a copyright, the mother provides an organic contribution of part of herself, shared thresholds of blood. In spite of the critiques of anthropomorphism that have ferreted out the humanist Man in Western discourse, neither metaphysics nor its critiques have theorized the materiality upon which the Symbolic rests; as Irigaray says, "The bodily in man is what metaphysics has never touched." In order to understand motherhood and gender relations, the "bodily" has to be the starting point, the physical relation between the mother and this unsymbolized Other within her.

There is no word for this Other, no sign; it is neither something nor somebody; this collapse, as the abortion debate shows, pits women as violently and profoundly against each other as no other issue does. Christian culture tries to insert itself into, to penetrate, this mutual singularity with intense determination before the mother has time to take charge, to make sure that she does not master this process. Because her control is usurped by religion, by science, and by law, which inscribe themselves retroactively, the mother is very likely to be turned into a filter, a thoroughfare, a mediating threshold for the passage of the child into the hands of society. The child becomes an obligatory donation rather than a gift.

This motherhood can obviously be the Symbolic's inscription of the mother so that she desires a child, a son, as a phallic substitute for her own lack. But it may also *not* be that; it may instead imply possibilities of semiotic disruption of attempts at cohesion by the Symbolic, for it might signify "the reunion of a woman-mother with the body of her mother," a body that is

> one toward which women aspire all the more passionately simply because it lacks a penis: that body cannot penetrate her as can a man when possessing his wife. By giving birth, the woman enters into a contract with her mother; they are the seam of continuity differentiating itself. She thus actualizes the homosexual facet of mother-

hood, through which a woman is simultaneously closer to her instinctual memory . . . and consequently more negatory of the social,
symbolic bond. (Kristeva 1980, 238, 239)

Though the dangers and risks of appropriation by the discourse of
the heterosexual mother and its homophobic Christian variants are so
enormous, perhaps it is possible at least to acknowledge a momentary
contiguity of lesbian theory and theories of the maternal. There is a
female contract here that fluidly destabilizes the points of application of
the oedipal contract, which must enforce its version of identity in order
to build its constructions.

The homosexual-maternal facet "is a whirl of words," displacement, rhythm. It slips between and around the Symbolic, accession to
which "is an appeasement that turns into melancholy as soon as the child
becomes an object, a gift to others, neither self nor part of the self, an
object destined to be a subject, an other" (Kristeva 1980, 239). This
melancholy has to do with the loss of the child, but it is also the loss of
the mother and the body through "the implacable violence which constitutes any symbolic contract."[11] This separation has only been figured as
castration, as loss of the *penis,* not the separation from the womb. Most
especially, it has not been figured as the separation the *mother* experiences, one that is excessive to such figuration; it is *more* than that.

Pregnancy is an original event, the enactment of the incorporation
of biology and the Symbolic, "thus instilling the subjectless biological
program into the very body of a symbolizing subject, this event called
motherhood," where life and discourse come together and where civilization's claims are both the most tenuous and its attempts at domination
most intense. The pregnant body is located precisely at the center of the
needs of power, where life must enter discourse and be disciplined, the
exact center of the rhetoric of bio-power as the "maternal body slips
away from the discursive hold and immediately conceals a cipher that
must be taken into account biologically and socially" (Kristeva 1980,
241). It is also the silent center, written about and claimed by Christians
and feminists alike but only rarely articulated by the mother/daughter
inside the symbolic Mother because of yet another division of intellectual
labor, this time between childless women and those with children, who
usually have few resources and are, for the most part, their sole caretak-
ers. They are denied uninterrupted time, though intellectual labor is
notoriously dependent on solitude and long stretches of time. The ro-

mantic valorization of fragments and self-lessness that one finds in much avant-garde literature and theory takes on a very different character when it is a forced condition of work.

Childbirth in Kristeva's description replaces the primal scene as a fantasy of origin; the sense of giving birth is "incest turned inside out, flayed identity. Giving birth: the height of bloodshed and life, scorching moment of hesitation (between inside and outside, ego and other, life and death), horror and beauty, sexuality and the blunt negation of the sexual" (Kristeva 1982a, 155). The bleeding of Kennedy's "lesson" fuses, intermingles with new life, the *requirement* to be a mother on Thelma's part bleeding into the *desire* to be one, compulsion and intent becoming inseparable.

Any attempt to articulate whatever "motherhood" might be hovers over this dangerous terrain; it cannot be used to guarantee female creativity or female power or even female intersubjectivity. Introducing motherhood into discourse instead simply involves taking care not to fall back into privileging the image of the Mother (with its erasure of women) or the prescription that all women be mothers. But all women *had* mothers, and, if we remain alert to the dangers, perhaps a slow subversion of the material and linguistic contract can come about, keeping intact two inseparable but not identical levels, the level in which specific subjects make decisions and act and the level of the Symbolic, in which decisions are already made for them.

Motherhood, which exists in this nebulous symbolic range, must also be connected over and over to its material nature. While trying not to reduce its emotional impact, one must also define the mother-child relationship as one that essentially enforces her other domestic role; because of her obligations to her child, the woman appears to be most obvious choice to provide the male with free labor. In Delphy's description the institution of marriage constitutes the collective attribution of childcare to women and the collective exemption of men, in effect exempting them "from the basic costs of reproduction" (1984, 104). Men partially assume the burden of financial care for the child and mother, but only temporarily, as the story of child support payments after divorce shows. His assumption of the costs of the child is used to appropriate both her childcare labor *and* her domestic labor, provided for his comfort. Her lack of control of her own reproduction essentially also robs her of control of her own labor; the social definition of child rearing as women's responsibility not so coincidentally enables society to appropriate her other domestic labor as well. Her involvement in reproduction does not cripple her; she is, instead, crippled by the social requirements having to do with her labor in a family that allows the male to appropriate her labor in exchange for her children's upkeep.

Kristeva, who takes the most ambiguous and indirect stands in relation to feminism, has written her maternity into her theory. She also approaches another dangerous but crucial intersection in the articulation of motherhood through her openness to what she calls the "crisis" of religion, with *religion* defined in terms of desire as the phantasmic necessity on the part of particular speaking subjects to "provide for themselves a representation (animal, female, male, parental, etc.) in place of what constitutes them as such, in other words, symbolization" (Kristeva 1982c, 32).

Religion may have to do with this desire for a representation, but it has also been the masculine institution that has most nearly succeeded in usurping motherhood: "What does this desire for motherhood correspond to? . . . For want of an answer to this question, feminist ideology leaves the door open to the return of religion, whose discourse, tried and proven over thousands of years, provides the necessary ingredients for satisfying the anguish, the suffering, and the hopes of mothers."[12] Christianity reclaimed the mother into its organizing system without, however, revalorizing her, and, in so doing, it has provided solace for many women, in spite of its ultimate arrangement for the benefit of heterosexual males and its blatant reinforcement of the right of the male to the female body: the right to appropriate her labor power to control her sexuality. The difficulty facing feminist theory is to approach this close connection between religion and motherhood and attempt to understand it sympathetically and patiently. It is especially difficult because of its location along the fault line of the sacred and the erotic, the violent and the intimate—in short, along the fault line of sacrifice. The mother and daughter conversation will be a long one.

Going in Style

This particular mother and daughter conversation has to do with theatricality as performance, and it is centered on the difference between the concepts of the enunciation and of the enunciated. Resistance to the oedipal Symbolic manifests itself as style in an enunciative strategy on the part of subjects highly trained by ordinary life to notice the foreign nature of the oedipal sentence and to resist it. Since the material of the language they have to work with has been prefabricated, their enunciations take on a duplicity that turns the *form* of the utterance, its twisting and contortion, into the *message*.

These enunciations work to resist the Symbolic's predetermination through *style,* which can show that the purpose of their speaking is "to thematize the displaced element" (Kristeva 1982b, 88), which cannot yet be spoken. The style of their manipulation of words is thus like the style of popular ingenuity that manipulates mass-produced objects differently. Words, like commodified objects, have the potential to drain and empty the subjects who inadvertently find their identities reflected back to them as empty. Taking those objects and touching them, leaving personal marks of use on them, may be one way to resist the emptiness. Subjects are not outside these words; that is, they come to subjectivity *through* language. But neither are they wholly *inside* them either. There is always an excess.

Kristeva suggests that the logic of the *enunciation,* the informative kernel or message, is an earlier organizer of meaning than the logic of the *enunciated,* or syntax, in the development of speech.[13] These levels are temporally sequential, as the child first develops language according to the principle of binarism. A subject, who at this stage is also developing the ability to distinguish between pleasure and pain, can emphasize one of two poles. She can emphasize either: (1) "I say what I like"; or (2) "I say to be clear," to make myself understood. There are, thus, two poles from which the binary message can be interpreted, that of the speaker's position (the first example) and that of the addressee (the second). This binarism immediately slips into universal syntax: "I say for you, for us, so that we can understand each other better" (Kristeva 1982b, 89). The binary message has slid from "I" as the point of pleasure to "you" as addressee and then to the impersonal third term "he," the generic male subject, which establishes a "universal" syntax, at least for now. Chronologically different in their moments of emergence, these two poles nevertheless become inseparable at a later date, like the intermixture of the semiotic and Symbolic.

What relates the logic of the enunciation, or message, to the logic of the enunciated, or syntax—what *marks* the individuality of specific speaking subjects in ways we can try to interpret—is style, the interpretive function itself, not only for the critic but also for the speaking subject, whose articulations are in every sense acts of interpretation; "it is thus that the subject of enunciation is born" (Kristeva 1982a, 196). Style connects the logic of the message and the logic of syntax *and their two corresponding subjective structures* ("I" for me and "I" for you). If these two inseparable subjective structures are conflated here, rather than being articulated in their intermingling, the linguistic contract will succeed in smothering difference, in overwriting it.

As Kristeva describes it, style marks the emotion or drive caught as a precipitate in the relationship between message (example 1) and syntax (example 2). Like the traces of hands on mass-produced objects, style, in this expanded, discursive sense, might refer to the specific markings on words and, in particular, on subjects conceptualized as lexemes, subjec*ted* by and resistant to a particular sociohistorical context, in this case, "that of Christian, Western civilization and its lay ramifications" (Kristeva 1980, 211). Grasping oedipal words as objects, treating words as things and surrounding them on all sides, slipping between them and through them personal touches and slight variations, allows popular ingenuity to practice a kind of guerrilla activity on Oedipus' narrative. The act of enunciating and the contents of the enunciation may not yet allow meaning to originate from a female direction because of the space and the grammatical form that limit what women can say or what can be *heard,* connecting this notion of speech to Fraser's subaltern counterpublics. The supposedly neutral public sphere of discourse, the community of language such as the one Habermas and the class of intellectuals Winkler described proposes, with their bracketing of power differences, does not account for the political nature of style. But Nancy Fraser does: "Unequally empowered social groups tend to develop unequally valued cultural styles" (1990a, 64).

Female activity might be read as it thematizes itself as what is being indirectly talked about in all the linguistic encounters in *'night, Mother.* Reading for style might make it possible to interpret those subjects' different symbolic capacities to account for the influence of power in the evaluation and hierarchizing of different kinds of style. In the style that marks the difference between two separate performances, "I say to mean" and "I say to be heard," mingled subject positions come together, their enunciative strategies mixing with normative syntax to produce a dialogic sentence. The old formalist literary concept of style can be redefined and expanded so that, in talking about language, we are actually talking about *discourse.* Thus, poetic and grammatical forms can be seen to be connected to the organization of the *socius.* Then the concepts of style and poetics can be seen as elements of a political poetics that depends on embodied enunciation, a *performance*.

By historicizing those performances in discourse, we can read the historical specificity in the use of words and symbols marked by the way the subject of the enunciation was born into language, emerged into subjectivity, was subject*ed*. "And it is in remembering this path that the subject rediscovers, if not [her] origin, at least [her] originality" (Kristeva 1982b, 89).

Jessie and Thelma have thematized their absence from the world of Oedipus by indirect and sideways allusions, by citations from the past coded as references to material objects, by words that do not in themselves mean much but that are given as peace offerings or gifts or knives—words that mean, but they do not mean quite what they say. The arrangement and ordering of the photographs, the arrangement of the interior of the house, and, finally, the arrangement and ordering of the words that pass between them allow them various moments of control.

Oedipus' grip is always tenuous, as glimpses through its cracks make possible quite specific rebellions, such as Jessie's suicide, which might be positive in its context; Thelma's resistance, on the other hand, is an impassioned determination to stay alive. These glimpses and their specific responses may share an affinity with a kind of interpretation Walter Benjamin describes: "the obscure impulse of the animal [which] detects, as danger approaches, a way of escape that still seems invisible," a way of escape not visible from the top down. The image of a redefined animal intelligence that peers closely at the world, reads it in its most minute significations without smothering it in abstractions, and glimpses ways through and around its attempted closures may help locate the missing sites of female activity. Benjamin suggests the need to differentiate this first notion of the animal from a different notion of animality in bourgeois society:

> This society, each of whose members cares only for his own abject well-being, falls victim, with animal insensibility but without the insensate intuition of animals, as a blind mass, to even the most obvious danger, and the diversity of individual goals is immaterial in face of the identity of the determining forces. (1978, 71)

Like woman, mother, and nature, the animal has to be wrested out of the grips of the oedipal Symbolic.

A single sentence of Thelma's, in its ironic indirectness and back-handed resistance, its moment of afterthought, reevaluates and wanders away from the ostensible meaning of the sentence, which works dialogi-cally as a conversation with herself as well as with Jessie. The second part of the sentence subtly disagrees with the first, contorting the coher-ence of Oedipus enough to leave a space for a glimpse of a difference. The social requirement, speaking to be understood in the first part of the sentence, the syntax, where I mean what I say, is surreptitiously, obliquely reconsidered, taken back, in the second part, the place of the message, where I say what I mean and where I acknowledge an excess to the normality required by the contract: "You're as normal as they come, Jessie, for the most part." Thelma speaks a sideways glance.

Chapter 6

The Space Where Speaking Bodies Evolve: Rosario Castellanos

One may urge that the censure does not touch the art of the dramatic
poet, but only that of the actor.
—Aristotle

Y cuál es mi lugar, señor, entre tus actos?
—Rosario Castellanos

Surely it was time someone invented a new plot, or that the author
came out from the bushes . . .
—Virginia Woolf

The Christian logic of purity, whose organizational effects showed up
so strikingly in the imagery of Adrienne Kennedy's plays and in the
spatial organization of Norman's, was also important to the history of
Spain's colonization of Mexico and to the subsequent independence and
revolutionary periods. Its influence continues today in late capitalism,
where the feminized debris of Third World cheap labor becomes the
chief resource of Free Trade negotiations in an information society. This
logic of purity was evident from the moment the Spanish conquistadors
left their own society, which was, argues Jean Franco, "preoccupied with
purity of blood"; the Spain they left had already "cleansed" itself by
expelling Jews and Moors. In colonial Mexico it was the Church whose
duty it was to safeguard purity, especially as the central site of that duty
was the control of the reproductive bodies of white Spanish women in
the New World in the interests of race and inheritable property. In order
to do so, it privileged two locations, "the pulpit and the confessional—
and two genres of discourse—the sermon and the confession—through

which a celibate male was authorized to warn, harangue, interrogate, educate, and interpolate the population" (Franco 1989, xiii).

Franco, whose historical work on women in Mexican culture I will draw on extensively before discussing Rosario Castellanos's play, *The Eternal Feminine,* argues that this structure worked differently in New Spain than it had in Europe. The majority population in New Spain was made up of African slaves, mulattoes, and indigenous men and women as well as people of mixed blood; nonwhites greatly outnumbered Spaniards and criollos. Thus, white women, whose "purity" was crucial to the continuation of Spanish culture and power in the New World, were subject to intense surveillance and control, this enforced immobility intimately connected to the racism expressed even in the structure of the home, with its protected interior patio and exterior iron grates. Within this phobic, cultural structure, where mixture was always already a fact, the figure of the mother almost inevitably assumed a sacred connotation, as it came to embody certainty and security. This connotation was eventually extended to the *madre patria* during the struggle for independence.

The institution of marriage was central to social organization and to the disciplining not only of women but of other feminized groups as well. As J. I. Israel writes:

[In the sixteenth century] the various evil effects of vagabondage in Mexico made both the administration in Mexico City and the government in Spain highly sensible of the political advantages of matrimony and the human family. The vast majority of the Spaniards in Mexico had left their womenfolk and families behind in Spain and this, the government soon realized, was not only a major cause of unruliness in the Spaniards who were free to wander where they pleased stealing from the wretched Indians and debauching their women, but, since the Spaniards were predatory and disruptive as well as vagrant and rootless, seriously impeded the administration of those who were married and settled, namely the Indians. Accordingly, the second *Audencia* and Viceroy Mendoza, with the encouragement of the clergy, made strenuous efforts to drive the Spaniards into matrimony, and, in the case of those who were already married, to induce them to bring over their wives from Spain. Lands and other concessions in and around the Spanish new towns were assigned only to married men of residence, as also were *corregimientos* and other bureaucratic posts. (1975, 12)

And as Franco argues, the organization of this protected space of the family inevitably introduced its own "contamination," just as the family in the Greek polis dependent on slaves and female labor introduced threat into its most intimate spaces: "Blacks, mulattoes, and indigeneous women (and men) were perceived to be the dangerous guardians of the erotic arts, all the more perilous since, as servants and slaves, they penetrated to the heart of the home" (1989, xiv).

During the colonial period the convent rather than the home became a center of women's culture, a place where at least two discourses were developed. One surrounded the woman as mystic. As the Church limited scholastic theology to the clergy, women in convents were allowed to discuss and write about areas of feeling, their writing important to a Church involved in protecting its power in the face of the development of scientific thought in Europe. Women helped develop the areas of spirituality and mysticism that could counter that influence. The other discourse was represented by Sor Juana Inés de la Cruz, where the supposed irrationality of mysticism was separated from a discourse in which a woman could learn and write, even though the letters, journals, poems, and texts produced were the property of the male clergy and could be confiscated, read at will, suppressed, or published. Sor Juana constructed a new kind of subject—the woman as writer of a theological poetics that drew on a religious tradition, connecting an author's abilities to interpret to God's ability to interpret the universe. This connection, because it now involved a woman author, produced a temporary conceptual dislocation: a woman as author moved into a space theologically and culturally reserved only for men. Such a position very early challenged the exclusion of women from what Franco calls truth activities, that is, the production and writing of discourses having to do with belief and knowledge.

During the National period (1812–1910), the organization of purity worked differently for it had now to legitimate criollo influence in setting the pattern for postrevolutionary Mexican nationalism. The liberal intelligentsia of this period drew on European models from the Enlightenment and metropolitan culture in order to construct a national culture centered in a modernized Mexico City. This culture, argues Franco, "whitened" the *léperos*—slang for the poor, the uneducated, the indigenous—by attempting to clean them up through education, conduct books, civilizing literature, and a special kind of instructive calendar. During this period a liberal secular attack was focused on the Church, but, because secular culture was centered in urban areas, rural areas were left in the hands of the clergy, or they remained in a kind of limbo.

The structure of the family, which had been important both to colonial bureaucratic and church control, was also central to this nationalism, but it worked differently for different groups. The Holy Family model, in fact, broke up certain activities in the indigenous communities that had depended on an extended family structure for symbolic production, artisan work, dance, fiestas, economic production, and reproduction. Capitalism was later "articulated with the hacienda and the mine, both of which disciplined the work force not only through direct repression but also by using the paternalistic discourse of the Church." These practices of domination produced discourses that valorized the family, on which ideological, economic, and biological reproduction was centered, coexisting "with plantation and mining enclaves in which the family was broken up altogether" (Franco 1988, 505).

The institutions of literacy and cultural production during modernization were in the hands of the male intelligentsia, which challenged women's loyalty to the masculine clergy of the Church but did not challenge the subordination of women to male dominance in the family. Intellectuals advocated the virtues of patriotism, the work ethic, and a belief in progress, as the label of "lazy" came to refer to the effects produced by the colonial system and the Church. Secular male writers produced novels that were, in most cases, allegories of national development dealing with public matters such as the nation and its politics; the secular intelligentsia took on the role of teachers of women, indigenous people, mulattoes, blacks, and other groups. This paternalistic role resulted in what Sylvia Molloy calls *aniñamiento,* or the reduction of women and other groups to the status of children in need of Europeanized education to turn them into adults.

The rise of Mexican nationalism, with its roots in criollo nationalism prior to independence in 1821 and on through the Revolutionary period (1910-17), produced a shift in the construction of femininity. Franco argues that postrevolutionary society was dynamized by populist nationalism, its rhetoric obscuring the real nature of the Mexican state as an instrument of capitalist modernization. Because of the interconnection between certain kinds of families, certain kinds of bodies, and the mode of production, nationalism was focused on the construction of the "decent" bourgeois body. Such a construction needed the disciplined family as a dependable site of its organization; a "decent" family could distinguish itself from lower groups because of its behavior, respectability, and tastes. The threat of mixture and miscegenation continues to be counteracted symbolically by a homogenized cultural imagery of the modern nation, the roots of this homogenization to be found in literacy that attempts to mold the diverse racial many of Mexico into the One in the identity of the Mexican citizen. The imagery of the patriarchal family, which had formerly been influenced by the clergy and by the authors of the literature of the educated classes, now reaches a far wider audience because of mass media and cinema.

Sacred Spaces, Virgins, and Mothers

Modernization and the growth of the culture industry intersected with a critique of nationalism in Mexico in 1968, the year when seven hundred students were killed at the plaza of Tlatelolco in Mexico City. This was an important period for feminism in Mexico, which found ways to align itself with other forms of political struggle earlier than did Anglo-American and French feminism. In terms of contemporary Mexican culture, Franco argues that the project for feminists involves writing a *prehistory* of Mexican culture that is prefeminist. That is, research into the activities of women in Mexican history must describe their activities not as if those activities were feminist, because that would imply an ahistorical assumption that they had the power to "change the story or to enter into dialogue" (Franco 1989, xxiii). Rather, a prehistory must look at the ways women "resorted to subterfuge, digression, disguise, or deathly interruption." In particular, a part of that interruption has to do with "revealing the mortal female body that sustains the male hero" (xx).

Rosario Castellanos's play *The Eternal Feminine* does that by staging and parodying Mexican history, whose telling has been a long patriarchal monologue, its coherence dependent on the exclusion of other groups from cultural production, or truth activities. The play theatricalizes and multiplies the kinds of disguises and deceptions that marked women's prehistory, ultimately calling into question any kind of confidence in the stories of "History" itself, precisely because, as Barthes sadly lamented, history is a story told by men to men.

The Eternal Feminine targets the constructed imagery of the Mexican Woman in history where her power is ostensibly celebrated but is, in reality, a distorted double image of the powerful, phallic mother side

by side with the weak and despised Woman. Castellanos's own family
were white landowners in Chiapas, a state in southern Mexico that is
predominantly indigenous. She was an early feminist, her master's thesis
at the National University entitled "On Feminine Culture," characterized by Elena Poniatowska as "the point of departure for the contemporary women's movement in Mexico" (Julian Paley, introduction to Castellanos 1988a, 22). Castellanos, who died in an accident at the age of
forty-seven while serving as Mexico's ambassador to Israel, worked in
San Cristobal with an educational puppet theater for the National Indigenist Institute, whose projects were aimed at acculturation and modernization of the indigenous population. The situation of indigenous
women in Chiapas brought into sharp relief the overlapping structures
of racism, male dominance, the Arab and Spanish cultural practices toward women that had been integral to colonialism, and North American
imperialism (Cypess 1989, 492). At the time she wrote the play, argues
Franco, Castellanos believed that the only way to improve conditions
for indigenous people, blacks, and women was through acculturation,
an approach that her play presents with far more ambiguity and suspi-
cion than her work with the Institute would suggest. Her writing, however, rarely presents indigenous women as active participants in the
production of culture, and she privileged literacy in a way that could not
account for the disciplinary effects of education.

Yet she well understood that a feminist movement required the
politicization of privileged women like herself. The farce of an eternal
feminine becomes inseparable from the farce of a feminism isolated from
the circumstances of the poor. The play's primary focus, however, is the
relationship between the absence of women from those activities—like
literature, the writing of history, and other intellectual disciplines involved in the cultural production of "truth"—and the representations of
women that become history.

The Eternal Feminine takes its mocking title from Goethe's *Faust,*
an exemplary text from the Enlightenment canon that influenced the
development of the secular intelligentsia and its members' notions of
literacy and metropolitan culture during modernization in Mexico. Castellanos's three-act play is far too long to be presented successfully, as
Kirsten Nigro has argued (1980), and it needs serious editing. But it sets
out the symbolic imagery of women, beginning with the image of the
mother, focusing first in hilarious fashion on *marianismo,* the cult of
female superiority in spiritual matters and in the virtues of self-sacrifice

exaggerated to give women power, particularly in middle- and upper-class Mexican families. *Marianismo* functions as a counterpart to *machismo* (Stevens 1973). In a structure of passive causality, phallocentric Catholicism constructs the not-male to appear almost superhumanly powerful, reinforcing female behavior that works in the interests of that phallocentric structure. The culture of *marianismo* includes the self-sacrificing "Mother like a god," the *mater dolorosa,* and the cult of the Virgin Mary, in its specific Mexican form as the dark Virgin of Guadalupe.

The Virgin of Guadalupe was originally revered at a shrine in Spain, that particular tradition transferred to Guadalupe Hidalgo in Mexico in the sixteenth century after an Amerindian, Juan Diego, in 1531 reported to Archbishop Zumarraga a miraculous vision of the Virgin on the hill Tepeyacac, the site of the worship of an Aztec virgin goddess. Miguel Hidalgo y Costilla, the priest who helped lead Amerindians and criollos in the war for Mexican independence in the nineteenth century, later used the banner of the Virgin of Guadalupe as his standard.

The Virgin of Guadalupe came to represent a certain model of femininity. As Sandra Messinger Cypess argues, the Virgin represents the virtuous feminine attributes of forgiveness, succor, piety, virginity, and saintly submissiveness, her usefulness also pronounced during the Nationalist period when the representation of the nation required an incorporation of indigenous people into images of the Mexican nation. The other side of this virtuous femininity is the Eve, Malinche image, that Castellanos draws on later in the play.

But the Virgin's functions for women in Catholicism have always been highly ambiguous, providing both oppressive constraints as well as, simultaneously, representations to satisfy the affective needs of maternal bodies. As Kristeva argues in "Stabat Mater," it is perhaps no accident that in Europe, feminism emerged out of Protestant countries, for in the imagery of Catholic theology, there is an aesthetic figuration of the female body, even though that figuration reabsorbs the female body into "the tightest parenthood structure," relying on "the female representation of an immortal biology" (Kristeva 1987b, 243, 251). The key question in discussions of the Virgin is: In what ways do representations of the Virgin Mary provide solace to women who are mothers that they do not find anywhere else? How might the excess to that resorption of femininity within the maternal be theorized to describe those "particularities of the maternal body [that] compose woman into a being of folds, a catastrophe of being that the dialectics of the trinity and its supplements would be unable to subsume"? And in what ways does not taking the maternal seriously lay women "open to the most fearsome manipulations, not to mention blinding, or pure and simple rejection by progressive activists who refuse to take a close look" (1987b, 260, 261)?

Sacred Spaces, Politics, and Archaic Subjects

Discussions of the Virgin or of *marianismo* must take into account political activity that has circled around that representation in recent years, in particular, in the violence by highly armed military regimes in combination with capitalist development in Latin America. In an important article "Killing Priests, Nuns, Women, and Children" Franco argues that military violence began to target formerly sacred sites and people—in particular, religious women and, most importantly for my argument, mothers. In circumstances in which religion and traditional moral rights were organized around the Church and its strictures, formerly safe sanctuaries such as churches, the home, and Indian communities became sites of resistance to military regimes:

> In Latin America, this sense of refuge and the sacredness that attaches to certain figures like the mother, the virgin, the nun and the priest acquire even greater significance, both because the Church and the home retained a traditional topography and traditional practices over a very long period, and also because during periods when the state was relatively weak, these institutions were the only functioning social organizations. (Franco 1985, 416)

But Franco argues that these formerly immune sites came under assault, as the traditional power of the family and the Church came into conflict in the 1950s and 1960s with capitalist development, which brought more women into the work force. Like Free Trade currently, this earlier form of capitalist expansion depended on cheap labor and urban underclasses, with leftist political movements and movements of national liberation coming into conflict with such development. As a result, highly technologized counterinsurgency campaigns were funded and supported by the First World, and, in particular, by the United States.

A result of this militarist, capitalist counterinsurgency has been the sacrilege of the intrusion of public violence into the sacred space of the home, which, as in other cultures, was itself obviously "a male-idealized otherness (the Utopia) [which locked] women into this pacific domesticity" (Franco 1985, 417). The mother in this system "[was] not only sanctified by this function but [was] converted into the temple of the species, whose bodily configuration is identical to that of the home," and the structure of the house marked it as a private and protected space, built around an enclosed patio, with windows barred to the outside: "A prison yes, but one that could easily be idealized as a sanctuary given the violence of political life" (418). It was in taking advantage of this space that "homes became hiding places, bomb factories, escape hatches, people's prisons. From the signifier of passivity and peace 'mother' became a signifer of resistance" (419).

The home and its constrictions thus made possible a kind of resistance. Franco advises an ambiguous revaluation of this domestic space:

> It is some time since Herbert Marcuse drew attention to the terrors of a desublimated world, one in which such spaces and sanctuaries had been wiped out. His analysis and that of Horkheimer can be seen as overburdened with nostalgia for the *gemütlich* interior of European bourgeois family life in which all the children played instruments in a string quartet. But even if we can no longer accept the now challenged Freudian language of his analysis, he undoubtedly deserves credit for monitoring the first signals from an empty space once occupied by archaic but powerful figures. Feminist criticism based on the critique of patriarchy and the traffic in women has rightly shed no tears for this liquidation of mother figures whose power was also servitude. Yet such criticism has perhaps underestimated the oppositional potentialities of these female territories whose importance as the *only* sanctuaries became obvious at the moment of their disappearance. (Franco 1985, 420)

It was not only in this more recent violent period that women's spaces need to be reinvestigated. Both the Church and the institutions of the developing bourgeoisie depended on what Franco calls the "anachronism" of women—on their anachronistic loyalty to the Church and its icons of maternity, as well as on their loyalty to a homebound existence that assured the separation of the public and the private and, through that separation, legitimation of the middle-class structure.[1] Franco argues that this historical process must be theorized in terms of anachronis-

tic, or *archaic,* subjects—women, indigenous people, the poor—their belief systems necessarily archaic,

> for no other options were open to them. At the same time this very
> anachronism provided them with "regions of refuge," with tradi-
> tions, moral rights, and spiritual bonds to particular territories
> (often organized around devotion of saints) that could be explosive
> when the state encroached on them. In contrast, the intelligentsia
> was a secular group, empowered by writing and therefore isolated
> from the culture of the majority of the population.

It was, she says, the "female territory of the house that allowed private
and family memory to be stored; these archaic values, quite alien to the
modern world, continued to flourish" (1988, 505–6).

John Berger and Jean Mohr's study, *Another Way of Telling,* helps
develop this relationship between women and certain experiences one
might classify, very carefully, as "universal," moments in which a kind
of connection to eternity suggests itself: moments of mourning, trance,
dream, passion, near-death, music—summit moments, or spaces of
popular memory. Berger and Mohr, drawing on Walter Benjamin and
Marx, argue that one of the effects of modernization from the eighteenth
century on was to change the experience of time so that those lyrical, or
universal, moments which seemed to establish a connection to eternity
and to timelessness, were increasingly seen simply as punctuations in a
speeded-up time or history. Those moments that had been experienced
as time*less* had once been experienced in common with members of a
community, linked to collective experiences. In "Women's Time" Kristeva traces the relationship between women and cyclical, or repetitive,
kinds of events such as the collective ones described by Berger and
Mohr. Yet those moments in modernized, capitalist cultures increasingly
came to be experienced privately or alone, as history speeded up so that
it changed faster than did any individual life. Similarly, eighteenth-cen-
tury notions of progress excluded many other cultural ways of making
sense of experience, ways that might be called "archaic" or "naive":

> The principle of historical progress insisted that the elimination of
> all other views of history save its own was part of that progress.
> Superstition, embedded conservatism, so-called eternal laws, fatal-
> ism, social passivity, the fear of eternity so skilfully used by

churches to intimidate, repetition and ignorance: all these had to be swept away and replaced by the proposal that man could make his own history. And indeed this did—and does—represent progress, in that social justice cannot be fully achieved without such an awareness of the historical possibility, and this awareness depends upon historical explanations being given.

Nevertheless a deep violence was done to subjective experience. (Berger and Mohr 1982, 107)

Opposition in people's lives to this speeded-up time was an opposition to the conflation between time and history, that is, the conflation between the rate of change (history) and the passage of time that made it difficult to read their experiences in relation to either one. The resistance to violence done to subjectivity, to people's very experience of themselves, by this speed-up was "often mystified and dangerous: both fascism and racism feed upon such protests" (Berger and Mohr 1982, 105). They continue: "Today what surrounds the individual life can change more quickly than the brief sequences of that life itself. The timeless has been abolished, and history itself has become ephemerality. History no longer pays its respects to the dead: the dead are simply what is passed through" (107).

But in attempting to deal with the violence done to subjectivity, the significance of women's activities in preserving popular memory has been devalorized, and leftist theory has been trapped "within a negative eros, one that values the violent confrontation with death over community and life," argues Franco (1988, 512). That is, in leftist theory and in much poststructuralist theory those things associated with community, ethics, and life have been coded as negative, sentimental, or "feminized." A certain unacknowledged virility has handicapped the development of political theory and theories of interpretation, portraying the intellectual as someone in danger of being immersed by, submerged in, the "masses" or sentimentality and emotion. Because the masses are most often represented as feminized, faceless, and fluid and because sentimentality and emotion are discredited as feminine, the gendered intellectual responds in fear of the loss of identity.

But the project is stalled if it only remains there. Franco insists that a political resistance, a project of *dissidence,* involves retheorizing the kind of resistance that may occur in cultural spaces that have been feminized. Such a valorization would also involve the realization that "violence, while necessary in self-defense, as in present-day Central America, is not the only way to be revolutionary." In fact, it may be revolutionary to focus on an ethics whose theoretical structure is closer to motherhood, which implies redefining the way the term *mother* is used:

> Mothering is not simply tied to anatomy but is a position involving a struggle over meanings and the history of meanings, histories that have been acquired and stored within unofficial institutions. While "mothers of subversives" is univocal, stripped of any connotation but that of reproduction, "mothers of the disappeared" signals an absence, a space that speaks through a lack—the lack of a child—but also a continuing lack within the government of any participatory dialogue, of any answer to the question of how their children disappeared. (Franco 1988, 514)

Dissidence in the cultural context of *prehistory* (what might also be called naive history) "generally occurs as a clash of discourses, which is not an abstract dialectic but a lived 'noncoincidence'" (Franco 1989, xxii). That is, rather than an agonistic, tragic confrontation between two symmetrical positions in a dialectical opposition, dissidence, according to this model, is defined as a reaction to circumstances that reveal a "lived noncoincidence" among the various discourses within which one is subjected. Before the feminist movement in Mexico, Franco argues, this "lived noncoincidence" was "generally experienced by women in serialized fashion, that is, by singular experiences" that did not have a discourse of feminism to connect them. Castellanos's play is written about precisely the kind of unease, or discomfort or clash, that makes itself felt when cultural images, and, in particular, images of the "nature" of women clash against their lives and experiences.

The recognition of this experience of lived noncoincidence works rather like the notion of dramatic character developed in Kennedy's work, with character seen as a poetic trope that serves as a matrix for overlapping discourses and foregrounds the constructedness and changeability of a lived truth, or a true delusion that does not add up. Thus, the spectator of *The Eternal Feminine* watches episode after episode of staged noncoincidences in which the clash between overdetermined cultural imagery of female bodies onstage, the kinds of mortal female bodies that sustained the male narrative, produces a break. In dramatic terms such a break can also be described as "the break that is introduced, that introduces itself, in the psyche of the spectator between something [she or he] accepts as real and something toward which [she or he] refuses a judgment of truth in order not to accord it the status of anything more than an image. But these two 'somethings' are *the same* scenic sign," argues Anne Ubersfeld about the theatrical image (1981, 316–17). The recognition of that clash, the split produced out of the same scenic sign of the female body, is perceived at first as if the clash were a singular or isolated experience. Then more and more clashes are joined together, not as serialized or separated events, but, instead, as events that come to be connected by Castellanos's relentless, farcical retelling of the pre-history of Mexican women.

Masquerade, Farce, Noncoincidence: Where Speaking Bodies Evolve

Castellanos's play foregrounds the possibilities and dangers of the masquerade described by Joan Rivière and traced in an earlier chapter, the ambiguity of the active manipulation of the image within the masculine Symbolic with "pretended submissions and hypocritical compromises." "Machismo," says one of the ladies at the end of the play,

> is the mask which Tonantzin [the name of the virgin mother goddess of the Aztecs; the hill where Tonantzin was worshipped is now the site of the Shrine to the Virgin of Guadalupe] hides behind in order to act with impunity. Bad faith, in the Sartrean sense of the word, is what makes our backbones so flexible. But one shouldn't trust us. When we bow down, it is not to submit but to stretch the cord that'll let the arrow fly.[2]

The play foregrounds the gap opened up by "playing" with this imagery of the Virgin, of the mother, of woman, by implicating the spectator: "The spectator's act of looking at an image activates a process of psychic investment organized around either narcissistic or voyeuristic identification," argues Abigail Solomon-Godeau (1985, 127). Or both. The concept of identification is here problematic because it still suggests a self-identical subject capable of identifying with another such subject, two atoms in equilibrium. Yet because subjectivity is dependent on systems of difference, the self-identity of the atomistic subject proves to be a mirage; my "I" can only identify itself in a very specific mutual relationship, much of which is out of my control as a "spoken" subject. Thus, it always depends on an other, on others, on the Other, available only by means of a language system (defined as systems of signification that included sound, touch, materiality—freed, as Eco would have it, from the blackmail of the linguistic model).

The term *identification* can be used to describe the temporary association between particular subject positions of spectator and image, a shimmering narcissistic, voyeuristic, theatrical alternation that allows us both to follow the process of "subjection" and the process of resistance, analyzing both where the spectator as subject is not and where she thinks she is. Or as Solomon-Godeau says, the spectator begins to forge "identificatory paths not with individual characters but with the discursive contradictions their narratives express" (1985, 127). Like the poststructuralist notion of writing, this space of the performance of subjectivities breaks "decisively with myth and representation to think itself in its literality and its space," all the while redefining that literality as the real unreal, or rather, as farce. The images of women depend upon a "dramatic economy whose 'geometrical locus' is not representable (it is performed and performs itself [il se joue])" (Phillipe Sollers, quoted in Kristeva 1984, 232).

Castellanos's farce wavers between foregrounding the split, implicated subject and the more objective one that Brecht (and, according to Kristeva, Marx) relied on—the subject who can stand back and come to some kind of conclusion about reality. It complicates Brecht's modernist trust in the ability to interpret the world correctly by a process of defamiliarization because such Brechtian objectivity becomes more difficult the closer one gets to the cultural images of the body, where the question of the female subject who enters discourse has to be analyzed. In the oedipal Symbolic it is the female who comes to represent physicality and corporeality—*even though,* and this is a complicated point, the privileged body is masculine. That is, the oedipal subject is a Man in a man's body (the Body with a head), which must try to distance itself and abstract itself away from its own femininity and physicality, as those are associated with the female body (the body without a head).

Spectators who are to be activated, made active as thinkers involved in Brechtian critical pleasure, must thus read these performed women in very complicated ways, as more than the "two somethings," the something the spectator accepts as real and the something toward which she refuses the status of truth in order not to accord it the status of anything more than an image. For women in abjected bodies there is an excess, a residue left over from these two somethings. An unsignifiable excess produced by "the collision of consciousness (including sexual identity) with internalized, impossible models" (Solomon-Godeau 1985, 122) undercuts Brechtian confidence in clear critical distinctions by "mixing up" the intellectual and the physical, the head and the body, refusing to let them fall into a tragic opposition.

Castellanos's playfulness with symbolic imagery is involved in redistributing *capacity,* or agency, to women in a "school for spectators" with intimate differences. In this respect her drama lends itself to a juxtaposition to the work of Anne Ubersfeld, a French theorist of drama, whose works *Lire le théâtre* and *L'école du spectateur* bring together poststructuralist, psychoanalytic, and Brechtian theory. But Castellanos undercuts Ubersfeld's otherwise useful analysis in a particular way. Ubersfeld argues that the oxymoron is the rhetorical mark of theater itself, the rhetorical figure within which the *materiality* of objects and bodies produces an unreal real space of concrete illusion, where subjectivity as character reveals itself most clearly as a construction. The psychoanalytic notion of construction, which has always underwritten linguistic concepts of subjectivity, helps describe the intermingling of the real and the Symbolic in an aesthetic relationship, for constructions, according to Laplanche and Pontalis, aim at the "reconstitution of a part of the subject's childhood history in both its real and its phantasy aspects" (1973, 88). According to Freud, the construction "owes its convincing power to the element of historical truth it inserts in the place of the rejected reality" (1953a, 268), paradoxically masking a reality while at the same time telling a truth about what produced it. A historical production that is nevertheless fictional tells a truth about its structuration, its itineraries of seeing, hearing, and interpreting (Ubersfeld 1981, 306).

The oxymoron on which Ubersfeld relies for the trope of theater and on which deconstruction rests produces its effects by the contiguous arrangement of two words whose meanings are opposite: *ignorant knower,* the *fictional real.* But another rhetorical figure may work even better to displace the oxymoron and to point to the necessity of a gendered concept of theater and theory, as both drag along their history of constraint by the requirements of tragedy. This other trope, *metathesis,* retains its surface coherence, its shape, while an *internal* exchange of letters occurs within a single frame, or word, for example, substituting the word *revelant* for *relevant*. In a Symbolic whose rules are written by Oedipus, an oxymoron like *blind seer* or *ignorant knower* more closely resembles a metathesis; its contiguous oppositions are not so much oppositions as internal exchanges of the Same within a single word, Oedipus. His name, then, figures the logical space of the equation between man and human, encompassing such concepts as the master/slave dialectic while containing them within the masculine plot space. This equation easily guarantees that the logical requirements of tragedy will provide the palimpsest for drama in general.

Ubersfeld tries to step to the side of the metatheses that she calls an oxymoron as the privileged figure of theatricality and constuctedness in general. She then posits a polysemic dialectics, what she calls a "thèse voyageuse" that moves without settling, or hovers, over multiple points of identification and application and numerous and diffuse spectatorial judgments, though she must continually return to metatheses that threaten to throw her back into the oedipal dialectical model she wants to escape.

Yet her analysis helps call attention to the "geometrical locus" of the dramatic economy, the space where speaking bodies evolve.

In the Salon of the Masquerade

The Eternal Feminine consists of three acts made up of short fantastical scenes tied together by the hour it takes for a woman to have her hair done at a beauty salon. The main character, Lupita, falls asleep and has dreams that foreground various stereotypes of Woman. These are both cited and undercut as versions of them are produced, but these versions prove to be more than the diversions commodity culture offers in a society where that commodity culture, argues Franco, provides the social glue that linked together the liberal intelligentsia during modernization in Mexico. The commodification of culture is in many ways centered on the female body, as fashion became the first system of signifiers with no reference except differentiation itself, establishing a link between women and commodification, between a clothed female body and the fetishistic object of desire (Franco 1989, 249).

Castellanos describes her characters as exaggerated caricatures and admonishes cast and crew to remember a line from Cortázar: "Laughter always digs more tunnels than tears" (273). This laughter also reveals something that Castellanos's character Lupita, whose name is derived from the name of the Virgin of Guadalupe (Cypess 1991, 124), will have discovered by the play's end, when she finds herself left all alone on the edge of the stage. This is not the laughter of one who observes and knows. It is, instead, a laughter that uncomfortably arises out of subjectivity and the intimate relationship to a culturally constructed body itself, as site of the theater of contradiction. It also marks the ambiguous inseparability of comedy and melancholy, which marks the form this drama takes—farce, "which in certain moments becomes sentimental, intellectual, or grotesque" (273).

But it also points to, even though Castellanos does not develop it further, the very particular relationship between North and South, or "First" and "Third" worlds, for, says Franco, in speaking about Mexico, analysts must look at the relationship between advanced capitalism and societies of scarcity, the kind of mixture that constitutes Mexican culture and economic circumstances. And looking at the structures of advanced capitalism from the perspective of scarcity produces another form of farce, another process of defamiliarization, for advanced capitalism then appears "not only replete but also grotesquely reified . . . the becalmed sea traps not the colonized but the colonizers" (Franco 1988, 515).

This farce makes ridiculous the invisibility of what is most blatantly visible, as Castellanos's use of the genre has a double effect in tracing the itinerary of seeing and hearing. Farce as genre depends on coarse, vulgar humor, "belly laughs," for its effects, and it uses exaggerated, caricatured types of characters. But Castellanos foregrounds an inherent contradiction in farce itself, which generally finds humor in improbable or ludicrous situations. For her farce finds humor in making the *visible* visible and showing how these exaggerated, caricatured types of characters are not improbable and ludicrous but *probable* and ludicrous.

Castellanos's play consists of scenes acted almost entirely by women characters acting out other women characters, a kind of house of mirrors for women. Besides being organized by time—the hour spent under the hair dryer—the drama is arranged to comment on the reason for Lupita's presence in the beauty salon: it is the day of her wedding. That fact sets off an explosion of caricatures and warnings. But though Lupita begins her movement toward the wedding, she never actually reaches it, except in a dream. She is on a dreamlike treadmill that seems to move forward but goes nowhere. As she experiences grotesque dreams and nightmares after falling asleep under the dryer, she begins to suspect that they are a sign that this *novio*, this fiancé, is not for her: "But I don't have another one. And it was even hard to find him, to make him fall in love, to convince him to marry me" (330).

The beauty salon in an affluent neighborhood in the Federal District in Mexico City establishes spatial relations between the characters, with its hair dryers lined up on the sides of the room, requiring a certain kind of person to fill it. All the people using those dryers are women, and the salon itself is a kind of threshold space, a temporary location in which women perfect their masquerades; it is neither private nor is it public in the sense in which *public* refers to a place where men valorize themselves through activity.[3] What the women do here is turn themselves into Woman by improving the veil, or the envelope, that will valorize them in the eyes of Man. The beauty salon often serves as a place where women get together for resistant conversations, but this one is more obviously determined by the male gaze, though the working-class employee, the hairdresser, becomes more and more active. When the salesman says of her, "What a charming girl! Where did she learn to ask questions?" she replies, "In a different place from where they taught you to answer them" (274). The women bring their bodies in to be prepared: their hair is washed and set; they are put under the dryers; their hair is combed out as if they are so many mannequins.

This kind of preparation, says Luce Irigaray, is a part of the masculine Symbolic's definition of Woman: "The 'physical vanity' of women, the 'fetishization' of her body—a process patterned after that of the model and prototype of all fetishes: the penis—are mandatory if she is to be a desirable 'object' and if he is to want to possess her. But no doubt she will in her turn seek to secure an increase in her price." But she is "price-less." Seeking to increase her price, to make herself valuable, she engages in disguise to cover what is the basis of the oedipal Symbolic— she has no value: "To sell herself, woman has to veil as best she can how price-less she is in the sexual economy" (Irigaray 1985, 114, 115).

Into this room steps a man, a salesman, who sees an opportunity for himself in this passivity he wants to increase. He has come to sell to the shop proprietor an electronic apparatus from the United States that, when inserted in the hair dryers, will produce dreams to divert the women, who, on average, spend fifty-two hours a year sitting doing nothing in the uncomfortable heat: "One must suffer to be worthy. Don't you think?" (275). A desire to provide amusement cloaks his real purpose—to make sure the customers keep coming back. Amusement is far from trivial; it can lead either to a new, critical interpretation through aggressive laughter, or, managed properly, it has another re-sult—pacification through psychological decompression. Parodic laugh-ter as a sign of revolt may also reinforce power by acknowledging revolt then bringing it back within controllable bounds, produced in a particu-lar form in order to make its management more efficient.[4] The salesman has invented something to ward off this danger, relying on his faith in technology. When the hairdresser asks what danger, he replies, "That women, without realizing it, might begin to think. The proverb says it: think the worst and you'll be right. Thinking, itself, is bad. It must be avoided" (276). Domestication in Castellanos's twentieth-century Mexi-can beauty salon no longer needs to be accomplished by open force, though force is never far away, as Tlatelolco proved. Pacification is accomplished more efficiently through amusement and diversion.

The salesman's catalog includes a number of fantasies the women might choose: to be beautiful; to incite mad passion; to arouse the envy of other women; to have a husband who gets a raise; to find a good, cheap maid; to be pregnant; to find that one is not pregnant; to have children who get high grades; to become a widow with a huge pension. In response to complaints that these dreams are very ordinary the sales-man replies that there are, of course, more refined ones at a higher price.

In the manner of a game show host, he turns to the audience, after putting the apparatus in Lupita's dryer, and introduces the multilayered acts the women will perform for each other. Lupita acts Lupita in her own dream, a speeded-up version of what her life will be like after her marriage to Juan. This act is made up of a number of segments: The Honeymoon, The Annunciation, Cruel Reality, The Apotheosis. In each what the Woman is ideally supposed to do turns out to be ridiculous, but many of the cartoonlike women actively try to fulfill them, their masquerade having sunk into their skin, become "epidermalized." In particular, Castellanos focuses on women's participation in the imagery of the self-abnegating, powerful mother, who is, as Lupita's mother says self-righteously, "a lamb of sacrifice, she has just immolated herself to satisfy the brutal appetites of the beast" (281). (When her mother says this Lupita responds in amazement: "What beast?") Her mother contin-ues: if the mother is a decent woman, she will be rewarded, but she must never expect to be happy; if she is happy, she will pretend she is not. Sacrifice founds this image: "Although in many cases, it may cost you your life. And, always, your youth and beauty. Oh, but to be a mother . . . to be a mother" (284). Lupita, excited, pregnant, is being turned into Lupita the martyr, motherhood proving to be the site where myth has most powerfully transformed history into nature.

As the scene changes, another Lupita is transformed into a woman who looks more and more like her aging furniture, as she and it are confined to the house and rapidly deteriorate; her appearance matches that of the furniture. She sits in her living room watching a more active version of herself on television, where another Lupita II finds that her husband is having an affair with his secretary, shoots them both, and becomes a celebrity, the "autoviuda," or self-made widow. The active Lupita II is interviewed about her crime, which has made her a national heroine; she, of course, vows to compensate for the murder by making a pilgrimage on her knees to the shrine of the Virgin of Guadalupe. Lupita I, "with the indelible mark of her life as a housewife," the physical effects of domestic work inscribed on her body, can only sit and watch, responding to advice that she should change her life by replying that, when things change, they only get worse.

Lupita I and Lupita II, observing each other and commenting on each other's actions, play around with the stereotype of the housewife. While Lupita II rebels, Lupita I insists on imitating what she perceived her mother and her grandmother before her to be, trying to match the static image of mother she has been taught. As the parrot in her room says of her, "This Lupita is a fanatic for stability [*una maniática de la inmutabilidad*]. Persons, times, fashions. If she were in charge, there wouldn't have been any history" (292).

But her last scene takes place on Mother's Day, which finds her joyously dancing "on your grave, Juanito." She mocks all the things he had demanded from her and celebrates her current life, paid for by his pension, the house arranged as she wants it, the bed "mine, completely mine, and at night I turn and roll over from left to right and from right to left and I don't bump into . . . what I bumped into when you were here" (293).

But here solitude is interrupted by a knock at the door. Selected by lottery to be honored in her old age as a kind of representative mother and in the same room where she and the furniture have spent their indistinguishable lives, she receives mountains of gifts from a carnival barker who tells her she has paid her debt "to nature and to society by becoming a mother [*al convertirse en madre*]" (295). It is in homes like hers, he says, a cipher of all the other middle-class homes in Mexico, that "the Mexican people's dearest essence [*Mexicanidad*] is preserved."

She is not alone, he says: "Solitude doesn't exist for those who have sacrificed themselves for others" (296). Isolated, she also is smothered by goods. This celebration of Mother's Day has been organized by the BGT chain of stores: B, buy; G, good; T, things. Almost asphyxiated by the piles of perfume and goods presented to her for Mother's Day, a "pyramid that buries her," and screaming "Help me! Help! Get me out of here! I'm suffocating! I'm suffocating. . . . Help me . . . Help," Lupita awakens hysterically back in the salon.

Versions/Diversions of Woman

The second act of the play puts women in situations where they can re-act other images of Woman in Mexican history. Lupita is once again under the hair dryer, but this time the apparatus has been adjusted by the hairdresser employed by the shop proprietor to make the dreams more scandalous; Lupita will eventually refer to them as nightmares. After she falls asleep she becomes a character who wanders onto the site of a carnival, this carnival suggests a liberatory space where hierarchies are played with and overturned. In this one there are a number of freak shows and a wax museum. The first performance she observes is a satire of the Garden of Paradise, which features "a show for the whole family, a performance recommended by both the ecclesiastic and civil authorities" (297). Lupita pays a peso to watch the events leading up to the Fall, but she is the only spectator, the other carnivalgoers having found this performance far too didactic. The character who plays Eva (Eve), awakened from her nap by the spotlights, chats with Lupita about the interest Women's Lib seems to be taking in Eve, whose story passes "like chewing gum: in everyone's mouth."[5] In an ambiguous way she is both the real Eve and this sideshow freak; she has been, she says, dreaming for centuries that someone would come and tell the story of paradise correctly. Maybe Lupita will be the one, she suggests.

As the show begins, Eve is named by Adam:

Adam: . . . and don't you forget it: your name is Eve. Repeat that. Eve.
Eve: Why?
Adam: (Confused, and, naturally, angry.) What do you mean, why? A decent woman doesn't ask those questions. She obeys and that ends it.
Eve: I don't see the reason for it.

Adam: (who does not see it either but trying to conceal it.) You love to oppose everything, to make yourself interesting. Why don't you follow everyone else's example? Look. *(Acting out what what he says)* You are called a tree. T-r-e-e. And, you, an ant. A-n-t. Without a *u*, because with one it's your father's sister.

Eve: I don't hear anyone answering at all.

Adam: That's precisely what I want you to learn. Not to talk back.

Eve: How do you expect a tree or an ant to reply if they're mute? That's not even funny! Why don't you talk with a parrot? Because he can answer you back, right?

(298)

When she asks whom he plans to talk to after all this naming, Adam says, "I'm not talking *to* anyone. I'm speaking *for*. I speak with Posterity. . . . I place the problem on a spiritual plane and you reduce it to its most vulgar biological elements." He then describes the job God assigned him in exchange for crowning creation with a consciousness—Adam's. He must catalog whatever exists "to put it in order, to take care of it, and to make all His creatures subject to His law." He insists that Eve accept his name for her, and she agrees, though conditionally: "That's the pseudonym under which I'll go down in history. But my true name, the one *I* call myself, that I won't tell anybody. And much less to you" (299).

As Eve sits and watches Adam enjoy the intellectual pleasure of his cataloging, she begins to find paradise boring. Boredom here and in the stories of other characters proves to be, as Franco argued in her study of Mexican women, one of the motors of history. The concept of paradise as an eternal present of stopped time is deceptive, for in this paradise God and Adam enjoy the pleasures of mastery and transformation through naming. This masterful naming both causes and depends on the gap between the name (or signifier) and the always escaping referent that is, nevertheless, approachable only through those signifiers. The gap of the noncoincidence of signifier and signified produces history and time as well as the way each of those is represented. God and Adam have thus, by giving Eve eternity or space, guarded time for themselves, along with the pleasures of intellectual transformation. Oedipus' privilege, like Adam's, is not the motionless self-identity of presence; it is, instead, the privilege of reserving for himself the power to transform and act, an active *making present* of his *presence* through production, doing, naming.

With the help of the serpent—"another walking rib"—who is a political exile from several other paradises who finds this one with its promise of eternity and stopped time to be cleverly, deceptively arranged—Eve decides to eat the apple and then go to work growing different kinds of plants whose leaves will be used as clothes for all seasons in a post-Fall world. The enforced immutability of a paradise with no transformation, no past or future, is rejected; such a paradise, Castellanos seems to suggest, is the privilege offered to the housewife Lupita.

The Lupita who is now spectator at the carnival is scandalized by this scene and dashes out, only to find herself at another performance in a wax museum where statues of women in Mexican history come to life to re-act themselves, repeating history with a difference, though, she says, "I believe I'm the only one here who has the right to give an opinion because I paid for my ticket." Lupita is to be treated to female performances at the wax museum by such characters as La Malinche, Sor Juana de la Cruz, Doña Josefa Ortiz de Domínguez, the Empress Carlota, Rosario de la Peña, and Adelita. Rather than attempting to set history straight by acting themselves as "what we were. Or, at least, as what we think we really were" (304)—the ways they passed into history—they set about dismantling the received version. Similarly, as Sandra Messinger Cypess argues, this use of fantasy draws on the apparatus of science fiction to juxtapose contemporary characters and historical or mythical figures as "iconic presentations brought onstage as revenants to highlight the coercive power of recurring cultural paradigms" (1990, 157). The play thus contrasts a somewhat realistic scene, though it is also highly caricatured (or maybe reality, for women, *is* caricature), to other scenes organized more overtly according to the conventions of fantasy, allowing the supposedly "immortal images of institutionalized myths to regain their mobility and dynamism" (Cypess 1990, 157).

As they act, Lupita is to guess who is who, to try to pin them back to the reified historical version, but the act of imitation has already shattered the "original" image naturalized by history and myth. When Lupita tries to identify the characters she finds that the new, playful version casts such doubt on the historical one that she can neither identify nor identify with the "real" Sor Juana or La Malinche, whose images draw on the cultural resources of Mexican culture. An important distance is produced between the image and its playful reenactment.

In each sequence the actor satirizes the historical image and suggests that the masculine historical version may have described how some men saw these events, but that version is so distorted it allows women to play around and make up all kinds of other versions and be just as close to the truth, whatever that might have been. Sandra Messinger Cypess's *La Malinche in Mexican Literature* is a complex study of the historical usage of La Malinche as discursive signifier, a usage that both constructed and reinscribed her at various moments in the interests of different groups in power. La Malinche, she argues, "may be considered the first woman of Mexican literature, just as she is considered the first mother of the Mexican nation and the Mexican Eve, symbol of national betrayal" (Cypess 1991, 2); the story of La Llorona also often follows this theme. This discursive construction was central to Mexico's telling itself its own history. The discursive image of La Malinche was produced "largely through fiction and can therefore be studied as a literary construct," but only on condition that literature be defined as a social institution. Within this construct "La Malinche has been transformed from a historical figure to a major Mexican and Latin American feminine stereotype, a poly-semous sign whose signifieds, for all their ambiguity, are generally nega-tive" (Cypess 1991, 2). In fact, Cypess suggests, the name La Malinche can best be studied as a palimpsest, whose workings are analogous to the way Aztecs, Mayans, and other tribes built pyramids on top of one another and the Catholic church built its cathedrals and churches on top of pre-Hispanic sites, the main cathedral in the plaza of Mexico City an example of this structuration. The Church of the Virgin of Guadalupe is another such site, built on a sacred hill dedicated to an Aztec virgin goddess.

La Malinche's figurations were used in opposition to those of the Virgin of Guadalupe, for La Malinche's image was eventually recoded to suggest uncontrolled sexuality. This layered figuration initially refers to the woman who translated Nahuatl for Cortés during the encounter with the Aztecs. A Spanish aide to Cortés, Aguilar, spoke Maya, Cortés spoke Spanish, and La Malinche mediated between the two. Simply tracing her name, as Cypess points out, shows the complexity of its historical usages: "La Malinche is called Malinal, Malintzin, Malinche, or Doña Marina. Malintzin is formed from her Nahuatl birth name, Malinal, and Marina was given to her at her Christian baptism; La Mal-inche is the syncretic, mestizo form" (Cypess 1991, 2).

La Malinche's birthdate and the details of her life are traceable through Spanish texts of the period—in particular, the letters of Cortés and, more extensively, Bernal Díaz del Castillo's *The Conquest of New Spain* and the writings of Cortés's biographer and secretary, López de Gómara. The exact place and date of her birth are unknown, either 1502 or 1505 in Oluta, Painala, or Jaltipán, and she was most likely the daughter of a cacique, or member of the privileged and educated class (Cypess 1991). Probably educated as a noble, she was sold into slavery to Mayan traders after her father's death, her mother's remarriage, and the birth to her mother of a son, whose inheritance had to be safeguarded. She was then sold to Tabascans, who gave her as a gift, with nineteen other women, to Cortés.

Besides her work as negotiator and translator for Cortés, La Malinche is also credited by Bernal Díaz with warning Cortés of an ambush as he made his way to Tenochtitlan by Cholulans under order from Moctezuma. Cypess traces this particular story in relation to La Malinche's image as traitor to find, again, selective usage of the historical record, flawed as it is; Castellanos's play refers to this incident as well. The Tlaxcalans, who were enemies of the Cholulans, had also warned the Spaniards of an attack, as had other women slaves, though the legend assigns blame only to La Malinche. Studies of the Conquest suggest that the Mexican argument that one woman could have brought down Aztec civilization is, of course, unsupportable; the defeat was influenced by the hostility and resentment created by the brutality of the Aztecs against other Amerindian groups as well as by the Aztec concept of the religious nature of war and the association of that tradition with Quetzalcoatl, which led to interpretations of Cortés's arrival in relation to Quetzalcoatl's return. Yet it was only Malinche's involvement with Cortés that led to the coining of the word *malinchista* to refer to the most serious kind of betrayal, that of one's own community or, later, of one's nation.

La Malinche gave birth to a son by Cortés before she was given to another Spaniard, Juan Jaramillo, as wife. Her usefulness to Cortés was represented in his own letters as strategic, but Díaz, who admired her independence, intelligence, and beauty, draws on the Spanish literary form of the chivalric romance, in particular the story of a Christian knight, Amadis de Gaul, to transfigure her into a noble lady.

La Malinche's discursive usefulness took a number of forms, its influence most profound during what Cypess calls the two liminal periods of Mexican history, 1521–28, the time of the conquest, and 1810–21, the period of transition from colonial rule to nationhood. During the period of the Conquest La Malinche's imagery constructed her as an aristocratic Hispanic lady, and she was given the name Doña Marina. Cypess argues that Spanish colonial culture reinscribed her as Great Mother, protector of foreigners, a biblical heroine responsible for bringing together Amerindian and European cultures through her son by Cortés, Don Martín, the first *mestizo*. She also came to represent the conquered Great Lady, an object of desire which found an analogy in the relation of domination between Spain and its object of desire, New Spain. This historical moment was especially important because it established the figurative relationship between male and female in Mexican history: "This was the period during which the political and cultural consequences of European dominance in the Americas were set. The conquest was the crucial event in the formation of male-female relations" (Cypess 1991, 8).

During the colonial period Malinche was largely ignored, but after the War of Independence writers transformed her from the Spanish model of a noble lady to a mother figure, thus redefining her in Mexican rather than Spanish colonial terms. Many of the characteristics that had been positively inscribed by Spanish writers took on negative connotations, Cypess argues; she became the Desirable Whore/Terrible Mother, as her biblical associations were shifted to refer to Eve and the serpent. She was figured as both the snake and the Mexican Eve, the traitor and the temptress, with these images rationalizing the Amerindian failure to overcome the European conquistadors.

By 1870 she is represented as the "seller of her nation." Because the most influential and even normative modern treatment of La Malinche is to be found in Octavio Paz's *Labyrinth of Solitude,* Cypess shows how Paz's grandfather, Ireneo Paz, had already condensed the Cortés-Malinche relationship into one symbolic of the European-Amerindian encounter, rewriting the complexities of the military and political circumstances in terms of a sexual encounter. His version, however, romanticized La Malinche in the interests of providing a positive symbol of *mestizage,* an image for "a nationalism that strives to incorporate the Indian within the paradigm of Mexican identity" (10).

But it was Octavio Paz who extended the analogy between the Spanish Conquest and sexuality, or, more specifically, rape, and who figuratively organized La Malinche's position into the site of blame for that rape, drawing on imagery already available by referring to her as La Chingada, the violated one, here the violated mother of all Mexicans. Paz describes that imagery as "the representation of the cruel incarnation of the feminine condition" (Cypess 1991, 11). La Chingada is defined in this way: "The person who suffers [the action of the verb *chingar*] is passive, inert, and open, in contrast to the active, aggressive, and closed person who inflicts"; the "mother forcibly opened, violated, or deceived," "an inert heap of bones, blood, and dust. Her taint is constitutional and resides . . . in her sex" (1961, 77, 79).[6]

This biological, fatalistic vision of femininity, then, is used as a metaphor to describe the failure of Mexican virility, its inability to resist either Spanish Conquest or First World imperialism. This Mexican virility has, in fact, been tainted as feminine because it resembles the condition of a raped woman, because its passivity found no ritual celebration of transcendence, as Oedipus' did. Its weakness as feminine made possible its violation by colonialism and imperialism, the term *malinchista* referring to "the individual who sells out to the foreigner, who devalues national identity in favor of imported benefits" (Cypess 1991, 7). But before any Mexican men had sold out, it was La Malinche who had already done so and provided the model for all later betrayals. The usefulness of the metaphors of rape and whore are, thus, in Paz's account, completely distanced from any economic or political analysis of women's lack of access to power. This oversight is not simply a Mexican macho phenomenon; it marks many other masculinist discourses as well.[7] It is a *constitutive* oversight that means that even figurative descriptions of rape and prostitution—like the duet, marriage, and the family—have more to do with men than they do with women.[8]

La Malinche, like La Chingada, absorbs the guilt, diverting it from actor to receiver, subject to object, but in the performance La Malinche stages for Lupita in Castellanos's play she actively assumes the power history has deceptively assigned her and manipulates Cortés like a puppet, advising him to spread the rumor that he has ordered his ships burned as a heroic act to keep his men from fleeing. That rumor will cover up what she says actually happened—one of his men fell asleep while smoking in his bunk. To Cortés she advises more tolerance toward that sailor: "You should be more tolerant. Tobacco is a vice your soldiers have just discovered. It's our way of repaying the gift of syphilis that you brought to us" (305). She also tells him to keep his armor on in order to fool the Indians into believing he is the god Quetzalcoatl: "In your armor you seem like a god." Following her suggestions with great pleasure he contemplates himself in the mirror she hands him after grooming him: "True. And this role of god fits me to a T" (305).

La Malinche situates Moctezuma as one of those to blame:

Malinche: I would like Moctezuma to drink a cup of his own bitter chocolate. He's a cruel master.
Cortés: More cruel than me?
Malinche: You're brutal because you're in a hurry. He thinks he's the owner of eternity.

Playing the role of manipulator of the manipulator, La Malinche then feeds Cortés more stories, gets him dreaming of wealth, power, and glory, and finishes her scene in this way: "While Cortés rambles on, Malinche polishes his armor, combs his hair, etc. When his appearance seems satisfactory, she goes to the door of the tent and calls to those who wait outside" (306).

This version acted by La Malinche disappoints Lupita, who expected a romantic story about a love intrigue between Marina and Cortés. What's love, asks La Malinche, to which Sor Juana replies in a didactic tone: "Probably the lady is referring to love, a genuinely Western product, an invention of Provençal troubadours and of the Castilian ladies in twelfth-century European castles. Probably Cortés, in spite of his stay in Salamanca, never knew it or practiced it" (307).

The next character acts the story of Rosario de la Peña, famous as a muse to intellectuals in the nineteenth century and as the cause of the suicide of the poet, Manuel Acuña, though, as Rosario says to Sor Juana, the legend of his suicide is a lie, as are all legends. Now she will tell the truth, and the scene begins with her visit to Acuña's garret to announce her love to him. He is horrified at her passion and her suggestion of marriage; his poetry—in particular, his "Nocturno a Rosario"—requires an Ideal, which her appearance before him destroys: "You were my ideal love, ergo, impossible," he shrieks as he recoils from her in horror. "With the step you've just taken, you've destroyed everything. My dearest illusions: those of living in a fantasy world in which you would always be in love with me and I would always be satisfied . . . 'And between us, my mother, like a God!'" (308). The last part of his speech draws on an actual poem by Acuña:

How beautiful it would have been to live beneath some roof
the two of us, in one soul, the two of us in one breast,
and between us, my mother, like a God![9]

Rosario then discovers that, in spite of his talk of pure, idealized love, Acuña has been conveniently living with an earthy laundress who takes care of his domestic and sexual needs, freeing him to idealize both Rosario and his mother. The laundress is now pregnant. Rosario promptly invites the laundress to her literary gatherings, and the scene ends with Acuña's suicide, followed by the laundress's response: "My God! He has spattered blood all over the clean clothes! Now I have to wash them all over again" (310).

The next performer, Sor Juana Inés de la Cruz, was a *mestiza* poet and writer in the seventeenth century who entered the convent of Santa Paula of the Hieronomite order in 1669 at the age of eighteen. Sor Juana, as Franco says, "not only trespassed, at least symbolically, on clerical terrain but directly defied the clergy's feminization of ignorance" (1989, 23). Juana wrote poems, plays, theological texts; her description of the Virgin situated her as the very matrix of Christianity, representing her as a thinker who also knew the secrets of the universe, "a sovereign Doctor of the Divine Schools who teaches wisdom to all the angels" (Franco 1989, 52).

To write Sor Juana developed a whole repertory of strategies, at times insisting on her identity as a woman writer, at other times writing as an impersonal subject or adopting a male persona, at still other times using a fictionalized "I" or relying on allegorical characters (Franco 1989, 29). As Franco says about her plays, she borrowed the discourses of students and copied black, indigenous, and regional speech; she wrote some of her poems in Nahuatl, relying on parody, allegory, and mimicry in order to gain anonymity—pretending to be obedient and self-denigrating—while at other times insisting on the importance of her position as a female author. In her later life, however, she acceded to the pressures of the Church's authority and gave up her writing, music, and study.

But Sor Juana's historical circumstances resemble the circus sideshow that Castellanos constructs, for "she found herself transformed into a fairground freak, something of a new World marvel who was constantly on show, exhibited, as she herself recognized, as a 'rare bird' because she was a woman who wrote on religious matters and a nun who wrote profane poetry" (Franco 1989, 23). Juana is disappointing to Lupita because she ridicules the historical explanation of her entry into the convent. Legend has it that it was because of an impossible love, whereas this character says it was because of her repugnance at the thought of marriage. In this sequence Celia, a young female friend, teasingly says of Juana "that beneath her petticoats are naught but syllogisms" (312). She says this perhaps unknowingly to Juana herself, who is dressed as a young boy in erotic acting that plays on cross-dressing and the ambiguity of gender identity. Celia may or may not know the boy is a girl; she may or may not be erotically attracted to a male and/or a female in a flirtation between Celia and her/him, Juana. The attraction between the two women confuses the women watching, who, in panic, insist on the paradigm of heterosexuality and want to keep the categories more distinct.

The next historical character, Josefa Ortiz de Domínguez, the criolla wife of a *corregidor,* or district governor, in Guanajuato in 1810, participated in the rebellion against Spain. Having been raised in an orphanage, her interest in the conditions of the Indians and *mestizos* brought her into collaboration with Father Miguel Hidalgo in the struggle for Mexican independence. Eventually, she was arrested and imprisoned for many years, and, on her release from prison, she became estranged from her family because of her belief that they had participated in compromising and betraying the independence movement (Cotera 1976, 38). To the heroic aura of Josefa's legendary exploits Castellanos adds the issue of boredom as one of history's motors, attempting to wrest it out of its trivial connotations, which may have to do with its association with women's domestic lives. Marx developed the relationship between the degradation of workers' lives and the degraded forms of work they were required to do; Castellanos draws on similar insights about the relationship between the kind of work required in the domestic sphere and the consequences for the lives of women required to do that work, of not having control over their own labor.

Adelita, the final performer in this segment, is a character who appears in Mexican *corridos,* popular ballads of the revolution of 1910–17. In the play she is a character who was active in the Mexican Revolution as a *soldadera,* one of the women who accompanied the men, prepared the meals for them, and sometimes fought along with them. Adelita, according to Diane E. Marting's notes to the play, was probably modeled on a woman from Durango who was actively involved in the revolution (1988, 365n). Here Adelita proves to understand the revolution better than the two colonels she is guarding, identical in their uniforms and identical in their reasons for fighting the revolutionary insurgents: they both fight because someone, anyone, gives them a gun. They are, she says, fighting other people just like themselves in a long, bloody,

confusing revolution, while the "piñata," here meaning the system, remains unbroken: "Big and fat, swaying high above us all, full of sweets,
fruits, of gifts to be given, to divide among everyone. The piñata is the
rich" (329). The poor, blindfolded, swing out, not at the piñata but at
each other. The political party that has ruled Mexico since the revolution
is called the Institutional Revolutionary Party *(Partido Revolucionario In-
stitucional, PRI)*, yet it is corrupt and linked with North American capitalist interests.

The revolution was, however, a period in which women were active participants, and feminist congresses began to debate the question
of women's emancipation in the public arena. Sor Juana's surprised response to Adelita's version of the revolution is to say that she thought
the Mexican Revolution had succeeded, whereupon Adelita points to
Lupita and asks: "If it had triumphed, would this girl be here? Would
there still be girls like her, with parents like hers, with sweethearts like
hers, with a life like hers?" But Lupita, who is both in and out of the
frame of these play acts as an ideal spectator, congratulates herself on her
middle-class luck and perspective: "Well, then I compare myself with
you, with any of you, I think that I was very lucky and that I hit the
jackpot" (329).

Both actor and spectator, Lupita's character foregrounds the sub-
ject/object status of the cultural image of Woman; she is both subject and
object of the spectacle, doubling the space of the spectator as she acts the
role of spectator. Both are spectator/characters and must "construct—
and no one can do it for [her or him, *lui*]—the relation between the real
and one's experience of it . . . the production onstage always says not
how the world is, but how the world is that the scene presents"
(Ubersfeld 1981, 259).

Thus, the spectator, who is here doubled, is coproducer of the
drama and introduces the specificity of her body into the multiple points
of diffuse judgments she must make to piece together the constructs of
actors and director. Ideally, she does this through an expanded notion
of artistic activity of a kind not confined just to an aesthetic sphere, as it
has been defined historically, but extended to the practical sphere of the
world. Each aesthetic judgment, in a revised aesthetic that is much more
like artisanal activity, has to do with what Michel de Certeau calls the
"capacity to produce a new ensemble from a pre-existent relationship. . . . [Each judgment] will constitute an artistic production, arising
out of the incessant inventiveness of practical experience" (Ubersfeld

1981, 289n). Such capacity involves the manipulation of representations "by those who are not [their] makers" (de Certeau 1984, xii). The "same scenic sign" establishes a relationship between itself and the *spectator's* body, bringing into the evaluation the displacing gaze, not that of the subject/voyeur but of the subject/object/abject, the Outsider inside who "writes [herself] into the interior of the text; it is for [her] that the director rewrites T' [the stage production] according to T [the written text]" (Ubersfeld 1981, 304; my translation). In the last analysis it is in and by the spectator that the performance is produced.

The female interpreter "acts" or performs a dialogue between a real body and images whose constructions are iconic of the relationships that construct the world in a gender-specific way: "the figurations have sexual connotations . . . awakening in each spectator unconscious images or perhaps conscious ones, in a rapport with the spatiality of [her or his] body." These figurations, like subjectivity, arise out of "an interrelation of bodies—[out of] the complex transactions which take place during infancy between our bodies and those around us" (Eagleton 1983, 163). A dramatic production like this one foregrounds that capacity of active production—while traditional drama reserves that capacity for the writer and the director, rather than for the spectator. Such feminist drama may, in fact, be involved in a subtle, slow process of redefining the artist as artisan, gradually insisting on the interaction between the aesthetic and the practical, which, paradoxically, might bring the feminist playwright closer to Aristotle's notion of the dramatic poet as a "maker" of drama, not a "creator."

Castellanos's playfulness with imagery and the real involves the female interpreter in a game that is very much like the game she plays outside the theater. She plays the unique and specific signification of her body and its relation to the bodies of actors in this theatrical discourse against the conventional imagery, participating in a performance that is "a game, but also a daily undertaking" (Kristeva 1980, 78).

The Greek stage erected barriers against representations of active women, preventing the spatialization of the female body from taking effect and indirectly preventing that body itself from entering "reality." Such an exclusion had other effects: "The exclusion of the represented has the paradoxical conclusion of negating all possibility of distance. It is the negation [of a represented image] which permits the interval between what is shown and what is thought" (Ubersfeld 1981, 317; my translation). But in *The Eternal Feminine,* the salesman and his catalog of images have introduced more representations onto Castellanos's stage through the reproduction upon which capitalism depends; colonialism requires mimics, and capitalism requires the multiplication of participants in its economy, the multiplication of consumers. The oedipal drama at first excluded any representations proper to women, allowing no women onstage.

But in the age of mechanical reproduction Oedipus attempts to control the disguises of women by producing differences without much difference. The salesman's function in introducing multiple representations is, paradoxically, constraint; ostensibly introducing more and more possibilities for women, he is actually introducing more and more of the Same kind of possibility, increasing representation while constraining it, keeping it within limits, "bringing it back within the field of unity (that of the subject and the State)," as Kristeva argued, disciplining it in a masquerade of the Same. The poetic masquerade, on the other hand, emphasizes the multiple, simultaneous roles the subject plays, the refusal of the actor/subject to be glued to a narrative, the transgression based on a nonrepresented focal point that has no origin or teleology, a transference based on something besides the father.

Castellanos's farce tries to subvert the salesman's power and to decondition the spectator's gaze by revealing the scaffolding of the image; the salesman cannot keep up with all the representations he introduces, and they stray, their multiplication making visible "the map of the voyager [the interpreter], the itinerary of seeing and hearing." It becomes difficult and even ridiculous for the spectator "to regard the world according to the codes it has taught [her or him]."

Shortcircuits: Playing (with) Woman

The last act, which swamps the spectator with more and more stereotypes of women, directs those stereotypes like bursts of laughter at the title of the play, The Eternal Feminine, whose claim to universality is now ludicrous, if it had not been already. The final act finds Lupita facing yet another complication on her way to marriage, as the predictable trajectory of the woman in the oedipal narrative, the journey to the marriage bed, is once again stalled.

A shower of sparks caused by a shortcircuit ended act 2 and threw the Lupita of the dream back into the beauty salon. The problem that produced the sparks and blackout could not be blamed on the dryers themselves, by definition: "The drier, the driers rather, are the most modern ones made in the United States. For that reason they can't be defective. We reject that possibility. But I wonder. . . . Perhaps these mishaps really are a warning against this marriage" (330).

Because the power is off (or the dryer is broken), Lupita's hair is left wet, heavy, ugly—certainly not suitable for a wedding. The only alternative is to try on wigs, and, once again, Lupita is faced with various possible representations, as she is temporarily turned into the person for whom each wig is named, in a section entitled "The Life of a Single Woman": a spinster, a prostitute, a mistress, a celebrity owned by her manager-husband, a politician owned by her party, a female astronomer Daddy's girl who encounters bad times when Daddy dies, a journalist censored by her employer so that her written words can only indirectly say what she wants to about male power. As Lupita tries on her last wig, she becomes an elegant, intelligent career woman whose academic degree has made her more "conscious of her femininity, more careful of her appearance . . . but she lets it be understood that she is ready to give up her independence at the first convenient occasion" (349).

The last fragment of act 3 takes place in a room that is a mixture of parlor and classroom, "so frequent among the ladies of the Mexican bourgeoisie who have just discovered that culture is an adornment and who dedicate to culture, if not their most arduous efforts, at least their best hours" (349); it focuses on the wives of affluent men, who are being educated about women's liberation. Their session, which was originally to have been a lecture on The Function of the Pedestal in the Colonial Architecture of New Spain but is quickly changed in order to talk about the play *The Eternal Feminine,* proves to be a satirical mockery of affluent liberation that extends only to the edge of the social class the women occupy. Most of the women are naive, in spite of, or perhaps because of, their privilege; as one says, "I don't set any store by motherhood, matrimony and all that paraphernalia. Let our principles perish, but save the servants." Other women, however, have been able to piece together a critique of their own positions and to try to articulate it in Mexican terms: "It's not good enough to imitate the models proposed that are answers to circumstances other than our own. It isn't even enough to discover who we are. We have to invent ourselves" (356).

But the group is so mixed, the disagreements so great, that their seminar around the grand oak table disintegrates into chaos and pandemonium, with some of the women screaming for freedom from hair rollers and others for revolution. Lupita, after telling them they are behaving like "ill-bred nobodies," furiously throws off the wig and stamps on it. She once again finds herself back in the salon, having refused all the wigs. But the exasperated proprietor, after picking up the demolished wig, tells her that the only female images she can give Lupita are the ones that already exist: "If you don't like anything I've offered to you, well, fix your own hair just as you darn well please. . . . Pay me what you owe me and we're through. The rest is *your* problem" (357).

But Lupita turns to the audience, as if looking for help: "My problem?"

She has now turned into the mirror that makes the audience possible, and, like the audience in *Between the Acts,* the people in this audience may squirm at being confronted with their own implication in the representations she has tried on and discarded. At the end of the play both she and they seem to be out of focus, in and out of the frame, on a threshold between—or among—representations. This is a sudden, contemplative moment following chaotic, noisy pandemonium. In the suddenness of this shift in pace Lupita's question takes on a poignancy that will not allow the play to conclude, that leaves both character and audience not with a period but with a question mark, the punctuation that marks lived noncoincidences.

Afterword

Modern theatre does not take (a) place.

—Julia Kristeva

[Style] is to be found in those features in which discrepancy appears: in the necessary failure of the passionate striving for identity.

—Theodor Adorno

The difficulty is that it is hard to work on the first stage [new subjects] when one is already thinking about the second [humanity's new mutual relationships].

—Bertolt Brecht

Il est essentiel que le spectateur ne se contente pas de donner sens à ce qui *se raconte,* mais observe ce qui *se fait* sur la scène . . .
. . . la question sans réponse: le corps de l'autre et notre propre corps.

—Anne Ubersfeld

Political poetics, feminist theory, and drama can finally be brought together because each circles around the historicity of the subject, a reading of that historicity made possible by defining textuality in such a way that the interrelationship between grammar and materiality is unavoidable. The written or enacted text, argue Oswald Ducrot and Tzvetan Todorov, in a discussion of Kristeva's notion of textuality as productivity, "makes work of language" by opening a gap between, on the one hand, the language of everyday use in representation and comprehension and, on the other, the underlying nature of signification itself, signification as signifying practices "where the meaning and its subject sprout . . . from within the language and its very materiality" in a play of combinations that is radically foreign to the language of communication. The *work* of the practice of language "deposits on the line of the speaking subject a signifying chain" (358); it "*makes a meaning* rather than expressing it," and it is immediately and intimately connected to the

275

social circumstances within which that meaning is made (Ducrot and Todorov 1979, 358, 359).

In such a translinguistic process, one that involves both bodies and symbols, "the scene of signification cannot be said to be because it is always in the process of being," its textual logic ultimately characterized as "the contingent distribution of infinite significance" (Ducrot and Todorov 1979, 358–59). This work of the practice of language means that questions of meaning are intrinsically and always questions of human work and struggle intimately arising out of what is in constant mixture within language—matter. Those questions of meaning are based very precisely on differences, on which an ethics might also be based, an ethics of respect for the foreignness of Otherness, a foreignness that structures our own most intimate relationship to ourselves: "On the basis of the other, I become reconciled with my own otherness—foreignness, that I play on it, live by it . . . in a journey into the strangeness of the other and of oneself, toward an ethics of respect for the irreconcilable" (Kristeva 1991, 182).

Both Aristotle's and Kristeva's poetics bring together materiality and grammar, both are about the activity not of expressing meaning but, rather, of *making* it, but there is a difference between the poetic subjects of the two theories. Aristotle's *Poetics* is an aesthetic theory for political man; as Vernant argued, when Aristotle defined man as a "political animal," "it was because Reason itself was in essence political" (1982, 130). Kristeva's theory of the political nature of meaning, the process of productivity in which the embodied speaking subject is made readable in poetic language, finds that literature "represents the ultimate coding of our crises, of our most intimate and serious apocalypses" (1982a, 208). Aristotle's poetic subject is a man of the polis, who first disrupts, then participates in reordering, the affairs of state in the interests of the Same, of men like himself; it is the logic of the Sign. Kristeva's, too, is disruptive and resistant but in the interests of shifting the very notion of the subject, shattering it in its deepest figurations while simultaneously acknowledging the involvement of bodies in symbolization.

Both kinds of aesthetic, political subjects depend on a "we," a social collectivity within and against which the subject may be distinguished. Subjects of the symbolic contract of Western culture have been produced according to a disciplinary sacrificial logic within which certain members of the collectivity are excluded from the active production of representation, their representations instead made available for exchange by other members, their control of representations sacrificed to the coherence of the group, of civilization.

This symbolic logic of the exchange of symbols relies on figurations of scapegoats, who are assigned the guilt for things that cannot be controlled—evil, corporeality, random natural phenomena, the arbitrary, death. Active subjects, in this logic, can "define" themselves only if there is something or someone to which they can be contrasted in a binary opposition or a normative system of classification, whose structure produces a borderline category, the abject—the residue, the excess, which results from both the process of separating the developing human ego from its objects and from the attempt to separate masculinity from femininity: "For abjection, when all is said and done, is the other facet of religious, moral, and ideological codes on which rest the sleep of individuals and the breathing spells of societies. Such codes are abjection's purification and repression" (Kristeva 1982a, 207). All women, all nonwhite people, all Jews, all gays and lesbians, are associated with the abjected feminine within the psychosymbolic, sociohistorical context Kristeva calls "Christian Western civilization and its lay humanist variants" (1982c, 24). And that civilization has perhaps reached a point of crisis: "Lacking illusions, lacking shelter, today's universe is divided between *boredom* (increasingly anguished at the prospect of losing its resources through depletion) or (when the spark of the symbolic is maintained and desire to speak explodes) *abjection* and *piercing laughter*" (Kristeva 1982a, 133).

Or it may not lead to laughter. It may, instead, lead to the recognition of suffering in a postmodern moment in which phallic power is in a paranoid shambles and no form of justice reveals itself, a moment in which neither past nor future gives promises. This postmodern moment does not look tragic so much as it seems to be situated in a "nondramatic, willed, unnameable sadness" (Kristeva 1989, 239), a mourning not for the dead father but for the missing mother damaged and brutalized by that Symbolic. That sadness does not "lend itself to description [but is] accessible through inspirations, tears, blank spaces between words" (243). For, in light of the monstrous violence that has marked the twentieth century, silence can no longer be equated only with enigmatic mystery. It has just as much to do with brutality:

What these monstrous and painful sights do damage to are our systems of perception and representation. As if overtaxed and de-

stroyed by too powerful a breaker, our symbolic means find themselves hollowed out, nearly wiped out, paralyzed. On the edge of
silence the word "nothing" emerges, a discreet defense in the face
of so much disorder, both internal and external, incommensurable.
(1989, 223)

The social group that attempts to achieve order and coherence
through a purifying cultural logic is no longer the nation-state; instead
the nation-state is transcended by a cultural similarity identified by
means of a symbolic denominator having to do not just with production
but also with biological reproduction and its symbols.[1] Roland Barthes's
essay, "Taking Sides," with which this study began, was, in the final
analysis, an essay about the truth value of the word *we,* the word whose
presuppositions determine what "we" think of as history and how "we"
conceptualize the speaking subject. The "we" Barthes was talking about
was a Eurocentric, masculine one dependent on sacrifice, a "socio-his-
torical conjuncture (patriarchal ideology, whether Christian, humanist,
socialist, or so forth)" (Kristeva 1982c, 24), which depended on the
sacrifice of corporeality represented by femininity, a sacrifice abstracted
over time to become a series of taboos and logics. The sacrifice in some
ways tames and lessens violence among the proper members of the
group, but it justifies legitimate violence against Outsiders and hidden
violence against deviant insiders, that is, Inside Outsiders. Any group
whose coherence depends on casting out an Other, on defining itself
over and against Others, risks duplicating this violent logic of tragedy.

There is another violence for which the symbolic contract attempts
to console its members, an original violence, the separation from an
imagined fullness that, in Lacan's version of the Symbolic, founds language. The status of this imagined fullness, from which every speaking
being is separated, is represented in Western culture by the archaic mother.

Because the equilibrium and stability of every subject is in intricate
ways affected by the equilibrium of the particular society in which the
subject is subjected, the Western subject, too, depends on the sacrifice
of its femininity. The feminine, the abject, the corporeal, are all
sacrificed to the purity of masculinity and, more specifically, white masculinity, in a very particular racial form. Female subjects thus both
sacrifice the feminine within themselves and experience themselves as
the feminine that is sacrificed. They "live the sacrifice" within the
group implied by Benveniste's notion of the impersonal "*il,*" the ge-

neric "he" that institutes universal syntax. As Barthes so carefully showed, acts of knowing by men of reason "illuminate [their] own solitude and [their] own particularity. Each is an act of darkness casting a brilliant light on the couple constituted by [knower and known] . . . knowledge thereby illuminates its own solitude and its own particularity; manifesting the very history of its division, it cannot escape it" (1972, 166). That particularity is interpreted by Barthes as tragic solitude, but there are other interpretations, and this particularity could just as easily suggest possibility rather than limitation, the possibility of naive history, or histories.

When naive history is written, when the mimics and the masqueraders, the thetic actors, put into play the process whose foundation is their exclusion and appropriation, an instability troubles the social and personal equilibrium that is the goal of a cultural logic: "The more or less beautiful image in which I behold or recognize myself rests upon an abjection that sunders it as soon as repression, the constant watchman, is relaxed" (Kristeva 1982a, 13). That instability brings an increase in attempts to produce order by force; it foregrounds the "increasingly dark caverns of male paranoia."

Naive history both draws attention to the violent, paranoid nature of oedipal bonding and calls into question the arrogance of its "we." "The community of language as a universal and unifying tool," its power to express a symbolic bond and common interest, is demystified, dispersed: "Dispersed are we; who have come together," drones the gramophone in *Between the Acts*. The subject and verb are reversed from their usual order; they are "out of order," as *dispersed* carries the weight of the sentence, not the *we*. In fact, the pronoun *we* is here frail and weak, questioning, longing for an answer to what cannot even be formulated as a question, in contrast to the usual arrogance of *we,* which, in its oversights, presumes a shared understanding so deep and clear it need not even be acknowledged.

But in Woolf's sentence, *we* has shattered into lonely, but not atomistic, units, some masculine, some feminine, people who happen to be contiguously arranged in a group because they share corporeality, a group of townspeople watching a play performed outdoors, a play no one can really understand because it is fragmented, experimental, and perforated by natural intrusions like cows, rainstorms, mud—and Others. Onstage is mingled with offstage, the spectators sharing only a cultural familiarity, a language, and the similarity of being alive.

The second clause of Woolf's sentence begins with an almost impersonal, isolated *who,* a relative pronoun that should be linked to *we* because, grammatically, it should not be able to stand by itself in an independent clause. The British punctuation of the semicolon rather than a
comma between phrases, from a North American reading, problema-
tizes the independence even further.

The sentence walks obliquely into its meaning. Kristeva quotes
Céline about such a simple sentence that does far more than it says:
"Style is a certain way of doing violence to sentences . . . of having them
slightly fly off the handle, so to speak, displacing them, and thus making
the reader himself displace his meaning. But ever so slightly! Ever so
slightly!" (Céline, quoted in Kristeva 1982a, 203).

Woolf's sentence has reversed the confidence of *we.* How can the
sentence make sense if *we* means "dispersed" as well as "joined together," if it is based on a logic of both/and rather than either/or? For
the spheres to be connected, in Nietzsche's conceptualization only a
stammering translation was possible, an aesthetic relation mediated by
force. But Woolf's delicate sentence reveals its search for a way around
(or through) binary logic; rather than being a translation between the
two spheres produced by a subject and an object, it "naively" originates
in a different, excessive space where the identities of subjects and objects,
translators and translated, are all mixed up, confused.

What kind of group or collectivity can possibly emerge from this
dispersion which, nevertheless, can only recognize itself *as* dispersion
because it still differentially depends on the oedipal concept of "we," on
a society and language based on meritocracy and the democracy of prop-
ertied, racially pure males? If the "we" that founds the language of men
of reason is actually a particular, specific, small group of speaking subjects whose status is universalized in symbolic language, how can "we"
as a community conceptualize another kind of society? What kind of
language is possible, or, as Audre Lorde asks, "What does the we-bird
see with who has lost its I's?" (quoted in Kintz 1989, 130).

The writer of Woolf's sentence positions herself as much in the
dispersed as in the *we,* yet the sentence retains a kind of sad, loving
meaning, reclaiming likeness by muddying it, showing that it is the
shared likeness of corporeality, life, even the shared likeness of mortal-
ity. The weight of the sentence falls on *together.* All the while the sentence acknowledges that any kind of "we" might still, at this historical
moment, be sacrificial, from which comes its sadness. Will it be women,
will it be people of the Third World, who, recognizing both togetherness

and sacrifice, will yet again be responsible for keeping "us" together, for "socializing male paranoia"?

The next sentence in Woolf's paragraph tells how the music from the gramophone can be heard over the dispersal of the confused, parting audience: *"But* the gramophone asserted, *let us retain whatever made that harmony"* (1941, 196). But what harmony? The fact that they momentarily came together to watch a play nobody understood? That they were in harmony in not understanding? That they separately heard the music together? That nothing is excluded, not even the mechanical "voice" of the gramophone—not the mud, not the cows, not the villagers, not the idiot—from the group called "us"?

Woolf points toward a different notion of harmony, one not dependent on the sacrificial nature of language's harmony, a way *we* can be together without being *We;* her sentence hangs onto the slightest but strongest desire to be with others, to mix back in whatever has been abjected: "O let us, the audience echoed (stooping, peering, fumbling), keep together. For there is joy, sweet joy, in company" (Woolf 1941, 196). There is sad joy in company. Miss Whatshername, the play's director and anonymous author, has resisted sacrifice, refusing to exclude filth and materiality in the way the founding rituals of Judeo-Christian culture did but, instead, mixing them back in: "What she wanted, like that carp (something moved in the water) was darkness in the mud; a whisky and soda at the pub; and coarse words descending like maggots in the waters" (203). Materiality is included rather than purified, mixture not threatening so much as productive. Likeness is muddied: "The mud became fertile. Words rose above the intolerably laden dumb oxen plodding through the mud. Words without meaning—wonderful words" (212). Words and coarse, common material inch toward a different space where, says Ursula LeGuin, there "is no away to throw to" (1985a, 487).

If there proves to be no "away" to throw to, how can the symbolic contract that bonds by means of throwing away keep itself together? If language always involves the violence of separation and of sacrifice, how can a symbolic system sustain itself differently? Kristeva suggests a way, a symbolic contract within which *every* subject interiorizes the separation or the foreignness that constitutes coming to subjectivity within language and admits it is a mixture, de-agonizing it, *de-dramatizing* the social unit, deconstructing the tragic notion of drama in the interests of a different kind of drama. Such an internalization of sacrifice might constitute an ethics, "a femininity which assumes the moment of castration, the passage through the *symbolique,* not at the price of repressing the maternal *chora*, but in order precisely to put castration in play by mobilizing within the *symbolique* the return of the repressed." Such a revision of language might provide a different space for organizing difference, "provided we hear in language—and not in the other, nor in the other sex—the gouged-out eye, the wound, the basic incompleteness that conditions the indefinite quest of signifying concatenations" (Kristeva 1982a, 133).

Reworking the symbolic bond would also mean retheorizing the "fullness" that has been represented by the archaic mother who could have satisfied all our desires if only she had not left us, an archaic mother whose power over us and failure of us justifies our resentment, fear, and awe of her as well as our revenge against her. Society relieves its guilt by blaming her and justifying violence against her and all those associated with her horrifying femininity: "Under the cunning, orderly surface of civilizations, the nurturing horror that they [push aside] by purifying, systematizing, and thinking; the horror that they seize on to build themselves up and function" (Kristeva 1982a, 210).

The separate spheres Nietzsche described might best be called the Language of the Family, but perhaps it is possible to change the organization of language, or the Symbolic, keeping at it, trying to get rid of the negligent father, the paranoid self-reproducing sons, and the archaic mother, telling the story naively from other directions, from the direction of mother and daughter and from sites of Otherness structurally linked to people othered across the globe by the First World purified masculine subject, perhaps speaking languages of other kinds of families, careful family discussions like this one between a brother and a sister. Here the unspoken is not nothing; it signifies: "But, brother and sister, flesh and blood was not a barrier, but a mist. Nothing changed their affection; no argument; no fact; no truth" (Woolf 1941, 26). We come together dispersed; "what she saw he didn't; what he saw she didn't—and so on, *ad infinitum*," together in their dispersal, thinking differently yet thinking the same because they can still speak together, the words not meaning as much as the mere fact that they are spoken. The unspoken—the intersubjectivity of the word—constitutes its meaning, part of an oblique, slow search, not for Home but for shelter. The unspoken has to do with different kinds of subjects, abject "feminine" ones—outside themselves, beside themselves, each beset with a longing to make sure the other lasts against all odds.

Notes

Introduction

1. John Mowitt's "Performance Theory as the Work of Laurie Anderson," *Discourse* 12, no. 2 (Spring–Summer 1990): 48–65, is an important discussion of the inseparability of theories of performance and the performance of theory. I have discussed this question more fully in "Gendering the Critique of Representation: Fascism, the Purified Body, and Theater in Adorno, Artaud, and Maria Irene Fornes," *Rethinking Marxism* 4, no. 3 (Fall 1991): 83–100.

2. A very concrete example of the relevance of questioning the model of unity can be found in the work of Ann Travers and Susan Johnston, two graduate students in sociology who have written about their work organizing opposition to the Oregon Citizens Alliance proposal of a constitutional amendment that would list homosexuality as "abnormal behavior" and eliminate human rights or civil rights protection from discrimination for gays and lesbians. See their paper, "Coalitions without Consensus: Challenges for Lesbian and Gay Organizing in the 1990s," describing their experience as activists in the Campaign for a Hate Free Oregon, or the No Hate PAC.

3. An essay by Mary Carpenter Wilson is one of the few to make the very specific criticism of theory's relationship to older women on campus, assuming, as theorists do, whether they are male or female theorists, that it is the subject position of *young* women which is at issue, either as rebellious or seductive daughters or as daughters seeking to become agents. Older women are either ignored or ridiculed. See her "Eco, Oedipus, and the 'View' of the University," *Diacritics* 20, no. 1 (Spring 1990): 77–103.

4. See, in particular, these chapters: "Menstruation, Work, and Class"; "Premenstrual Syndrome, Work Discipline, and Anger"; "Birth, Resistance, Race, and Class"; and "Menopause, Power, and Heat" (Emily Martin, *The Woman in the Body: A Cultural Analysis of Reproduction* [Boston: Beacon Press, 1987]).

5. Régis Durand's work suggested this terminology: "On Aphanisis: A Note on the Dramaturgy of the Subject in Narrative Analysis," *MLN* 98, no. 5 (December 1983): 860–70.

6. "Toute théorie du 'sujet' aura toujours été appropriée au 'masculin'" (Luce Irigaray, *Speculum de l'autre femme* [Paris: Les Editions de Minuit, 1974], 165).

7. In Western metaphysics there is a long tradition of "coincidences" that deserve more study. In Rousseau's "On the Inequality of Men," for example, and in Marx's description of the formation of the family there is a moment of coincidence in which force is erased from the description and a couple spontaneously—coincidentally—appears.

8. *Interpellation* is Louis Althusser's term for the way ideology works to recruit or to transform individuals through the category of the subject, calling on individuals as particular kinds of subjects. Various discourses "hail" or call subjects: "Hey, you there!" (Louis Althusser, "Ideological State Apparatuses," *Lenin and Philosophy and Other Essays*, trans. Ben Brewster [New York: Monthly Review Press, 1971, 174]).

9. Luce Irigaray, *Ce sexe qui n'en est pas un* (Paris: Les Editions de Minuit, 1977), 87.

10. *New Larousse Encyclopedia of Mythology* (London: Hamlyn, 1959), 162.

11. *Thespian* here means a subject of King Thespis. The use of *Thespian* to refer to an actor is derived from the name of the Greek poet Thespis, who introduced the prologue and speech into Greek drama as it developed from improvisation to enacted text. See Gerald Else's discussion of the development of dialogue in Greek drama in *Aristotle's Poetics: The Argument* (Cambridge: Harvard University Press, 1957).

12. *New Larousse* (1959), 162. *Fading* is the term used to translate what happens in the process of the formation of the subject within language: "There where it was just now, there where it was for a while, between an extinction that is still glowing and a birth that is retarded, 'I' can come into being and disappear from what I say" (Jacques Lacan, *Ecrits: A Selection*, trans. Alan Sheridan [New York: Norton, 1977], 300).

13. Klaus Mann, writing in exile after the rise of the Nazis, relies on the metaphor of the echo: "Do our pleas for help thrown toward incertainty fall into a void? We wait for something like an echo, even if it is still vague and far away. There where one has called so strongly, there must be at least a little echo," in Ariane Mnouchkine, *Mephisto: Le roman d'une carrière d'après Klaus Mann*. Paris: Editions Solin and Théâtre du Soleil.

14. Foucault's view of language changes after *Historie de la folie*, which associated madness with writing as otherness. In his later works, in particular *Les mots et les choses*, he steps back from an espousal of this modernist view of writing and historicizes modernism by showing why it occurs as a conceptual possibility in the late twentieth century. See John Rajchman, "Foucault, or the Ends of Modernism," *October* 24 (Spring 1983): 37–62.

15. These oppositions change, depending on the circumstances. Jane Tompkins's study of silent men in Hollywood westerns finds that the right to determine speech is claimed by the hero, whose power is reflected in his right to keep silent while the woman chatters. This structure is still based on this binary

opposition between those who control speech and those whose speech is controlled (Public lecture, University of Oregon, May 1989).

16. I have more fully argued this point about the circulation of the feminine as textuality in deconstruction in "On Performing Deconstruction: Postmodern Pedagogy," *Cultural Critique* 16 (Fall 1990): 87–107; and "In-Different Criticism: The Deconstructive 'Parole,'" in *The Thinking Muse: Feminism and Modern French Philosophy,* ed. Jeffner Allen and Iris Young, 113–35 (Bloomington: Indiana University Press, 1989).

17. Aristotle wanted to show that the polis was "like an extended family, since it was formed by the merging of villages that themselves were a merger of households. He noted that the *oikos,* the domestic family, is a natural community, a *koinonia*" (Jean-Pierre Vernant, *The Origins of Greek Thought* [Ithaca: Cornell University Press, 1982], 130).

18. For the complexities and even duplicities of public speaking, see John J. Winkler, "Laying Down the Law: The Oversight of Men's Sexual Behavior in Classical Athens," *The Constraints of Desire: The Anthropology of Sex and Gender in Ancient Greece* (New York: Routledge, 1990), 45–70.

19. "*Tragôidoi* perform not to express the spirit of Dionysos but to display the polis's finely tuned sense of discipline and impulse, of youth's incorporation into a competitive harmony of tribes and age classes" (John J. Winkler, "The Ephebes' Song: *Tragôidia* and *Polis,*" *Representations* 11 [Summer 1985]: 51).

20. Vernant continues: "Thus restored to its historical setting, philosophy casts off the character of pure revelation that scholars have sometimes bestowed upon it, proclaiming that in the youthful science of the Ionians timeless Reason became incarnate in Time. The Milesian school did not witness the birth of Reason; rather, it devised a kind of reasoning, an early form of rationality. . . . When Aristotle defined man as a 'political animal,' he emphasized what differentiates Greek reason from today's reason. If in his eyes *Homo sapiens* was *Homo politicus,* it was because Reason itself was in essence political" (*Origins,* 130).

21. Amarty Sen, in a very different context, connects issues of social perception of women to the maintenance of female deprivation. In particular, she studies parts of the world where there is a lower ratio of women to men and finds a very complex matrix of reasons for it. One of the most important factors in this imbalance has to do with social perceptions of the worth of women, perceptions that structure academic studies as well as more overt political decisions. The dimensions of this imbalance and neglect are simply missing from scholarship and statistics because these women themselves are missing:

> In view of the enormity of the problems of women's survival in large parts
> of Asia and Africa, it is surprising that these disadvantages have received
> such inadequate attention. The numbers of "missing women" in relation to
> the numbers that could be expected if men and women received similar care
> in health, medicine, and nutrition are remarkably large. A great many more
> than a hundred million women are simply not there because women are
> neglected compared with men. If this situation is to be corrected by political

action and public policy, the reasons why there are so many "missing" women must first be better understood. We confront here what is clearly one of the more momentous, and neglected, problems facing the world today. ("More Than 100 Million Women Are Missing," *New York Review of Books* 37, no. 20 [20 December 1990]: 61–67)

Chapter 1

1. Teiresias, the blind priest who "sees" what Oedipus cannot, has other interesting connections. He lived seven years as a woman and seven years as a man and was gifted with the ability to see things from the perspective of both genders. Zeus and Hera, arguing over the question of which gender enjoyed greater sexual pleasure, turned to Teiresias for the answer, which was that women's pleasure was nine times greater than that of men.

Teiresias lost his sight when he accidentally happened upon the naked Athena, the goddess of chastity, bathing. She punished him by blinding him but gave him the gift of prophecy as a compensation. He also foretold the death of Narcissus.

2. The specific differences between Sophocles and Aristotle risk being collapsed here, and they are considerable. As Gerald Else says, "Tragedy in its greatest days comported things that were not dreamt of in Aristotle's philosophy" (*Aristotle's Poetics: The Argument* [Cambridge: Harvard University Press, 1957], 446).

Sophocles represented a period in which ethos was important, with *ethos* defined as the integration of practical needs and thought into one moral, political approach to the world. The aristocratic man whose deeds and thinking were integrated with the needs of the state was the exemplary man.

Aristotle's work represented a shift toward an epistemology in which thought was in some ways separated from the practical sphere and was privileged over ethos. The philosopher was the exemplary figure of his version of society, followed by the aristocratic political man. Aristotle's interpretation of Sophocles has had more influence on the "subject" of the West, institutionalizing both its logic and its rhetoric.

3. Else implies an opposition between melodrama and tragedy, with tragedy the obvious, clearly superior form. The gendering of this opposition is of particular importance.

4. Another study that needs to done is a feminist collection and analysis of the possible variants of the Oedipus tale, on the order of the studies done by Vladimir Propp, *Edipo all luce del folclore,* ed. Clara Strada Janovic (Turin: Einaudin, 1975).

Narrowing the focus of drama to stories of a very few families did not occur until the second half of the fifth century, the period of the development of Athenian democracy.

5. "What is the answer to the question? The problem. How is the problem resolved? By displacing the question" (Michel Foucault, "Theatrum Philoso-

phicum," *Language, Counter-Memory, Practice*, trans. Sherry Simon and Donald Bouchard [Ithaca: Cornell University Press, 1977], 185).

6. Teresa de Lauretis, *Alice Doesn't: Feminism, Semiotics, Cinema* (Bloomington: Indiana University Press, 1984).

7. Propp's study of the historical roots of the Oedipus story, "Edip v svete fol'klora," *Serija filologičeskich nauk* 9, no. 72 (1944): 138–75, still has not been published in English. Neither has *The Historical Roots of the Fairy Tale* (*Istoricheskie korni volshebnoĭ skázki* [Leningrad, 1986]). The reception of Propp's work would make an interesting study, since he is frequently characterized as an ahistorical formalist. Yet *Las raíces históricas del cuento*, trans. José Martín Arancibía (Madrid: Editorial Fundamentos, 1974), first published in Spanish in 1946, almost twenty years after *The Morphology of the Folktale*, is striking because of its political and historical interests. Every structure is linked to the tensions between particular social organizations; they are not presented as universal, ahistorical forms. The different reception of these two works can be related to the effects of the cold war on academic scholarship.

8. In a rich chapter tracing the emergence of an epistemological paradigm that does not rely on a binary opposition between rationalism and irrationalism, "Morelli, Freud, and Sherlock Holmes," in *The Sign of Three: Dupin, Holmes, Peirce*, ed. Umberto Eco and Thomas Sebeok (Bloomington: Indiana University Press, 1983), Carlo Ginzburg shows how the social sciences in the late nineteenth century began using a methodology similar to that used in medicine today, a methodology that relied on abductive reasoning based on reading symptoms and small details, intuitive guesses based on probabilities. This type of reasoning is not necessarily restricted to an educated elite but is also found in uneducated hunters, women, mariners, etc., in all geographic locations. It is also used by physicians trained to read the signs of the body and by detectives like Sherlock Holmes, who intuit and predict from obscure details, rather than reasoning deductively from predetermined concepts.

9. The use of the concept of *role* here does not refer to a simple character role. Rather, it is meant to suggest a subject position constructed and made possible by the logical requirements of the texts and, ultimately, by and in language, in its broad material sense used by Julia Kristeva. The Sphinx and Jocasta are subjected in language that is organized within a particular cultural logic. They are not "people" or "characters" but, instead, the poetic matrix of various subject positions, in the same sense that the ego is the matrix of multiple historically determined judgments and identifications, but it is never singular or separate from discourse. This concept of dramatic character will be discussed more fully in chapters 3, 4, 5, and 6.

10. This reading is suggested by the work of Teresa de Lauretis.

11. This discussion is based on two articles by Jurij Lotman: "The Origin of Plot in the Light of Typology," *Poetics Today* 1, nos. 1–2 (1974): 161–84; and with B. A. Uspenskij, "Myth—Name—Culture," in *Soviet Semiotics: An Anthology*, ed. and trans. Daniel P. Lucid, 233–52 (Baltimore: Johns Hopkins University Press, 1977).

12. Lotman draws on Roman Jakobson's article, "Shifters, Verbal Categories, and the Russian Verb," in Lotman and Uspenskij, "Myth," 246n, for this discussion.

13. The oedipal plot is not universal, but its effects have influenced the history of Western metaphysics and representation to such an extent that, temporarily in this study, plot and oedipal plot will be used interchangeably.

14. Sophocles, *Oedipus the King*, trans. David Grene, in *Greek Tragedies* (Chicago: University of Chicago Press, 1960), 1: 122. Further references to this translation will be cited in the text.

15. A similar pattern in a different context shows up in a review of Hollywood movies where rich white men find themselves impotent in one way or another, movies like *Regarding Henry*. Georgia Brown suggests that a claim is made in such movies that "the emblems of power and potency are failing." (BMW cars break down; medical degrees are useless against a robber's bullet, etc.) "Well," she argues, "this is what Hollywood believes the ordinary have-not audience would like to *think* is taking place" ("Apocalypse Now and Then," *Village Voice* 36, no. 53 [December 1991] : 52).

16. *New Larousse* (1959), 321.

17. Melanie Klein relates the metaphor of paths and roads to the "geography of the mother's body" in a discussion of children's difficulties with learning geography and orientation. See Melanie Klein, "Early Analysis," *Love, Guilt, and Reparation* (New York: Delta Books, 1975), 98.

And *aporia*, as Else reminds us, means "roadlessness."

18. According to Else (*Aristotle's Poetics*) the ritual of the expulsion of the *pharmakos* was different from ostracism or the exile of a tyrant. The first had to do with getting rid of an internal contaminant who had little direct power, the second with the expulsion of someone powerful who threatened to take control.

19. Meaghan Morris, in "The Pirate's Fiancée," characterizes the paradox bluntly: "The circular form . . . is one beloved of classical ('masculine') intelligibility fondling its own limits—the paradox" (*Michel Foucault: Power, Truth, Strategy* [Sydney: Feral Publications, 1979], 161).

20. This possibility of waiting is the same as the lot of women in marriage, as Benveniste's tracing of the etymology of *marriage* showed. Waiting can be equated with a condition or state as opposed to activity, the *nominal* as opposed to the *verbal*.

21. Suicides are effective devices for preserving the plot's symmetry because they occur within the spaces of chance, the arbitrary, the random. Aristotle described these random events as episodic temptations that threaten to divert the poet from his unified plot. The events in a dramatic plot must move forward regularly in a certain way, but episodes or stories about particularities along the way divert us from the plot: "At each joint, so to speak, between two 'parts' of the play which ought to fit tightly together—there is a wrench in the continuity" (Else, *Aristotle's Poetics,* 326). [Or maybe a wench?] The device of the suicide helps control these episodic temptations.

Homer, according to Aristotle, was the only poet strong enough to be able to use episodic structure without being seduced by it.

22. Aristotle's system includes two different kinds of universals. One kind, with which tragedy deals, has to do with pragmatic universals. The other concerns metaphysical universals, and the man of tragedy does not concern himself with these; only philosophers do.

23. Furthermore, women soon come into opposition to civilization and display their retarding and restraining influence—those very women who, in the beginning, laid the foundations of civilization by the claims of their love. Women represent the interests of the family and of sexual life. The work of civilization has become increasingly the business of men; it confronts them with ever more difficult tasks and compels them to carry out instinctual sublimations of which women are little capable. Since a man does not have unlimited quantities of psychical energy at his disposal, he has to accomplish his tasks by making an expedient distribution of his libido. What he employs for cultural aims he to a great extent withdraws from women and sexual life. His constant association with men, and his dependence on his relations with them, even estrange him from his duties as a husband and father. Thus the woman finds herself forced into the background by the claims of civilization and she adopts a hostile attitude to it. (Sigmund Freud, *Civilization and Its Discontents,* ed. James Strachey [New York: Norton, 1961], 50)

Julia Kristeva, in *Soleil noir: Dépression and mélancolie* (Paris: Editions Gallimard, 1987), offers a very different interpretation of the "inability" of women to carry out "instinctual sublimations." Because it is so much more difficult for girls to replace their original love object, the mother, with the father than it is for little boys, who are able to retain their original love object, Kristeva argues that girls must carry out far more rigorous and difficult sublimations than do boys.

24. Patricia Jagentowicz Mills's *Woman, Nature, and Psyche* (New Haven: Yale University Press, 1987) is an important discussion of the circularity of the public and private in the active plot space of the masculine thinker in Hegel's dialectic and his discussion of Antigone, or "the irony of the tribe." The master/slave dialectic participates in a similar paradoxical opposition that is always already in the space of the masculine subject yet effaces this fact in order to claim universality.

25. The relationship between this logic based on One and monotheism in the West will be developed in chapter 3.

26. The law of the developing Greek state introduced a conflict between the archaic taboo (and the right of the family to punish blood murder) and the democratic equality of citizens within the law (the right of citizens to determine guilt). The state eventually took over punishment for kindred murder, and law replaced vengeance.

Chapter 2

1. Gerald Else, *The Origin and Early Form of Greek Tragedy* (Cambridge: Harvard University Press, 1965), 86.

2. Gerald Else, *Aristotle's Poetics: The Argument* (Cambridge: Harvard University Press, 1957), 377. He isolates an important difference between Sophocles and Aristotle. In Sophocles there is an emphasis on speech that expresses *character* (ethos as habitual, unreflective behavior). By Aristotle's time this had changed to an emphasis on speech that expressed *thought* (intellectual, reflective, generalizing expression).

3. *American Heritage Dictionary of the English Language,* New College ed. (Boston: Houghton Mifflin, 1980).

4. Claude Lévi-Strauss in Kaja Silverman, *The Subject of Semiotics* (New York: Oxford University Press, 1983), 20. Lévi-Strauss's analysis claims universality for his rules of exchange, but they may only apply to very particular segments of Western culture, which sees the world in its own image. The rule of exogamy not only defines appropriate sexual partners but appropriate gender identities.

5. Language participated in this opposition. The word *barbarian* originated in the description of non-Greek languages as "babble."

6. One story has it that the Olympic athletes competed in the nude because a woman had once sneaked into their midst to participate in their exercises. To prevent such mixing of females in this male activity, the athletes took off their clothes, making difference easily distinguishable and exposing the fakes.

7. Finley gives an example of the analogy between slaves and animals: "The Greeks may have coined the contemptuous word *andrapoda* (man-footed beings) for slaves collectively, on the model of *tetropoda* (quadrupeds)" (M. I. Finley, *Ancient Slavery and Modern Ideology* [New York: Viking Press, 1980], 99).

8. Finley, *Ancient Slavery,* 95. Pierre Gravel's description of this inscription bears repeating:

> One can in effect read the terms of reason's desire which animates *homo rationalis* in the maxims he inscribes on the fronts of his courts. One can read the terms of that desire equally well in the signs he traces on the bodies of the people upon whom he inflicts corporal punishment (*supplice*) or in the disgrace and shame with which he charges those he wants to exclude. In one of these cases, one reads what he poses for himself as the infinity of his own desire. In the other what must be produced so that that desire can be maintained. (*Pour une logie du sujet tragique* [Montréal: Montréal University Press, 1980], 70; my translation).

9. Finley, *Ancient Slavery,* 67. The English word *family* is derived from the Latin *familia,* which means "family, household, servants of a household." *Familia* is derived from the word *famulus,* which means "servant."

10. Michel Foucault, quoted in an interview with Hubert L. Dreyfus and Paul Rabinow, *Michel Foucault: Beyond Structuralism and Hermeneutics* (Chicago: Chicago University Press, 1983), 232. Again, the implied reader is masculine.

11. Foucault in Dreyfus and Rabinow, *Michel Foucault,* 233. Foucault's study of the Western subject focused on Athens because its culture still functions as an ideal. But he is critical of the Greek subject: "The Greek ethics was linked to a purely virile society with slaves, in which the women were underdogs whose

pleasure had no importance, whose sexual life had to be only oriented toward, determined by, their status as wives."

At another point in the interview Foucault responds to the following question:

Q. It looks like nonreciprocity was a problem for the Greeks all right, but it seems to be the kind of problem that one could straighten out. Why does sex have to be virile? Or is it that it's not just a little problem, because if you try to bring in the pleasure of the other the whole hierarchical, ethical system would break down?

A. That's right . . . (Dreyfus and Rabinow, *Michel Foucault*, 233)

12. Page duBois, *Centaurs and Amazons: Women and the Pre-History of the Great Chain of Being* (Ann Arbor: University of Michigan Press, 1982), 146. She says elsewhere: "Faced with conflict, with the disintegration of the traditional analogical model of differentiation, the philosophers of the fourth century did not extend their definition of the human subject to include all kinds. Instead, in an attempt to fix the form of the city in an unchanging, internally differentiated pattern, there evolved a new rationalization of social relations. Those relations comfortable to the elite of the city were attributed to natural qualities which were described in terms of a hierarchy of difference" (133).

13. Sue-Ellen Case has also traced the status of women on the Greek stage as masculine representations of women in *Feminism and Theatre* (New York: Methuen, 1988), 5–27.

14. The attempt to prevent violence among males in the circle of equals made violence acceptable in two other ways: (1) the invisible violence of the domestic space; and (2) legitimate violence against Outsiders.

15. Sophocles, *The Women of Trachis*, trans. Michael Jameson, in *The Complete Greek Tragedies*, vol. 2: *Sophocles* (Cambridge: Harvard University Press, 1978), 298. Further references will be cited in the text.

16. According to the glossary of Gregory Dickerson's translation of *The Women of Trachis* the floral imagery Sophocles used in reference to Iole and Deianeira builds on the more technical medical term *anthos*, which means "pustulant efflorescence."

17. The rest of the passage connects the mark of inscription with its use in reproducing the logic of culture as the logic of property: "He told me / what property from our marriage I should take and how he wished the portions of ancestral land to be divided up among the children" (284).

18. In some cultures part of a young boy's initiation consisted of being dressed as a girl. This disguise was a prelude to the moment in the ceremony when he became a man, when male and female were definitively separated.

Herakles had been condemned to spend a year with Omphale, the queen of Lydia, who bought him when he was offered as a nameless slave. He had been punished for stealing the tripod of the Pythia, the oracle at Delphi, where he had gone to be purified for the murder of Iphitus. His fury at the Pythia was caused by her refusal to purify him.

While he was enslaved, he dressed as a woman and engaged in weaving.

But he also had time for adventures: capturing the Cercopes, killing the king of Aulis, ridding the river Sagaris of a giant serpent, and throwing Lityerses into the sea. Impressed by these achievements, Omphale freed him.

19. Catherine MacKinnon has defined the private as "everything women have been equated with and defined in terms of men's ability to have" ("Feminism, Marxism, Method, and the State: Toward a Feminist Jurisprudence," *Signs* 8, no. 4 [1982] : 636).

20. As Freud says, "It is our impression that more constraint has been applied to the libido when it is pressed into the service of the feminine function, and that—to speak teleologically—Nature takes less careful account of its demands than in the case of masculinity" ("Feminity," *The Standard Edition of the Complete Psychological Works of Sigmund Freud,* ed. James Strachey [London: Hogarth Press, 1953], 131).

21. Guilt is also associated with judgments made about one's inferiority, as the study of melancholia showed: "This trouble, as is well known, is characterized in particular by self-accusations, self-denigration and a tendency towards self-punishment that can end in suicide. Freud showed that we are faced here with an actual splitting of the ego between accuser (the super-ego) and accused" (Jean Laplanche and J. B. Pontalis, *The Language of Psychoanalysis,* trans. Donald Nicholson-Smith [New York: Norton, 1973], 425).

22. Jacques Donzelot and Michel Foucault have studied the class nature of policing male violence within the family. In the late nineteenth and early twentieth centuries the state's policing of working-class families increased, but psychoanalysis continued to ignore male violence within the affluent families that could afford its services. See Jacques Donzelot, *The Policing of Families,* trans. Robert Hurley (New York: Pantheon, 1979).

23. Herakles's past has already been marked by a confusion between god and father. His mother was Alcmene, who was seduced by Zeus, who came to her disguised as her husband, Amphitryon. Amphitryon arrived soon afterward and capitalized on this god/husband indistinguishability. Twins were born to Alcmene; one was Herakles, the other a weak, cowardly, duplicitous son named Eurystheus, obviously the son of Amphitryon. Much of Herakles's legendary career was spent trying to outwit Hera, who was responsible for his Twelve Labors. Through her trickery Eurystheus was born first, condemning Herakles to do his brother's bidding and, indirectly, Hera's.

Chapter 3

1. Foucault's discussion of the death of the author, a discussion which too quickly bypasses race and gender specificity, can be found in "What Is an Author?" in *Language, Counter-Memory, Practice,* ed. Donald F. Bouchard, trans. Donald F. Bouchard and Sherry Simon, 113–38 (Ithaca: Cornell University Press, 1977).

2. Teresa de Lauretis's work on conceptualizing an "elsewhere" can be found in *Technologies of Gender* (Bloomington: Indiana University Press, 1984).

3. See the work of Augusto Boal on Aristotle's *Poetics* and the way it

privileges the status quo over transformation: *Theater of the Oppressed,* trans. Charles A. and Maria-Odilia Leal McBride (New York: Theatre Communications Group, 1985).

4. Freud's development of the rhetorical tropes of condensation and displacement, articulated with Lacan's and Jakobson's discussions of contiguity and similarity in the workings of the unconscious and textuality, make for a much more complicated notion of resemblance and iconicity in the development of the propping of signification on the body. See Kaja Silverman, *The Subject of Semiotics* (New York: Oxford University Press, 1983).

5. See Pierre Gravel, *Pour une logie du sujet tragique* (Montréal: University of Montréal Press, 1980). Luce Irigaray adds:

Is it necessary to add, or repeat, that woman's "improper" access to representation, her entry into a specular and speculative economy that affords her instincts no signs, no symbols or emblems, or methods of writing that could figure her instincts, make it impossible for her to work out or transpose specific representatives of her instinctual object-goals? The latter . . . will only be translated into a *script of body language. (Speculum of the Other Woman* [Ithaca: Cornell University Press, 1985], 124)

6. Freud's "Negation" (*Complete Works,* vol. 19 [1961]) is an important study of the relationship between the formation of bodily boundaries, of subject and object, by means of judgments based on the not-yet-subject's experience of the difference between the inside and outside of the body. Because bodies are not all alike, these judgments will thus be specifically organized according to gender. This way of analyzing the "étayage," or "propping," of signification on the body that is a description of the mixture of symbol and body makes a constantly revised psychoanalytic methodology important here.

7. See the development of the aesthetic relation between symbol and phantasm in the work of Jean Laplanche, in particular *Life and Death in Psychoanalysis,* trans. Jeffrey Mehlman (Baltimore: Johns Hopkins University Press, 1976).

8. Madelon Sprengnether discusses this point extensively in *The Spectral Mother* (Ithaca: Cornell University Press, 1990).

9. Maria Irene Fornes writes of a resistance to separation in this way: "It is as if words are dampness in a porous substance—a dampness which becomes liquid and condenses. As if there is a condensation that is really the forming of words. I want to catch the process of the forming of thought into words . . . the *devil* passed the word around that in the beginning was the word and . . . it's sinister to think that. Can you imagine? I don't know why words want to become authoritarian" (Scott Cummings, "The Visions of Maria Irene Fornes, *Theater* [Fall–Winter 1985]: 55).

10. When the hierarchy is in relation to *logos,* man is close, woman is distant.

11. Luce Irigary's concept of masquerade refers to the role of Woman that many women do not realize is a role but take seriously and try to play well, unlike Rivière's analysand, who tries to manipulate it. Irigaray's concept of mimicry, on the other hand, suggests the possibility that women can manipulate the images.

Chapter 4

1. See Cynthia Chase, "Primary Narcissism and the Giving of Figure: Kristeva with Hertz and de Man," in *Abjection, Melancholia and Love: The Work of Julia Kristeva*, ed. John Fletcher and Andrew Benjamin, 124–36 (London: Routledge, 1989); Paul de Man, *Allegories of Reading: Figurative Language in Rousseau, Nietzsche, Rilke, and Proust* (New Haven: Yale University Press, 1979); Jacques Derrida, *Limited, Inc.* (Baltimore: Johns Hopkins University Press, 1977); and Shoshana Felman, *The Literary Speech Act: Don Juan with J. L. Austin, or Seduction in Two Languages*, trans. Catherine Porter (Ithaca: Cornell University Press, 1983).

2. Pierre Bourdieu, *Distinction: A Social Critique of the Judgement of Taste*, trans. Richard Nice (Cambridge: Harvard University Press, 1984).

3. This also involves reanalyzing *kinship* in order to historicize it and to compare it to the universalized kinship model of Lévi-Strauss. His "universal," like Freud's, is written retroactively. The system of organization which produced the nuclear family has concentrated on weakening other kinds of kinship systems:

> Imperialist assaults on families take many forms. In the first place, families as sources of power frequently constitute real threats to the authority of the invader. Just as imperialists are concerned to dominate and exploit the pre-existing state apparatus, economic system, and religious institutions, so also they seek to eliminate the corporate power of kin groups, especially in those societies which are organized around lineages. Various colonial strategies, such as the forcible introduction of private property in land to replace communal ownership and control, are mechanisms for breaking down the organizational strength of families, as well as for facilitating the appropriation of land for commercial uses of the "export sector." The Western preference for small, father-headed families does not simply reflect an ethnocentric bias toward the "Christian" norm, but is part of a larger strategy of "divide and rule." (Mina Davis Caulfield, "Imperialism, the Family, and Cultures of Resistance," *Socialist Revolution* 4, no. 20 [October 1974]: 71)

4. The period of the marriages of Frederick III and of Maximilian I, which increased the Hapsburgs' hereditary holdings, produced the motto: "Let others wage war; thou, happy Austria, marry."

5. A study of this interpretation of the play can be found in Rosemary K. Curb, "Lesson I Bleed," in *Women in the American Theatre*, ed. Helen Krich Chinoy and Linda Walsh Jenkins [New York: Theatre Communications Group, 1987], 50–56.

6. *Oedipus the King* opened with the early harvest festival of the Thargelia in the spring. At this ceremony it was common to bring forward two *pharmakoi* whose expulsion could save a city from some kind of calamity. Frequently, one was female, the other male. They represented the spirits of vegetation in general, but, in particular, "they masqueraded as the spirits of fig trees" (Sir James Frazer, *The Golden Bough* [New York: Macmillan, 1950] 1: 672).

They wore strings of black and white figs around their necks, and, as they were paraded through the city, they were beaten on their genitals with the branches of fig trees. According to Frazer, this custom was related to a process called caprification, "the artifical fertilisation of the cultivated [domesticated] fig trees by hanging strings of wild figs among the boughs" (673). Frazer interprets this as an instance of imitative magic in which the figs around the necks of the male and female were to assist the "marriage" in the fig orchard. Sometimes the two human beings were also expected to mate.

7. Bourdieu, *Distinction*, 95.

8. In the area where I live, this channel is used part of the day by Pat Robertson's Christian Broadcasting Network. One of the ads for "Bonanza," now a rerun, shows Hoss Cartwright standing tall and taking two short Native Americans in each hand then banging their heads together.

9. George Mosse's work on the historical construction of the "decent" bourgeois body in *Nationalism and Sexuality: Respectability and Abnormal Sexuality in Modern Europe* (New York: Fertig, 1985) traces the relationship—in nineteenth- and early twentieth-century England, France, and Germany—between periods in which homosexuality was tolerated and those where it came into conflict with both nationalism and a middle-class ideology of decency. His study focuses particularly on the rise of fascism.

10. See, in particular, Kaja Silverman's *The Subject of Semiotics* (New York: Oxford University Press, 1983); and the introductions by Juliet Mitchell and Jacqueline Rose to *Feminine Sexuality: Jacques Lacan and the école freudienne* (New York: W. W. Norton, 1982).

11. See Mark Poster's study of the relation between electronic communication and poststructuralist theories of writing, *The Mode of Information: Poststructuralism and Social Context* (Chicago: University of Chicago Press, 1990).

12. See Jennifer Wicke, "Postmodernism: The Perfume of Information," *Yale Journal of Criticism* 1, no. 2 (Spring 1988): 145–59.

13. Timothy Murray, "Screening the Camera's Eye: Black and White Confrontations of Technological Representation," *Modern Drama* 28, no. 1 (March 1985): 115.

14. As Guy Debord says, "The critique which reaches the truth of the spectacle exposes it as the visible *negation* of life, as a negation of life which *has become visible*" (*The Society of the Spectacle* [Detroit: Black and Red, 1983], passage 10).

15. For a study of the film *Now, Voyager*, see the screenplay and introduction by Jeanne Thomas Allen, *Now, Voyager* (Madison: University of Wisconsin Press, 1984).

16. The psychologist in this film functions as a placeholder for the therapeutic Law through whose legitimation female independence, in this system, must circulate.

17. Another of Kennedy's plays is a study of an African-American Vietnam veteran and the relation between his death at the hands of the police after his return and the racist nature of the Vietnam War. See *An Evening with Dead Essex* in *Theater* 9 (Spring 1978): 66–78.

18. The history of this film and a discussion of Steinbeck's relation to

anticommunism can be found in *Viva, Zapata! The Original Screenplay,* ed. and with an introduction by Robert E. Morsberger (New York: Viking, 1975).

19. Thomas Byrne Edsall and Mary D. Edsall, *Atlantic Monthly* 267, no. 5 (May 1991): 53–86. Their study quotes the Analysis Group, a Democratic polling firm:

> These white Democratic defectors express a profound distaste for blacks, a sentiment that pervades almost everything they think about government and politics. Blacks constitute the explanation for their [white defectors'] vulnerability and for almost everything that has gone wrong in their lives; not being black is what constitutes being middle class; not living with blacks is what makes a neighborhood a decent place to live. . . . These sentiments have important implications for Democrats, as virtually all progressive symbols and themes have been redefined in racial and pejorative terms.
>
> The special status of blacks is perceived by almost all of these individuals as a serious obstacle to their personal advancement. (56)

Chapter 5

1. One example of very different reactions can be found in Clive Barnes's review of the play:

> Lovely performances both, and the audience at the preview I attended responded to them, and apparently, the play itself, with unfeigned pleasure.
>
> Indeed this pleasure was so evident that I felt a passing pang of disappointment at being an odd man out unable to identify with it. Yet finally I was reminded of some remark made by the mother in the course of her chatter designed to divert the daughter from her intent.
>
> She says: "Things don't have to be true to talk about them." Well, that goes for playwrights as well as people, but nevertheless they have to be—let us say—true enough.
>
> For me, at least, *'night, Mother* is a worthy try, but just not true enough. (*New York Theatre Critics' Review:* 1983, 334)

2. "We can no longer assume that the bourgeois conception of the public sphere was simply an unrealized utopian ideal; it was also a masculinist ideological notion that functioned to legitimate an emergent form of class rule" (Nancy Fraser, "Rethinking the Public Sphere: A Contribution to the Critique of Actually Existing Democracy," *Social Text* 25–26 [1990]: 62).

3. Fraser, "Rethinking the Public Sphere," 61. She says at another point: "I do not mean to suggest that subaltern counterpublics are always necessarily virtuous; some of them, alas, are explicitly anti-democratic and anti-egalitarian; and even those with democratic and egalitarian intentions are not always above practicing their own modes of informal exclusion and marginalization" (67).

4. Delores Hayden lists five categories of people not specifically included in the ritual of the American Dream of home ownership: (1) white women of all classes who were expected to live in their husbands' homes; (2) white elderly working-class and lower-class men who remained in the inner city; (3) minority men of all classes who were at first legally excluded from many suburban tracts

("the FHA [Federal Housing Administration] actually had agents whose job it was to keep minorities out, and they pressured any builder or lender who didn't agree"[55]. It was also difficult to obtain loans for houses in inner-city or "red-lined" areas.); (4) minority women of all classes who frequently became domestic workers, cleaning the houses of white women's husbands; and (5) the minority elderly of all classes (Delores Hayden, *Redesigning the American Dream: The Future of Housing, Work, and Family Life* [New York: W. W. Norton, 1984]).

5. Delores Hayden, *Redesigning the American Dream,* 34. Indirectly, Jeremy Bentham's project of organizing and disciplining people by architecture is relevant here. Bentham's Panopticon was a design for a prison that would operate with maximum efficiency; it was originally a plan developed to keep the urban poor from starving and to do so at the least expense to British taxpayers. The design of the building arranged people in tiers with a single supervisor in the center; it had "folding beds ranging in size from cradles for babies to bunks for adult males—reflecting the preoccupation with body measurements first developed by slave-ship owners and ultimately a staple of *existenzminimum* (minimum existence) housing. The basic design, Bentham thought, could be used as a poorhouse, an orphanage, a penitentiary, a hospital, a mental asylum, or a school" (Hayden, 112).

Only prison officials adopted the plan directly, but it was very influential in other areas. As Bentham said, "Morals reformed—health preserved—industry invigorated—all by a simple idea in architecture." The relationship between architecture, the organization of space, and the reproduction of a certain kind of culture makes discussions of the spaces of "home" especially important. See Marsha Ritzdorf's work on zoning laws in the United States and Mimi Abramovitz's *Regulating the Lives of Women: Social Welfare Policy from Colonial Times to the Present* (Boston: South End Press, 1989) in which she discusses the "family ethic" that guides social welfare policy and works to the disadvantage of all who do not fit the nuclear family model.

6. The African-American author John Edgar Wideman's description of the relationship between him and his brother, one a Rhodes scholar, the other a convicted criminal, traces the prison as device for the organization and treatment of difference through the construction of deviance (*Brothers and Keepers* [New York: Holt, 1984], 51).

7. Julia Kristeva's *Strangers to Ourselves,* trans. Leon Roudiez (New York: Columbia University Press, 1990), discusses the notion of strangeness as the most familiar and, paradoxically, promising relationship to difference. Such a relationship involves a "strangely familiar" identification or empathy with Others because that relationship of irreconcilable strangeness is similar to the relationship to the otherness of one's own body and the unconscious.

8. George Mosse's work on nazism foregrounds the danger of relying on concepts that initially appear innocent to a North American audience. Feminist theory has to break apart and historicize the uses made of certain concepts, for, as Mosse says, fascism, too, was an "attempt to personalize the abstract" (George Mosse, *Nationalism and Sexuality, Respectability and Abnormal Sexuality in Modern Europe* [New York: Fertig, 1985, 95]). Similarly, attempts to revalorize popular

culture must keep a historical gaze on what Mosse argues was the "genuine popularity of Nazi literature" (52), and, finally, it is not only movements of the Left or feminist movements that are concerned with solidarity, but it was "all fascism—more than any other revolutionary impetus between the wars—[that] stressed the idea of a community" (98).

9. Julia Kristeva, "Women's Time," *Signs* 7 (1982): 23. See also the work of Jessica Benjamin, *The Bonds of Love: Psychoanalysis, Feminism, and the Problem of Domination* (New York: Pantheon, 1988); and Nancy Chodorow, *The Reproduction of Mothering: Psychoanalysis and the Sociology of Gender* (Berkeley: University of California Press, 1978).

10. Alice Jardine, in *Gynesis: Configurations of Woman and Modernity* (Ithaca: Cornell University Press, 1985), argues that European literature may best by analyzed according to the oedipal paradigm, while North American literature written by men may best be read in terms of the story of Orestes, a paradigm that focuses on the son, rather than on the father.

11. "From the point of view of social coherence, which is where legislators, grammarians, and even psychoanalysts have their seat, motherhood would be nothing more than a phallic attempt to reach the Mother who is presumed to exist at the very place where (social and biological) identity recedes" (Julia Kristeva, *Desire in Language: A Semiotic Approach to Literature and Art,* ed. Leon Roudiez, trans. Thomas Gora, Alice Jardine, and Leon Roudiez [New York: Columbia University Press, 1980], 242).

12. Kristeva, *Desire in Language,* 239. She also treats religion in great detail in *Powers of Horror*:

At the doors of the feminine, at the doors of abjection, we are also, with Céline, given the most daring X-ray of the "drive foundations" of fascism. For this indeed is the economy, one of horror and suffering in their libidinal surplus value, which has been tapped, rationalized, and made operative by Nazism and Fascism. Now neither theoretical nor frivolous art, stirred by epiphenomena of desire and pleasure, has been able to touch that economy. Such desiring art could only offer a perverse negation of abjection, which, deprived in other respects of its religious sublimation (especially considering the state of bankruptcy of religious codes beween the two wars, most particularly in Nazi and Fascist circles), allowed itself to be seduced by the Fascist phenomenon. (*Powers of Horror: An Essay on Abjection* [New York: Columbia University Press, 1982], 55)

13. The term *enunciation* (*énonciation*) is used here in the broad sense to mean "an act in the course of which . . . sentences are actualized, assumed by a particular speaker in specific spatial and temporal circumstances."

The enunciation is distinguished from the utterance (*énoncé*), which is "a sequence of sentences, identified without reference to any specific circumstances of occurrence (the sentences may be pronounced, transcribed by means of various writing systems, or printed" (Oswald Ducrot and Tzvetan Todorov, *Encyclopedic Dictionary of the Sciences of Language* [Baltimore: Johns Hopkins University Press, 1979], 323).

Chapter 6

1. See the discussions of the historical relationship between the public/private split and the rise of the bourgeoisie in Nancy Fraser, "Rethinking the Public Sphere: A Contribution to the Critique of Actually Existing Democracy," *Social Text* 25–26 (1990): 56–80; Emily Martin, *The Woman in the Body: A Cultural Analysis of Reproduction* (Boston: Beacon Press, 1987); George Mosse, *Nationalism and Sexuality: Respectability and Abnormal Sexuality in Modern Europe* (New York: Fertig, 1985); and Adrienne Rich, *Of Woman Born: Motherhood as Experience and Institution* (New York: W. W. Norton, 1986).

2. Rosario Castellanos, *The Eternal Feminine*, trans. Diane E. Marting and Betty Tyree Osiek, in *A Rosario Castellanos Reader*, ed. Maureen Ahern (Austin: University of Texas Press, 1988).

3. Sandra Messinger Cypess argues that the beauty salon constitutes a liminal space of possible transition. Drawing on the work of Victor Turner, she defines *liminal* as, "a complex and dramatic period in which one is moved in accordance with a cultural script" ("Shades of the Past: Revenants on the Mexican Stage," *Cincinnati Romance Review* 9 [1990], 155). This transitional dramatic space, however, also provides the possibility for generating new myths, symbols, and paradigms, a point Cypess develops in "From Colonial Constructs to Feminist Figures: Re/visions by Mexican Women Dramatists," *Theatre Journal* (December 1989): 155.

4. "Capitalism leaves the subject the right to revolt, preserving for itself the right to suppress that revolt. The ideological systems capitalism proposes, however, subdue, unify, and consolidate that revolt, bringing it back within the field of unity (that of the subject and the State)" (Julia Kristeva, *Revolution in Poetic Language*, trans. Margaret Waller [New York: Columbia University Press, 1984], 210).

5. Castellanos plays on the idiom, "andar de boca en boca," to pass from mouth to mouth as rumor or gossip (*Eternal Feminine*, 298).

6. Jean Franco argues that Paz located in La Malinche "the Mexican disease," which forced her sons to "reject the feminine in themselves as the devalued, the passive, the mauled and battered, as *la chingada*, the violated, the one who has been screwed over, fucked, and yet is herself the betrayer" (*Plotting Women: Gender and Representation in Mexico* [New York: Columbia University Press, 1989], xix).

7. As important to feminism as the work of Walter Benjamin is, he, nevertheless, falls into this same pattern in the way he figures reactionary historicism. He chooses the whore as a metaphor for the kind of historians whose writing works hand in hand with capitalism, selecting a *victim* of that very system to be the privileged metaphor for the *victimizer*, following the model of passive causality.

As he says in the "Theses on the Philosophy of History": "The historical materialist leaves it to others to be drained by the whore called 'Once upon a time' in historicism's bordello. He remains in control of his powers, man enough to blast open the continuum of history" (Walter Benjamin, *Illuminations*, ed. Hannah Arendt, trans. Harry Zohn [New York: Shocken Books, 1976], 262).

8. In relation to these concepts that ostensibly are about women, see Tania Modleski, *Feminism without Women: Culture and Criticism in a "Postfeminist" Age* (New York: Routledge, 1991).

9. This is Castellanos's description of Acuña's garrett: "Darkness. An extremely poor attic apartment appears. It belongs to a young romantic of nineteenth-century Mexico who would like to appear as a young romantic of nineteenth-century Paris. Manuel Acuña has all the noble signs of malnutrition, insomnia, and, perhaps, some addiction. Feverish, with dark circles under his eyes, he writes a few lines and then, standing up, he recites" (*Eternal Feminine*, 307).

Afterword

1. Robert Reich's *The Work of Nations: Preparing Ourselves for Twenty-First Century Capitalism* describes the change from a political analysis of nationalism based on the mode of production and land boundaries to one in which the construction of myths of nationalism are far more abstract and necessary. This is so precisely because corporate economic activity is, in fact, *not* national but, instead, global. And this corporate activity is based on the symbolic exchanges of the mode of information (New York: Alfred A. Knopf, 1991).

Bibliography

Abramovitz, Mimi. 1989. *Regulating the Lives of Women: Social Welfare Policy from Colonial Times to the Present*. Boston: South End Press.

Allen, Jeanne Thomas. 1984. *Now, Voyager*. Madison: University of Wisconsin Press.

Allen, Jeffner, and Young, Iris, eds. 1989. *The Thinking Muse: Feminism and Modern French Philosophy*. Bloomington: Indiana University Press.

Althusser, Louis. 1971. *Lenin and Philosophy and Other Essays*. New York: Monthly Review Press.

Angus, Ian, and Jhally, Sut. 1989. *Cultural Politics in Contemporary America*. New York: Routledge.

Aponte, Barbara Bockus. 1987. "Estrategias dramáticas del feminismo en *El eterno femenino*." *Latin American Theatre Review* 20, no. 2: 49–58.

Aristotle. 1984. *The Complete Works of Aristotle: The Revised Oxford Translation*, vols. 1–2. Ed. Jonathan Barnes. Princeton: Princeton University Press.

———. 1987. *The Poetics*. Trans. Richard Janko. Indianapolis: Hackett.

Barnes, Clive. 1983. *New York Theatre Critics' Reviews* 44, no. 4: 334.

Barthes, Roland. 1972. "Taking Sides." *Critical Essays*, trans. Richard Howard. Evanston, Ill.: Northwestern University Press.

Bataille, George. 1970. "L'Abjection et les formes miserables," in *Essais de sociologie*. Vol. 1 of *Oeuvres completes*. Paris: Gallimard.

Baudrillard, Jean. 1991. "La guerra del golfo no ha existido, según Baudrillard." *El País* (20 May): 19.

Benjamin, Jessica. 1988. *The Bonds of Love: Psychoanalysis, Feminism, and the Problem of Domination*. New York: Pantheon.

Benjamin, Walter. 1976. *Illuminations*. Ed. Hannah Arendt. Trans. Harry Zohn. Indianapolis: Hackett.

———. 1982. *Reflections*. Trans. Edmund Jephcott. New York: Pantheon.

Benveniste, Emile. 1973. "The Indo-European Expression for 'Marriage.'" *Indo-European Language and Society*. London: Faber.

Berger, John. 1977. *Ways of Seeing*. London: British Broadcasting Corporation and Penguin.

Berger, John, and Mohr, Jean. 1982. *Another Way of Telling*. New York: Pantheon.

Bhabha, Homi. 1984. "Of Mimicry and Man: The Ambivalence of Colonial Discourse." *October* 28 (Spring): 125–33.

———. 1989. "Remembering Fanon: Self, Psyche, and the Colonial Condition." In *Remaking History: Discussions in Contemporary Culture*. Eds. Barbara Kruger and Phil Mariane, 131–50. Seattle: Bay Press.

Binder, Wolfgang. 1985. "A *Melus* Interview: Adrienne Kennedy." *Melus* 12, no. 3 (Fall): 99–108.

Blau, Herbert. 1987. "The American Dream in American Gothic: The Plays of Sam Shepard and Adrienne Kennedy." *The Eye of Prey*. Bloomington: Indiana University Press.

Boal, Augusto. 1985. *Theater of the Oppressed*. Trans. Charles A. and Maria-Odilia Leal McBride. New York: Theatre Communications Group.

Bourdieu, Pierre. 1970. *Reproduction in Education, Society, and Culture*. Trans. Richard Nice. London: Sage.

———. 1976. "Marriage Strategies as Strategies of Social Reproduction." *Family and Society: Selections from the Annales*. Trans. Patricia Ramun and Elborg Forster, 117–44. Baltimore: Johns Hopkins University Press.

———. 1977. *Outline of a Theory of Practice*. Trans. Richard Nice. Cambridge: Harvard University Press.

———. 1979. *La Distinction: Critique social du jugement*. Paris: Les Editions de Minuit.

———. 1984. *Distinction: A Social Critique of the Judgement of Taste*. Trans. Richard Nice. Cambridge: Harvard University Press.

Bovenschen, Sylvia. 1977. "Is There a Feminine Aesthetic?" *New German Critique* 10 (Winter): 111–37.

Brecht, Bertolt. *Brecht on Theater: The Development of an Aesthetic*. Trans. John Willett. London: Methuen, 1988.

Brown, Georgia. 1991. "Apocalypse Now and Then." *Village Voice* 36, no. 53 (31 December): 52.

Brown, Lloyd W. 1970. "Black Entitles: Names as Symbols in Afro-American Literature." *Studies in Black Literature* 1 (1970): 61–78.

Burgin, Victor. 1990. "Geometry and Abjection." In *Abjection, Melancholia and Love: The Work of Julia Kristeva*. Eds. John Fletcher and Andrew Benjamin, 104–23. New York: Routledge.

Butler, Judith. 1990. *Gender Trouble: Feminism and the Subversion of Identity*. New York: Routledge.

Carpenter, Mary Wilson. 1990. "Eco, Oedipus, and the 'View' of the University." *Diacritics* 20, no. 1 (Spring): 77–103.

Carpignano, Paolo, et al. 1990. "Chatter in the Age of Electronic Reproduction." *Social Text: Theory/Culture/Ideology* 25–26: 33–55.

Case, Sue-Ellen. 1988. *Feminism and Theatre*. New York: Methuen.

———. 1988–89. "Toward a Butch-Femme Aesthetic." *Discourse* 11, no. 1 (Fall–Winter): 56–73.

Castellanos, Rosario. 1984. *El eterno femenino: farsa*. Mexico City: Fondo de Cultura Económica.

————. 1988a. *Meditation on the Threshold*. Tempe: Bilingual Press/Editorial Bilingue.

————. 1988b. *A Rosario Castellanos Reader*. Ed. Maureen Ahern. Trans. Diane E. Marting and Betty Tyree Osiek. Austin: University of Texas Press.

Caulfield, Mina Davis. 1974. "Imperialism, the Family, and Cultures of Resistance." *Socialist Revolution* 4, no. 20 (October): 67–86.

Chase, Cynthia. 1984. "Book Review." *Criticism* 26, no. 2: 193–201.

————. 1989. "Desire and Identification in Lacan and Kristeva." In *Feminism and Psychoanalysis*. Ed. Judith Roof, 65–83. Ithaca: Cornell University Press.

————. 1990. "Primary Narcissism and the Giving of Figure," In *Abjection, Melancholia and Love: The Work of Julia Kristeva*. Eds. John Fletcher and Andrew Benjamin, 124–36. London: Routledge.

Chodorow, Nancy. 1978. *The Reproduction of Mothering: Psychoanalysis and the Sociology of Gender*. Berkeley: University of California Press.

Cotera, Martha. 1976. *Diosa y Hembra: The History and Heritage of Chicanas in the United States*. Austin: Information Systems Development.

Cummings, Scott. 1985. "The Visions of Maria Irene Fornes." *Theater* (Fall/Winter): 51–57.

Curb, Rosemary K. 1987. "Lesson I Bleed." In *Women in the American Theatre*. Eds. Helen Krich Chinoy and Linda Walsh Jenkins. New York: Theatre Communications Group.

Cypess, Sandra Messinger. 1989. "From Colonial Constructs to Feminist Figures: Re/visions by Mexican Women Dramatists." *Theatre Journal* (December): 492–504.

————. 1990. "Shades of the Past: Revenants on the Mexican Stage." *Cincinnati Romance Review* 9: 154–64.

————. 1991. *La Malinche in Mexican Literature: From History to Myth*. Austin: University of Texas Press.

Davis, Gerald L. 1985. *I Got the Word in Me and I Can Sing It, You Know: A Study of the Performed African-American Sermon*. Philadelphia: University of Pennsylvania Press.

Debord, Guy. 1983. *The Society of the Spectacle*. Detroit: Black and Red.

de Certeau, Michel. 1984. *The Practice of Everyday Life*. Trans. Steven F. Rendall. Berkeley: University of California Press.

DeCrow, Karen, and Seidenberg, Robert. 1983. *Panic and Protest in Agoraphobia: Women Who Marry Houses*. New York: McGraw-Hill.

de Lauretis, Teresa. 1984. *Alice Doesn't: Feminism, Semiotics, Cinema*. Bloomington: Indiana University Press.

————. 1987. *Technologies of Gender*. Bloomington: University of Indiana Press.

de Man, Paul. 1979. *Allegories of Reading*. New Haven: Yale University Press.

Deleuze, Giles, and Guattari, Felix. 1977. *Anti-Oedipus*. Trans. Robert Hurley, Mark Seem, and Helen R. Lane. New York: Viking.

Delphy, Christine. 1984. *Close to Home: A Materialist Analysis of Women's Oppression*. Trans. Diana Leonard. Amherst: University of Massachusetts Press.

Derrida, Jacques. 1981. *Dissemination*. Trans. Barbara Johnson. Chicago: University of Chicago Press.

Devor, Holly. 1989. *Gender Blending: Confronting the Limits of Duality*. Bloomington: Indiana University Press.

Diamond, Sara. 1989. *Spiritual Warfare: The Politics of the Christian Right*. Boston: South End Press.

Doane, Mary Ann. 1982. "Film and the Masquerade: Theorising the Female Spectator." *Screen* 23, nos. 3–4 (September–October): 74–87.

———. 1987. *The Desire to Desire: The Woman's Film of the 1940s*. Bloomington: Indiana University Press.

Dolan, Jill. 1988. *The Feminist Spectator as Critic*. Ann Arbor: UMI Research Press.

Dollimore, Jonathan. 1990. "The Cultural Politics of Perversion: Augustine, Shakespeare, Freud, Foucault." *Genders* (Summer): 1–16.

Donzelot, Jacques. *The Policing of Families*. Trans. Robert Hurley. New York: Pantheon.

Dreyfus, Hubert L., and Rabinow, Paul. 1983. *Michel Foucault: Beyond Structuralism and Hermeneutics*. Chicago: University of Chicago Press.

duBois, Page. 1982. *Centaurs and Amazons: Women and the Pre-History of the Great Chain of Being*. Ann Arbor: University of Michigan Press.

Ducrot, Oswald, and Todorov, Tzvetan. 1979. "Semiotics against the Sign." *Encyclopedic Dictionary of the Sciences of Language*. Trans. Catherine Porter. Baltimore: Johns Hopkins University Press.

Durand, Régis. 1983a. "On Aphanasis: A Note on the Dramaturgy of the Subject in Narrative Analysis." *MLN* 98, no. 5 (December): 860–70.

———. 1983b. "Theatre/SIGNS/Performance: On Some Transformations of the Theatrical and the Theoretical." In *Innovation/Renovation: New Perspectives on the Humanities*. Eds. Ihab Hassan and Sally Hassan, 211–24. Madison: University of Wisconsin Press.

Eagleton, Terry. 1983. *Literary Theory: An Introduction*. Minneapolis: University of Minnesota Press.

Eco, Umberto, and Sebeok, Thomas, eds. 1983. *The Sign of Three: Dupin, Holmes, Peirce*. Bloomington: Indiana University Press.

Edsall, Thoman Byrne, and Mary D. 1991. "Race." *Atlantic Monthly* (May): 53–86.

Eisenstein, Zillah R. 1988. *The Female Body and the Law*. Berkeley: University of California Press.

Else, Gerald. 1957. *Aristotle's Poetics: The Argument*. Cambridge: Harvard University Press.

———. 1965. *The Origin and Early Form of Greek Tragedy*. Cambridge: Harvard University Press.

Fabre, Geneviève. 1983. *Drumbeats, Masks and Metaphor: Contemporary Afro-American Theatre*. Trans. Melvin Dixon. Cambridge: Harvard University Press.

Faludi, Susan. 1991. *Backlash: The Undeclared War against American Women*. New York: Crown.

Fanon, Frantz. 1967. *Black Skin, White Masks*. Trans. Charles Lam Markmann. New York: Grove Press.

Felman, Shoshana. 1983a. "Beyond Oedipus: The Speciman Story of Psycho-analysis." *MLN* 98, no. 5 (December): 1021–52.

———. 1983b. *The Literary Speech Act: Don Juan with J. L. Austin, or Seduction in Two Languages*. Trans. Catherine Porter. Ithaca: Cornell University Press.

Finley, M. I. 1980. *Ancient Slavery and Modern Ideology*. New York: Viking.

Foucault, Michel. 1977a. *Discipline and Punish: The Birth of the Prison*. Trans. Alan Sheridan. New York: Pantheon.

———. 1977b. *Language, Counter-Memory, Practice*. Trans. Sherry Simon and Donald Bouchard. Ithaca: Cornell University Press.

Franco, Jean. 1985. "Killing Nuns, Priests, Women, and Children." In *On Signs*. Ed. Marshall Blonsky, 414–20. Baltimore: Johns Hopkins University Press.

———. 1988. "Beyond Ethnocentrism: Gender, Power, and the Third World Intelligentsia." In *Marxism and the Interpretation of Culture*. Eds. Cary Nelson and Lawrence Grossberg, 503–15. Urbana: University of Illinois Press.

———. 1989. *Plotting Women: Gender and Representation in Mexico*. New York: Columbia University Press.

Fraser, Nancy. 1990a. "Rethinking the Public Sphere: A Contribution to the Critique of Actually Existing Democracy." *Social Text: Theory/Culture/Ideology* 25–26: 56–80.

———. 1990b. "The Uses and Abuses of French Discourse Theories for Feminist Politics." *Boundary 2* 17, no. 2 (Summer): 82–101.

Frazer, Sir James. 1950. *The Golden Bough*, vol. 1. New York: Macmillan.

Freud, Sigmund. 1953a. "Constructions in Analysis." *The Standard Edition of the Complete Psychological Works of Sigmund Freud*, vol. 23. London: Hogarth Press.

———. 1953b. "Femininity." *The Standard Edition of the Complete Psychological Works of Sigmund Freud*, vol. 22. London: Hogarth Press.

———. 1957a. "A Special Type of Choice of Objects Made by Men." *The Standard Edition of the Complete Psychological Works of Sigmund Freud*, vol. 11. London: Hogarth Press.

———. 1957b. "The Taboo of Virginity." *The Standard Edition of the Complete Psychological Works of Sigmund Freud*, vol. 11. London: Hogarth Press.

———. 1961a. *Civilization and Its Discontents*, ed. James Strachey. New York: Norton.

———. 1961b. "Negation." *The Standard Edition of the Complete Psychological Works of Sigmund Freud*, vol. 19. London: Hogarth Press.

———. 1965. *The Interpretation of Dreams*. New York: Avon.

Gates, Henry Louis. 1988. *The Signifying Monkey: A Theory of African-American Literary Criticism*. New York: Oxford University Press.

Glaspell, Susan. 1987. *Trifles* in *The Plays of Susan Glaspell*. Ed. C. W. E. Bigsby. New York: Cambridge University Press.

Goffman, Erving. 1974. *Frame Analysis: An Essay on the Organization of Experience*. Cambridge: Harvard University Press.

Gravel, Pierre. 1980. *Pour une logie du sujet tragique*. Montréal: University of Montréal Press.

Griffin, Gail. 1990. "Alma Mater." *Profession* 90: 37–42.

Grosz, Elizabeth. 1989. *Sexual Subversions: Three French Feminists.* Boston: Allen and Unwin.

Habermas, Jürgen. 1989. *The Structural Transformation of the Public Sphere: An Inquiry into a Category of Bourgeois Society.* Cambridge: MIT Press.

Harrison, Paul Carter, ed. 1974. *Kuntu Drama: Plays of the African Continuum.* New York: Grove Press.

———, ed. 1989. *Totem Voices: Plays from the Black World Repertory.* New York: Grove Press.

Hayden, Dolores. 1984. *Redesigning the American Dream: The Future of Housing, Work, and Family Life.* New York: W. W. Norton.

hooks, bell. 1989. "Reflections on Race and Sex." *Zeta Magazine.* (July–August): 57–61.

———. 1990. *Yearning: Race, Gender, and Cultural Politics.* Boston: South End Press.

Irigaray, Luce. 1974. *Speculum de l'autre femme.* Paris: Les Editions de Minuit.

———. 1977. *Ce sexe qui n'en est pas un.* Paris: Les Editions de Minuit.

———. 1979. *Et l'une ne bouge pas sans l'autre.* Paris: Les Editions de Minuit.

———. 1985. *Speculum of the Other Woman.* Ithaca: Cornell University Press.

———. 1988. "And the One Doesn't Move without the Other." *Signs* 7, no. 1 (Autumn): 60–67.

Israel, J. I. 1975. *Race, Class, and Politics in Colonial Mexico: 1610–1670.* Bath: Oxford University Press.

Jameson, Fredric. 1990. *Signatures of the Visible.* New York: Routledge.

Janko, Richard. 1987. *Aristotle: Poetics.* Indianapolis: Hackett.

Jardine, Alice. 1981. "Introduction to 'Women's Time.'" *Signs* 7, no. 1 (Autumn): 5–12.

———. 1985a. *Gynesis: Configurations of Woman and Modernity.* Ithaca: Cornell University Press.

———. 1985b. "Men in Feminism: Odor di Uomo or Compagnons de Route?" *Critical Exchange* 18 (Spring): 44–60.

Jeffords, Susan. 1989. *The Remasculinization of America: Gender and the Vietnam War.* Bloomington: Indiana University Press.

Joyrich, Lynn. 1990. "Critical and Textual Hypermasculinity." In *Logics of Television: Essays in Cultural Criticism.* Ed. Patricia Mellencamp, 156–72. Bloomington: Indiana University Press.

Kaplan, Amy. 1988. *The Social Construction of American Realism.* Chicago: University of Chicago Press.

Kennedy, Adrienne. 1971. *Funnyhouse of a Negro* in *Contemporary Black Drama.* Eds. Clinton Oliver and Stephanie Sills. New York: Charles Scribner.

———. 1987. *The People Who Led to My Plays.* New York: Alfred A. Knopf.

———. 1988. *In One Act.* Minneapolis: University of Minnesota Press.

Kintz, Linda. 1989. "In-Different Criticism: The Deconstructive 'Parole.'" In *The Thinking Muse: Feminism and Modern French Philosophy.* Eds. Jeffner Allen and Iris Young, 113–35. Bloomington: Indiana University Press.

———. 1991. "Gendering the Critique of Representation: Fascism, the Purified

Body, and Theater in Adorno, Artaud, and Maria Irene Fornes." *Rethinking Marxism* 4, no. 3 (Fall): 83–100.

Kissel, Howard. 1983. *New York Theatre Critics' Reviews* 44, no. 4: 336.

Klein, Melanie. 1975. *Love, Guilt, and Reparation.* New York: Delta.

Klein, Richard. 1983. "In the Body of the Mother." *Enclitic* 7, no. 1: 66–75.

Kluge, Alexander, and Negt, Oskar. 1990. "Selections from 'Public Opinion and Practical Knowledge': Toward an Organizational Analysis of Proletariat and Middle Class Public Opinion." *Social Text* 25–26: 24–32.

Koestenbaum, Wayne. 1989. *Double Talk: The Erotics of Male Literary Collaboration.* New York: Routledge, Chapman and Hall.

Kristeva, Julia. 1973. "The System and the Speaking Subject." *Times Literary Supplement* 12 (October): 1249.

——. 1974. *La révolution du langage poétique.* Paris: Editions du Seuil.

——. 1976. "Signifying Practice and the Mode of Production." *Edinburgh Magazine* (Winter): 64–75.

——. 1980. *Desire in Language: A Semiotic Approach to Literature and Art.* Ed. Leon Roudiez. Trans. Thomas Gora, Alice Jardine, and Leon Roudiez. New York: Columbia University Press.

——. 1980a. *Pouvoirs de l' horreur: essai sur l'abjection.* Paris: Seuil.

——. 1981. "Women's Time." *Signs* 7: 13–35.

——. 1982a. *Powers of Horror: An Essay on Abjection.* New York: Columbia University Press.

——. 1982b. "Psychoanalysis and the *Polis.*" *Critical Inquiry* 9, no. 1 (September): 77–92.

——. 1984. *Revolution in Poetic Language.* Trans. Margaret Waller. New York: Columbia University Press.

——. 1987a. *Soleil noir: Dépression and mélancolie.* Paris: Editions Gallimard.

——. 1987b. "Stabat Mater." *Tales of Love.* Trans. Leon Roudiez. New York: Columbia University Press.

——. 1987c. *Tales of Love.* Trans. Leon Roudiez. New York: Columbia University Press.

——. 1989. *Black Sun: Depression and Melancholia.* Trans. Leon Roudiez. New York: Columbia University Press.

——. 1990. "The Adolescent Novel." In *Abjection, Melancholia and Love: The Work of Julia Kristeva.* Eds. John Fletcher and Andrew Benjamin, 1–23. London: Routledge.

——. 1991. *Strangers to Ourselves.* Trans. Leon Roudiez. New York: Columbia University Press.

Lacan, Jacques. 1977. *Ecrits: A Selection.* Trans. Alan Sheridan. New York: W. W. Norton.

Lacoue-Labarthe, Phillippe. 1989. *Typography: Mimesis, Philosophy, Politics.* Cambridge: Harvard University Press.

Lacoue-Labarthe, Phillippe, and Nancy, Jean-Luc. 1990. "The Nazi Myth." *Critical Inquiry* 16, no. 2 (Winter): 291–312.

Laplanche, J. 1976. *Life and Death in Psychoanalysis.* Trans. Jeffrey Mehlman. Baltimore: Johns Hopkins University Press.

Laplanche, J., and Pontalis, J. B. 1973. *The Language of Psychoanalysis*. Trans. Donald Nicholson-Smith. New York: W. W. Norton.

LeGuin, Ursula. 1985a. "Not Being Singleminded." *Always Coming Home*. New York: Harper.

———. 1985b. "She Unnames Them." *New Yorker* 60, no. 49 (21 January): 27.

Lehman, Lisa. 1977. "A Growth of Images." *Drama Review* 21, no. 4 (December): 42–48.

Lévi-Strauss, Claude. 1969. *The Elementary Structures of Kinship*. Boston: Beacon Press.

Lotman, Jurij. 1974. "The Origin of Plot in the Light of Typology." *Poetics Today* 1, nos. 1–2: 161–84.

———, and Uspenskij, B. 1977. "Myth—Name—Culture." In *Soviet Semiotics: An Anthology*. Ed. and trans. Daniel P. Lucid, 233–53. Baltimore: Johns Hopkins University Press.

Lucid, Daniel Peri. 1977. "Introduction." *Soviet Semiotics: An Anthology*. Baltimore: Johns Hopkins University Press.

MacCannell, Dean. 1984. "Baltimore in the Morning . . . After: On the Form of Post-Nuclear Leadership." *Diacritics* 14, no. 2 (Summer): 43–60.

MacKinnon, Catherine. 1982. "Feminism, Marxism, Method, and the State: Toward a Feminist Jurisprudence." *Signs* 8, no. 4: 635–58.

Mann, Klaus. 1979. *Mephisto: Le roman d'une carrière d'après Klaus Mann*, Ariane Mnouchkine. Paris: Editions Solin and Théâtre du Soleil.

Martin, Emily. 1987. *The Woman in the Body: A Cultural Analysis of Reproduction*. Boston: Beacon Press.

Marx, Karl. 1978. "The German Ideology." *The Marx-Engels Reader*. Ed. Robert C. Tucker, 2d ed. New York: W. W. Norton.

———. 1987. *Capital*, vol. 1. New York: International Publishers.

Mills, Patricia Jagentowicz. 1987. *Woman, Nature, and Psyche*. New Haven: Yale University Press.

Mitchell, Juliet, and Rose, Jacqueline. 1982. Introduction to *Feminine Sexuality: Jacques Lacan and the Ecole Freudienne*. Eds. and trans. Juliet Mitchell and Jacqueline Rose. New York: Norton.

Modleski, Tania. 1991. *Feminism without Women: Culture and Criticism in a "Postfeminist" Age*. New York: Routledge.

Molloy, Sylvia. 1984. "Dos lecturas del cisne: Rubén Darío y Delmira Agustini." In *La sartén por el mango*. Eds. Patricia Elena González and Eliana Ortega, 57–69. Rio Piedras, Puerto Rico: Ediciones Huracán.

Montrelay, Michèle. 1978. "Inquiry into Femininity." *m/f* 1: 83–101.

Morris, Meaghan. 1979. "The Pirate's Fiancee." *Michel Foucault: Power, Truth, Strategy*. Sydney: Feral Publications.

Morsberger, Robert, ed. 1975. *Viva Zapata! The Original Screenplay*. New York: Viking.

Mosse, George. 1985. *Nationalism and Sexuality: Respectability and Abnormal Sexuality in Modern Europe*. New York: Fertig.

Mowitt, John. 1990. "Performance Theory as the Work of Laurie Anderson." *Discourse* 12, no. 2 (Spring–Summer): 48–65.

Müller, Heiner. 1984. *Hamletmachine and Other Texts for the Stage*. Ed. and trans. Carl Weber. New York: Performing Arts Journal Publications.

———. 1990. *Germania*. New York: Semiotext(e).

Murray, Timothy. 1985. "Screening the Camera's Eye: Black and White Confrontations of Technological Representation." *Modern Drama* 28, no. 1 (March): 110–24.

New Larousse Encyclopedia of Mythology. 1959. London: Hamlyn.

Nietzsche, Friedrich. 1979. "On Truth and Lying." *Philosophy and Truth: Selections from Nietzsche's Notebooks of the Early 1870s*. Ed. and trans. Daniel Breazeale. New York: Humanities Press.

Nigro, Kirsten. 1980. "Debunking the Eternal Feminine." *Journal of Spanish Studies, Twentieth Century* 8, nos. 1–2: 89–102.

Norman, Marsha. 1983. *'night, Mother*. New York: Hill and Wang.

———. 1984. "Lillian Hellman's Gift to a Young Playwright." *New York Times* 2 (26 August): 1.

Nye, Andrea. 1990. *Words of Power: A Feminist Reading of the History of Logic*. New York: Routledge.

Omi, Michael. 1989. "In Living Color: Race and American Culture." In *Cultural Politics in Contemporary America*. Eds. Ian Angus and Sut Jhally, 111–22. New York: Routledge.

Pagels, Elaine. 1981. *The Gnostic Gospels*. New York: Vintage.

Papanek, Hannah. 1984. "False Specialization and the Purdah of Scholarship— a Review Article." *Journal of Asian Studies* 44, no. 1 (November): 127–48.

———. 1985. "Class and Gender in Education-Employment Linkages." *Comparative Education Review* 29, no. 3 (August): 317–46.

Paz, Octavio. 1961. *The Labyrinth of Solitude*. Trans. Lysander Kemp. New York: Grove Press.

Petro, Patrice. 1990. "Feminism and Film History." *Camera Obscura* 22 (January): 9–28.

Phillips, Rachel. 1983. "Marina/Malinche: Masks and Shadows." In *Women in Hispanic Literature: Icons and Fallen Idols*. Ed. Beth Miller, 97–115. Berkeley: University of California Press.

Polan, Dana. 1986. *Power and Paranoia: History, Narrative, and the American Cinema, 1940–1950*. New York: Columbia University Press.

Pollitt, Katha. 1990. "When Is a Mother Not a Mother?" *Nation* (31 December): 825.

Pomeroy, Sarah. 1975. *Goddesses, Whores, Wives, and Slaves: Women in Classical Antiquity*. New York: Schocken.

Poster, Mark. 1990. *The Mode of Information: Poststructuralism and Social Context*. Chicago: University of Chicago Press.

Propp, Vladimir. 1974. *Las raíces históricas del cuento*. Trans. Jose Martin Arancibía. Madrid: Editorial Fundamentos.

———. 1975. *Edipo all luce del folclore*. Ed. Clara Strada Janovic. Turin: Einaudin.

Rajchman, John. 1983. "Foucault, or the Ends of Modernism." *October* 24 (Spring): 37– 62.

Rapping, Elayne. 1991. "Daytime Inquiries." *Progressive* (October): 36–38.

Reich, Robert. 1991. *The Work of Nations: Preparing Ourselves for Twenty-First Century Capitalism.* New York: Alfred Knopf.

Rilke, Rainier Maria. 1985. *The Notebooks of Malte Laurids Brigge: A Novel.* Trans. Stephen Mitchell. New York: Vintage.

Ritzdorf, Marsha. 1987. "Challenging the Exclusionary Impact of Family Definitions in American Municipal Zoning Ordinances." *Journal of Urban Affairs* 7: 15–25.

Rivière, Joan. 1929. "Womanliness as a Masquerade." *International Journal of Psycho-Analysis,* vol. 10: 303–13. London: Institute of Psychoanalysis.

Rogin, Michael. 1987. *Ronald Reagan: The Movie and Other Episodes in Political Demonology.* Berkeley: University of California Press.

Rose, Jacqueline. 1986. *Sexuality in the Field of Vision.* London: Verso.

Rossaud, Jacques. 1978. "Prostitution, Youth, and Society." *Deviants and the Abandoned in French Society: Selections from the Annales,* vol. 4. Baltimore: Johns Hopkins University Press.

Russo, Mary. 1986. "Female Grotesque: Carnival and Theory." In *Feminist Studies/Critical Studies.* Ed. Teresa de Lauretis, 213–29. Bloomington: Indiana University Press, 213–29.

Saxton, Alexander. 1990. *The Rise and Fall of the White Republic: Class Politics and Mass Culture in Nineteenth-Century America.* New York: Verso.

Seltzer, Mark. 1984. *Henry James and the Art of Power.* Ithaca: Cornell University Press.

Sen, Amarty. 1990. "More than 100 Million Women Are Missing." *New York Review of Books* 37, no. 20 (December 20): 61–67.

Silverman, Kaja. 1983. *The Subject of Semiotics.* New York: Oxford University Press.

Solomon, Alisa. 1990. "Dicks Nix Crits." *Village Voice* 25, no. 4 (23 January): 92.

Solomon-Godeau, Abigail. 1985. "Reconstructing Documentary: Connie Hatch's Representational Resistance." *Camera Obscura* 13–14: 114–47.

Sophocles. 1957. *Women of Trachis.* Trans. Ezra Pound. New York: New Directions.

———. 1960. *Oedipus the King.* Trans. David Grene, in *Greek Tragedies,* vol. 1. Chicago: University of Chicago Press.

———. 1978a. *Women of Trachis.* Eds. and trans. Gregory Dickerson and C. K. Williams. New York: Schocken.

———. 1978b. *The Women of Trachis.* Trans. Michael Jameson. *The Complete Greek Tragedies,* vol. 2. Cambridge: Harvard University Press.

Spencer, Jenny. 1987. "Norman's *'night, Mother:* Psycho-drama of Female Identity." *Modern Drama* 30, no. 3 (September): 364–75.

Sprengnether, Madelon. 1990. *The Spectral Mother.* Ithaca: Cornell University Press.

Stevens, Evelyn P. 1973. "*Marianismo*: The Other Face of *Machismo* in Latin America." In *Female and Male in Latin America.* Ed. Ann Pescatello, 89–102. Pittsburgh: University of Pittsburgh Press.

Stoller, Robert. 1967. "Facts and Fancies: An Examination of Freud's Concept of Bisexuality." In *Women and Analysis: Dialogues on Psychoanalytic Views of Femininity*, ed. Jean Strouse, 343–64. New York: Dell.

Suleiman, Susan Rubin. 1990. *Subversive Intent: Gender, Politics, and the Avant-Garde*. Cambridge: Harvard University Press.

Tanner, Nancy. 1974. "Matrifocality in Indonesia and Africa and Among Black Americans." *Woman, Culture, and Society*. Palo Alto: Stanford University Press.

Taylor, Clyde. 1988. "The Master Text and the Jeddi Doctrine." *Screen* 29, no. 4 (Autumn): 96–104.

Theweleit, Klaus. 1987. *Male Fantasies*, vol. 1: *Women, Floods, Bodies, History*. Trans. Stephen Conway in collaboration with Erica Carter and Chris Turner. Minneapolis: University of Minnesota Press.

———. 1989. *Male Fantasies*, vol. 2. *Psychoanalyzing the White Terror*. Trans. Erica Carter and Chris Turner. Minneapolis: University of Minnesota Press.

Tompkins, Jane. 1989. Lecture delivered at the University of Oregon, Eugene.

Travers, Ann, and Johnston, Susan. 1992. "Coalitions without Consensus: Challenges for Gay and Lesbian Organizing in the 1990's." Paper presented at the Fascisms: Roots, Extensions, Replays Conference at the University of Oregon, Eugene, April.

Ubersfeld, Anne. 1978. *Lire le théâtre*. Paris: Editions Sociales.

———. 1982. *L'école du spectateur: Lire le théâtre*, vol. 2. Paris: Editions Sociales.

Vernant, Jean-Pierre. 1974. *Mythe et société en Grèce ancienne*. Paris: François Maspero.

———. 1977. *Mythe et tragédie en Grèce ancienne*. Paris: François Maspero.

———. 1982. *The Origins of Greek Thought*. Ithaca: Cornell University Press.

———. 1988. *Myth and Tragedy in Ancient Greece*. New York: Zone Books.

Watt, Douglas. 1983. *New York Daily News* (1 April): 18.

Weitzman, Lenore. 1985. *The Divorce Revolution: The Unexpected Social and Economic Consequences for Women and Children in America*. New York: Free Press.

West, Cornel. 1989. "Black Culture and Postmodernism." In *Remaking History: Discussions in Contemporary Culture*. Eds. Barbara Kruger and Phil Mariana, 87–96. Seattle: Bay Press.

Wideman, John Edgar. 1984. *Brothers and Keepers*. New York: Holt.

Williams, Sherley Anne. 1978. "Introduction." *Their Eyes Were Watching God*. Urbana: University of Chicago Press.

Winkler, John. 1985. "The Ephebes' Song: *Tragôidia* and *Polis*. " *Representations* 11 (Summer): 26–62.

———. 1990. *The Constraints of Desire: The Anthropology of Sex and Gender in Ancient Greece*. New York: Routledge.

Woolf, Virginia. 1941. *Between the Acts*. New York: Harcourt Brace Jovanovich.

Yudice, George. 1990. "For a Practical Aesthetics." *Social Text: Theory/Culture/Ideology* 25–26: 129–145.

Zeitlin, Froma. 1985. "Playing the Other: Theater, Theatricality, and the Feminine in Greek Drama." *Representations* 11 (Summer): 63–94.

Žižek, Slovaj. 1989. *The Sublime Object of Ideology*. New York: Verso.

Index

Abductive reasoning, 287n.8
Abjection, 111–12, 138, 222, 253, 277; and *chora,* 189; and cultural logic, 113–14; and Oedipus complex, 112–13, 120–21, 220; and parody, 138; and separation, 112, 116
Abortion, 231
Abraham, Roger D., 150
Achelous (*The Women of Trachis*), 77
Active/passive opposition: Aristotle on, 24–25, 43, 65, 76, 106, 285n.17; and cultural reproduction, 74; and female hostility, 89; and goodness, 64–65; and guilt, 80, 81, 82; and homosexuality, 72; and Inside/Outside opposition, 69, 78; and language, 61; and marriage, 22–23, 55; and masculine passivity, 45, 61–62; and masquerade, 130, 131, 133; and mythological plot, 42–45; and naming, 260; and oedipal plot, 44–45, 260; and patrilineal secession, 44, 59; and public/private opposition, 25–26; and resistance to fusion, 65; and Sphinx, 47–48, 59; and suicide, 55–56; and television, 197; and waiting, 44, 55, 288n.20. *See also* Female agency; Female agency, invisibility of
Acuña, Manuel, 266, 300n.9
Adam (*The Eternal Feminine*), 259–60
Adelita (*The Eternal Feminine*), 268–69
Aesthetic dismissal of women, 196–97, 199–200

African-American culture, 145, 147, 162; family in, 154–55; misogyny in, 148–49; mulatto theme, 165; Signification, 149–50. *See also* African cultures
African cultures, 143, 146; and family, 154–55; Kuntu drama, 147–48, 159–60; masks, 153; totem animals in, 162, 170
Age, 209, 213
Agnes (*'night, Mother*), 218, 219
Agora, 25–26, 27
Althusser, Louis, 15, 284n.8
Amazons, 68, 69, 73, 77, 92
"Ambiguity and Reversal: On the Enigmatic Structure of *Oedipus Rex*" (Vernant), 45–46
Ames, Adrienne, 182
Anachronism, 247–48
Ancient Greece: and colonization, 126; female absence from polis, 3, 4, 27–28, 45–46, 73; homosexuality in, 3, 72; initiation in, 32; Inside/Outside opposition in, 68, 69–71, 290n.8; marriage in, 3, 66, 91; military organization in, 26–27, 32–33; spatial ordering in, 25–28; subordination in, 72, 290–91nn.11, 12. *See also* Democratic Greek state; Greek tragedy; Patrilineal secession
Angus, Ian, 145, 179
Animals, 88, 162, 237; owls, 162, 164, 167, 169–70, 171–72, 185; and patri-

Mobility. *See* Active/passive opposition

Moctezuma, 263, 265–66

Mode of information, 145, 179–81, 190, 300n.1

Modernism, 252, 284n.14

Modernization, 248–49, 254

Mohr, Jean, 215, 248–49

Molloy, Sylvia, 242

Monotheism, 104, 114. *See also* Christianity; One, logic of

Montrelay, Michele, 130

Morphology of the Folktale (Propp), 36

Mosse, George, 297–98n.8

Mother: in *A Movie Star Has to Star in Black and White,* 183; and daughter, 107, 219–21, 225–29; desire of, 110–11, 124, 134; and family discourse, 105, 106–7, 110, 219–20; in *Funnyhouse of a Negro,* 162–63; and Gulf War, 166, 193, 194; and masquerade, 131, 132, 134; sadness for, 277; and son, 92–93, 95; in *The Owl Answers,* 165, 167, 169–70. *See also* Maternal body; Motherhood; Mother/wife; Oedipus complex; *specific characters*

Motherhood, 42, 217, 222, 264; and coagulation, 11, 122–23, 124; and crossroads, 288n.17; and domestic space, 247; as fantasy, 124; and feminist theory, 12, 121, 230, 234; and knowledge production, 125; as martyrdom, 257–59; and patrilineal secession, 37; and purity, 240; and religion, 231, 234; and resistance, 250; and separation, 124–25, 220, 232, 278; and social coherence, 298n.11; and Symbolic, 118, 231–32; and Virgin Mary, 245–46; and women's labor, 233–34. *See also* Maternal body; Mother/wife; Older women

Mother/wife, 37, 40, 75, 76; fusion of, 50–51, 52–54; silence of, 84, 92, 95. *See also* Maternal body; Mother; Mother/wife

Mots et les choses, Les (Foucault), 284n.14

Movie Star Has to Star in Black and White, A (Kennedy), 157, 176–93; *A Place in the Sun,* scenes in, 187–89; and cinematic body, 181–82; dialogue in, 185; female specificity in, 176, 177; and mirror stage, 189–91; and mode of information, 179–81; *Now, Voyager,* scenes in, 181, 183–84, 185–86, 187, 295n.16; scenes of, 183–89; and *The Owl Answers,* 182, 183, 185; *Viva, Zapata!,* scenes in, 185, 186–87, 192–93

MTV, 196

Mulatto theme, 165–66, 169. *See also* Bastard imagery

Müller, Heiner, 191

Murray, Timothy, 181, 193

Mythological naming, 41–42, 52

Mythos, 32, 33, 35–36

Naming, 19–20, 21, 259–60, 260; and family, 51–52; mythological vs. logical, 41–42, 52; and Oedipus complex, 223, 224

Narcissus, 16, 286n.1

Narrative, 34

National Indigenist Institute, 244

Nationalism, 241–43, 245, 264, 268–69, 300n.1

Negt, Oskar, 213

Nessos (*The Women of Trachis*), 74, 78, 79, 87, 93

New Testament, 105, 115, 163. *See also* Christianity; Monotheism

Nietzsche, Friedrich, 21, 23, 32, 115, 280; on delusion, 14, 18; and family, 282; on madness, 20; on plot, 33, 44; on translation, 30

'night, Mother (Norman), 197–99, 207–30; critical reception of, 197–98; language in, 215–18, 220, 235; mother-daughter relationship in, 219–20, 219–21, 225–29; role of Dawson in,